The Philosophy of Rawls

A Collection of Essays

Series Editors

Henry S. Richardson
Georgetown University

Paul J. Weithman
University of Notre Dame

A GARLAND SERIES
READINGS IN PHILOSOPHY

ROBERT NOZICK, *ADVISOR*
HARVARD UNIVERSITY

Contents of the Series

Opponents and Implications of
A Theory of Justice

Edited with an introduction by

Henry S. Richardson
Georgetown University

GARLAND PUBLISHING, INC.
A MEMBER OF THE TAYLOR & FRANCIS GROUP
New York & London
1999

Library of Congress Cataloging-in-Publication Data

Opponents and implications of a theory of justice / edited with an
introduction by Henry S. Richardson.
     p. cm. — (The philosophy of Rawls ; 3)
     "A Garland series, readings in philosophy."
     Includes bibliographical references.
     ISBN 0-8153-2927-x (alk. paper)
     1. Rawls, John 1921– Theory of justice. 2. Justice.
I. Richardson, Henry S. II. Series.

JC578.O66 1999
320'.01'1—dc21   99-048610

Printed on acid-free, 250-year-life paper
Manufactured in the United States of America

Contents

Series Introduction

John Rawls is the pre-eminent political philosopher of our time. His 1971 masterpiece, *A Theory of Justice*, permanently changed the landscape of moral and political theory, revitalizing the normative study of social issues and taking stands about justice, ethics, rationality, and philosophical method that continue to draw followers and critics today. His *Political Liberalism* (rev. ed., 1996) squarely faced the fundamental challenges posed by cultural, religious, and philosophical pluralism. It should be no surprise, then, that turn-of-the-century searches of the periodical indices in philosophy, economics, law, the humanities, and related fields turn up almost three thousand articles devoted to a critical discussion of Rawls's theory. In these Volumes we reprint a wide-ranging selection of the most influential and insightful articles on Rawls.

While it was impossible, even in a collection of this size, to reprint all of the important material, the selection here should provide the student and scholar with a route into all of the significant controversies that have surrounded Rawls's theories since he first began enunciating them in the nineteen-fifties — issues that the Introductions to each Volume of this series delineate. Eight criteria guided our selection. First, these volumes form part of a series devoted to *secondary* literature. We reprint no articles by Rawls: most of these have just appeared together for the first time in his *Collected Papers*.[1] Second, we reprint only self-contained articles published in English, rather than selections from books or articles in other languages. Third, the articles reprinted here are all *about* Rawls's view, as opposed to being original reflections inspired by Rawls's work. Fourth, we aimed for a broad coverage of controversies and of the main features of Rawls's theory that they surround. Since the Volumes are organized in terms of these controversies, we include very few overall assessments or book reviews. Some central elements of Rawls's theory, while relatively novel and well-articulated, have not been controversial enough to draw critical fire in the secondary literature. The Volume Introductions mention many of these features. Fifth, we aimed to include the most influential articles that have appeared. In identifying these, we used a systematic search of the citation indices to supplement our own judgment. Naturally, we also took special notice of pieces cited by Rawls himself. Sixth, we sought to reprint articles by a large number of authors representing the widest possible range of points of view. In some cases, this meant refraining from reprinting a certain article because its author was already well represented in the selections. Seventh, we have sought to exhibit through our selections the broadly interdisciplinary influence of Rawls's writings. We have included articles by political theorists, economists, lawyers, religious thinkers, and social scientists as well as by philosophers. Eighth, we have favored including articles that are now relatively hard to find. For this reason, with the exception of H.L.A. Hart's exceptionally influential essay, we refrained from including any of the fine articles that were reprinted in Norman Daniels's 1975 collection, *Reading Rawls*,[2] which the reader interested in the early reception of Rawls's views should consult.

Utilizing all of these selection criteria did not leave us without painful choices. The secondary literature on Rawls is so deep that another set of five volumes could cover all the main issues with a completely non-overlapping set of fine articles. Some articles unfortunately had to be cut because of their sheer length: dropping one of them allowed us to include two or three others. Others, more arbitrarily, fell victim to the high permissions costs set by their initial publishers. We particularly regret that it proved impossible to find a short enough, self-contained essay by Robert Nozick that would have represented his trenchant libertarian critique of Rawls. While we do include (in Vol. 3) some of the secondary literature that responds to and picks up on Nozick's influential arguments, one should consult Nozick's *Anarchy, State, and Utopia* (1974) to appreciate their richness, subtlety, and power.[3]

The five volumes are arranged in roughly chronological order. The first volume includes articles on Rawls's early statements of his view and on its central contractarian ideas. Volume 2 covers the two principles of justice as fairness and Rawls's most general ideas about their justification. Volume 3 focuses on the concrete implications of Rawls's view and on the debates between Rawls and his utilitarian, perfectionist, libertarian, conservative, radical, and feminist critics. Volume 4 treats of Rawls's moral psychology and his attempt to accommodate the value of community. Volume 5, on Rawls's most recent work, is entitled "Reasonable Pluralism."

The serious student of Rawls's initial impact is greatly assisted by *John Rawls and His Critics: An Annotated Bibliography*, put together by J.H. Wellbank, Denis Snook, and David T. Mason, which catalogues and provides abstracts for most of the secondary literature in English prior to 1982.[4] While this work was of great help with that earlier period, completing the onerous task of collecting and sorting through the voluminous secondary literature, which has since continued to balloon, would not have been possible without the able and thorough research assistance of Rachael Yocum. We are grateful to the Dean of Georgetown College and to the Graduate School of Georgetown University for their generosity in supporting this research assistance.

Henry S. Richardson
Paul J. Weithman

Notes

[1] John Rawls, *Collected Papers*, ed. Samuel Freeman (Cambridge, Mass.: Harvard University Press, 1999).
[2] Norman Daniels, ed., *Reading Rawls* (N.Y.: Basic Books, 1975).
[3] Robert Nozick, *Anarchy, State, and Utopia* (N.Y.: Basic Books, 1974).
[4] J.H. Wellbank, Denis Snook, and David T. Mason, *John Rawls and His Critics: An Annotated Bibliography* (New York: Garland, 1982).

Volume Introduction

This volume reprints articles representing criticisms of Rawls's justice as fairness, as presented in his 1971 book, *A Theory of Justice* [*TJ*],[1] that involve comparing his view to distinctly identifiable opposed points of view, and also covers attempts to extend the principles of justice as fairness, or his style of social contract view, beyond the subject-matter of the basic structure of society, to which *TJ* largely confines itself. The opposed points of view fall into two classes: those regarding which *TJ* itself compares the merits of justice as fairness (utilitarianism, perfectionism, and libertarianism) and those it does not (here grouped as conservative, leftist, or feminist).

Comparison of the two principles of justice as fairness (whose content is the focus of Vol. 2) with alternative principles is built into the argumentative strategy of Rawls's social contract procedure. The parties in the original position (OP) — whose motivational and cognitive states are defined by Rawls and justified on the basis of ideals that, he hopes, "we do in fact accept" (*TJ*, 587) — are not asked to devise principles, but rather to select among a relatively small number of alternative principles that seem worthy of consideration. The principal alternatives besides justice as fairness are utilitarianism, perfectionism, and libertarianism.[2]

As noted in the Introduction to Vol. 1, Rawls describes the principal aim of *TJ* as being to develop a well-articulated and richly-defended alternative to the utilitarian view, which defines right and wrong in terms of the aggregate happiness of individuals. Utilizing the social contract apparatus as a way of smoking out the fundamental assumptions of different theories, Rawls distinguishes sharply between two kinds of utilitarianism: classical utilitarianism, typified by Jeremy Bentham's, which holds that right actions as those that maximize the *sum* of individuals' utility; and average utilitarianism, typified by John Harsanyi's, which instead directs one to maximize the *average* level of individuals' utility.[3] This differentiation is somewhat surprising, as the concrete recommendations of the two versions do not differ except where variable population size comes into play. The latter, as Harsanyi argues, emerges naturally from a social contract procedure in which, as in Rawls's, the parties to the contract choose without knowing which position in society they would occupy, but also without some of the other moral constraints that Rawls builds into the OP. Classical utilitarianism, by contrast, can be arrived at either (1) by simply concluding that, happiness being the only good, all that matters is how much of it there is and not how it is located in individuals, or (2) by utilizing the alternative imaginative device of a sympathetic spectator who decides what ought to be done "when he has made the rounds of all the affected parties, so to speak" (as Rawls suggests, TJ, 186). Accordingly, Rawls claims, "classical utilitarianism fails to take seriously the distinction between persons" (TJ, 187). The contest between justice as fairness and average utilitarianism thus hinges largely on whether the parties to the OP, behind the veil of ignorance, would favor maximizing their expected welfare or would, instead, be drawn to principles that would protect them more securely against unacceptable outcomes.   In other words, would they be drawn to anything like the "maximin" principle, which says to pick the option that has the highest level for the worst-off person (see the Introduction to Vol. 1). The comparison between justice as fairness and classical utilitarianism, by contrast, depends more upon how moral theory ought to take account of the separateness of persons.

The articles reprinted here reflect each of these lines of inquiry. David Lyons's early article criticizes Rawls's view from a utilitarian direction, arguing from that point of view against the assumptions that lead Rawls in the direction of maximin (for more general critical consideration of maximin, see Vol. 1). Gregory S. Kavka's article, which takes up the differentiation between the two forms of utilitarianism discussed in the last paragraph, is especially useful in raising interesting and problematic issues about how to conceive of possible people from the point of view of the OP. He notes difficulties that arise from the fact that the principles of justice to be chosen, applying as they do to the basic structure of society, will apply to many generations of individuals. Whereas Kavka concludes that these difficulties indicate that Rawls's way of treating inter-generational justice is inelegant and ad hoc, Brian Barry's article, also reprinted here, argues that they reveal deeper problems with Rawls's view.

Rawls understands by "the principle of perfection" the view that society ought to be arranged so as to promote the achievement of some relatively richly-described good, such as human cultural excellence or human flourishing as described by Aristotle (TJ, sec. 50). Rawls's main argument against it is quite simple: it is that, given the pluralism of views that set the subjective circumstances of justice (see the Introduction to Vol. 1), the parties in the OP do not agree on any such standard of goodness. The perfectionist view, not prominent while Rawls was preparing TJ, has since been ably defended and developed.[4] While the communitarian critique of justice as fairness discussed in Volume 4 often leans on an unstated principle of perfectionism, there are relatively few articles in the literature that criticize Rawls's argument against the principle of perfection in the terms he presented it. The reprinted article by Kai Nielsen finds these arguments of Rawls's question-begging.

While Rawls does describe a libertarian opponent within TJ ("liberal equality": see pp. 65, 73), a stronger and more sharply opposed libertarian position was put forward in Robert Nozick's brilliant 1974 book, Anarchy, State, and Utopia.[5] Pursuing a different strand of the social contract tradition and starting from the assumption that individuals have certain rights, Nozick used the idea of a state of nature (absent government) to build an argument that individuals would freely consent only to a minimal state. In particular, they would not consent to the sort of (re-)distributive role that Rawls's difference principle (Vol. 2) seems to assume that government must take. Nozick's alternative theory of distributive justice was historical. Simplifying somewhat, his view is that if one can assume that initial holdings of property were justly acquired, then as long as subsequent transactions are mutually consensual, the resulting pattern of property holdings is just, whatever it is. Attempts by government to interfere with this free result in order to satisfy some abstractly-stated standard of distributive justice will unjustifiably violate individuals' property rights. Such efforts will always be necessary, for liberty will lead to any aimed-at pattern of distribution being upset by consensual transactions.

The philosophical debate about the relative merits of Rawls's and Nozick's positions has centered on the appropriate way to understand claims of desert. A natural way to put the libertarian position is to say that individuals deserve to reap the fruits of their labor, and that redistributive efforts take from some what they deserve. Rawls holds, to the contrary, that the notion of desert is applicable only within an institution or a set of rules, and one must first determine whether that set of rules is fair or just (*TJ*, sec. 48). This is what his justice as fairness, in developing principles of justice to apply to the basic structure of society, attempts to do. *Within* a just basic structure, such claims do arise; but to signal that they arise only relative to a just set of arrangements, Rawls prefers to call them "legitimate expectations." Hence, a key question to ask in assessing the disagreement between Rawls and the libertarians is whether one can imagine consensual economic transactions occurring without a basic structure of social institutions (such as property and contract law) already in place. If one can, then one can perhaps imagine the kind of evolution out of a state of nature that Nozick describes occurring without depending on a basic set of social institutions. If, on the other hand, one believes that the idea of "consensual" economic transactions is parasitic on a set of basic social conventions that helps settle which threats are coercive and which are not, then one will have reason for going along with Rawls's view that one must take the basic structure into account as a separate step in developing a theory of social justice (see *PL*, 262–5).

The pieces reprinted here address the disagreement between Rawls and the libertarians in these terms. The article by Allen Buchanan carries Nozick's idea about liberty upsetting patterns to a higher level of generality. He notes that the basic structure will need to include institutions that allow for social change. Buchanan suggests that Rawls's theory can cope with this problem in this form, as well as in the form originally posed by Nozick. George Sher's essay, by contrast, seeks to undercut Rawls's shift from desert to legitimate expectations. He points out that Rawls's position on this seems to assume that one must deserve that on which one bases one's claims (such as one's abilities and talents). This assumption he finds questionable. This debate about desert and its basis, having been widened in the 1980s by Michael Sandel's criticisms (see Vol. 4),[6] is ongoing, as witness the relatively recent article by Stephen W. Ball.

The debate engendered by Nozick's libertarian critique of Rawls reminds us that Rawls takes the basic structure of society to be the sole subject-matter to which the principles of justice as fairness are addressed. Both these principles and his social contract apparatus, however, have proved attractive and useful to ethical theorists with other problems in view. In *TJ*, indeed, Rawls remarks that "it is clear that the contractarian idea can be extended to the choice of more or less an entire ethical system" (17). However that may be, Rawls himself has moved, if anything, in the opposite direction, insisting now (in *PL*) upon presenting and defending justice as fairness as an account of political justice and not as a part of a comprehensive moral view. Others, however, have made their own efforts to extend the view.[7] In his article here, Thomas E. Hill, Jr., thoughtfully discusses the obstacles facing any such attempt at extension. Specifically, he notes the features of the OP that seem specific to political ethics and inappropriate for generating principles of personal ethics. There are many kinds of questions of political ethics, however. To make his argumentative task simpler, Rawls limits his attention to the basic institutions of a single nation. Noting the artificiality of this restriction of the theory's scope, Charles R. Beitz's article early raised important issues about how the theory might generalize to the international arena. Thomas Pogge, who has published a series of reflections on this question since the early 1980s, takes account of Rawls's own article on the subject, "The Law of Peoples" (1993),[8] in the piece reprinted here.

Rawls's ideas have also been brought to bear on more specific topics. Some of these discussions emerge from some of the many concrete discussions that fill Part II of *TJ*, which describes an exemplary set of social institutions in order to check the fit between the implications of his principles and our more concrete considered judgments. One of the issues he there touches upon (sec. 55) is civil disobedience, an issue at the forefront of public conversation during the civil rights struggles of the 1960s and 70s. Joel Feinberg's reprinted article puts Rawls's stance on civil disobedience under pressure, in part as a way to raise questions about the way that his view generates conclusions about such relatively concrete matters. Some concrete issues are excluded from the consideration of the parties in the OP by Rawls's idealizing assumptions. For instance, he has the parties assume that all persons in the society for which they are choosing principles are fully cooperating members. Thus, issues involving the disabled are set aside, as too difficult to deal with in a first cut at a theory of social justice. Even farther from Rawls's intention is to apply the view to non-human animals and to the natural environment. The article by Michael S. Pritchard and Wade L. Robison argues nonetheless for the former extension, urging that it yields a distorted view of the basic structure to ignore issues of cruelty to other animals. Brent A. Singer's piece also treats issues involving animals and advocates including environmental goods in the list of primary goods.

The final third of this Volume is devoted to critiques that come from three perspectives not represented by principles that Rawls considers from within the perspective of the OP: conservatism, Marxist and related leftist positions, and feminism. Comparing Rawls to the *philosophes* of the French Revolution, Robert Nisbet's early, vividly argued criticism typifies the hostile conservative hostility to Rawls's sort of abstract theorizing and to his serious commitment to equality. Coming from an exactly opposite point of view, C.B. Macpherson's article attacks Rawls for *justifying* inequality (in the way the difference principle does: see the Introduction and the article by Van Parijs in Vol. 2). The reprinted article by Arthur DiQuattro defends Rawls against the Marxist critiques of Macpherson and others, arguing that Rawls's principles rule out a class society.[9]

There are many feminist perspectives, and many have generated criticisms of Rawls. A classic feminist critique is that by Susan Moller Okin, reprinted here.[10] Okin's criticism contrasts Rawls's reliance on reason with a more caring or emotionally-based approach to ethics and criticizes Rawls's seeming acceptance of the traditional family unit.[11] Amy R. Baehr's article further develops this line of criticism, answering some of the initial Rawlsian responses to Okin.

Henry S. Richardson

Notes

[1] John Rawls, *A Theory of Justice* (Cambridge: Harvard University Press, Belknap, 1971).

[2] Additional possibilities Rawls discusses include those (besides libertarianism) that arise from the four different interpretations of the second principle that he lays out on *TJ*, 65, "intuitionistic" conceptions that involve a plurality of principles without any priority ordering among them, egoistic conceptions, and mixed conceptions that blend the others in various ways. These possibilities are laid out on *TJ*, 124.

[3] Jeremy Bentham, "An Introduction to the Principles of Morals and Legislation," eds. J.H. Burns and H.L.A. Hart (London: Athlone Press, 1970). John C. Harsanyi, "Morality and the Theory of Rational Behaviour," in *Utilitarianism and Beyond*, eds. Amartya Sen and Bernard Williams (Cambridge: Cambridge University Press, 1982), 39–62.

[4] See, e.g., Martha C. Nussbaum, "Aristotelian Social Democracy," in *Liberalism and the Good*, eds. R. Bruce Douglass, Gerald M. Mara, and Henry S. Richardson (N.Y.: Routledge, 1990), 203–52; and Thomas Hurka, *Perfectionism* (Oxford: Oxford University Press, 1993).

[5] Robert Nozick, *Anarchy, State, and Utopia* (N.Y.: Basic Books, 1974).

[6] Michael J. Sandel, *Liberalism and the Limits of Justice* (Cambridge: Cambridge University Press, 1982).

[7] And see now the independent contractarian moral view developed in T.M. Scanlon, *What We Owe to Each Other* (Cambridge, Mass.: Harvard University Press, 1998).

[8] John Rawls, "The Law of Peoples," in *On Human Rights* (Basic Books, 1993), 41–231.

[9] For arguments urging that Rawls's own approach implies a more radically egalitarian stance than he has lately taken, see Thomas W. Pogge, *Realizing Rawls* (Ithaca: Cornell University Press, 1989) and Rodney G. Peffer, "Towards a More Adequate Rawlsian Theory of Social Justice," *Pacific Philosophical Quarterly* 75 (September/December 1994): 251–71.

[10] See also Susan Moller Okin, *Justice, Gender, and the Family* (New York: Basic Books, 1989).

[11] For a rebuttal of Okin's criticisms, see Sharon Lloyd, "Family Justice and Social Justice," *Pacific Philosophical Quarterly* 75 (1994): 353–71.

Further Reading

Bentham, Jeremy. "An Introduction to the Principles of Morals and Legislation." Burns, J.H., Hart, H.L.A eds. London: Athlone Press, 1970.

Harsanyi, John C. "Morality and the Theory of Rational Behaviour." In *Utilitarianism and Beyond*, eds. Amartya Sen and Bernard Williams, 39–62. Cambridge: Cambridge University Press, 1982.

Hurka, Thomas. *Perfectionism*. Oxford: Oxford University Press, 1993.

Lloyd, Sharon. "Family Justice and Social Justice." *Pacific Philosophical Quarterly* 75 (1994): 353–71.

Nozick, Robert. *Anarchy, State, and Utopia*. N.Y.: Basic Books, 1974.

Nussbaum, Martha C. "Aristotelian Social Democracy." In *Liberalism and the Good*, eds. R. Bruce Douglass, Gerald M. Mara, and Henry S. Richardson, 203–52. N.Y.: Routledge, 1990.

Okin, Susan Moller. *Justice, Gender, and the Family*. New York: Basic Books, 1989.

Peffer, Rodney G. "Towards a More Adequate Rawlsian Theory of Social Justice." *Pacific Philosophical Quarterly* 75 (September/December 1994): 251–71.

Pogge, Thomas W. *Realizing Rawls*. Ithaca: Cornell University Press, 1989.

Rawls, John. "The Law of Peoples." In *On Human Rights*, 41–231. Basic Books, 1993.

———. *A Theory of Justice*. Cambridge: Harvard University Press, Belknap, 1971.

Sandel, Michael J. *Liberalism and the Limits of Justice*. Cambridge: Cambridge University Press, 1982.

Scanlon, T.M. *What We Owe to Each Other*. Cambridge, Mass.: Harvard University Press, 1998.

THE JOURNAL OF PHILOSOPHY

VOLUME LXIX, NO. 18, OCTOBER 5, 1972

RAWLS VERSUS UTILITARIANISM *

IN *A Theory of Justice,* John Rawls† develops and defends a conception of justice that is centered on such notions as liberty and reciprocity. I am sympathetic to the general style of argument suggested by Rawls, but in this paper I wish to pay his specific arguments the respect they deserve by airing some serious reservations. I agree with Rawls that utilitarianism is the single most important type of theory with which he must contend, and I shall concentrate on Rawls's arguments to show the superiority of his principles to utilitarianism.[1]

I

Rawls is chiefly concerned to defend two principles. The *Greatest Equal Liberty Principle* concerns the distribution of liberty, and says that each person has an equal right to the most extensive basic liberty compatible with a like liberty for others. The second principle concerns the distribution of other "primary goods," such as income and wealth, power and authority. It has two parts, each of which is also called a principle; it says that social and economic inequalities are to be arranged so that they are (a) reasonably expected to be to everyone's advantage (this is the *Difference Principle*), and (b) attached to positions in society that are open to all (the

* To be presented in an APA symposium on *A Theory of Justice* by John Rawls, December 27, 1972; cosymposiasts will be Michael Teitelman and John Rawls: see this JOURNAL, this issue, pp. 545–556 and 556/7, respectively.

I am grateful to Robert S. Summers for his very helpful comments on an earlier draft of this paper.

† Cambridge, Mass.: Belknap Press, 1971. Parenthetical page references in the text will be to this book, unless otherwise noted. I shall keep such references to a minimum; most topics are discussed in several places in the book.

[1] Traditional forms of utilitarianism, that is, not including some recent forms of rule-utilitarianism; see Rawls, p. 182, note 31. I shall ignore differences among the several traditional forms, for they are irrelevant here.

1

Fair Equality of Opportunity Principle). According to Rawls, the violation of any of these principles is an injustice (60).[2]

Rawls claims that his principles take precedence over any others, and the result is a conception remarkably at variance with utilitarianism. Consider his Greatest Equal Liberty Principle. Rawls maintains that liberty may not be restricted save to secure the maximum liberty possible under concrete circumstances. And he stresses that limitations on liberty and inequalities of freedom cannot be justified on the ground that they promote the general interest—by affording, say, a higher standard of living. In contrast, utilitarians are committed only to serving the general welfare, not to securing equal or maximum liberty. Accordingly, utilitarians could so justify restrictions on freedom. Thus Rawls's conception of justice stands in conflict with utilitarianism.

It diverges significantly from utilitarianism even without his Greatest Equal Liberty Principle. The general interest (to which utilitarianism is committed) might require that the good of some persons be sacrificed in order to serve the greater good of others, but Rawls's Difference Principle would not permit this. According to Rawls, social inequalities are permissible only if everyone benefits from them: if a person is worse off than others are, justice is done only if he is nevertheless *better* off than he would be *without* the inequality.[3]

How can one defend such a substantive moral position? What kinds of argument are possible? It is sometimes thought that normative theories simply "account for" certain lower-level or more specific judgments, by serving as principles from which the latter could be derived. Rawls argues partly in this way, for he believes that his principles are most congruent with our strongest considered moral convictions. But Rawls recognizes that this "congruence" argument cannot be conclusive, because none of the relevant judgments can be considered incorrigible, and the fit between such judgments and any plausible conception of justice will never be perfect. Accordingly, he constructs a more direct "contractarian" argument. Whereas a congruence argument may seem to yield at best a rational reconstruction of one's moral convictions, Rawls ap-

---

[2] I am guided here by Rawls's simpler formulations; for a fuller statement, see 302ff. I shall avoid qualifications wherever possible, including those created by the Fair Equality of Opportunity Principle, which will hereafter be ignored because it is irrelevant to the issues of this paper.

[3] The principles actually concern "representative persons in the various social positions" (64). Sometimes Rawls suggests a concern only for the worst off, but this seems a simplification; see, e.g., 82f.

pears to consider his contractarian argument a *justification* for substantive principles—the strongest kind the subject will allow, and
a substantial argument at that.[4] According to this argument, Rawls's
principles of justice are those principles which "free and rational
persons concerned to further their own interests would accept in an
initial position of equality as defining the fundamental terms of
their association" (11).

The congruence argument is important, and I shall say a word
about it. But the contract argument is Rawls's main weapon, and it
requires most of our attention.

II

In his earlier paper, "Justice as Fairness," [5] Rawls suggested that
his principles were more congruent than utilitarianism is with our
strongest considered moral judgments, because, for example, they
"always" condemn such institutions as serfdom and slavery, whereas
for utilitarianism it is a contingent and therefore logically an open
question whether serfdom and slavery could be justified.[6] But there
was, in fact, *no* such difference between Rawls's principles and utilitarianism. The Greatest Equal Liberty Principle *of that paper*
could not absolutely exclude serfdom or slavery, for it was held to
express no more than a *presumption* in favor of equal maximum
liberty. Inequalities of liberty as well as of other social goods could
be justified by the reasonable expectation that everyone would
benefit.[7] (Note that the requirement was for *everyone* to benefit,
not for all to benefit *equally*.) It is a contingent question whether
serfdom or slavery would, under some conditions, lead to net benefits for all, even benefits that would not otherwise be obtainable. So
it became, on Rawls's earlier view, a contingent question whether
serfdom or slavery could be justified.

Today, in *A Theory of Justice,* Rawls eliminates some irregu-
larities that plagued his earlier conception. He segregates liberty
from the other social goods (making its distribution the concern of
the Greatest Equal Liberty Principle alone), and argues for the
"priority" of liberty—that it may not be traded for other benefits.
His new position may thus seem to exclude such arrangements as

---

[4] Though the contractual conditions themselves would seem to depend on
moral judgments of a general or abstract kind, concerning, e.g., the constraint of
impartiality on moral reasoning; see, e.g., Rawls, p. 130.

[5] *Philosophical Review,* LXVII, 2 (April 1958): 164–194.

[6] *Ibid.*, p. 188 (sec. 7, first paragraph).

[7] "The first principle holds, of course, only if other things are equal. . . . the
second principle defines how this presumption may be rebutted," *ibid.*, 166f (sec
2, third para.).

serfdom and slavery, for these presumably violate the now categorical Greatest Equal Liberty Principle. But Rawls seems to acknowledge (what is at any rate true) that his new position is *logically* compatible with serfdom and slavery. For Rawls, the priority of liberty is predicated on the existence of certain "favorable" conditions, in which liberties can be "effectively" established and exercised (152, 244ff). Under such happy circumstances, his libertarian "special conception" of justice, consisting of the principles so far described, is to apply. Under conditions less favorable to the establishment and exercise of liberty, the inviolability of liberty cannot be defended, compromises must be made, and the special conception gives way to what Rawls calls a "general conception" of justice. This is a generalized version of the Difference Principle, covering distributions of liberty as well as other goods, and saying that all "are to be distributed equally unless an unequal distribution of any, or all, of these values is to everyone's advantage" (62; cf. 303). It requires that everyone benefit from unequal distributions, but allows liberty to be exchanged for other benefits. The general conception thus resembles Rawls's view in "Justice as Fairness."

I do not mean to suggest that Rawlsian justice is indistinguishable from utilitarianism. I have already indicated some of the striking differences between the two positions. Even under unfavorable conditions, for example, Rawls requires that inequalities benefit all persons, whereas utilitarianism requires only that the general interest be served. The utilitarian would have one weigh all benefits and burdens, whereas Rawls says that benefits derived from inequalities that do not benefit everyone need not be considered. Much more could be said. But this means only that the two *conceptions* are different; that, for example, the considerations sanctioned by Rawls's principles are different from the utilitarian's. It does not show that they have significantly different practical implications. It does not show, for example, that some social arrangements that we judge, on reflection, to be unjust are approved by utility but not by Rawls's principles; nor does it show that such institutions are more likely under utilitarianism. Now, it may well be that Rawls's conception of justice *is* over-all more congruent with our considered moral judgments, in view of differing implications; but the examples of serfdom and slavery indicate that such differences will not be as striking as one might at first expect. It follows that the congruence argument for Rawls against utilitarianism is somewhat weaker than it may at first appear.

My main concern is, however, with Rawls's contract argument for his principles over utilitarianism. I wish to show how the implication of Rawls's full position undermine that argument.

III

The parties to Rawls's hypothetical contract are to reason from a self-interested standpoint based on how they would fare if society were regulated by this or that conception of justice. Because of the special circumstances in which their selection must be made, Rawls maintains that they would choose principles that allow the *least undesirable* condition for the *worst*-off members of society. In short, they will choose the least risky principles.

I shall return to the reasoning behind this mode of argument later. Right now I wish to emphasize that Rawls directs the parties' attention to *possible* (not *likely*) risks. And his strong belief that his supposedly less risky principles would be chosen over utilitarianism suggests the sort of contrast we considered before. It *looks* as if the parties are imagined to compare utilitarianism, which might permit serfdom or slavery, with Rawls's special conception of justice, including his *Greatest Equal Liberty Principle* which holds liberty inviolable and thus excludes those institutions. Rawls offers a short list of alternative conceptions of justice to be considered by the parties in the "original position" (or hypothetical choice situations) and then stipulates that each conception is to be regarded as holding "unconditionally, that is, whatever the circumstances of society" (125). The list includes utilitarianism (which of course *is* supposed to cover all cases) and Rawls's special conception of justice. Now, if the parties compare utilitarianism with Rawls's special conception, *of course* they will find the former riskier, by Rawls's test, for the worst-off presumably fare very badly under serfdom and slavery, which are compatible with utilitarianism but not with the special conception. And it is quite proper for the parties to compare utilitarianism and Rawls's special conception in the initial-contract argument, as we shall see. It is a mistake, however, to suggest that the competing conceptions of justice are to be regarded as applying in *all* circumstances. Rawls explicitly rules this out. There are at least two stages to the contract argument, one assuming conditions favorable to the effective establishment and exercise of liberty, another without that assumption. Rawls seems to conflate these stages in such a way as to make utilitarianism, misleadingly, appear less acceptable to the parties in the original position. I shall try to explain.

Rawls has perfectly good reason to develop his argument in stages. It suffices to mention that, given the choice situation as so

5

far defined, the results of the parties' deliberations may well be indeterminate (140). The range of problems that could be covered by
distributive principles and the alternatives to be considered need to
be restricted. Once that is done, and principles are chosen for ideal
circumstances, the argument is to be extended to cover the more
difficult problems as well as the more diverse circumstances of ordinary everyday life.

Rawls makes the selection of principles easier by stipulating that
the original position have certain additional features, which seem
to restrict the *applicability* of the principles initially chosen and
affect the comparison with utilitarianism. For example, the parties
are allowed to know that they can benefit from social cooperation
and that they need some way of adjudicating claims upon socially
distributed goods (128); this allows us to ignore some extreme cases
in which questions of justice can arise—and obliges us to disregard
what utilitarianism has to say about them. The parties are not to
consider all questions of distribution, but only those concerning the
"basic structure" of a society (7); the parties are initially to choose
principles only for the governance of a "well-ordered society" under
happy circumstances (4f, 245); they are to count on each others'
firm commitment to any principle that they can unanimously accept (145); they are to assume that the basic structure of their society will satisfy such principles (4f); and they are to take for
granted that favorable conditions obtain for the effective establishment and exercise of basic liberties (245).

Other important conditions laid down by Rawls are designed not
only to simplify the choice problem but also to guarantee the moral
quality of the outcome. For example, Rawls imposes certain constraints "associated with the concept of right" (130ff) and restricts
the alternative principles for consideration by the parties to "rec-
ognizably ethical" conceptions (125). Also, the parties are assumed
to have whatever general information is relevant to their deliberations, such as the principles of (true) social theory; but they are
deprived of specific information about their society, their own
status in it, their specific interests, and their natural endowments—
Rawls calls this a "veil of ignorance" (136ff). Given this knowledge
and lack of knowledge, each party must reason from the same premises; so, if any one forms a preference, universal agreement on the
point is presumably guaranteed (140). Also, moral principles are
supposed to be "general," and the veil of ignorance helps to meet
this constraint by preventing the contractors from rigging principles to serve their special interests (131). They are, as it were, forced
to decide impartially (190).

6

After the parties have chosen principles to govern in *ideal* circumstances, they are to lay down guidelines for less happy conditions—when, for example, institutions do not satisfy the shared conception of justice, or different conceptions compete for acceptance in society, or some persons pose a serious threat to the security of others (chap. IV). Rawls informally extends his argument to cover such cases. The results are highly complex, and it can be said that they express a bias toward liberty (152). But it would appear that Rawls's general conception of justice is most generally supposed to apply.

Thus, the *initial* contract argument is claimed to yield the special conception of justice, with liberty inviolable. But the special conception is *restricted* to certain favorable conditions; it has no direct application to other circumstances. The special conception is a special case or qualification of the general conception, the chief difference being that liberty is segregated and given priority (inviolability) under the special conception. Rawls's strategy of argument in the original position has a certain risk-averting character, which, once assumed, may seem most naturally to yield the general conception of justice. What the special conception requires, in addition, are reasons for the inviolability of liberty. These are contingent upon the favorable circumstances initially assumed. When those conditions no longer exist, the priority of liberty cannot be sustained and the general conception *simpliciter* results. For our purposes, it will be clearest to think of a two-stage argument against utilitarianism, first for the special conception under ideal conditions, second for the general conception under non-ideal conditions.

The contract argument does not seem so convincing when its limits and complexity are acknowledged. In the initial stage, we do not compare utilitarianism *simpliciter* with Rawls's principles; we must compare a Rawlsian well-ordered society, governed by the special conception of justice, under favorable conditions, with a utilitarian well-ordered society *under similar conditions*. We must allow the utilitarian all the advantages of Rawls's stipulations; we are not to consider utilitarianism under *all* conditions, but only under certain most favorable ones. Now, as I have remarked, utilitarianism does not change its shape or content under different social conditions, as Rawls allows his principles to do; so one may be tempted to argue that utilitarianism is riskier than Rawls' special conception, because there is a sense in which utilitarianism remains compatible with serfdom and slavery, even under favorable conditions, although Rawls's special conception rules them out. But this would be mistaken. Mere logical possibilities are not in ques-

7

tion here, or anywhere else in Rawls's argument. As the parties in the original position are assumed to know all the relevant general facts and principles about human interaction and social organization, they would restrict their attention to possibilities that are compatible with these contingent limitations. Their question is not whether utilitarianism *simpliciter* is logically compatible with serfdom or slavery, for example, but whether utilitarianism *under the favorable conditions assumed in the initial stage of the contract argument* could possibly approve such institutions. We have no reason to believe this. Until we know more about the relevant conditions, we must withhold judgment. This does not mean that utilitarianism can be rejected because of possible, though uncertain, risks. The parties in the original position are assumed to have the relevant general information, and they may very well be able to answer our question. Perhaps they can see that there are *no* such risks under utilitarianism in the relevant conditions. If so, the contract argument would collapse. At best, it stands in need of substantiation.

Similar considerations apply to the second stage of the contract argument. We no longer assume the most happy circumstances, and we must therefore compare utilitarianism with Rawls's general conception of justice. But both alternatives are logically compatible with arrangements like serfdom and slavery; so the striking contrast between them seems to disappear.

It might be thought that Rawls could reason as follows. The utilitarian criterion (promote the general interest) is logically weaker than the Rawlsian (benefit everyone), because the former allows the good of some to be sacrificed for the general interest, but the latter does not. So it is logically possible for there to be circumstances in which institutions sanctioned by utilitarianism would not be allowed by Rawls's conception of justice, and it is possible that the worst-off members of society would do worse under utilitarianism than under Rawlsian arrangements in the *same* circumstances. In a similar way, it could be argued that the worst-off members of society could perhaps fare worse under utilitarianism than under Rawls's principles *even within* arrangements like serfdom and slavery, and also that there are *more* logically possible circumstances in which very bad conditions would be experienced by the worst-off members of a utilitarian society than under Rawlsian arrangements. For reasons like these, it may seem to follow that utilitarianism is generally riskier by Rawls's test, which concerns the condition of the worst-off members of society. But this would be mistaken, largely for reasons already given. Logical possibilities are not in question here. The relevant question faced by the parties in the original position is whether there is *some contingently* possible condition of the worst-off members of society under utilitarianism that is worse than *any contingently* possible condition for them under Rawlsian arrangements. Under Rawls's own strictures, they must answer this question affirmatively if this central argument is to give them a reason for preferring Rawls's conception of justice to utilitarianism. Rawls has given us no substantive reason to accept this claim. I conclude, therefore, that the second stage of the contract argument also stands in need of substantiation.

It should be emphasized that Rawls offers many other considerations favoring his principles over utilitarianism. But I believe the argument just reviewed is the backbone of Rawls's contractarian claims, without which the others would have little significance.

IV

I wish finally to consider the reasoning *behind* the risk-aversion argument that I have criticized. Rawls observes: "There is an analogy between the two principles and the maximin rule for choice under uncertainty. This is evident from the fact that the two principles are those a person would choose for the design of a society in which his enemy is to assign him his place. The maximin rule tells us to rank alternatives by their worst possible outcomes; we are to adopt the alternative the worst outcome of which is superior to the worst outcome of the others" (152f).

Rawls wishes to show that his use of the maximin approach does not merely express an arbitrary aversion to risk. He admits that "the maximin rule is not, in general, a suitable guide for choices under uncertainty" (153). A more "natural" rule would have us maximize expectations, taking into account the likelihood of various undesirable outcomes as well as the probability of benefits (154). Such reasoning would lead to a form of utilitarianism; so Rawls's use of the maximin rule is obviously crucial. Rawls must defend his risk-averting argumentative strategy and then substantiate his arguments in the ways we have already indicated. Rawls says that "there appear to be three chief features of situations that give plausibility to this unusual rule" (154). I shall limit my comments to these features and to Rawls's arguments to show that they are aspects of the original position.

(1) In the original position, "knowledge of likelihoods is impossible, or at best extremely insecure" (154). Because a party in the original position is deprived of information about his own specific

9

circumstances (the "veil of ignorance"), he cannot reason that *he* is more or less *likely* to live well or badly under these or those conditions. He knows only the possible outcomes, not how likely they are. This appears to exclude any attempt to maximize expectations, which would lead toward utilitarianism (155f).

Rawls's claim seems false; probability calculations are possible in the original position. One is of course barred from basing one's calculations on, say, one's own personal good or bad fortune in the "natural lottery" or on the special conditions of one's own society; for these are unknown to the parties under the veil of ignorance. But the parties are assumed to have complete knowledge of theory and of facts that cannot serve special interests. I see no reason why one cannot use such information for calculating the likelihood of one's having certain natural endowments and the likelihood of one's society being in a certain broadly defined condition. Of course, a more specifically informed basis for calculating probabilities would be more satisfactory to the individual. It does not follow, however, that rationally respectable probability calculations are impossible. I conclude that, despite the veil of ignorance, the parties in the original position can still calculate to maximize general expectations, which Rawls admits is generally the most natural approach. It is therefore difficult to see why they would opt for the maximin rule, and not naturally incline toward utilitarianism.

(2) Rawls also claims that "the person choosing has a conception of the good such that he cares very little, if anything, for what he might gain above the minimum stipend that he can, in fact, be sure of by following the maximin rule" (154; cf. 156). But it is difficult to see how a party in the original position *could* reason in this way, since the veil of ignorance deprives him of information about his own conception of the good (his own rational plan of life). One could so reason *only* on the basis of a certain *likelihood* of having a certain conception of the good, or one within a broadly defined range. Rawls does in fact use a similar kind of argument, though not in such words in this place. He restricts his attention to the social distribution of what he calls "primary goods," such as liberty, income and wealth, and power and authority; for he supposes, quite plausibly, that these are things it is reasonable to believe that anyone would want, whatever his conception of the good (62, 92). But, of course, there *can* be extreme conceptions of the good, suited to this or that unusual individual, which place more or less value on one or another of these items. The argument for considering primary goods (rather than, say, sat-

isfactions) is thus based on the kind of actuarial calculation that I suggested could be made in the original position. Knowing the relevant general facts about humanity, one reasons in the original position that it is *most likely* that one will want freedom, wealth, power, and so on. But if one can reason in this way, as Rawls seems to admit, then significant probabilistic reasoning may also be possible in the original position, and the first condition does not obtain. Thus, the first and second features seem to be mutually exclusive.

(3) Rawls claims, finally, that "the rejected alternatives [e.g., utilitarianism] have outcomes that one can hardly accept" (154; cf. 156). But we have already seen that this is highly doubtful. Under favorable conditions, we have no reason to believe that utilitarianism *has* unacceptable conditions for the worst-off members of society; under other contingently possible conditions, we have no reason to believe that the worst conditions actually allowed by Rawls' principles are any better than those allowed by utilitarianism.

It therefore seems as if at least two of the claims underlying Rawls's use of the maximin strategy cannot be sustained. The original position does not have the requisite features. The contract argument therefore seems to stand on very shaky foundations.

DAVID LYONS

Cornell University

GREGORY S. KAVKA

RAWLS ON AVERAGE AND TOTAL UTILITY

(Received 25 April, 1974)

"If we foresee as possible that an increase in numbers will be accompanied by a decrease in average happiness or *vice versa*, a point arises which has not only never been formally noticed, but which seems to have been substantially overlooked by many Utilitarians." – Henry Sidgwick.[1]

As Sidgwick points out, utilitarians have been very remiss in failing to discuss a central theoretical problem of utilitarianism – the problem of whether, on utilitarian principles, one ought to seek to maximize total happiness or average happiness (happiness per capita). Given a fixed population, of course, the same acts or policies which maximize one will maximize the other. But when acts or policies affect the size of the world's population, we may face situations in which we have to choose between having a smaller total population with a higher level of average happiness and a somewhat larger population with a lower level of average happiness but a higher total amount of human happiness.[2]

Sidgwick himself opts for the total happiness alternative. As he puts it, "The point up to which, on Utilitarian principles, population ought to be encouraged to increase, is not that at which average happiness is the greatest possible, ... but that at which the product formed by multiplying the number of persons living into the amount of average happiness reaches its maximum."[3] But few other utilitarians have even discussed the issue, probably because it seems hard to imagine reasoned grounds for preferring one alternative to the other. Fortunately, however, help in dealing with the average versus total utility problem has recently arrived from a nonutilitarian source. John Rawls, in presenting his theory of justice, develops a theoretical framework within which we may discover the fundamental difference in viewpoint which underlies the average and total utility principles.[4] In this paper, I shall seek to extend Rawls' insights on the average versus total utility question by noting an important and illuminating point which Rawls seems to miss in his discussion. Thus, in section I, I will very briefly outline the theoretical structure of Rawls' theory and Rawls' own discussion of the average versus total utility

Philosophical Studies **27** (1975) 237–253. *All Rights Reserved*
Copyright © 1975 by D. Reidel Publishing Company, Dordrecht-Holland

question. In section II, I will present a proposal about the perspective which the total utility principle may be derived from and will answer certain objections to that proposal. Finally, in section III, I shall raise a query about the adequacy of Rawls' theory of justice based on the observations of section II.

I

Writing within the contractarian tradition, Rawls seeks to derive a conception of justice by identifying those principles which free, rational, and purely self-interested persons in an original position of equality would choose to govern the fundamental social institutions (i.e. the political constitution and basic economic and social arrangements) they are to live under. Aware that, under normal conditions, free and rational self-interested persons would not agree on principles of justice, Rawls adds an important new wrinkle to the contractarian position by stipulating that the parties in the original position be situated behind what he calls a *veil of ignorance*. That is, we are to suppose the parties in the original position to have no knowledge of such things as their personal place in society, their personal conception of the good life, their natural talents, specific psychological facts about themselves, the particular (historic, economic, and political) circumstances of their society, and what generation they belong to. The parties are supposed to have the general knowledge germane to their choice of principles – the knowledge that the circumstances of justice[5] obtain in their society and knowledge of the laws of sociology, economics, human psychology, political science, etc.

The point of the veil of ignorance, of course, is to insure that the parties in the original position cannot rig the principles which they choose to serve their own personal advantage. Since each member does not know what personal characteristics he has, he cannot choose rules which favor persons having those characteristics at the expense of other persons. Lacking any specific knowledge of their own nature and cricumstances, the parties would, out of rational self-interest, choose principles which give fair consideration to the interests of all persons regardless of their personal characteristics or circumstances.

This contractarian model of rational self-interested individuals choosing general principles for governing society from behind a veil of ignorance can be easily applied to compare and evaluate the average and total utility principles. Rawls notes that rational self-interested persons behind the veil of ignorance (and thus ignorant of their place in society) would prefer rules producing a higher average utility rather than rules producing a higher utility total but a smaller average.[6] This can be seen most easily if we suppose that the parties must choose between living in two different societies, each of which is totally egalitarian with respect to utility distribution, i.e. the utility of each member of society is the same and equal to the utility average.[7] If we suppose that egalitarian society S_1 has the higher utility average while egalitarian society S_2 has the higher total utility, it follows from the characterization of the parties in the original position as rational and purely self-interested that they would prefer to live in society S_1. For this merely amounts to preferring the certainty of obtaining a higher utility (namely, the utility average of S_1) to the certainty of obtaining a lower utility (the utility average of S_2). Any contrary preference would imply irrationality or benevolence which are ruled out by the characterization of the parties in question.

Having noted that the average utility principle would be preferred to the total utility principle from the perspective of rational self-interested parties making choices in the original position, Rawls asks what situation of choice would favor the total utility view over the average utility view. He mentions two perspectives from which the total utility principle would be preferred.[8] First, it would be preferred by a Humean ideal observor who has sympathetic pleasures of approval and sympathetic pains of disapproval in exact proportion to the pleasures and pains of each relevant individual. For such an observor's balance of approval (or disapproval) will be directly proportional to the total balance of pleasure over pain (pain over pleasure) for the relevant group and he would thus most approve of the social arrangements which produced the highest total utility for that group. Second, the total utility view would be chosen from the perspective of a rational self-interested person who expected to live the lives (or experience the experiences) of each of the relevant individuals in succession. For the utility which such an individual would expect would be equal to the total expected utility for the group of persons in question and, being rational and self-interested, this individual would seek to maximize his personal expected utility.

It is easy to see then why Rawls considers the average utility principle much superior to the total utility principle. For the average principle is preferred by rational self-interested parties deliberating in a setting in which they are deprived of knowledge which might lead them to make unfair or biased decisions. The total utility principle, on the other hand, is preferred only from perspectives which seem to involve breaking down the distinction between human individuals, lumping all human desires and interests together in some huge conglomerate, and then treating these as if they were the desires and interests of some strange (many-lived or all-observing and perfectly sympathetic) superperson. [9] If these were the only perspectives from which the total utility principle would be preferred, Rawls would probably be justified in declaring the superiority of the average utility principle. However, Rawls overlooks another perspective underlying the total utility view – a perspective which is closely related to the perspective of rational self-interested persons choosing principles behind a veil of ignorance. Only by examining this perspective, as I shall in the next section, may we make best use of Rawls' contractarian theory to bring out the fundamental difference in perspective underlying the average and total utility principles.

II

The parties in the original position, behind the veil of ignorance, do not know their individual characteristics, their social position, or what generation they belong to. This renders them unable to bias the principles of justice they choose to favor their own interests over the interests of other persons. But there is one fact about himself that each party is assumed to know and which could, in theory, be affected by the principles chosen in the original position. This is the fact that he exists. Although the principles of justice chosen might well profoundly affect societal population policies and thus determine whether or not certain persons will or will not come into existence at all, the parties in the original position are allowed knowledge that they will exist under the chosen rules. Hence, one might say that Rawls' conception of the original position involves a (possibly justifiable) bias in favor of those already existing in the sense that it favors the interests of existing persons over the interests which would exist if certain persons who might or might not exist were brought into existence.

What this suggests is that it might be illuminating to extend the veil of ignorance to shroud the question of existence and to think of the parties in the original position as rational and self-interested *possible* persons choosing principles for governing the fundamental institutions of the society whose population policies will affect whether or not they will exist and in which they will live *if* they come into existence. In fact, it turns out that if we make certain assumptions which seem reasonable for representing the conditions of choice for possible persons in the original position, we can easily show that rational self-interested possible persons in the original position would choose those principles expected to lead to the highest total utility for the society in question in preference to principles expected to lead to a higher average but lower total utility.[10]

The conditions of choice are represented by the following five assumptions:

(1) *Possible person P, the chooser in the original position, is rational and purely self-interested.* This implies, among other things, that in choosing between two courses of action, he will in circumstances not involving risk choose the course which will yield him the higher personal utility. It also implies that under conditions of uncertainty he will choose the course which promises the higher *expected* personal utility, at least in cases in which the action having the lower expected personal utility is as risky or riskier than the action having the higher expected personal utility.

(2) *Personal utilities are quantitatively representable on a scale of (positive and negative) real numbers with '0' representing the utility of not existing at all.* The claim of quantitative representability is philosophically controversial, of course, but it is a common assumption or goal of utilitarian theories. Placing the utility of non-existence at the crossover point between net positive utility and net negative utility seems entirely natural since not existing entails experiencing neither happiness nor unhappiness.

(3) *P is confronted with a choice between two or more sets of principles. For each set of principles, he is told what the relevant society's utility average, utility total, and population would be under those principles.[11] The utility average in every case is larger than zero.* The stipulation that all utility averages are higher than zero amounts to saying that under any of the sets of principles, on average, life in that society is worth living.

(4) *Under any of the principles under consideration, the utility distribution within the society in question would be completely egalitarian, i.e. the personal utility of all individuals would be equal.* This assumption allows

us to avoid complications relating to the distribution of utility within society. Since neither the average or total utility principle gives any consideration to questions of distribution, we can reasonably make this simplifying assumption for the purposes of comparing these two principles.

(5) *The chances of a possible person existing under a given set of principles is directly proportional to the population size of the society in question when governed by those principles. That is, there is a positive constant n (which may be though of as the total number of possible persons) such that* (i) *n is larger than the population the society would have under any given set of principles under consideration, and* (ii) *the chances of a possible person existing under a given set of principles is equal to the population under those principles divided by n.* This assumption is meant to represent in precise terms the intuitive notion that the larger the population of the society in question is, the larger are the chances that any given possible person will actually exist. This notion is captured by treating the pool of possible persons as consisting of a fixed finite number of members from which members of the population are chosen at random so that the chance of a given possible person coming into existence is the quotient of the total population and the size of the pool of possible persons.

From these assumptions, we now derive the conclusion that a possible person P in the stated position will choose those rules for society which will maximize total utility. For convenience, we shall introduce the following abbreviations:

(a) Let 'U_R', 'U_E', and 'U_N' represent respectively (i) the expected utility for possible person P if set of principles R were to be applied to the society in question, (ii) the expected utility for P given that he exists in the society under R and, (iii) the expected utility for P given that he does not exist at all. Assumption 2 implies, of course, that $U_N = 0$.

(b) Let 'A_R', 'T_R', and 'P_R' represent respectively (i) the average utility of the society under principles R, (ii) the total utility of that society under principles R and, (iii) the population of the society under principles R. Of course, it follows from the definition of average utility that $A_R = T_R/P_R$.

(c) Let 'C_R' represent the probability that P will exist if principles R govern the society in question.

Now U_R, the expected utility for P if rules R are chosen, will be the weighted average of P's expected utility if he exists and if he does not (with the weights representing the probabilities he will or will not exist if principles R are adopted.) In other words, $U_R = (C_R U_E) \times (1-C_R)(U_N)$ and, since $U_N = 0$, we may conclude that $U_R = C_R U_E$. But, according to assumption 5, $C_R = P_R/n$ where n is the constant of assumption 5 (the number of possible people). Furthermore, it follows from assumption 4 that $U_E = A_R$ and hence that $U_E = T_R/P_R$. By substitution we obtain: $U_R = (P_R/n)(T_R/P_R) = T_R/n$.

Since n is a constant, the possible person's expected utility is proportional to the total utility of the society under the set of principles in question. As a rational self-interested individual seeking to maximize his expected utility (if the risks are comparable), P will choose that set of principles (of the alternatives available) which promises to result in the greatest *total* utility. This much is implied by assumption 1 provided the risks involved in opting for the rules producing the highest total utility are not greater than the risks involved in another choice. But, by any reasonable measure of risk, the risks are as great or greater in opting for rules producing a higher average utility in the society but a lower total utility. If we measure risk in terms of the level of the worst possible outcome, there is an equality of risk since non-existence and a resultant utility of zero is the worst possible outcome in either case.[12] If we measure risk in terms of the likelihood of the worst outcome occurring, it is clear that the probability of non-existence must be greater in a society with a lower total but higher average utility since the lower population of this society implies according to assumption 5 a greater risk of non-existence. Finally, if we measure risk in terms of spread between the best and worst possible outcomes, the average utility of the society will be the measure of risk[13] and hence the risk is greater in the society with higher average utility but lower total than in the society with lower average and higher total.

We may conclude then, that on the given assumptions, rational self-interested possible persons in the original position would prefer the total utility principle to the average utility principle. In fact, in the given assumptions, the parties would prefer the total utility principle to *any* principle or principles for governing society's fundamental institutions, since their expectations are directly proportional to the society's total utility.[14] What this shows is that Rawls' conception of the original position reveals a much closer connection between the average and total utility principles than Rawls himself recognizes. They represent respectively the principles which persons or possible persons in the original position would choose to govern society, questions of distribution aside. The only difference in the perspectives leading to the two utility principles lies in the making or omission of the assumption that the parties know that they will exist. This confirms the intuitive pre-theoretic notion that the supporter of the total utility principle is, unlike his average utilitarian counterpart, concerned not only with the happiness of those who do and definitely will exist but also with the possibility of producing more human happiness by seeing that more vessels of happiness (i.e. persons) come into existence. This concern for the potential happiness of those who might or might not exist which underlies and characterizes the total utility view is represented in the contractarian model by conceiving of the original parties as being possible rather than actual persons.

At this point, we must confront an objection which will surely be raised to the above analysis. According to this objection, the above analysis is vitiated by the fact that it makes no sense to speak of possible persons, or at least makes no sense to speak of possible persons making choices. Furthermore, it might be objected that if it did make sense to speak of possible persons, it would be unreasonable to suppose, as we have in assumption 5 above, that there are only a finite number of these strange entities. These are serious objections and I would now like to respond to them by briefly considering Rawls' own views about the role of the original position in his theory.

According to Rawls, one should not think of the original position as a gathering of all actual or possible persons. Rather, the original position is merely an analytical device to capture the idea that the reasoning which one uses in arriving at principles of justice must satisfy certain restrictions and conditions, e.g. this reasoning may not rest on assumptions about one's own particular characteristics or place in society. As Rawls puts it, "To say that a certain conception of justice would be chosen in the original position is equivalent to saying that rational deliberation satisfying certain conditions and restrictions would reach a certain conclusion."[15] My reference to possible persons in the original position can be similarly interpreted as an analytical device which represents placing certain restrictions upon the reasoning process leading to a choice of fundamental principles for governing society. In particular, speaking of possible rather than actual persons in the original position amounts to adding to Rawls' restrictions on the process of rational deliberation the condition that one's existence is not to be taken for granted but rather that it is assumed one's chances of existence will be directly proportional to society's population under a given set of principles.

Furthermore, even if one insists on conceiving the original position as a hypothetical convention of actual persons deliberating under certain conditions of ignorance, we can represent the notion of possible persons choosing from behind the veil of ignorance to his satisfaction in two different ways. First, we may conceive of the parties in the original position as being actual rational *trustees* whose sole concern is to carry out the commission of maximizing the expected utility of their clients by choosing fundamental social principles for their clients to live under from behind an expanded veil of ignorance. The expanded veil of ignorance prevents the trustees from knowing who their clients are, what their personal characteristics and places in society are, etc. Furthermore, the expanded veil of ignorance prevents each individual trustee from knowing whether his own client exists at all. Instead, each trustee has the information that the chances of his client existing will be directly proportional to the population which results from the implementation of the chosen principles. Those who are squimish about the notion of possible persons making choices in the original position, may everywhere replace this notion by the notion of actual rational trustees making choices under the conditions just stated.

Second, we might conceive of the parties in the original position as rational self-interested persons choosing rules to govern a society S under the following conditions: (i) they are ignorant of their own personal characteristics, place in society, etc., (ii) they know that they will live their lives either in S under the rules they choose or in an alternative society S' in which everyone's net utility is zero, and (iii) they know that the probability that they will live in S (as opposed to S') is directly proportional to the population of S under the chosen rules.[16] By thus replacing the limbo of non-existence by existence in a zero-happiness society S', we are able to present an alternative analytical device that places the desired restrictions on the deliberation process without making any reference to possible people or their choices.

Having demonstrated how we might eliminate reference to possible persons from the representation of the choice situation, let us briefly consider an objection which might arise from those who are willing to countenance possible people in this context. Such persons might object that while there are such things as possible people, there are an infinite number of them and hence that assumption 5 above is mistaken in identifying the number of possible persons as being a finite constant. This objection may be answered in either of two ways. First, we might suggest a physical interpretation for the concept of possible persons such that the constraints of assumption 5 are satisfied. We might, for example, identify possible persons with actual human eggs of which there are certainly a finite number which is larger than the human population which could be brought into existence by even the most dedicated human effort to produce as many people as possible. Second, we may note that treating the constant n as representing the total number of possible persons from which actual populations are drawn, is merely a heuristic device to give backing to the claim that chances of existence are directly proportional to population size. Those who accept possible people and find this device more puzzling than helpful may regard assumption 5 as merely the precise specification of the vague intuitive notion that a larger population means a greater chance that a given possible person will exist.

III

To reveal the fundamental difference in perspectives underlying the average and total utility principles, we have explored the consequences of extending the veil of ignorance to cover the question of existence. In so doing, however, we have operated totally within the confines of the simplifying assumption that utility distribution would in all cases be totally egalitarian. Rawls, in developing his own non-utilitarian theory of justice, is vitally concerned with distributive questions, and in fact argues that the parties in the original position would prefer the following two principles of justice to either the average or total utility principle as fundamental principles for governing society:

(1) Each person is to have an equal right to the most extensive liberty compatible with a similar liberty for others.

(2) Social and economic inequalities are to be arranged so that they are both (a) reasonably expected to be to everyone's advantage, and (b) attached to positions and offices open to all.[17]

The question I wish to raise is whether Rawls' two principles of justice remain plausible when we extend the veil of ignorance to cover the question of existence, i.e. when we conceive the parties in the original position as being possible people (or their rational trustees) rather than actual persons. I submit that when we conceive the original parties as merely possible people, a serious problem arises with respect to Rawls' principle 2a, the so-called *difference principle*. Rawls explicates the difference principle as requiring that all inequalities in the distribution of primary goods, i.e. goods it is rational for any person to want – rights, liberties, income, opportunities, and self-respect, be justified in terms of being to the absolute advantage of the representative man in the worst off social position.[17a] In other words, the difference principle requires maximizing the expectations of the representative person of the group which is worst off with respect to the possession of primary goods. But, if we conceive of the parties in the original position as merely possible persons (or their trustees), there are two ways of interpreting the difference principle and either way leads to difficulties. On the first interpretation, we include among the groups or classes whose representative's plight is to be considered the class of possible persons who do not exist under society's population policies. But clearly the representative non-existent person is going to be the worst off with respect to primary goods among all the relevant representative men,[18] and hence the only inequalities justified by the difference principle on this interpretation are those leading to population increases which would increase the expectations with respect to the possession of primary goods of the average non-existent possible person.[19]

On the second interpretation of the difference principle, we assume that it refers only to the advantages of those who exist and thus that the class of non-existent possible persons is not considered a relevant group whose representative's expectations with respect to the possession of primary goods must be taken into account in justifying inequalities. This interpretation amounts to leaving Rawls' principles of justice as they are. But now the question arises as to whether rational self-interested possible persons in the original position would choose as fundamental social principles exactly those principles which Rawls argues they would choose if they knew they would exist, rather than some different set of principles designed to strongly encourage and facilitate population growth up to the point where limits on natural resources make life not worth living for the average citizen. It seems clear that they would not.

If we agree that extending the veil of ignorance to encompass the question of existence would make it improbable that the parties behind that veil of ignorance would select Rawls' two principles as their fundamental principles of justice, it seems incumbent upon Rawls to explain why it is not appropriate to extend the veil of ignorance in this manner. In other words, reasons must be given for holding that, in deriving and defending principles of justice, it is appropriate to employ an analytical device which assumes the relevant parties' ignorance of their own personal characteristics and even what generation they belong to but allows them to have the knowledge that they will exist whatever principles are chosen. Are such reasons available? We can best bring forth the considerations favoring and disfavoring Rawls' restriction of the veil of ignorance, I think, by comparing two alternative interpretations of the original position.

According to the *present time of entry* interpretation of the original position, which Rawls favors, the parties are to be conceived as already living together under certain social institutions.[20] In choosing principles of social justice, they are choosing principles which will govern their relationships and institutions in the future. It follows from this conception that while the parties behind the veil of ignorance do not know what particular generation they belong to, they do know that they all are members of the same generation (or at least are living at the same time). It also follows that the parties know that their choices will not effect the past, i.e. will have no influence on the rules and actions of previous generations.

By contrast, on the *atemporal* interpretation of the original position, the parties are not only totally ignorant of what generation they are in but also cannot assume that they are all in the same generation. Furthermore, the parties are to choose principles on the assumption that these principles will govern society's operations from the *first* generation onward. In other words, the parties may not assume that they have a common fixed temporal location from which they are choosing principles to govern the future. Rather, without knowing where they will fall on the timeline of generations, the parties are to choose the best principles to govern society from start to finish. Each party thus must be concerned not only with the direct effects of the chosen principles on him during his lifetime, but also the indirect effects of these principles in determining (via their influence on earlier generations) what kind of social world he is born into.

What is especially significant for our purposes about the atemporal interpretation of the original position is that if we adopt it, we are forced to reject the assumption that the parties know that they will exist and we must instead treat the parties as possible people. This is because conceiving the choice of principles as affecting society from the first generation onward raises the possibility that the principles a party chooses might affect his own chances of existence. It is clear, for example, that among the whole array of logically consistent social principles which the parties could consider is the principle 'Do not allow the birth of children and painlessly dispose of any children who are born in violation of the rule'.[21] If this rule were put into effect successfully from the first generation onward, there obviously would be no members of future generations. Now if we assumed à la Rawls that the parties know that they will exist whatever principles they choose, it would follow that the parties can conclude from the information available to them that they are all members of the first generation (or members of the second generation who are destroyed at birth.) But allowing the parties this knowledge is inconsistent with our description of the atemporal interpretation of the original position which includes the provision that each party is totally ignorant of what generation he belongs to. The solution is to drop Rawls' assumption and take the parties to be self-interested possible people. Then it makes sense for the parties to consider the 'no children' rule and each of them will, of course, reject it on the grounds that it would prevent his own existence unless he were lucky enough to be a member of the first generation.

Having noted how adoption of the atemporal interpretation of the original position in place of the present time of entry interpretation would require us to treat the parties as possible people, let us examine the relative advantages and disadvantages of these two interpretations. The main advantages of the present time of entry interpretation are (i) that it makes it easier to imagine oneself being in the original position, and (ii) it connects the choice of principles to the motivations of actual persons in the real world. Thus, except for the requirement that the parties are deprived of specific knowledge of the features of themselves and their societies, the original position on the present time of entry interpretation is not that much different from the super constitutional convention which would result if members of a contemproary society all got together to change by discussion and general consent the rules they are presently functioning under. These advantages of the present time of entry interpretation are significant given the nature of the enterprise in which Rawls is engaged: explicating our concept of social justice by seeking principles of justice which thoughtful people will be willing to accept upon careful reflection. By constructing the original position so that we can view the parties as simply being ourselves deprived of all knowledge which could lead to our making biased choices, Rawls makes it seem quite plausible that we should upon reflection accept the resulting principles as an explication of our concept of justice.

The strengths of the atemporal interpretation of the original position come to the fore when we turn to the problem of justice between different generations.[22] For Rawls, this problem primarily manifests itself in the question of how much saving will be done by each generation to benefit future generations. On the atemporal interpretation of the original position, no special assumptions are needed to insure that the parties choose fair savings rates for each generation since it will be in the self-interest of each party to do so to insure that his own generation benefits appropriately from the savings of earlier generations. On the present time of entry interpretation, however, since the parties know that they are all in the same generation and that their choices will not affect the actions of previous generations (who will have saved at a certain rate already), they will have no self-interested reason to choose social rules incorporating a fair rate of saving. Rawls is forced to deal with this problem by adding the additional motivational assumption that each party in the original position cares about some of those in the next generation and that each person in the next generation is cared about by someone in the original position.[23] But it is not clear that this assumption is sufficient to insure justice with respect to the savings issue. For example, it seems perfectly consistent with this assumption that the parties choose principles which force cutting the population in half by the next generation and thus allow themselves to devote fewer resources to saving for future generations' needs and more resources to present consumption. This would seem to be a perfectly rational course of action consistent with Rawls' motivational assumptions but it hardly seems a case of being fair to future generations.

Even if we agree that Rawls can insure justice between generations by adding his motivational assumption, he sacrifices a degree of theoretical simplicity in the process. He is forced to add an inelegant and inexact assumption about motivation to replace the simpler assumption that the parties are purely self-interested. Addition of this assumption leaves room for raising the potentially embarrassing question of how strong each party's concern for those in future generations is as compared with his concern for his own well-being. The inelegance of the present time of entry interpretation compared to the atemporal interpretation is also evident when we look at the issue of what knowledge is allowed to the parties. On the atemporal interpretation, *all* knowledge of specific personal, social, or generational features is ruled out. The veil of ignorance, we might say, has a sharp clean edge. On the present time of entry interpretation, however, each party knows that his generation is the same as the generation of each of the other parties. The veil of ignorance has a slightly jagged edge.

What I wish to suggest then is that, in adopting the present time of entry interpretation and treating the parties as real persons, Rawls has opted for a conception of the original position which the thoughtful reader can get a fairly clear intuitive grasp on. This makes it easier than it might be to follow Rawls' reasoning to his two principles of justice and to assent to or dissent from his endorsement of those principles. But for these advantages Rawls pays the price of not being able to adequately handle the problem of justice between generations and of ending up with a theoretical structure which is less elegant and simple than it might be. In my view this is too high a price. I believe that Rawls would be on stronger philosophical ground if he adopted the atemporal conception of the original position, allowed the veil of ignorance to shroud the question of real existence of the parties therein, and sought to determine what principles of social governance would be chosen by the parties under these new conditions.[24]

University of California, Los Angeles

NOTES

[1] *The Methods of Ethics*, New York – Dover, 1966 (1907), p. 415.
[2] I assume, as Sidgwick does not, that we may limit our attention to human happiness and need not concern ourselves with the happiness or unhappiness of animals.
[3] *Ibid.*, pp. 415–6.
[4] See John Rawls, *A Theory of Justice*, Cambridge, Mass., Harvard University Press, 1971, especially chapters one and three.

[5] For discussion of the circumstances of justice, see *Ibid.*, Section 22.

[6] See especially *Ibid.*, pp. 163–4.

[7] This simplifying assumption allows us to avoid problems concerning rational choice in conditions of uncertainty and risk. Of course, such considerations and questions of distribution are central to the derivation and defense of Rawls' own two principles of justice. As far as the intramural utilitarian dispute between the average and total views is concerned, however, questions of distribution *per se* may be ignored.

[8] See *Ibid.*, section thirty.

[9] See *Ibid.*, p. 27.

[10] This result has been arrived at independently by Derek Parfit. It is mentioned briefly by R. M. Hare in 'Rawls' Theory of Justice-II', *Philosophical Quarterly*, July 1973, p. 245.

[11] Of course, the values of any two of the trio 'utility average, utility total, population' determine the value of the third.

[12] It follows from assumptions 2, 3, and 4 that zero utility is the worst possible outcome.

[13] Since zero utility is the worst possible outcome and the average utility level is the best (and only other) possible outcome.

[14] This assumes, of course, that from the point of view of the parties behind the veil of ignorance the best way to maximize total utility is to choose the total utility principle as society's fundamental rule rather than choosing as fundamental principles certain more specific rules intended to promote total utility.

[15] *A Theory of Justice*, p. 138.

[16] This approach was suggested to me by Warren Quinn.

[17] See *Ibid.*, p. 60.

[17a] Actually, due to the priority of the first principle of justice, a stricter condition must be satisfied to justify inequalities in the distribution of liberty and opportunity: such inequalities must be necessary to raise society to a general level of well-being in which equal liberty can be enjoyed by all. See *Ibid.*, pp. 60–3, 542–3.

[18] Another way of putting it is that this representative lacks the one fundamental primary good whose possession is a prerequisite of the possession of all other primary goods – life itself.

[19] These expectations are increased, of course, in accordance with assumption 5 of the last section, by decreasing the likelihood that a representative person who is non-existent (under status quo social principles) would be non-existent (under the new rules encouraging population growth.)

[20] Although Rawls never explains his use of the phrase 'present time of entry interpretation', it is possible to reconstruct his view on the basis of his comments on pages 140 and 292 of *A Theory of Justice* and his earlier sketch of the original position in 'Justice as Fairness', *Philosophical Review* (April 1958) section 3.

[21] Besides being logically consistent, this principle satisfies the further constraints which Rawls imposes on principles to be considered in the original position. For discussion of these constraints, see section 23 of *A Theory of Justice*.

[22] *Cf.* Hare, *op. cit.*, pp. 243–4.

[23] Actually, in explaining his motivational assumption, Rawls adds the stipulation that the concern of the parties in the original position for the members of the next generation 'is for different individuals in each case.' (*A Theory of Justice*, pp. 128–9) As I see it, there are two ways of interpreting this stipulation. Let C_x represent the set of all and only those persons in the next generation whom party X in the original position cares about. On the first interpretation, the stipulation says that for any two

distinct parties X and Y in the original position, $C_X \cap C_Y = \emptyset$. In other words, no individual in the next generation has two people in the original position who care about him. On the second interpretation, the stipulation says that for any distinct parties X and Y in the original position, $C_X \neq C_Y$. In other words, no two people in the original position care about exactly the same people in the next generation. Now the first interpretation of the stipulation, together with the assumption that each party in the original position cares about someone in the next generation, implies the very strong conclusion that the population of the next generation cannot be less than the population of the generation of those in the original position. Since Rawls must have been aware of this implication and could hardly have intended to endorse such a conclusion without explicit mention of it, we are forced to reject the first interpretation. On the second interpretation, however, the stipulation is implausible since it is inconsistent with the possibility of a husband and wife caring about their children and no one else in the next generation. Furthermore, I cannot see what the point of the stipulation is on this reading of it. I propose, therefore, to ignore this aspect of Rawls' motivational assumption.

24 I am grateful to John Perry, Tyler Burge, and David Braybrooke, referee for *Philosophical Studies*, who, while disagreeing with me on some basic points, have made helpful critical comments which have enabled me to improve this paper in several respects.

BRIAN BARRY

RAWLS ON AVERAGE AND TOTAL UTILITY: A COMMENT

(Received 17 August, 1976)

In his recent article (*Philosophical Studies* 27 (1975), 237–53) Prof. Kavka has, I think, inadvertantly driven a further nail into the coffin of hypothetical contractarianism. That he did not notice he was doing this is to be explained partly by the fact that he did not pause to ask how plausible his conclusions were and partly by the fact that the conclusions he drew, though implausible, were less implausible than those actually pointed to be his analysis.

Kavka is surely right in suggesting that it is inconsistent with the logic of *A Theory of Justice* to posit that the people in the original position are contemporaries and know they are. For the force of self-interest would then lead them to choose principles that ignore the interests of their successors. Rawls' 'motivational assumption' – that the people in the original position *do* care about their successors – is clearly an interloper, only too apparently designed to produce the desired results.

An alternative, which Kavka does not mention, is the idea put forward by David Richards in *A Theory of Reasons for Action* (Oxford: Clarendon Press, 1971), according to which 'the class of members of the original position includes, in a hypothetical sense, *all* persons, who have lived, live now, or will live' (Richards, p. 81). But this is subject to the objection that Kavka makes against Rawls, namely that 'the parties in the original position are allowed knowledge that they will exist under the chosen rules' (Kavka, p. 240). If they endorse policies that by using up resources and creating pollution make the tenure of human life on the planet shorter than it might have been, they have no need to worry because they know that *they* will still exist. There is, indeed, some kind of incoherence in the whole idea that we can have a given population of people choosing policies which will, among other things, affect population. How can they choose if their very presence is consistent with one policy but not others?

It does therefore look as if the 'rational contractor' model, in order to make sense of relations between generations – including but not restricted to

Philosophical Studies 31 (1977) 317–325. *All Rights Reserved*
Copyright © 1977 *by D. Reidel Publishing Company, Dordrecht-Holland*

population policy — must follow Kavka in making use of the idea that the contractors are 'potential persons.' But if this leads us in bizarre directions, it provides further reasons for doubting the validity of the whole approach. I want to argue, with the help of Kavka's article, that this is indeed the case.

Naturally, we must begin by determining the population of 'possible persons.' Kavka believes that any number will do as long as it is finite, because the conclusions are invariant with respect to the number of possible persons. This happens to be correct for the two decision-rules considered by Kavka — maximizing the minimum utility and maximizing the average utility — but is not true for other decision rules. It does therefore matter in general what the number is, and it is much larger than Kavka envisages. He offers a 'physical interpretation' such that we 'identify possible persons with actual human eggs' (Kavka, p. 246). But the number of possible persons defined physically is the number of unions of one sperm and one egg that might have come about in the history of the human race — a number that presumably outstrips the number of atoms in the universe by a tidy margin.

It needs to be emphasized that the notion of 'rationality' does not set very narrow constraints on choices between different odds of different outcomes. We can say that it would not be rational to take a lower probability of a given utility rather than a higher probability of that same utility, and that it would not be rational to take a lower rather than a higher utility if they are offered with equal probability. But if we are prepared to allow a variety of attitudes to risk to be consistent with rationality (and I do not see how we can refuse to) we cannot set closer limits on rational choice.

The rule that expected utility is to be maximized (i.e. that one should maximize the sum of all the products of utility and probability of obtaining that utility) is rational for someone who is perfectly risk-neutral but not for anyone else. For any other choice function, it may come about that the choice to be made changes even if the utilities and the *relative* probabilities of their occurrence stay the same. In other words, from the fact that someone prefers $p_1 u_1$ to $p_2 u_2$ it does not follow that he must in consistency prefer $p_{1/n} u_1$ to $p_{2/n} u_2$, where n is any arbitrarily large number.

Suppose, for example, that I am told a million dollars is to be distributed randomly among n people (of whom I am one), and I can choose whether there will be one prize of a million dollars or ten of a hundred thousand dollars each. If I wish to maximize expected utility, I need not enquire what number n is. All I need to decide is whetehr a one-tenth chance of a million is worth more or less to me than the certainty of a hundred thousand. That will give me my answer, whatever the actual odds against getting either prize may be, so long as they are in the ratio ten to one. If (as is usually assumed) money has decreasing marginal utility for me, I will choose to have the lump sum divided into ten prizes.

But if I do not care to commit myself to maximizing expected utility, I cannot say what I prefer until I know what number n is. Suppose $n = 10$. I may then prefer the certainty of a hundred thousand dollars to a one-tenth probability of a million. But suppose instead that the lump sum is to be distributed among all the people currently alive. My chance of getting a prize at all is extremely small, but I may rationally prefer one chance in three billion of winning a million dollars to one chance in three hundred million of winning a hundred thousand dollars. When choosing between such remote probabilities, why not have a fling?

If we bear in mind the infinitesimal probability that any given potential person has of existing under any possible arrangement, we must surely wonder whether we want to be bound by the choices that we would ascribe to these potential people. For them, the choice between different societies is a choice between contingencies none of which has more than the most minute chance of arising. Why should the choice between principles to govern interpersonal and intergenerational relationships be determined by the way in which one chooses between alternative contingencies when all of them are vanishingly remote?

Kavka is, however, right in saying that the number of potential persons does not have any effect on the results derivable from the rule that the average utility of all potential persons (whether or not they become actual) is to be maximized. Formally, if p_i is the probability that the ith outcome will occur and u_i is the utility that will be received from the ith outcome and there are n possible outcomes, $\sum_{i=1}^{n} p_i u_i$ is to be maximized. The general statement of the requirements for maximizing expected utility can be simplified if it is known that all n outcomes have an equal chance of occurring and that the sum of probabilities is unity. The probability of each outcome is then $1/n$ and the way to maximize expected utility is to maximize $u_1(1/n) + u_2(1/n) + \ldots u_{n-1}(1/n) + u_n(1/n)$ which may be written $\sum_{i=1}^{n} u_i/n$. It follows that if n is fixed, $\sum_{i=1}^{n} u_i/n$ is maximized when $\sum_{i=1}^{n} u_i$ is maximized. Thus, if each potential person in the original position has an equal chance of being any (existent or non-existent) person, and each is seeking to maximize expected utility, each will agree on the rule that the total utility of all (existent and non-existent) people is to be maximized.

The next step is to move from this to Kavka's conclusion that the total utility of all people who actually come to exist is to be maximized. This follows on two conditions: that the utility of each non-existent person is zero and that the average utility of all existent persons is positive. If we assign a value of zero to the utility of each non-existent potential person, then clearly the total utility of all non-existent potential persons is zero. We can therefore disregard them and say that the total utility of all potential persons is the same as the total utility for all existent persons. Total utility for potential people is therefore maximized when total utility for existent people is maximized *provided* that the maximum total utility is positive. If the maximum total utility is negative, then clearly total utility is maximized when no people come into existence.

These are about the weakest assumptions capable of generating the result that the total utility of all potential persons is maximized when the total utility of all existent persons is maximized. (I have not followed Kavka's proof, because it uses unnecessarily strong assumptions.) This means that it is crucial to assign a value of zero to non-existence. Suppose, for example, that utility runs from plus ten to minus ten, and that non-existence is assigned a score of minus one unit. The total utility of all potential people now becomes a huge negative amount, since non-existent potential people are so numerous. It might at first sight appear, however, that total utility is still maximized when the total utility of those who exist is maximized. But this is not so.

If we want to maximize the total utility of those who exist, it would obviously be better not to bring into existence anyone with a negative utility from living, because this would lower the total. But if non-existence scores minus one, we would increase the total utility of all potential people (or more precisely reduce the disutility of all potential people) by bringing into existence a person who gets a negative utility from living, provided the utility is higher than minus one. The rule now becomes that we should add one to the utility of each existent person and maximize that total. Similarly, the proviso that the human race would be better not to be brought into existence if the average utility of those who live is negative now has to read that the human race should not be brought into existence if the average utility of those who live is lower than minus one. Conversely, of course, if we were to assign non-existence a value of plus one, we would have to maximize the utility of those who exist after subtracting one unit from each person's score, and it would be better not to bring the human race into existence unless its members average a score of at least plus one unit.

Kavka supports an assignment of zero value to non-existence as follows: 'Placing the utility of non-existence at the crossover point between net positive utility and net negative utility seems entirely natural since not existing entails experiencing neither happiness nor unhappiness' (Kavka, p. 241). But this is something of an equivocation. Surely it would be more accurate to say that not existing entails not experiencing either happiness or unhappiness.

It seems to me that there are four ways of treating the value of non-existence in relation to that of existence. The first is to say that the two cannot be brought into relation. It does not make sense to equate non-existence with being happy, or being unhappy, or being poised between the two. This has a certain appeal, but it would seem to disallow the judgment (made by the person concerned or some other) that someone was made better off by having his life saved or that somebody (with gross physical defects, say) would have been better off not to have been born.

The second is to say, with Kavka, that the value of non-existence should be that corresponding to the borderline between net happiness and net unhappiness. This is not unreasonable, but is by no means inevitable because a case can be made out for either of the remaining alternatives.

Thus, the third possibility is to say that non-existence is worse than a hedonically neutral existence. If we think of being a potential person reflecting on existence as analogous to being an actual person reflecting on non-existence, it is easy to make this look plausible. Many people who would say their lives are on balance unhappy would still, I think, not regret having been born; and not everyone who expects the balance of his life to be unhappy commits suicide.

Finally, if we fight clear of the idea that potential non-existent people are conscious entities in the 'Never-never land' of *Peter Pan*, waiting to be born, we can make quite a plausible case for the opposite line. If we imagine ourselves given the task of acting on behalf of a non-existent potential person, might we not argue as follows? 'Being non-existent is really not too bad, since you don't know about it. It's hardly worth being brought into existence on the strength of an average expectation that one will be just barely on the credit side of the happiness/unhappiness ledger. Why not insist on a fairly substantial positive expectation of happiness?' Clearly, the way to formulate this demand would be to say that non-existence should be ascribed a positive value.

Although I myself find the last of the attractive, I do not want here to extend the argument between them. What I do want to suggest is that there is something wrong with a theory that makes our position on population policy depend in a fundamental way upon the answer that we give. If a contractarian approach to population entails dealing with potential people (as it appears to) and if dealing with potential people entails that we have to assign a value to non-existence (as it clearly does) the conclusion I wish to suggest is that there is something wrong with the contractarian approach.

The maximin criterion, which Kavka also considers in the context of choice by potential people, produces such odd results that it seems to me to cast further doubt on the reasonableness of the criterion itself as well as the contractarian approach rather than to offer useful guidance. Kavka adds an extra curiosity by carrying out the discussion in terms of primary goods. Why maximin should be discussed in these terms when maximizing expected value was discussed in terms of utilities he does not explain. In any case, it is surely clear that defining the maximin principle in terms of primary goods cannot be defended. Once we exist, we want primary goods (let's concede) but it doesn't follow that as potential people we would want to exist in order to have primary goods. As Kavka notes, one has to exist in order to have any of the Rawlsian primary goods. Indeed, he suggests in a footnote (fn. 18, p. 252) that the representative non-existent potential person 'lacks the one fundamental primary good whose possession is a prerequisite of the possession of all other primary goods — life itself.' Whether or not we treat life as a primary good, however, it may be agreed that 'the representative non-existent person is going to be the worst off with respect to primary goods among all the relevant representative men' (p. 247).

Now the clear implication of this (which Kavka does not recognize) is that on the maximin principle all states of affairs that can actually be achieved are ranked equally. For, as we have seen, the number of potential people is so vastly in excess of the number of people who could exist under any set of arrangements that under any set of arrangements there will be non-existent people. Since all non-existent people are equally badly off in terms of primary goods, the worst-off representative person is equally badly off in all possible states of affairs.

Kavka's own solution is both incoherent and inconsistent with the rationale of maximin as a decision-rule. He continues the sentence quoted above by saying 'and hence the only inequalities justified by the difference principle on this interpretation are those leading to population increases which would increase the expectations with respect to the possession of primary goods of the average non-existent possible person' (p. 247). The point is continued in a footnote (fn. 19, p. 252) which reads: 'These expectations are increased, of course, in accordance with [the assumption of a finite number of potential people], by decreasing the likelihood that a representative person who is non-existent (under status quo social principles) would be non-existent (under the new rules encouraging population growth).'

This is incoherent because any rule produces a set of non-existent people but different rules produce different sets and we cannot therefore speak of trying to improve the prospects of the set of non-existent people. It is inconsistent with the rationale of maximin because the whole idea is to talk about the levels of possible outcomes and get away form probabilistic expectations. The worst-off potential person (on the primary goods criterion) is one who doesn't exist. We can't get away from that by saying that the worst-off representative potential person can be regarded as existing a little bit because some non-existent people may exist after all.

The conclusion that Kavka reaches − that as many people as possible should be brought into existence − cannot be derived from the argument that this minimizes the number of worst-off people, since the maximin criterion is not concerned with the *number* of worst-off people. However, we could derive his conclusion from a modification of Rawls's maximin criterion that is a natural extension and has sometimes been suggested. This is the idea that if the worst-off person is equally badly-off in two situations, we go to the next worst-off in each situation, and if one of those is better off than the other we say that situation is preferable. If the next worst-off are equally badly-off we go up one further, and so on until we find a tie-breaking pair. Clearly, it is an implication of this extension of Rawls's maximin principle that if there are in two situations a number of people who are equally worst-off, but there are fewer worst-off people in one than the other, the one where there are fewer is preferable. We can imagine ourselves matching one non-existent person in each situation against a non-existent one in the other, until we finally run out of non-existent people in one. We then match the existent person in that situation with a further non-existent person in the other and declare the first the winner, since something beats nothing in terms of primary goods.

Oddly enough, Kavka does not offer any reflections on his conclusion, which we have seen can be derived validly by an extension of maximin to break ties. Yet surely it is simply insane to suppose that we ought to maximize the total number of people ever born so as to give as many potential people as possible the chance of getting some primary goods (even if little more than life itself). The absurdity of trying to serve the interests of potential people is surely brought out starkly by the conclusion. It is perhaps if anything brought out even more starkly by the implication of the unmodified Rawls maximin criterion, which is that all states of affairs are equally just, however the people alive in them fare, because there are some non-existent potential people in all of them.

Does the craziness of the conclusion follow from the use of primary goods rather than utilities? Certainly, the conclusion is altered if we switch to utilities, but in a way that I am inclined to think casts even further doubt on the maximin criterion. Before saying what that conclusion is, I should note that Kavka, in the paragraph following the one I have been quoting, restates his own conclusion in a way that involves utilities, though he does not draw attention to the shift. He now says that what would be chosen would be 'some different set of principles [from those put forward by Rawls] designed to strongly encourage and facilitate population growth up to the point where limits on natural resources make life not worth living for the average citizen' (p. 247). However, as a statement of the implications of maximin for utilities this again fails because of an illegitimate use of averaging. Whether or not the *average* person who is alive is better off alive than non-existent is neither here nor there for a potential person who is following a maximin criterion. The question he has to ask himself is what the worst possible outcome would be under various alternatives. (This may be made clearer if it is recalled that the person in Rawls's 'original position' is supposed not to worry about the average obtainable under alternative arrangements but to concentrate on the minimum he might obtain.)

Let me offer what seems a safe statement. There is no imaginable rule for the conduct of human affairs that would not result in there being at least one person in the history of the human race who would regret having been born. If we are prepared to attach a value to non-existence, then I take it this must mean that — whether the value of non-existence is positive, negative or zero — it is possible to be worse-off by being alive than by being non-existent. As I have already remarked, I am far from happy with the whole notion of attaching a value to non-existence, but unless we are prepared to countenance it at least in order to see where it gets us I do not see how the business of ascribing choices to potential people who may exist or not can be got off the ground at all.

If I am correct, then, in saying that some human life has a value lower than non-existence under any set of arrangements, it immediately follows what decision potential people following a maximin rule will take. They will opt not to bring the human race into existence. For it is clear that the worst possible outcome that one might obtain from existing is worse than the guaranteed outcome from not existing. There is, of course, no reason why we should not embrace this as the correct answer if we choose. But if we find the answer unreasonable, we have a further case for thinking that the maximin criterion is no better as a guide to making large decisions than it is as a guide to making smaller ones.

Center for Advanced Study in the Behavioral Sciences,
Stanford, California

THE CHOICE BETWEEN PERFECTIONISM
AND RAWLSIAN CONTRACTARIANISM

KAI NIELSEN
University of Calgary

It is Rawls' claim that when we compare his conception of justice with its rivals (average utility, classical utility, and the different kinds of perfectionist theories) that his theory at least appears (a) "to match our common sense convictions more accurately" and (b) more adequately extrapolates to previously unsettled cases[1] (p. 332). While Rawls takes utilitarian accounts to be his most serious rivals, I want here to examine whether Rawls has demonstrated or even made convincing 1) his claim that his principles give a more adequate conceptualization of the basis of justice and morality than does perfectionism and 2) his further and related claim that there is "no basis for acknowledging a principle of perfection as a standard of social justice" (p. 330).

I shall argue that Rawls has not made a compelling case here. If I am not mistaken in the essentials of my argument, and if some reconstruction of Rawls' critique of perfectionism cannot be made which will show such a critique to be essentially sound or at least more compelling than it now appears to be, then his overall theory will be rather considerably weakened, for part of its plausibility turns on his ability to show that rival accounts are inadequate or at least suffer from even greater difficulties than does his own account.

Rawls begins his examination of what he calls "the principle of perfection" by pointing out that there are two variants of the principle (p. 325). In the first—let us call it "extreme perfectionism"—the principle of perfection is the sole principle of a teleological theory which directs "society to arrange institutions and to define the duties and obligations of individuals so as to maximize the achievement of human excellence in art, science and culture" (p. 325). The following quotation from Nietzsche's *Schopenhauer as Educator* illustrates this posture: "man-kind must work continually to produce individual great human beings—this and nothing else is the task—for the question is this: how can your life, the individual life, retain the highest value, the deepest significance? ... Only by your living for the good of the rarest and most valuable specimens."[2] Whether the greatest

---

[1] *A Theory of Justice* (Cambridge, Mass.: Harvard University Press, 1971). References to *A Theory of Justice* are given in the test. There are important remarks about his appeal to considered judgments and the rationale for extrapolation from them on pp. 316–320 of the book. I have critically examined this matter in my "On Phliosophic Method," *International Philosophical Quarterly*, (September, 1976).

[2] Quoted in *ibid.*, p. 325.

number are made happy or not, whether equal liberty is furthered or not, whether all men are taken to be of equal concern or not, the cultural achievements of humankind must be preserved. If, for example, slavery was necessary to attain and preserve the achievements of the Greeks in philosophy, science, and art, then slavery was morally justified in those circumstances.

A second form of perfectionism—let us call it "moderate perfectionism"—is a form of intuitionism in which the principle of perfection is accepted as only one (though a very crucial one) of several irreducible ultimate standards. Such a view can be more or less perfectionist depending on the weight given to the claims of excellence and culture. Applied moderately and reasonably, as a kind of moral basis for conservativism, perfectionists, as a counterpoint to the egalitarianism advocated by Rawls, could argue against the difference principle for a limit to the redistribution of wealth and income once the subsistence needs or the most basic needs of people—including, of course, the least favored stratum of society—have been met. Such a redistribution should be halted when subsistence needs have been met and where such a redistribution tends to undermine the preservation of cultural values; that is to say, instead of using the expenditures in such a situation to enhace the happiness and relieve the suffering and alienation of the more unfortunate strata of society, one should use it to preserve and to add to the flourishing of the arts, sciences, and cultural amenities of life.

Let us consider Rawls' arguments against this moderate form of perfectionism. (In doing this I shall consider some of his criticisms of extreme perfectionism as well, for he believes, and rightly, that they apply to both variants.) Many of his criticisms depend on an appeal to what would be chosen in the original position. Persons in the original position do not "share a common conception of the good by reference to which the fruition of their powers or even the satisfaction of their desires can be evaluated," so they can hardly "have an agreed-on criterion of perfection that can be used as a principle for choosing between institutions" (p. 327). Such a conception would be utterly empty and inapplicable for them. But this would not be so for rational, impartial people in everyday life capable of a sense of justice, and, if the methodological device of the original position has the effect of excluding consideration of such a substantive theory *simply on those grounds,* i.e., that "O.P"'s (people in the original position) cannot understand or assess such conceptions, then we have in that very fact good grounds for rejecting or at least seriously questioning the use of that methodological device. What we need to know is whether rational and impartial persons in normal circumstances would have good grounds for adopting Rawls' principles of justice rather than either extreme or moderate perfectionism. To say, at least of extreme perfectionism, that a rational person would not adopt such a principle because it might lead to some curtailment of his own liberties and indeed even to a loss of freedom altogether is not yet to make a non-question-begging criticism of perfectionism, for we have to be given a reason why rational, impartial human beings might not adopt the teleological ideal-regarding principles of perfectionism, principles which commit them to the claim that in certain circumstances some personal liberties (including, perhaps, their own) may "fall before the higher social goal of maximizing perfection," of raising or maintaining the level of culture (p. 327).

Only if we were justified in claiming that a man acts rationally not *if*, but *only if*, he seeks to maximize that which is in his self-interest will such a claim undermine perfectionism. But such a claim about rationality is quite arbitrary; if Rawls is committed to such a conception of rationality, then so much the worse for his conception of rationality.[3] If, alternatively, Rawls is saying that, as a simplifying device, we will stipulate that rational persons will take no interest in one another's interests, then so much the worse for such simplification. There are no sufficient reasons for believing that all or even most rational and impartial persons in everyday life operate in accordance with that simplifying device. To set it up so that they must do so, and then to point out that such people will opt for the principle of greatest liberty rather than the principle of perfection, is too obvious a gerrymandering to require further comment. Where is it written or established that no rational man can risk his freedom to further or protect the sciences and the arts?

Rawls—moving to a different kind of objection—cannot, without radically changing his own position, reject perfectionism on the grounds that it is a doctrine which captures nothing which is even tolerably clear, for he avers that "comparisons of intrinsic value can obviously be made" and that, as he puts it, "clearly there are standards in the arts and sciences for appraising creative efforts, at least within particular styles and traditions of thought. Very often it is beyond question that the work of one person is superior to that of another. Indeed, as he points out himself, the freedom and well-being of individuals, when measured by the excellence of their activities and works, is vastly different in value (p. 328). He agrees that the judgments we make here are not so vague that they must fail on that account as a basis for assigning rights.

To point out, as Rawls does, that justice as fairness "allows that in a well-ordered society the values of excellence are recognized" and that "human perfections are to be pursued within the limits of the principle of free association" is not to the point, for the question is one of priority. Even moderate perfectionism must generally give greater

---

[3] I have argued against such a conception of rationality in my "Principles of Rationality," *Philosophical Papers* 69 (1972), and in "Rationality and Egoism," *Studi internazionali di filosofia*, (1975).

weight to principles of perfection than to the Rawlsian principles of justice.

Rawls rightly argues that the principle of perfection provides an insecure foundation for equal liberties and would depart widely from the difference principle. A criterion of perfection will be such that rights in the basic structure are to be assigned so as to maximize the total intrinsic value. And even the moderate perfectionist and the Rawlsian contractarian will not find a basis for a lower-level agreement in a mutual commitment to the indispensability of human equality, for the equality of rights does not follow from the equal capacity of individuals for the higher forms of life. It may well not even be true that we have such equal capacities, but even if we do, that by itself would not commit a perfectionist who accepted it to a Rawlsian doctrine of equal rights as well. From the fact (if it is a fact) that impartial rational agents would commit themselves to a principle of perfection it does not follow that they would be, if they are consistent, committed to a conception of right which would in turn commit them to the principle of equal liberty. Maximization of the total of intrinsic value (defined in perfectionist terms) may or may not be compatible with a principle of equal liberty. Whether it is or not will depend on particular circumstances. Thus in a perfectionist account there is no secure foundation for a key pillar of justice as fairness, namely, the principle of equal liberty.

However, against Rawls, it could be responded, "So what?" Perhaps it is more reasonable and, morally speaking, better to stick with a principle of perfection with different principles of justice subordinate to that principle. Why must it be the case, and indeed is it the case, that rational and impartial people with a capacity for a sense of justice must opt for the priority of a principle of equal liberty rather than the priority of a principle of perfection when the two are in conflict? As far as I can see, Rawls has done nothing to show that they must or even that they should.

It would be reasonable for Rawls to respond that in arguing about morals and in arguing morally, it should be evident that at "some point we cannot avoid relying upon our intuitive judgments" (p. 320). In the above argument we were forgetting that in comparing the adequacy of these rival moral postures, we must at some point appeal to our *considered convictions* (p. 318). He might add that we need, as well, to develop more fully the consequences of these principles; indeed, we need to develop them in detail and see where they lead (p. 319). In particular, we need to see whether they have consequences that conflict with our considered convictions. Some of these considered convictions, Rawls reminds us, "are fixed points ... that we seem unwilling to revise under any foreseeable circumstances" (p. 318). The point, Rawls could claim, is that justice as fairness harmonizes better with our considered convictions, including those deepest convictions which are fixed points we are not willing, except purely in theory, to revise (pp. 381–20).

We must, however, be careful with the use of "we" and "our" here. Rawls has not succeeded in drawing implications from the perfectionist principle which clash with any such considered convictions of mine. I am not trying, as Hare and Singer do, to challenge such an appeal to considered convictions; I am only remarking (accepting at least for this discussion, the legitimacy of such an appeal) that in appealing to such considered convictions, Rawls has not, as far as I can see, given us grounds for opting for justice as fairness over perfectionism.[4]

It may be the case that Rawls' considered convictions, including his most fixed considered convictions, differ rather radically from mine. If that is so, and if we are both rather representative of different groups of people, then Rawls' account is in deep trouble. Why should we accept as normative for humankind the considered convictions of his particular group? If, as I think more likely, Rawls' considered convictions and mine are not very different, then Rawls is also in deep trouble, for he has not been able to achieve a reflective equilibrium between, on the one hand, principles, rational beliefs, the facts in the case and, on the other, our considered convictions which will register against perfectionism and for justice as fairness. In either case he has not shown why rational, informed, impartial men with a sense of justice (a moral understanding) should opt for his two principles rather than the traditional teleological principles of perfectionism.

Where we accept a moderate perfectionism and do not insist on any claim that the principle of perfection provides the sole ultimate criterion for what we are to do, Rawls is particularly vulnerable. Moderate perfectionists argue that we are to balance fundamental moral principles, including the principle of perfection and Rawls's two principles of justice, much as W. D. Ross argued that we should balance what he called *prima facie* duties, sometimes shifting in favor of one weighting of the principles and sometimes another. Through engaging in this activity, we come to appreciate in a particular circumstance what is suitable to the situation. The moderate perfectionist, like a pluralist such as Ross, is contending that we cannot reasonably generalize beyond this. (Indeed, it seems to me that such a perfectionist is a rather distinctive kind of pluralist.)

Rawls tells us that so construed the principle of perfection, as distinct from his principles, will not provide us with a single standard of social justice. "Criteria of excellence," he claims, are too "imprecise as political principles and their application to public questions is bound to be unsettled and idiosyncratic" (p. 330). Presumably, his

---

    [4] R. M. Hare, "Rawls' Theory of Justice' I," *Philosophical Quarterly* 28 (1973): 144–55; Peter Singer, ' Sidgwick and Reflective Equilibrium," *Monist* 58 (1974): 490–517.

remarks about their public ascertainability made two pages earlier and at least seemingly in conflict with this last remark, were meant as part of some narrower tradition and community of thought. The claim is that we can, using Rawls' account, determine rather more exactly than can the perfectionist what we are to do. We know on Rawls' account rather exactly when liberty or freedom can be restricted, namely when it violates some obligation or natural duty or interferes with the basic liberties of others. And, as the least favored stratum can be identified by its index of primary goods, we can apply the difference principle fairly precisely, for we can ascertain in a rather straightforward manner "what things will advance the interests of the least favoured" (p. 320).

Indeed, as Rawls recognizes, ethical principles are, as we have known at least since Aristotle, vague, but, he continues, "they are not all equally imprecise, and the two principles of justice have an advantage in the greater clarity of their demands and in what needs to be done to satisfy them" (p. 321). Perfectionist principles, he claims, are less determinate: with them there is less general agreement. The consensus model would not work nearly as well for perfectionism, for over such matters "we are likely to be influenced by subtle aesthetic preferences and personal feelings of propriety; and individual, class and group differences are often sharp and irreconcilable" (p. 331).

Surely, if there actually is such a comparative non-vagueness, it counts in favor of the principles of justice as fairness over the principle of perfectionism. Yet how decisive this is is far from evident. Matters such as personal feelings of propriety can, at least in theory, be eliminated. Moreover—to take a distinct consideration—perhaps the Rawlsian doctrine in counterdistinction to perfectionism does not leave enough scope for *ideal-regarding* considerations? In defending perfectionism one might argue against Rawls, as Stuart Hampshire has, that Rawls' account suffers from a one-sided emphasis in explaining "the virtue of justice, and even more the other essential virtues, as rational consequences of planned cooperation in a rational social setting."[5] Hampshire queries whether this is the most fundamental role of justice or of morality, and goes on to claim that "to adopt the moral point of view ... is to think what kind of character and aims men should have, or try to have, and what kind of life they should lead."[6] To have a moral point of view is among other things, but still quite centrally, to have a *conception*, vague though it may be, "of the wholly admirable man, and of the entirely desirable and admirable way of life."[7] But this is—or so it seems—to commit oneself

---

[5] Stuart Hampshire, "What Is the Just Society?" *New York Review of Books* 18, No. 3 (1972), p. 38.

[6] *Ibid.*

[7] *Ibid.*

to a form of perfectionism as a still more fundamental feature of morality than anything to which Rawls appeals.

Rawls admits that such perfectionist conceptions are involved in morality but denies that they are as fundamental as are his principles of justice in thinking about the necessary bases of rational cooperation for a well-ordered society. However, as Hampshire points out, where such a postion is taken, it is not obvious how the issue can be rationally settled as to the comparative *adequacy* of Rawlsian contractarianism and moderate perfectionism. Hampshire further remarks plausibly, as Nowell-Smith has as well, that this indecisiveness is inescapable in moral philosophy.[8] But Hampshire, admittedly indecisively, offers as "evidence" for perfectionism the following "considerations capable of determining the intellect"—considerations of the same order of rigor as the ones to which Rawls feels that he can legitimately appeal (p. 125). The "evidence" in question is from the history of reflective moral opinions and from the psychology of moral sentiments, respectively.

The kind of reflective moral opinion Hampshire is appealing to centers around the claim, reflected in the moral beliefs of many intelligentsia, that it is not the justice of the prevailing practices and institutions which are at the center of moral concern but a conception of what kind of person to become and of what kind of relations are ideally to obtain among people. Such an argument from the psychology of moral sentiments stresses that the virtue of justice is more "associated with the conceptions of guilt and innocence, of law and due procedures of law, of separation, of impartiality in judgment," and is less centrally associated "with the rational distribution of goods in society."[9] On Rawls' own positive account just the opposite is the case.

To this I think Rawls could and should respond, particularly to the point about the psychology of moral sentiments, that although genetically and historically speaking these ideas have had a very considerable role and indeed that an understanding of their origins should not be lost, yet when one reconstructs the basis—the rational foundation—of morality, the conceptions Rawls refers to and utilizes are more central, for without a basis of rational cooperation—a basis for adjudicating conflicting claims, aims, and interests and for setting out the grounds of human cooperation—the other moral considerations referred to by Hampshire would have no point. The considerations of justice Hampshire talks about and the possibility of finding a truly admirable way of life, a rational and thoroughly desirable life plan, are dependent for their very possibility on the considerations Rawls concerns himself with. Thus in that obvious way they are more funda-

---

[8] *Ibid.*, pp. 38–39. See also P. H. Nowell-Smith, "A Theory of Justice?" *Philosophy of the Social Sciences* 3 (1973).
[9] Hampshire, "What Is the Just Society?" p. 39.

mental than the others; i.e., the others depend on them. If *they* are not coherently set out and rationally justified, the rest would be a shambles.

There is a lot of metaphor here which may resist more literal statement, but, that consideration aside, even if Rawls' considerations provide the base, it does not follow that the rest of the edifice is less important. My house would not stand without its foundations, and it would not be the house it is without its basement, but it by no means follows that my basement is the most important room in my house. Perhaps, as Hampshire points out, Rawls' considerations give us the theory of the kind of social order—a theory of just institutions— which provides the machinery "that makes a desirable, natural and admirable way of life possible," but from that it does not follow that such considerations, rather than considerations about what constitutes the most truly desirable way of life—with its concern for *ideals* of perfection—are at the core of moral philosophy, i.e. an inquiry into the reasonable foundations of morality.

What we must recognize from the above discussion is that we have not yet settled, as Rawls thinks we have, the issue of whether justice as fairness or perfectionism provides the more adequate articulation of the foundations of morality or even the foundations of social justice.[10] Perhaps we should say something eclectic such as this: neither gives the whole or even the most central aspects of the picture of what morality is all about, but both, perhaps with conceptions taken from utilitarianism as well, are essential and indeed essentially complementary in any more adequate account of morality. And perhaps this in effect points to the superiority of some form of pluralism encompassing all of these elements and eschewing anything like priority rules.

---

[10] Rawls might stick to his guns and respond that in much of what I have said I have assumed mistakenly that the standard of perfection is a principle of justice; on the contrary, though it is a moral principle and a principle concerning which moral arguments can be made, it is *not* a principle of justice. This perhaps is true, but even if it is true it would not touch the essentials of my argument. Rawls acknowledges that perfectionist principles are rational moral principles. The crucial question involved in the above argument is whether Rawls has shown that his principles, rather than the perfectionist principles, should be said to be the most basic elements of morality and which principles, where they conflict, should take pride of place. Rawls claims that the principles of justice as fairness should take pride of place. My argument has been that he has not established this essential point, and my argument would hold here even if (a) perfectionist principles are not principles of justice and (b) the moral terrain is so complex that we should not say that either form the most basic elements of morality but that they both are indispensable parts of the moral terrain. See here Stephen Toulmin, "Is There a Fundamental Problem in Ethics," *Australasian Journal of Philosophy* 33 (1955): 1–19.

ALLEN BUCHANAN

DISTRIBUTIVE JUSTICE AND LEGITIMATE EXPECTATIONS

(Received 11 December, 1974)

Robert Nozick argues that Rawls's difference principle is liable to a fundamental instability. According to Nozick, an 'end-state' theory of distributive justice is any theory which holds that "the justice of a distribution is determined by how things are distributed (who has what) as judged by some structural principle(s) of distribution," [1] Nozick claims that no end-state principle, including Rawls's difference principle, "can be continuously realized without continuous interference into people's lives" because allowing individuals freedom to transfer goods to one another (through gifts, exchanges, etc.) would lead to departures from the specified end-state.[2]

Rawls's difference principle requires that social and economic inequalities be arranged so as to be expected to benefit maximally the worst off group.[3] Any transfer of goods which could be expected to interfere with the establishment or preservation of the distribution required by the difference principle is prohibited by that principle. Nozick concludes that the difference principle is unacceptable because it prohibits a large class of actions, namely, transfers of goods, which are not unjust and whose prohibition constitutes an intolerable limitation on individual liberty. But even if Rawls can rebut Nozick's instability objection, there is another, more serious sort of instability objection to which the difference principle – and any end-state principle – may be liable.

It is generally acknowledged that problems of rectifying past injustices present an awesome challenge to any theory of justice. Recent philosophical literature has focused on the plight of 'victims' of 'compensatory justice'. The most forceful complaint of one who is disadvantaged through efforts to rectify past injustice is not simply that his wants have been thwarted, but also that, as a result of rectificatory policies, his rational long-term planning and consistent execution of plans have worked against him. Quota systems for university admissions illustrate this point well.

Philosophical Studies **28** (1975) 419–425. *All Rights Reserved*
Copyright © 1975 by D. Reidel Publishing Company, Dordrecht-Holland

On reflection we feel that the thwarting of a non-minority applicant's desire to attend law school is not the *only* harm done him when he is rejected as a result of a quota system. We feel he has been harmed in another, deeper way: the introduction of a quota system (at approximately the time of his application) undercuts his effectiveness as a rational planner and executor of plans. The applicant counted on conditional access to a certain position and bent his efforts to fulfilling the conditions. But very late in the game the rules specifying the conditions were abruptly changed. Knowledge of the change came too late for him.

Due consideration of cases of this sort may lead us to conclude that, *since the previous arrangement was after all unjust,* rectificatory measures are justified. We may conclude that measures necessary to correct an *unjust* scheme are justified even if they involve disrupting the long-term plans of persons who played no significant role in the creation or preservation of the unjust scheme and who have not even benefitted from it significantly. At least we may conclude that rectification and its attendant disruptions are justified if the previous system was *extremely* unjust.

My objection to Rawls's difference principle is two-fold. (1) It makes the justness or unjustness of societies, actions and expectations alarmingly transient. (2) It may (as a consequence of (1)) require gross and frequent disruptions of individuals' framing and execution of long-term plans, even when applied to schemes which were *not* (previously) *unjust.* Suppose at time T_1 the difference principle is satisfied by the basic structure b of a society S: at T_1 social and economic inequalities are arranged so as to be expected maximally to benefit the worst off. But suppose that at T_2 certain new facts come to light. Due to technological innovations, or due to the discovery of new economic facts, certain new socio-economic arrangements become feasible. Granted these new facts, it is no longer the case that the existing structure b is expected maximally to benefit the worst off. There is now a different basic structure, b', which is feasible and which does satisfy the different principle. The basic structure at T_1 *was just* (according to the different principle) – but now, at T_2, it is *unjust.* Since we have a duty to establish and support just arrangements, a change of the basic structure is required.

The basic structure of a society, as Rawls himself points out, provides the all-embracing framework in which individuals frame and execute their long-term plans. Yet the super-rule which determines which of these rules are valid – the difference principle – is a principle whose continued satisfaction requires changing those rules *whenever* they no longer define a system in which social and economic inequalities are expected to be to the greatest benefit of the worst off.

Now as Rawls also frequently notes, the rules of the basic structure determine the legitimacy of individuals' expectations. But as previously just Rawlsian basic structures become unjust instantaneously in the light of new information about how to maximize the benefit of the worst off, so previously legitimate Rawlsian expectations *lose their legitimacy* just as instantaneously.

Consider the following examples of disruptive institutional change which may be required by the continued satisfaction af the difference principle.

(i) It is determined at T_1 that it is to the greatest benefit of the worst off to establish certain new health services. New medical technician careers are created. Institutions are established and staffed with persons specially trained to inculcate the relevant skills in others. Persons plan and train to enter these new occupations: expectations are encouraged by the institutional arrangements. At T_2 the medical technician program, or a large part of it, is scrapped. New information, or perhaps the development of new automatic diagnostic equipment, indicates that a different health service system is a better way of improving the lot of the worst off. The expectations generated by the previously just scheme now have no legitimacy at all. The situation is worse than the quota system case. It is not simply that the conditions of access to certain positions have abruptly changed. Rather, the positions themselves have been abolished.

(ii) Rawls emphasizes[4] that while the difference principle may be consistent with private ownership of the means of production under some conditions, in other circumstances it may require a transition to public ownership. Suppose that at T_1 a private ownership scheme satisfies the difference principle. But suppose that at T_2 new information or new conditions indicate that public ownership of the means of production is required if we are to satisfy the difference principle. The previous institution of private property and the expectations generated by it lose all legitimacy.

As with the non-minority applicant in the rectificatory case, the strongest grievance of a person who is disadvantaged by such institutional changes is not simply that his wants have been thwarted. His functioning as a rational planner and executor of long-range plans has been undercut by his society's attempts to continue to satisfy the difference principle. Continued satisfaction of the difference principle – or any and-state principle – has all the tribulations of rectificatory justice, but none of its consolations. We cannot say: but after all, the previous scheme was *unjust*.

It might be thought that a theorist can cope with the problem of instability and disruption by invoking the notion of the rule of law. The right to life under the rule of law was conceived by its seventeenth century advocates primarily as the right to life under the protection of standing general laws as opposed to life under the uncertainty of 'government by arbitrary decree'. The root idea behind the case for the rule of law is that of providing a stable, relatively permanent framework of expectations within which rational planners can consistently and effectively pursue their ends. The disruptive effects of continued satisfaction of the difference principle are similar to the disruptive effects of 'government by arbitrary decree'. Hence one might argue that the difference principle (or some other end-state principle) can be made tolerable if it is constrained by a strong principle of the right to life under the rule of law.

Now Rawls does list this right among the basic liberties of his first principle of justice. His discussion of the rule of law, however, neither raises the problem of instability, nor suggests any way of resolving it.[5] Moreover, the notion of the rule of law itself appears too lean to provide what is required. For what is needed is nothing short of *a theory of institutional change* – a set of systematically related principles defining institutions for institutional change.

Rawls tells us that in *A Theory of Justice* he presents only the ideal part of the theory of justice. He does not offer a nonideal theory to cover the problems of noncompliance and of the rectification of past injustices.

The theory of rectificatory justice is a nonideal theory of institutional change. The problem of instability sketched above, however, is a problem of institutional change in ideal theory. It is neither a problem of noncompliance nor of the rectification of past injustices. What is required here is a theory of how to *maintain* the justness of a scheme over time, where maintaining justness requires *institutional change*.

Though the rectificatory theory of justice and the theory needed to prevent instability in the continued satisfaction of an end-state principle are both theories of institutional change, their contents, presumably, will be quite different. For surely the fact that the previous arrangement, along with the expectations generated by it, was just in the one case, but unjust in the other, will make a great difference in determining the rules for institutional change in the two sorts of cases.

Having put the problem, I would now like to suggest what I believe to be the only strategy which offers any promise of solving it. Rawls's difference principle itself may provide the key to an adequate theory of institutional change. The plausibility of this strategy depends on a fact which has not received adequate emphasis. Though the difference principle does require goods such as income to be distributed in certain ways, what it primarily distributes is life-prospects or long-term expectations.[6] To determine whether a system of institutions is just, we are to view it from the position of the worst off: the system is just only if it maximizes the life-prospects of the worst off. If we include institutions for institutional change in the set of institutions to which the difference principle is applied, we can take into account the effects of instability and disruptions on the life-prospects of the worst off.[7]

Now it will not be plausible to argue with respect to many individual disruptive changes that they are not to the greatest benefit of the worst off, especially in cases where the changes will occur only in positions occupied by members of better off groups. But the prospects of the worst off include their prospects of ascending to higher positions, of enjoying the benefits of those positions, and of being able to continue to enjoy those benefits. Maximizing their expectations, then, will require taking into account the stability of institutional arrangements, since liability to future disruptions decreases their present expectations, other things being equal.

To determine in each case whether a particular proposed institutional change is to the greatest benefit of the worst off might be such an enormously complex affair that it would require an excessive outlay of time and resources. If this were so, it might not be to the greatest benefit of the worst off to apply the difference principle in this direct way. Further, the knowledge that institutional arrangements were liable to revision at any time, as a result of direct application of the difference principle, might itself undermine individual security to such an extent that expectations in general, including the expectations of the worst off, were diminished.

I will not elaborate these arguments here. They have familiar analogs in arguments to show the superiority of rule over act utilitarianism. If they can be adequately developed, it may be possible to construct an adequate theory of ideal institutional change for Rawls's theory at least. Though the difference principle itself neither constitutes nor entails such a theory, it may provide its foundation. The theory would consist, presumably, of principles defining institutions of institutional change which serve to minimize disruption and to compensate the victims of disruption. The theoretic justification for any such principle would consist in showing that the system of principles of institutional change of which it is an element defines a system of practices which works to the greatest benefit of the worst off.

I should also like to suggest that the difference principle itself may provide the key to the solution of Nozick's instability objection as well. Nozick's objection implies that the attempt to satisfy and to continue to satisfy the difference principle puts severe restrictions on property rights to the goods it distributes. We will not be free to use these goods in important ways, since using them in these ways disrupts the distribution the difference principle requires.

If, as Nozick assumes, the difference principle prohibited transfers of goods, it would constrict property rights to the point of making them all but useless. But such a constriction of property rights would *decrease*, rather than increase the expectations of the worst off in two ways. First, it would severely limit their freedom to use whatever property they have. Second, it would undercut their expectations of gaining property in the future and of being able freely to use it in the pursuit of their ends. These are two reasons for thinking that, other things equal, the difference principle will *not* prohibit private transfers.

My claim is not that the difference principle would require an 'absolute' capitalist property right guaranteeing complete freedom to dispose of one's goods as one wishes. I only suggest that the application of the difference principle will require a complex theory of property which weighs the advantages of strong property rights against their disadvantages. The acceptability of a theory which includes a distributive principle such as the difference principle will depend in part on the acceptability of its theory of property. At present Rawls lacks a theory of property. But whether, as Nozick assumes, the difference principle will in general probihit private transfers of goods will depend on the content of that theory.

Similarly, the need for a theory of institutional change in the ideal theory part of a theory of justice will be present in any theory of justice which includes an end-state principle of distribution. The lack of a theory of institutional change, like the lack of a theory of property, is nothing less than a major theoretical defect. Until a corresponding ideal theory of institutional change is adequately developed, the acceptability of a principle of distribution simply cannot be determined. For until the ideal theory of institutional change is developed, we cannot determine whether significant measures for continued realization of the prescribed distribution are compatible with the stability of legitimate expectations so essential to us as rational agents.

University of North Carolina
at Chapel Hill

NOTES

[1] Nozick, *Anarchy, State, and Utopia*, Basic Books, New York, 1974, p. 153.
[2] Nozick, p. 163.
[3] Rawls, *A Theory of Justice*, Harvard University Press, Cambridge, 1970, p. 78.
[4] *Ibid.*, p. 274.
[5] *Ibid.*, pp. 235–243.
[6] *Ibid.*, p. 92.
[7] This point was suggested to me by S. L. Darwall.

GEORGE SHER

Effort, Ability, and
Personal Desert

A familiar argument in recent social theorizing is that because no one deserves either his native talents or his ability to exert effort, no one can be said to deserve any advantages made possible by his talents or abilities. The premises of this argument are perhaps most clearly stated in the following well-known passage from *A Theory of Justice*:

> It seems to be one of the fixed points of our considered judgments that no one deserves his place in the distribution of native endowments, any more than one deserves one's initial starting place in society. The assertion that a man deserves the superior character that enables him to make the effort to cultivate his abilities is equally problematic; for his character depends in large part upon fortunate family and social circumstances for which he can claim no credit. The notion of desert seems not to apply to these cases.[1]

If these contentions are correct, and if Rawls is also correct in concluding from them that no one deserves "the greater advantages he could achieve with [his natural endowments],"[2] then personal desert will play no role at all in determining which system of distributing goods is just. At best, the connection will work the other way around: a social system which is just for other reasons may itself determine a (logically secondary) sense in which people deserve things. But, as

1. John Rawls, *A Theory of Justice* (Cambridge, Mass.: Harvard University Press, 1971), p. 104. See also pp. 15, 75-76, 310-315, and passim.
2. Ibid., p. 104.

© 1979 by Princeton University Press
Philosophy & Public Affairs 8, no. 4
0048-3915/79/040361-16$0.80/1

Rawls insists, personal desert will not be among the *fundamental* facts of morality at all.[3]

In this essay, I want to argue against this way of showing that people never deserve things for reasons prior to or independent of social conventions. My attempt to rebut the anti-desert argument will proceed in three stages. In the first stage (sections I and II), I shall try to interpret Rawls' influential formulation of the argument as sympathetically as possible. In the second stage (sections III and IV), I shall contend that even when the argument *is* interpreted sympathetically, its normative premises do not support the conclusion that people rarely or never deserve things. In the third stage (section V), I shall raise some questions about the underpinning of one of the crucial normative premises itself. As this essay's thrust is primarily defensive, I shall not offer a detailed defense of any positive theory of personal desert, nor even try to decide whether such desert attaches primarily to effort or to achievement. My aim is merely to secure the moral import of personal desert against the Rawlsian attack, and so indirectly to cast doubt upon those theories of justice which are insensitive to it.

I

Before we can begin any evaluation of Rawls' argument against personal desert, we must get somewhat clearer about what that argument says. We have seen that Rawls wants to move from the premise that people do not deserve their character or abilities to the conclusion that people do not deserve the advantages which these "natural as-

3. Although Rawls has presented the most developed version of the anti-desert argument, an abbreviated version of it also appears in Richard Wasserstrom, "The University and the Case for Preferential Treatment," *American Philosophical Quarterly* 13, no. 2 (April 1976): 167. For related discussion, see also Thomas Nagel, "Equal Treatment and Compensatory Discrimination," *Philosophy & Public Affairs* 2, no. 4 (Summer 1973): 348-363; John Schaar, "Equal Opportunity and Beyond," in Anthony de Crespigny and Alan Wertheimer, eds., *Contemporary Political Theory* (Chicago: Atherton, 1970), pp. 135-53; and John Hospers, "What Means This Freedom?" in Sidney Hook, ed., *Determinism and Freedom in the Age of Modern Science* (New York: Collier, 1961), pp. 126-142.

sets" make possible. But why, exactly, does Rawls believe that people do not deserve their character and abilities in the first place?

Because Rawls mentions the social causes of our effort-making abilities, and because our other talents and abilities seem obviously to be caused as well, it may be tempting to interpret him as claiming that our natural assets are undeserved simply because they are caused. However, this claim is nowhere explicitly made by Rawls, and would in any event be no less controversial than the related claim that an agent is not responsible if his *act* is caused. For these reasons, I shall not attribute it to Rawls here. Instead, I shall take him to hold the more reasonable view that our natural assets are undeserved because they are brought into existence by events independent of anything we ourselves have done. A person may indeed take steps to develop his talents and increase his effort-making capacity; but his ability to take such steps must itself depend on some earlier complement of talents and effort-making abilities which are not the result of any such actions. Because of this, he may indeed be held unable to "claim credit" for any of these earlier talents or abilities.

If an agent's possession of an ability is not the result of anything he does, I shall refer to that ability as a *basic* ability of the agent. When it is formulated in terms of basic abilities, the complete anti-desert argument looks something like this:

(1) Each person M has some basic set of abilities, S_m, which includes an ability to exert effort, and which does not belong to him as a result of anything he does.

(2) If X does not belong to M as a result of anything M does, then M does not deserve X.

Therefore,

(3) M does not deserve S_m.

Moreover,

(4) Each action performed by M is made possible, directly or indirectly, by some subset of S_m.

(5) If M does not deserve X, and X makes Y possible, then M does not deserve Y.

Therefore,

    (6) *M* does not deserve to perform his actions, and neither does
        he deserve to enjoy any of the benefits which those actions
        make possible in their turn.

I do not know if Rawls would endorse this version of the argument as
his own. However, whether or not he would, the version is the one
which initially seems most likely to yield his conclusion and, in any
event, is worthy of consideration in its own right. For these reasons,
I shall confine my discussion to it in what follows. Is this argument,
or some further refinement of it, sound?

II

Although each step of the argument sketched above has some intuitive appeal, the argument surely cannot be accepted as it stands; for
premise (5), at least, is implausibly strong. If deserving the benefits
of our actions did require that we deserve everything that makes our
actions possible, then all such desert would immediately be canceled
by the fact that no one has done anything to deserve to be alive or to
live in a life-sustaining environment.[4] If this were the case, then
Rawls' insistence that people do not deserve their natural assets would
be quite superfluous. Moreover, as Alan Zaitchik has pointed out, anyone who accepts both (5) and "the truism that all deserving is deserving in virtue of some ground or other" will immediately be led
to a vicious regress: in order to deserve *Z*, *M* must deserve *Z*'s ground
Y, in order to deserve *Y*, *M* must deserve *Y*'s ground *X*, and so on.[5]
This regress shows again that (5) rules out the possibility of personal
desert for reasons quite independent of the (alleged) fact that we do
not deserve our natural talents or abilities.

    According to Zaitchik, the fact that (5) rules out the possibility of
personal desert, and so contradicts many people's "pre-theoretical
certainty that at least some people deserve something," is itself a
reductio of (5). It seems to me, however, that this particular way of

---

4. I owe this point to Wendy Lotz.
5. Alan Zaitchik, "On Deserving to Deserve," *Philosophy & Public Affairs* 6,
no. 4 (Summer 1977): 373.

dismissing (5) proceeds too quickly. If Zaitchik has correctly represented Rawls as intending to produce "a completely general argument which alleges that *no* desert theory could be true for the simple reason that no one ever deserves things,"[6] then we cannot appeal to our intuitive conviction that people *do* deserve things without begging the question against Rawls. What we can ask, however, is that Rawls' premises about personal desert should not be question-begging in their turn. Although they must of course be strong enough to yield the desired conclusion, Rawls' premises should also be uncontroversial enough to be acceptable even to persons initially sympathetic to personal desert. As we have stated it, premise (5) fails to satisfy this requirement. Can any alternative premise do better?

Perhaps one can. The basic problem with (5) is that it promiscuously allows M's desert of Y to be canceled by *all* undeserved necessary conditions for his having Y. Intuitively, this seems excessive because many such conditions are satisfied not only by M, but also by everyone else. *All* claimants to goods must satisfy such conditions as being alive and existing in life-sustaining environments; and so these conditions, though undeserved by M, do not give him an unfair advantage over anyone. In light of this, the obvious way to amend (5) is to construe it as requiring not that M deserve *all* the conditions necessary for his having Y, but rather only that he deserve those which are not shared by all rival claimants as well. This modification will in effect transform (5) from a statement of the conditions necessary for M's deserving Y *simpliciter* into a statement of the conditions necessary for M's deserving to have Y while someone else does not. When personal desert is consistently interpreted as involving a relation of this sort, (5) becomes

> (5a) If M does not deserve to have X while N does not, and X makes it possible for M to have Y while N does not, then M does not deserve to have Y while N does not.

By shifting from (5) to (5a), we can avoid both the charge that this premise is violated by universally satisfied necessary conditions

6. Ibid., pp. 373, 371.

for having Y and the charge that it leads to a vicious regress. Nevertheless, despite these gains, the shift to (5a) is not without costs of its own. For one thing, since the antecedent of (5a) is now cast in comparative terms, the earlier premises of the anti-desert argument will also have to be recast in this way if they are to mesh with (5a). Moreover, and more seriously, the shift to a comparative conception of desert will also require us to make new distinctions among the elements of a person's basic abilities. As long as personal desert was not construed comparatively, it was quite permissible to speak of one's whole basic package of abilities as either deserved or undeserved. However, once we shift to a comparative conception of desert, we must go beyond this. If M has a set of basic abilities $a_1 \ldots a_d, a_e$, and N has the smaller set $a_1 \ldots a_i$, then only M's special ability a_e will give him an advantage over N. Because this is so, the argument's earlier premises must be reformulated to factor out such shared basic abilities as $a_1 \ldots a_d$.

When both of the required alterations are made, the anti-desert argument emerges looking like this.

(1a) Each person M has some basic set of abilities, S_m, which includes an ability to exert effort, and which does not belong to him as a result of anything he does. Suppose S_m includes $a_1 \ldots a_d, a_e$, and S_n includes only $a_1 \ldots a_d$.

(2a) If X does not belong to M as a result of anything M does, then M does not deserve to have X while N does not.

Therefore,

(3a) M does not deserve to have a_e while N does not.

(4a) Let A be an action which a_e makes it possible for M, but not N, to perform.

(5a) If M does not deserve to have X while N does not, and X makes it possible for M to have Y while N does not, then M does not deserve to have Y while N does not.

Therefore,

(6a) M does not deserve to perform A while N does not, and neither does *M* deserve to enjoy the benefits of *A* while *N* does not.

There may be problems with the assumption that abilities are goods which people can deserve relative to others; for abilities, unlike other goods, are not transferrable among persons. But instead of pursuing these problems further, I want to raise a question of a rather different sort. Assuming that its treatment of abilities can be made intelligible, exactly what, if anything, will this version of the argument entail about personal desert in particular cases?

III

By demonstrating that the Rawlsian argument must be reformulated in comparative terms, we have already compelled a measure of retreat from its initial unqualified conclusion that nobody ever deserves anything. In its current form, the argument does indeed leave room for personal desert in cases where all the relevant parties have equivalent sets of basic abilities. However, if basic abilities are in fact generally *unequally* distributed, then this concession will leave essentially intact Rawls' central conclusion that personal desert counts for little or nothing. If we are to challenge this conclusion, we must examine more closely the claim that people's basic abilities vary systematically in significant ways. Since this claim is most controversial as it applies to the ability to exert effort, we may begin by considering this aspect of it. On what basis, exactly, can people be said to differ in effort-making ability?

Although Rawls is plainly committed to an environmental explanation of *how* people come to differ in effort-making ability, he offers no explicit defense of the prior claim that they *do* differ in this ability. Because of this, any discussion of the rationale for this claim must be quite speculative. As a first attempt at reconstructing that rationale, let us consider the argument that people are shown to differ in effort-making ability by the great differences in the efforts they actually make. If *M* applies himself assiduously to whatever task is at hand while *N*'s efforts are interspersed with evasion and procrastination, the argument might run, then *M must* have some effort-making ability which *N* lacks. *N* must indeed have some effort-making ability, since he does try sporadically; but whatever such ability *N* has, *M* must have that much ability plus some additional ability as well. For how else are we going to account for *M*'s additional industry?

Although this argument may have some initial plausibility, a closer look reveals its weakness. If we are going to infer superior effort-making ability directly from *M*'s additional industry, then we will have to do so on the basis of the more general principle that no one is capable of making any more effort than he actually does make. However, this principle, when brought to light, seems simply to be false. Even persons who would be acknowledged to have superior effort-making abilities are often inclined not to make the efforts necessary to accomplish their goals. Many goals, though desirable, are not worth the effort it would take to attain them; and others, though worth the effort, are blocked by conflicting goals. In light of this, there is obviously room for a distinction between the *possession* of an ability to exert effort and the *exercise* of that ability; and given this distinction, it is easy to understand the difference in *M* and *N*'s efforts without supposing that they differ in effort-making ability. To do this, we need only view the difference in their efforts as stemming from the different degrees to which they have exercised their common effort-making ability.

Given these considerations, we clearly cannot infer the conclusion that people differ in their effort-making abilities directly from the fact that they differ in their efforts. However, it remains possible to defend the different-ability thesis in a somewhat different way. Although persons who exert different amounts of effort always *can* be viewed as drawing differently upon similar effort-making abilities, this suggestion may seem implausible when the difference in their efforts is pronounced, systematic, and to the obvious disadvantage of the less industrious. In such a case, there is simply no good reason for *N* to refrain from exercising his effort-making ability; and so it may seem most reasonable to suppose that he does not have a full measure of that ability to begin with. If we defend the unequal-ability thesis in this way, we will in effect be deriving it, not as a logical consequence of the difference between *M* and *N*'s efforts, but rather via an inference to the best explanation of that difference.

This second way of defending the different-ability thesis is considerably more sophisticated than the first. However, it is not notably more successful. The different-ability thesis would indeed have more explanatory power than its rival if we could assume that *M* and *N* are always equally attentive to their own long-range interests, and are always equally concerned to advance these interests. However, in the current context, neither of these assumptions is legitimate. Anyone who accepts the equal-ability thesis will of course wish to maintain that when *N* fails to exert efforts that are plainly in his own long-range interest, he is either momentarily inattentive to those interests or else momentarily unconcerned to further them. And when the equal-ability thesis is supplemented by these premises, the resulting explanation of *N*'s lack of effort is every bit as plausible as its alternative.[7]

These considerations show that there are serious problems with the grounding of Rawls' contention that people commonly differ in effort-making abilities. However, there is also a further difficulty here. Even if we grant that this contention is both meaningful and well-grounded, its conjunction with the other Rawlsian premises will still not entail that *M* does not deserve the benefits of his superior efforts. According to (5a), a difference in *M* and *N*'s effort-making abilities will rule out *M*'s desert relative to *N* only if the difference in their abilities makes it *impossible* for *M* and *N* to exert equal amounts of effort. But not every difference in effort-making ability need have this effect. It is easy to see how *M* and *N* might differ in effort-making ability, but *N* might still take steps to match *M*'s superior efforts. For one thing, *N* can maintain a special vigilance against those distractions which he but not *M* finds attractive; for another, if *N* foresees difficulty in

7. Although I have argued against Rawls' uncritical assumption that people differ in effort-making abilities, I do not wish to suggest that Rawls has been the only philosopher to fall into this error. For another example of it, see my own earlier paper, "Justifying Reverse Discrimination in Employment," *Philosophy & Public Affairs* 4, no. 2 (Winter 1975): 165-167.

avoiding these temptations, he can always take action to avoid them, or to increase his ability to resist them. Of course, Rawls could always maintain that these steps, as well as N's efforts themselves, are blocked by N's lesser effort-making ability; but this contention becomes progressively more difficult to maintain as the range of N's inability is said to increase. Whatever it is that N cannot do, there are surely many things that he *can* do; and since there is no theoretical limit to the steps one can take to increase one's effort-making ability, the number of cases in which differences in such ability render differences in effort inevitable seems minimal at best. In light of this, even genuine differences in effort-making ability, should they exist, would seem unlikely to have the moral significance attributed to them by Rawls.[8]

IV

So far, we have seen that Rawls' anti-desert argument is plausible only if desert is understood comparatively; that on this interpretation desert is threatened only by unequal basic abilities; and that it is doubtful whether people's abilities to exert effort are unequal in the relevant way. The Rawlsian argument has thus evidently failed to discredit the thesis that personal desert may be established by conscientious effort. However, people manifestly *do* differ in abilities such as physical strength and intelligence, and so a parallel defense does not seem available for the further thesis that personal desert is established by superior achievement. Because of this, it is tempting to view Rawls' argument as showing, in effect, that personal desert is properly associated with effort rather than achievement. Although Zaitchik's approach to the Rawlsian argument differs substantially from mine, he has drawn a qualified version of this conclusion from it. It seems to me, however, that the truth lies elsewhere.

To see why this is so, let us again consider the argument advanced at the end of the preceding section. It was contended there that even if people *did* differ in effort-making abilities, those differences would

8. For the argument of this paragraph, I owe an obvious debt to Stuart Hampshire, *Thought and Action* (New York: Viking, 1959), chap. 3.

not inevitably lead to differences in efforts actually expended. By suitably compensating for his lesser effort-making abilities, N might have put himself in a position to exert the same amount of effort that M made; and if N could have done this, then his lesser effort-making ability was not a violation of (5a) at all. But surely something similar can be said for other differences in initial ability as well. Even if M is initially stronger or more intelligent than N, this difference will only entail that M does not deserve what he has achieved relative to N if the difference between them has made it impossible for N to achieve as much as M. However, differences in strength, intelligence, and other native gifts are rarely so pronounced as to have this effect. The far more common effect of such differences is merely to make it more *difficult* for the less talented person to reach a given level of attainment. He must work harder, husband his resources more carefully, plan more shrewdly, and so on. Because the latter differences do *not* combine with (5a) to yield any conclusions about desert, the Rawlsian premises are evidently compatible with desert for achievement in at least a large number of cases.

This conclusion is reinforced, moreover, by a careful reconsideration of (5a) itself. We were initially led to accept (5a) because it intutively seemed unfair for one person to enjoy benefits from which another has been barred through no act or omission of his own. However, on second glance, this unfairness may be largely mitigated if there is another, comparable benefit which the second person could have enjoyed instead. It is merely perverse for someone to remain deeply upset over his inability to become a professional athlete when he is perfectly capable of making a successful career in education or business. Because this is so, (5a) is actually *im*plausible when it is applied to particular benefits without regard to alternatives available. To make (5a) generally plausible, we must insist that it range not over particular benefits, but rather over general levels of well-being. Properly understood, (5a) should assert only that if M does not deserve to have X while N does not, and X makes it possible for M to achieve a particular level of well-being which N does not share, then M does not deserve to exist at *that level of well-being* while N does not. Since this alteration will permit even persons with very superior talents to deserve the benefits of their achievements as long as others are capable of attaining equivalent levels of well-being in other areas, its result will be to relax still further the constraints which the Rawlsian premises place upon desert for achievement.

Nevertheless, despite this loosening, some constraints clearly do remain. Even after we have allowed both for the greater efforts of the less talented and for the possibility of equivalent achievement in alternative areas, there will remain many cases in which one person has achieved a level of well-being which another could not possibly have achieved. This may be either because the first person's talents were so great, because the second person's talents were so minimal, or because the first person was just lucky enough to be in the right place at the right time. Moreover, there will remain many other cases in which a person of meager attainments could indeed have achieved more, but only through efforts which it would have been unreasonable to expect of him. In the former cases, and perhaps even in the latter, premises like Rawls' will indeed suggest that the person who has achieved more does not deserve the full benefit of his achievement relative to the other, but rather deserves only the proportion of it which the other could reasonably have been expected to match. Since every high achiever can be paired with some low achiever in this way, it seems to follow that few people can lay absolutely full claim to all the benefits they have achieved.

These considerations suggest that if the Rawlsian premises are correct, we cannot allow people to enjoy the full benefits of their achievements without permitting many persons to be better off than they deserve to be with respect to at least some others. Assuming that undeserved inequalities which do not bring appropriate compensating benefits are unjust, this concession may seem to tell heavily against allowing people to enjoy whatever they have achieved. In fact, however, the situation is more complicated than this; for even if allowing people to enjoy the benefits of their achievements does permit some undeserved inequalities, it may still come closer to giving everyone what he deserves relative to everyone else than any alternative. To see why this is so, consider a simplified situation in which M has much talent but has achieved much, while N has much talent but

has achieved little, and O has little talent and has achieved little.
In this situation, N and O may well deserve the same amount relative to each other; but M will deserve more relative to N than he
does relative to O. Because this is so, M's getting precisely what he
deserves relative to N will require that he *not* get precisely what
he deserves relative to O, and vice versa. In light of such cases,
it will almost certainly be impossible to allow everyone to get exactly
what he deserves relative to everyone else. At best, we can try to design a system in which as few people as possible get more or less than
they deserve relative to others. There is nothing in Rawls' argument
to suggest either that such a system will not allow most or all people
to enjoy most or all of the benefits they have achieved, or that its remaining undeserved inequalities will be so weighty as to render it
unjust. Because this is so, there remains at least one version of the
claim that people deserve to enjoy what they have achieved which the
Rawlsian argument leaves quite untouched.

V

Up to now, my criticisms of the Rawlsian argument have been mainly
internal to it. I have tried to show that even if we grant that people
deserve things relative to others only when their having them is their
own doing [(2a)] and only when their having them is not the result
of other undeserved differences [(5a)], we are still not forced to conclude that people do not commonly deserve things. In this last section,
I want to abandon this internal perspective, and turn my attention to
the grounding of premise (5a) itself. We saw earlier that the intuitive
argument for (5a) is that it allows personal desert only when no
claimant begins with any unfair advantage over another. However,
this intuitive appeal to fairness, when scrutinized, is itself open to
serious question.

The basic difficulty with the proposed defense of (5a) is that it presupposes a particular—and dubious—model of the way in which desert
is acquired. More specifically, the claim that M's desert relative to N
requires that M has had no unfair advantage over N will make sense
only if we view M's desert as arising through his besting N in a fair

competition. Because this is so, the proposed defense of (5a) will tacitly presuppose a competitive model of desert-acquisition. But even if competition for goods is *one* of the contexts which give rise to personal desert, it is surely not plausible to view it as the *only* context which does this. Instead, anyone who is initially sympathetic to personal desert will wish to hold that people may also come to deserve things in a variety of other ways: by working especially hard, by possessing special moral characteristics, or simply by exercising their own creative capacities in building houses, painting pictures, or otherwise producing or improving objects of value. There is, of course, ample room for disagreement about what a person may come to deserve in these ways, and also about the conditions which must prevail before any such desert can arise. Nevertheless, whatever the answers to these questions may be, it remains clear that such activities as extending effort and creating things are not simply variant forms of winning. Because this is so, the notion of an unfair advantage over one's competitors seem completely out of place where they are concerned.

In light of these considerations, the most plausible defense of (5a) appears to collapse when it is applied in non-competitive desert-creating contexts. However, it might still be argued that there are many extremely important desert-claims, such as claims by the best qualified to deserve jobs and other opportunities, which do indeed arise through victory in quasi-competitive situations. If this is correct, and if the "fairness" defense of (5a) succeeds in competitive contexts, then (5a) will remain correct for at least one significant class of cases. However, despite the initial appeal of these suggestions, there may be good reason to reject the competitive model of desert-acquisition even here; for a simpler account of the way desert arises in these cases may be available. Put briefly, the suggestion is that the best qualified claimant's desert may arise, not through any victory over his rivals, but directly from the comparative closeness of the "fit" between his qualifications and the requirements of the job or opportunity to be awarded.[9] Although a full defense of this suggestion would require

9. Cf. Feinberg's remark that desert, as opposed to rights, involves "that weaker kind of propriety . . . [which] is simply a kind of *fittingness* between

more discussion than can be provided here, the suggestion draws considerable support from the impressive variety of other contexts in which personal desert seems directly related to the "fit" between the relevant act or quality of the deserving party and the thing deserved. Such contexts include at least those in which persons who perform wicked acts are thereby said to deserve condemnation and punishment, those in which persons who act heroically are thereby said to deserve praise and reward, those in which persons with superior expertise are thereby said to deserve careful hearings, and those in which persons who suffer misfortune are thereby said to deserve our sympathy and understanding. In each of these contexts, personal desert appears to be grounded in nothing more than the especially appropriate nature of the deserved response; in none of them does such desert depend on the deserving party's competitive equality with others.[10] If something similar can be said about the relation between qualifications and desert of opportunities, then such desert too will be grounded in considerations independent of the competitive model, and so (5a) will fail for it as well.

Although these considerations suggest that many desert-claims have little to do with the competitive model which alone renders (5a) plausible, there may still be some desert-claims which do arise primarily through competitive victory. Specifically, claims to deserve profits generated by the exchange of goods in competitive markets may con-

---

one party's character or action and another party's favorable response, much like that between humor and laughter, or good performance and applause." Joel Feinberg, "The Nature and Value of Rights," in Samuel Gorovitz et al., eds., *Moral Problems in Medicine* (Englewood Cliffs, NJ: Prentice-Hall, 1976), p. 456. For further discussion, see Feinberg's important paper, "Justice and Personal Desert," in his *Doing and Deserving: Essays in the Theory of Responsibility* (Princeton, NJ: Princeton University Press, 1970), pp. 55-94. Also relevant, thought not restricted to personal desert, is Michael Walzer's discussion in "In Defense of Equality," *Dissent* (Fall 1973), pp. 399-408.

10. Of course, it is one thing to say that a person's desert may arise through his exercise of abilities not possessed by others, and quite another to say that his desert cannot be limited by concern for the future competitive position of others. For an account of desert which appears to allow for limitation on the latter grounds but not the former, see Lawrence Becker, *Property Rights* (London: Routledge and Kegan Paul, 1977), pp. 48-56.

ceivably be of this sort.[11] If they are, then such claims may indeed be constrained by something like (5a). However, even if this is so, (5a) will at best hold for a small subset of the claims to deserve goods which people advance, and so the crucial Rawlsian premise will still fail for the majority of such claims. There of course may be other routes to the conclusion that people rarely or never deserve things; and there may be independent reasons for systematically ignoring or overriding personal desert. However, pending the advancement of some further argument for these views, it seems clear that no satisfactory theory of justice can afford to ignore personal desert.

11. However, see Feinberg, "Justice and Personal Desert," pp. 88-94.

This essay has been much improved by the helpful criticism and suggestions of Alan Wertheimer.

Maximin Justice, Sacrifice, and the Reciprocity Argument: A Pragmatic Reassessment of the Rawls/Nozick Debate

STEPHEN W. BALL

California Polytechnic State University

I. INTRODUCTION

Theories of economic justice are characteristically based on abstract ethical concerns often unrelated to practical distributive results. Two decades ago, Rawls's theory of justice began as a reaction against the alleged 'sacrifices' condoned by utilitarian theory. One variant of this objection is that utilitarianism permits gross inequalities, severe deprivations of individual liberty, or even the enslavement of society's least well-off individuals. There are, however, more subtle forms of the objection. In Rawls, it is often waged without any claim that utilitarianism *does* in fact imply such gross deprivations in actual real-world circumstances. A second variant hinges, rather, on the milder claim that utilitarianism *could* condone such deprivations or sacrifices in some *possible* world—the objection being that utilitarianism improperly makes justice contingent, or uncertain, in this way. A third, still more abstract, variant would be that utilitarianism is flawed—not because of any practical distributive result, actual or hypothetical, but *in theory*—due to the way it treats individuals' interests, or the 'concept of persons' it presupposes.[1]

These themes, though not clearly delineated, not only are the cornerstone of Rawls's early theory, but continue to reverberate throughout his most recent essays of the 1980s. Thus, Rawls's theory was founded on a Kantian moral axiom about the 'inviolability' of the individual, and the early exposition was laced with many explicit contrasts to the sacrificial nature of utilitarianism. Similarly, the recent essays thematically stress the need to make basic individual rights and liberties more *secure*, less dependent on shifting historical

---

[1] These three lines of objection are critically analysed in my essays 'Economic Equality: Rawls Versus Utilitarianism', *Economics and Philosophy*, ii (1986), 225–44; 'Choosing Between Choice Models of Ethics: Rawlsian Equality, Utilitarianism, and the Concept of Persons', *Theory and Decision*, xxii (1987), 209–24; and 'Uncertainty in Moral Theory: An Epistemic Defense of Rule–Utilitarian Liberties', *Theory and Decision*, xxix (1990), 133–60.

  Utilitas Vol. 5, No. 2 November 1993

circumstances, or on abstract factual information that may be difficult to obtain.[2] Much of the current Rawls literature is written by and for Kantians, who, while endorsing different forms of Kantianism, appear united on the general thesis that utilitarianism is to be rejected for perpetrating (or not precluding) sacrifices. So ubiquitous and attractive is this criticism that Kantians now often regard it as enough merely to allude to such sacrifices, casually *en passant*, without feeling the need to argue the point in any detail.[3] Thus, the overarching claim of Rawlsian theory, and of any Kantian theory, is that *justice* must absolutely rule out such interpersonal *sacrifice*.

Nevertheless, the same objection has been turned around against Rawls himself, and this poses a more general problem in liberal theory which it is the purpose of the present essay to resolve. The Rawlsian insight against utilitarianism is that it characteristically allows sacrifice of individuals who are socioeconomically *less* advantaged, and therefore regarded as expendable for the collective good. As a corrective, Rawlsian justice is characterized by the so-called 'maximin' principle: i.e., the idea of maximizing society's minimum level of economic well-being.[4] While presumably eliminating 'sacrifice' at the *lower* end of the socioeconomic distribution, then, the maximin principle appears in fact so generous to the disadvantaged that it has been accused of requiring sacrifice at the other end: viz., the sacrifice of *more* favoured individuals. Critics as diverse as Arrow, Nagel and Nozick, have argued this objection.[5] Little attention is focused nowadays

---

[2] Cf. Rawls, *A Theory of Justice*, Cambridge, Mass., 1971, hereafter referred to as *TJ*, esp. pp. viii, 3, 26–9, 177–80, 586; with his 'The Idea of an Overlapping Consensus', *Oxford Journal of Legal Studies*, vii (1987), 14, 19–21. On the more positive theme of making basic rights and liberties more 'secure', cf. Rawls, 'Kantian Constructivism in Moral Theory', *Journal of Philosophy*, lxxvii (1980), 561, 563; and 'Justice as Fairness: Political not Metaphysical', *Philosophy & Public Affairs*, xiv (1985), 226. Still more recently, Rawls is concerned to define and defend his own distinctive form of 'individualism': 'The Priority of Right and Ideas of the Good', *Philosophy & Public Affairs*, xvii (1988), 251, 264, 267, 268–9.

[3] Illustrative is the recent Symposium on Rawlsian Theory, in *Ethics*, ic (1989), in which utilitarianism is only obliquely mentioned, and dismissed, in scattered references to its 'sacrifices', the contingent status of utilitarian rights, its 'merging of interests', etc. In philosophy of law, the same anti-utilitarian themes have been echoed in the Dworkin literature: cf. my 'Dworkin and His Critics: The Relevance of Ethical Theory in Philosophy of Law', *Ratio Juris*, iii (1990), 340–84, esp. § IV on 'Law and Politics'.

[4] The term 'maximin' will throughout be used (as a heuristically more graphic label) to designate the criterion of distribution, also known as the 'difference principle' (cf. *TJ*, pp. 75 ff., 302–3)—as distinguished from the principle, by the same name, for choice under uncertainty in Rawls's hypothetical choice model (the 'original position'): p. 152. For a synopsis, with detailed critical analysis of how Rawls's overall distributive conception works, see my 'Economic Equality: Rawls Versus Utilitarianism', 225–44, esp. 226–7.

[5] Kenneth Arrow, 'Some Ordinalist Utilitarian Notes on Rawls's Theory of Justice', *Journal of Philosophy*, lxx (1973), 257; Thomas Nagel, 'Rawls on Justice', in N. Daniels, ed., *Reading Rawls*, New York, 1974, p. 13 (repr. from *Phil. Review*, 1973 at p. 231); R. Nozick, *Anarchy, State, and Utopia*, New York, 1974, pp. 192–7.

on the maximin criterion itself—perhaps because many regard the Arrow–Nagel–Nozick line of argument as rendering it obsolete. In any case, this line of criticism continues to be relevant, for the reasons suggested above. On the one hand, liberal theories of justice, whether or not committed to the specific concept of maximinimizing, are heavily egalitarian, and therefore subject to the objection that they sacrifice at the top. On the other hand this objection is related to other prevalent, decision-theoretic criticisms about the basic approach to economic justice.

This essay will critically analyse the sacrifice-objection to liberalism in the context of the maximin principle, and in light of a possible defence of that principle based on the idea of *reciprocity*. Contrary to the objection, Rawls's theory contains an important, but largely ignored, argument to the effect that maximin justice offers a 'reciprocity' of advantages between all members of society, the less as well as the more favoured. Since the advantages to the less favoured are obvious, the argument is addressed to the so-called 'more favoured man'. This argument is formulated in several versions by Rawls, and was extensively criticized by Nozick. Nozick's critique rests on a misinterpretation of the reciprocity argument. The main defect is a failure to appreciate what may be referred to as the 'pragmatic' nature of the argument, viz., its reliance on rational self-interest, and empirical premises about moral psychology and socioeconomic conditions of cooperation, instead of on a direct appeal to liberal moral intuitions about fairness. Following a statement of the original reciprocity argument(s) in Section II, Nozick's view will be analysed and rejected in Sections III and IV. The reconstructed reciprocity argument will then be reassessed from a similarly 'pragmatic' perspective in Section V, and from a utilitarian point of view in Section VI. The upshot will be a limited defence of Rawlsian liberalism against Nozick, and a defence of utilitarianism against Rawlsian or Kantian objections.

A preliminary observation should be made about some of the above terminology. Admittedly, the key concept of 'sacrifice' is especially problematic. Indeed, it might be contended that sacrifice objections need not be taken seriously, since those who use them typically do not explain exactly what 'sacrifice' is. There are practical reasons for not dismissing all such arguments in this way. First, we have already seen that intuitions about sacrifice, whether or not fully formulated, do in fact play an important role in debates about justice. It would be nice, then, to have a more incisive treatment of this beyond merely calling for conceptual clarification. Hopefully, the following analysis will contribute to a better understanding of the limitations of 'sacrifice' objections. The same may be said with respect to the related notions of 'conflating persons', or the concomitant charge that conflationary

theories are not 'individualistic' enough. While the notions of sacrifice, or conflation or individualism (or, for that matter, 'liberalism') are
obscure, the present analysis should help clarify these concepts in the
process of criticizing popular arguments which assume them.

Secondly, however, much of this pertinent argumentation can be
considered without explicit reference to vague language. Nozick's
argument is not overtly couched in terms of sacrifice, for instance. In
fact, in defence of his own theory of justice, Nozick recognizes the
notion of sacrifice to be problematic, involving more than the mere
possibility of alternative distributions in which present disparities
between rich and poor could be reduced or reversed. Still, he goes on to
argue that the least advantaged in a Rawlsian society *benefit more*.[6]
This analysis, if correct, would imply a sense in which those who are
more advantaged—but 'benefiting (relatively) *less*'—would presumably
be sacrificing. It is also clear that the idea of 'benefiting less' here is
taken by Nozick to be charged with negative evaluative force, in the
same way that many moral theorists use the term 'sacrifice', or that
other political or economic theorists have used the concept of 'exploitation'.

Similarly, Rawls's problem of explaining maximin justice to the more
favoured man can be phrased without explicit reference to sacrifice.
Thus, for readers who do not have a pre-theoretical conception or
intuition about sacrifice, or do not find this notion or such claims
intelligible, an analysis of the reciprocity argument should still be a
significant undertaking. This indicates that the reciprocity argument
is nevertheless a crucial part of both Rawls's reaction *against* utilitarianism and his alliance *with* Kantianism. For Rawlsians, then, as
well as for critics who *do* find Rawls's pervasive claims about utilitarian 'sacrifices' intelligible (if not convincing), the reciprocity argument has *added* significance.[7]

---

[6] Nozick, *Anarchy, State, and Utopia*, pp. 193–4. Recently Joshua Cohen has given a
limited response to Nozick's problem by arguing that maximin should not threaten the
self-respect of the more favoured man: 'Democratic Equality', *Ethics*, xcix (1989), 740.
Cohen's argument, however, does not solve the problem here about *sacrifice* which
appears to be Nozick's real concern.

[7] I would like to thank Allan Gibbard for critical comments (on my use of the terms
'sacrifice', etc.) in response to an earlier form of my analysis of Rawls's reciprocity
argument, concentrated in Sections II–V of the present essay. Since writing this essay, I
note that Gibbard's recent book on rationality and moral psychology contains a number
of interesting suggestions of relevance to the present analysis. See A. Gibbard, *Wise
Choices, Apt Feelings: A Theory of Normative Judgment*, Cambridge, Mass., 1990. On the
above topic, cf. the observations that, among alternative cooperative schemes which are
'mutually advantageous', some are 'more advantageous' than others for a given person—
while other schemes contain 'poor terms', and morality generally requires (or is
intuitively perceived as requiring) 'genuine sacrifice': pp. 264, 298, 308, and cf. n. 23
below. In general, Gibbard's book may be viewed as highlighting the importance of the
topic of *reciprocity*, vis-à-vis (feelings about) fairness, in socioeconomic theory.

II. RAWLS'S RECIPROCITY ARGUMENT(S) TO 'THE MORE FAVOURED MAN'

The Arrow–Nagel–Nozick objection to the maximin criterion—viz., that it requires sacrifice from those at the top of the socioeconomic distribution, for the maximal advantage of those at the bottom—was in fact anticipated by Rawls as part of the initial exposition of his theory. This concern surfaces in arguments addressed to the 'more favoured man', i.e. to the 'representative' person in the upper stratum of society.[8] Rawls's problem is to show that maximin justice is 'reciprocally', or 'mutually', advantageous to those at the top as well as to those at the bottom. Since the latter *less* favoured class of persons is, *ex hypothesi*, receiving the *maximum* amount possible, the problem for the reciprocity argument is to explain the corresponding benefits to those in the *more* favoured class.

In examining the problem of reciprocity, the present analysis will dispense with several preliminary problems which have preoccupied critics. One set of problems may be referred to as 'technical' difficulties with applying the maximin criterion, or implementing it in a real economy: e.g., determining what or where the 'representative' strata or classes are, who actually inhabits them or which one is the 'bottom', or determining when the minimum is maximized. The intuitive idea of maximining nevertheless seems sufficiently clear for present purposes.

A related problem, which we will (dis)regard as preliminary, is that of why the maximin criterion should apply to *groups* ('classes' or 'strata'), instead of to *individuals*. Thus, one might ask why maximiners are not interested in maximizing the holdings of the actual *person* who is minimally well off, perhaps even worse off than the worst-off group. This objection may be construed as either decision-theoretic or ethical: the problem being that hypothetical choosers in Rawls's Original Position would care only about *individuals*, and/or that there may be some Kantian objection to treating individuals this way, i.e., collectively at the *group*-level, instead of more 'personally'.[9]

There are two replies. First, as a matter of practicality, it does not appear realistic to suppose that *any* theory of distributive justice could avoid group-level applications when dealing with real-world economies in large societies.[10] This implies, as a matter of decision theory,

---

[8] On the general idea of the *'representative* man', see Rawls, *TJ*, p. 64. (Rawls clearly means to refer to the gender-neutral 'person', and my pronoun usage throughout the present essay adequately reflects this.)

[9] Nozick, who poses the general problem about 'groups', does not delineate these variants, and does not consider the problem as merely preliminary: *Anarchy, State, and Utopia*, p. 190.

[10] I would like to thank Richard B. Brandt for helpful conversation with me on this point.

that it would not be *ad hoc* for Rawlsians to *stipulate* group-level motivation in the Original Position choice model. Additionally, as a matter of Kantian ethics, it should be permissible to discard any contrary 'Kantian' demand that required approaching economic justice in an unfeasible manner. Alternatively, then, if 'group' distributions involve some sort of 'sacrifice' to real-world individuals, this should be regarded as merely innocuous. A second reply, however, is again a point about mootness: Any such difficulty at the individual level becomes otiose, if maximin already requires entire groups to sacrifice for the benefit of other groups. It is thus the prospect of sacrifices between groups that properly occupies the present analysis.

A final preliminary problem here is terminological, and this has been addressed briefly in the preceding section. One such concern is about the meaning of 'sacrifice', and an ancillary problem, for some theorists, will be that of why Rawls *needs* to argue that maximin is characterized by 'reciprocity'. It has already been suggested that this philosophic quest is indeed a crucial part of the Rawlsian dichotomy between Kantianism and utilitarianism. Here we might further observe the practical point that the reciprocity argument is in fact prominent in Rawls's writings, and this fact itself provides extra support for the present thesis about its significance.

Rawls himself finds it significant enough to formulate the argument in three main versions. In the most elaborate one, the point of the argument is succinctly encapsulated in his observation that 'the social order [regulated by maximin] can be justified to everyone, and particularly to the least favoured'—i.e., setting up the problem with respect to the more favoured:

Now what can be said to the more favoured man? To begin with, it is clear that the well-being of each depends on a scheme of social cooperation without which no one could have a satisfactory life. Secondly, we can ask for the willing cooperation of everyone only if the terms of the scheme are reasonable. The difference principle, then, seems to be a fair basis on which those better endowed, or more fortunate in their social circumstances, could expect others to collaborate with them when some workable arrangement is a necessary condition of the good of all.[11]

This argument is almost a verbatim translation from an earlier formulation containing the same terminology. The notable addition of that earlier version—which Rawls classifies as belonging to 'the main idea' of his entire theory—is the explicit incorporation of the observation that maximin represents an agreement on the basis of which 'those better endowed, or more fortunate in their social position, *neither of*

[11] *TJ*, p. 103.

which they can be said to deserve', can expect the cooperation of the less favoured.[12]

A third main formulation of this argument appears in Rawls's later writing. First, the initial problem of reciprocity is posed with utilitarianism in mind:

Looking first at the situation of the less advantaged, the utility principle asks them to view the greater advantages of others who have more as a sufficient reason for having still lower prospects of life than otherwise they could be allowed. This is an extreme demand psychologically; by contrast, the maximin criterion assures the less favoured that inequalities work to their advantage. The problem with maximin would appear to lie with those who are better situated. They must accept less than what they would receive with the utility principle . . .

And then the argument that is supposed to solve that problem:

[But] two things greatly lessen their strains of commitment: they are after all, more fortunate and enjoy the benefits of that fact; and insofar as they value their situation relatively in comparison with others, they give up that much less. In fact, our tendency to evaluate our circumstances in relation to the circumstances of others suggests that society should be arranged so that if possible all its members can with reason be happy with their situation. The maximin criterion achieves this better than the principle of utility.[13]

This basic line of argument still reverberates in Rawls's most recent essays throughout the 1980s. On the one hand, there are further references to the putative 'sacrificial' character of the principle of utility—i.e. which presumably stands in contrast to the 'reciprocal' character of the maximin principle. On the other hand, there appear also to be more specific references to the more-favoured-man argument. In the development of Kantian 'constructivism', for instance, the theme of the 'social role' of justice emerges, as *connected* to the claim that the Rawlsian conception 'can be justified to all citizens', with 'fair terms of cooperation' expressing 'reciprocity and mutuality' that 'each participant may reasonably be expected to accept'.[14] Similarly, the criticism that Rawls's choice model is 'unfair to those with superior natural endowments' is rebutted not merely by a *tour de force* (or *coup de force*) appeal to a Kantian concept of persons, in which such natural assets are simply pronounced to be morally irrelevant, but rather again

[12] Ibid., p. 15, italics added, and the same idea about desert (or lack thereof) is reiterated at pp. 103–4. In the p. 15 version, Rawls credits Allan Gibbard as the originator of this intuitive line of argument. In conversation with me, however, Professor Gibbard has expressed reservations as to exactly what intuitions are involved here, and more general skepticism as to the theoretical need for this whole argument. The present essay addresses both of these concerns.

[13] 'Some Reasons for the Maximin Criterion', *American Economic Review*, lxiv (1974), 144.

[14] Cf. 'Kantian Constructivism in Moral Theory', 517, 528.

by appeal to the practical role of justice in promoting social cooperation.[15] This suggests that the Kantian concept of persons—though
admittedly prominent in Rawlsian theory, and increasingly more so in
the recent essays—is nevertheless not the irreducible, axiomatic value
that many critics have assumed it to be. The basic argument to the
more favoured man also appears implicitly in the new theme of
Rawlsian theory as 'political' (rather than 'metaphysical'), stressing
the need for cooperation, 'reciprocity or mutuality', and *therefore* the
idea that the *choice* of principles of justice should be abstracted from
personal information about one's natural endowment or the contingencies of the social world.[16] Finally, this same basic reciprocity argument
appears to be at least an important part of what underwrites Rawls's
more recent claim that utilitarianism 'quite possibly cannot' belong to
a stable political 'consensus'.[17] The suggestion is that the argument to
the more favoured man may be still more fundamental to Rawlsian
theory than the overtly Kantian postulates that have attracted more
attention. Alternatively, one might conclude that, in the core idea of
'justice as fairness', not even intuitions about *fairness* are fundamental, but rather a certain conception of fairness is itself *argued* for as a
practical requirement of cooperation between less favoured and more
favoured individuals.

III. NOZICK'S CRITIQUE

As it stands, the foregoing argument should be quite unconvincing—to
utilitarians, or to other ethical or political perspectives. The immediate problem, however, for any critic, is that of interpreting what the
intended argument is.

There appear to be two basic interpretations available. First, the
argument might be construed as purely prudential. Thus, the gist of the
argument certainly appears to be that more favoured individuals have
a straightforwardly practical or self-interested reason to accept maximin, in order to secure the cooperation of the less favoured. Additionally, in support of this interpretation, much of the argument appears to
be merely a matter of *empirical* psychology. Various claims about
empirical facts are suggested—all pertaining to what *in fact* is necessary for obtaining such cooperation. Secondly, an interpretation is
suggested by the ostensibly *moral* language involved: i.e., suggesting
that more favoured individuals are supposed to recognize maximin as a
'reasonable' or '*fair* basis' of cooperation, or to share a Rawlsian
intuition about what they *deserve*. The moral interpretation is perhaps

---

[15] Ibid. 550–1.
[16] 'Political not Metaphysical', cf. 232, 235–6.
[17] 'The Idea of an Overlapping Consensus', 12.

also suggested in the initial claim that maximin can be 'justified' to everyone.

This generates several distinct lines of objection. First, Rawls may be accused of confusing these two arguments. In the context of his choice model, the objection would be that prudential and nonmoral considerations, which are supposed to appeal to purely self-interested (or mutually disinterested) choosers *inside* of the Original Position, are being run together with substantive moral considerations which could presumably be convincing only to people *outside* in the real world. In any event, when the arguments are separated, neither seems very convincing. Thus, two more, separate lines of objection may be waged, corresponding to the arguments that emerge under these interpretations. Further, the argument from self-interest may be criticized as unconvincing *in* the Original Position, and to those who are more favoured in the real world. The hypothetical choosers, after all, are not real flesh-and-blood egoists, but rather their self-interested (i.e., 'mutually disinterested') motivation is subject to special decision-theoretic constraints, and consequently it is possible that the prudential interpretation of Rawls's argument to the more favoured man presents the *wrong kind* of self-interested considerations for use in the choice model.

If Rawls has not been careful to specify exactly which argument to the more favoured man he intends here, it should already be clear that many of his critics have not precisely targeted their criticisms, either. The more-favoured-man argument provides a helpful instrument for focusing various criticisms. No doubt, many who object to maximin 'sacrifices' are objecting directly on moral grounds, the claim being that maximin is not really *morally* 'justified' to the more favoured man. Others, however, may be using 'sacrifice' in a *morally neutral* sense, to assert that more favoured individuals have no prudential reason to accept maximin. Even this somewhat more incisive claim is again ambiguous, for the objection may be against the more-favoured-man argument as applied inside of the Original Position, i.e., to hypothetical choosers contemplating the prospect of being more favoured in the real world, *or* as applied outside to those who *are* so favoured. It might be thought that these latter two objections, making purely prudential or morally neutral points, are ethically insignificant, but both may be used indirectly as a basis for other objections to Rawls's ethical system. The first suggests that maximin could not be chosen by prospective 'more favoured' choosers in the Original Position, i.e., vitiating Rawls's proposed decision-theoretic *derivation*. The second claim might be used as a morally neutral premise to establish various other ethical results: e.g., that maximin 'sacrifices' (even if morally justified!) undermine at least the moral *contrast* which Rawls intends with utilitarianism—an insight which might, in turn, be used in defence of utilitarianism, or by others to attack both Rawlsian and utilitarian conceptions of 'liberal' justice.

Robert Nozick's argument is that Rawls is mixing up self-interested calculations and moral notions about the 'fairness' of maximin, and that maximin is not so 'reasonable' (presumably, either prudentially *or* morally) to favoured men and women in the real world. His attack centres on Rawls's conclusion that 'The difference principle, then, seems to be a fair basis . . .' on which the more favoured can get the less favoured to cooperate. Nozick raises four distinct objections; (i) that Rawls's conclusion does not follow from anything that Rawls has argued, and (ii) that it is in any case false:

The presence of the 'then' in this sentence is puzzling. . . . Rawls is merely repeating that it seems reasonable; hardly a convincing reply to anyone to whom it doesn't seem reasonable . . . A [the more favoured man] *does* have grounds for complaint. Doesn't he?[18]

Nozick's further suggestion in (ii), that maximin is unreasonable, itself appears to merge prudential and moral considerations, though he evidently intends both. Nozick's counter-argument nevertheless clearly indicates *to whom* maximin is supposed to be unreasonable: viz., to *real* more-favoured individuals *outside* the Original Position. Rawls's favoured-man argument must be so interpreted, according to Nozick, because 'trying to squeeze it into the original position makes it completely mysterious'—this because of (iii) the confusion of moral and nonmoral reasoning:

And what is thinking of what is 'fair agreement' . . . or a 'fair basis' . . . doing here anyway, in the midst of rational self-interested calculations of persons in the original position, who do not knowingly possess, or at any rate utilize, particular moral notions?[19]

Thus, *Nozick's* argument is addressed to real-world individuals, because he imagines Rawls to be addressing the favoured-man argument to such individuals: 'either to better-endowed individuals or to his readers, to convince *them* that the difference principle is fair'.[20]

Nozick's analysis here suggests another (possibly intended as distinct) reason for the aforementioned 'mystery': viz. (iv) a motivational or decision-theoretic problem of understanding what *concern*, for those *in* Rawls's choice model, the favoured-man argument could possibly answer. Thus, the hypothetical choosers cannot be answering themselves, *as* they contemplate the prospect of later be(com)ing more favoured out in the real world, for *at the moment* of this contemplation

[18] Nozick, *Anarchy, State, and Utopia*, pp. 196–7.
[19] Ibid. p. 197n.
[20] The outcome of Nozick's interpretative argument, later in the same note, ibid.

they have no such moral intuitions about fairness. Another possibility is that they are thinking about what *will* seem fair *after* they are more favoured. Nozick rejects this possibility on grounds that, out in the real world, the answer to the favoured man should be, 'You agreed to it (or would have agreed, if originally positioned)'. That proposed answer, however, is inadequate, for it raises the question of why real-world people should *care* about Rawls's choice model. Presumably, Nozick's point here should be instead that, out in the real world, the *moral* appeal should be directly to the *justice* of maximin, or (indirectly) the 'fairness' of the *choice*-conditions. So far, however, the point in (iv) appears parasitic on (iii): that the favoured-man argument requires substantive moral insights which are precluded in the Original Position. Additionally, as to the issue of what will *seem* fair to favoured individuals in the real world, Nozick's argument would appear to collapse back into (ii): the claim that maximin will in fact *not* seem fair to such real-world individuals—because of the (further) claim that it *really is not* fair.

IV. EMPIRICAL PREMISES AND RATIONAL SELF-INTEREST: NOZICK'S MISINTERPRETATION

The favoured-man argument can be defended from Nozick's attack. Three basic moves must be made in constructing this defence.

Contrary to Nozick's analysis, the present thesis is that Rawls's argument is based on an intelligible and important line of self-interested reasoning—from empirical, nonmoral premises. The first manoeuvre is to distinguish the 'argument *for* reciprocity', a label which we will use to designate all of the *non*moral part of the argument, in contrast to the *moral* 'argument *from* reciprocity'. Certainly the favoured-man argument contains much prudential material under the former heading, which is not merged with morality in any insidious way. The goal in this phase of the argument is simply to point out all of the benefits of maximin from the (ad)vantage point of the more favoured. In the next phase, given the fact that there *are* reciprocal benefits of this sort, the goal is to establish some point of superiority about maximin as a *moral* principle. Thus, Rawls's argument *need* not be construed as a confusion of moral and nonmoral considerations, though admittedly it *fuses* them in certain ways.

The next move is to (re)define *who* the more favoured man is. On the present view, the *moral* point just mentioned, in the argument *from* reciprocity, is primarily directed against, *utilitarians*. It is thus *not* addressed primarily at Lockeans or Nozickians—moral philosophers or decision theorists of this persuasion, or to real-world socioeconomically favoured individuals entrenched in these competing moral conceptions. Nor is the first, prudential phase of the favoured man argument addressed to the Nozickian individual regarded as a psychological type. This view helps rebut Nozick's suggestion that maximin will simply not seem 'reasonable' *to* some individuals. The proposal here is that the favoured-man argument need not be an attempt to convince such individuals, and can escape Nozick's charge that it is conclusory or question-begging.

The previous sections of this essay have linked the favoured-man argument with Rawls's thematic reaction against utilitarian 'sacrifices' perpetrated against the *less* favoured. Thus, the first phase of the favoured-man argument, *for* reciprocity, is plausibly viewed as an attempt to show that maximin does not in fact do the *same thing* in principle, merely to *more* favoured individuals, as utilitarianism is supposed characteristically to do to *less* favoured individuals. This interpretation provides also a rejoinder, then, to the objection that Rawls has undermined his own project by admitting, in the preface to the argument, that maximin can be justified *in particular to* the latter: In the context of the argument *against utilitarianism* this is merely to emphasize (the nonmoral fact) that maximin rectifies that 'particular' kind of sacrifice. So understood, this observation—which Rawls must take to be 'particularly' noteworthy for the later moral phase of his argument—is at least *compatible* with the contention that maximin is nevertheless an even-handed principle that does not involve partiality for those less off.

There remains the problem, posed by Nozick's challenge, of how the favoured-man argument can be 'squeezed' into Rawls's choice model purely in terms of rational self-interest. As suggested above, there is nevertheless a good deal of material appealing in a straightforward way to the practical 'interest' of the more favoured in securing economic *cooperation* from the less favoured. The arguments of Section II involve a nexus of empirical claims about what socioeconomic conditions are in fact 'necessary' for cooperation, what it takes to make individuals 'happy with their situations' and the extent to which this depends on 'comparisons with others', or what by contrast would be extremely 'demanding psychologically'. Indeed, so protrusive is this empirical line of argument that the references to moral notions appear to play merely a secondary, instrumental role. The primary claim is not about what *is* 'fair' or 'reasonable', but rather about what people in the real world *think* is fair or reasonable. Here the third move in defence of Rawls is to draw a distinction between *having* moral notions oneself, and merely knowing empirical facts about *moral psychology*. Although the fictional choosers in Rawls's choice model admittedly do not *have* moral insights themselves, there is nothing at all mysterious about their using information about psychological conditions that are necessary for a 'workable' scheme and cooperation in the real world. This distinction does much to assuage Nozick's decision-theoretic 'squeezing' problem.

The argument constructed from these interpretative manoeuvres can be schematized as follows:

(1) The satisfactory life (well-being, welfare, etc.) of favoured men requires, as a 'necessary condition', a workable scheme of social cooperation.

(2) A workable scheme of social cooperation requires the cooperation of 'others'—the *less* favoured.

(3) The stable cooperation of the less favoured requires *willing* cooperation.

(4) Their willing cooperation requires that they perceive the scheme of their society as governed by 'reasonable terms'.

(5) Their so perceiving the scheme requires that they perceive it as 'fair'.

(6) In order for a scheme of cooperation to be recognized as fair by the least favoured collaborators of society, it must be seen to minimize the 'undeserved' influences of 'natural endowment' and 'social position', i.e., it must embody the maximin principle.

(7) Therefore, the welfare of the more favoured man depends on the maximin principle.

This formulation allows exposure of several different mistakes in Nozick's analysis. On the one hand, his critique misses the key decision-theoretic distinction between *having* and *using* moral notions. It is thus incorrect for Nozick to say that the hypothetical choosers in the Original Position do not 'knowingly' possess, *or utilize* moral concepts, once we construe the idea of 'utilization' in the purely empirical, psychological sense just explained. 'Morality' is at best subordinate to the practical objectives achieved, from the standpoint of the favoured man. On the other hand, Nozick's critique misinterprets *whose* moral dispositions are being utilized. In the above schema, the claim is not about what *is* fair or reasonable, but only about what is *thought* to be; moreover, it is not the 'thought' of the *more* favoured Nozickian individual that counts here, but rather that of the *less* favoured. The issue is what they will (as a psychological matter) find 'reasonable', and thus tend (as another psychological matter) to cooperate with. Thus, for this pragmatic 'use' of moral notions, the overt references to moral judgement in the favoured-man argument must be viewed as shorthand abbreviations for cooperative states of mind generating desired behaviour, empirical spin-off properties of beliefs and actions. Without going far into functionalist Marxian theories about the relationship between moral beliefs and class interests, it is certainly plausible that *less* favoured individuals do indeed typically have notions of fairness or reasonableness roughly corresponding to what the above argument assumes them to be.

Similarly, the above schema demystifies Nozick's other difficulty here, as to what intelligible *concern* the more favoured could have in this argument: e.g., whether it is addressed to the real man or woman who knows that he or she *is* a more favoured individual, or to the originally positioned chooser contemplating be(com)ing one. On the present interpretation, *both* must be concerned about what it takes to secure the cooperation of the less favoured, and therefore what they must *think* is fair. Admittedly, we have seen that the favoured-man argument does continue with Rawls's observation that the *more* favoured 'can with reason be happy with their situation'. The appeal here is not to their sense of fairness, but to rational self-interest operating on empirical premises. Here, as though *conceding* the Nozickian insight that the more favoured may regard maximin as too generous to be 'fair' or just, Rawls's argument suggests two, connected, points: (i) the consolation that the more favoured in any event have more economic advantages than anybody else in society, but more importantly (ii) the prudential point that maximin *guarantees* these advantages as part of a *stable* system of cooperation. Again, the idea here with regard to the *more* favoured appears to rest essentially on the empirical, psychological thesis that, whatever contrary notions of abstract justice or fairness are no doubt prevalent among more favoured individuals, such individuals nevertheless have 'reason to be happy' with their situation under maximin, and reason to contribute their own cooperation to the system. Further, this psychological thesis about the motivation of the more favoured appears supported by the interaction of (i) and (ii): Presumably, the large economic advantages, referred to in (i), themselves directly tend to promote happiness, and this effect is accentuated by *interpersonal comparisons.* Additionally, the security factor in (ii) lends stability to both of these sources of satisfaction. And presumably this sense of security itself, the aware-ness that one's 'situation' is stable, is an additional source of happiness for the more favoured.

The above formulation in (1)–(7) may seem to put inordinate weight on the practical constraint of 'workability', or conditions of empirical *stability.* It may seem rather surprising that Rawls would think he can distinguish maximin from other distributive principles (of desert and natural endowment, etc.) on the sole basis of the *stability* of favours for the more favoured man. Several considerations, however, strongly recommend this construction of the argument. First, stability and workability are interchangeable, and the latter expression *is* explicit in Rawls's argument to the more favoured man. Secondly, 'stability' is elsewhere, and pervasively, stressed by Rawls himself—not only in arguing for his own conception of justice, as a stable or feasible basis of social cooperation, but with arguments against competing conceptions, either as having less 'relative stability' than maximin, or as being even *un*stable! Indeed, specifically in connection with the favoured-man argument, Rawls elsewhere appears to contrast his view of natural and social assets (as 'undeserved', or morally 'arbitrary') against competing conceptions on the basis of precisely this stark claim: 'Now both the liberal conception and that of natural aristocracy are *unstable*'.[21] Another instance of this mode of empirical argument, in Rawls's recent writing, would be the similar contention that utilitarianism cannot be part of a *stable* 'overlapping consensus'. If my analysis is correct, Rawls's reliance on a very 'practical', empirically oriented style argument is fundamental even in his earlier theory. This feature is crucial to understanding the favoured-man argument, as illustrated by Nozick's misinterpretation.

V. RAWLS'S MISINFORMATION: STABILITY, SOCIAL COOPERATION, AND INTERPERSONAL COMPARISONS

While eluding Nozick's critique, Rawls's favoured-man argument faces *other* serious difficulties. As it stands, the argument appears to rest on an obviously false empirical claim about stability, that the *maximin* principle really is a 'necessary condition' for the cooperation of the less favoured, or that in fact any economic distribution giving them less must be unstable. Intuitively, maximin certainly appears to pamper the poor far more than 'necessary' merely to bring about the desired level of cooperation. If the rich are interested only in this, maximin would not seem to be a very shrewd bargain.

As related to the formulation in (1)–(7), the implausibility of the above proposition about stability can be more closely traced to three false contentions: (i) The more favoured can elicit cooperation of the

---

[21] *TJ*, p. 74, italics added. Rawls contrasts his 'democratic' conception, designed to counteract the economic effects of both *natural* and *social* contingencies, as against the 'liberal' view which counteracts only the second (arbitrary) factor, and 'natural aristocracy', i.e. a free–market conception which counteracts neither. For further analysis of these conceptions, see my 'Choosing Between Choice Models of Ethics', 210–11, and esp. 213, at n. 8. For the '*relative* stability' argument, against utilitarianism, cf. *TJ*, § 76. In general, instability arguments are of course not unheard-of in political and economic theory. Cf. Jürgen Habermas on the 'threshold of tolerance' for economic conditions visà-vis the stability of moral *beliefs* in 'legitimacy': *Legitimationsprobleme im Spätkapitalismus*, Frankfurt a.M., 1973, pp. 90, 132 ff., 177; or the theme that there can be 'no [political] loyalty without [i.e., *belief in* moral] legitimacy': in Jürgen Habermas, *Moralbewußtsein und kommunikatives Handeln*, Frankfurt a.M., 1983, p. 72.

less favoured 'only if' they concede a scheme which is thought 'reasonable'; (ii) the less favoured find 'reasonable' only what fits their sense of 'fairness' or justice; (iii) the less favoured find anything less favourable than maximin to be unfair, unjust or unreasonable. Thus, as a matter of *moral psychology*, after all, the notion of *reasonableness* would seem much looser, or an easier requirement to meet, than that of *fairness* or *justice*. Similarly, the latter notions, even among less favoured individuals, would seem looser or easier to satisfy than the particular, and particularly stringent, notion of *maximin*. Alternatively, in the reverse direction, the notion that the less favoured should have the very *maximum* amount (of economic goods, etc.) that it is possible to give them, appears to go beyond what even the less favoured would insist on in the way of 'fairness', and surely *well* beyond what they would accept as passing a threshold standard of being at least 'reasonable'.

On the other hand, as an empirical matter, there appears to be much evidence that the less favoured will in fact *cooperate* in socioeconomic systems they find less than just, or perhaps even entirely 'unreasonable'. Historically, as regards merely the amenability to cooperate, it seems that the least advantaged socioeconomic classes may easily be, and often are, induced to cooperate in unreasonable (unfair, and certainly unRawlsian) circumstances, if only because they think (whether or not it is true) that things could get still more unreasonable for them if they do not cooperate. (Ordinary people, after all, and especially those who are socioeconomically less advantaged, are typically not the idealized rational maximizers of game theory, nor are they politically organized and unified as a bargaining unit in pursuit of their class interests!) Despite the preoccupation of Rawls's argument with the more favoured man, the *less* advantaged, too, must be concerned with social stability, and therefore with engaging the cooperation of the more advantaged, and before reading Rawls it would surely not occur to them (the less favoured) that they should 'expect' to get away with, or even demand as only 'reasonable', a distributive scheme that goes so far as to distribute to them no less than the very largest possible shares that *can* be given to them. As an empirical question concerning the practical matter of social stability, or soliciting the 'willing cooperation of everyone' to maintain 'some workable arrangement', it seems obvious that the more advantaged could get away with large and lucrative violations of maximin-justice to obtain still greater advantages without jeopardizing the security of their holdings, or the stability of a cooperative system that satisfies only the rather minimal requirement of 'working'. Perhaps the most dramatic evidence that they *could* do this is supplied not by historically oppressed socioeconomic classes, but by the fact that they *are* doing so in the United States today—a society which, on Rawls's own view, is 'riddled with grave injustice'.[22]

There are several ways to make the favoured-man argument appear more plausible. One is to stress the need for the '*willing* cooperation' of the less favoured.[23] Willingness is a matter of degree, and presumably, still purely in terms of empirical psychology, the least favoured are generally *more* willing to cooperate the more advantageous their situation is. This suggestion, however, can be given two interpretations. First, the concern for the 'willing' cooperation of the less favoured could be viewed as a directly *moral* appeal to the favoured man's sense of decency, or an attempt to evoke compassion for the plight of the disadvantaged. Here morality would operate as more than a sociological sedative administered for the appeasement of the less favoured. Secondly, this concern could be interpreted again in purely prudential terms. Of course, from the standpoint of the more favoured who are purely self-interested, it does not seem necessary that the less favoured cooperate *willingly*, but only that they cooperate. The present point, however, is that willing cooperation tends to be more stable than reluctant cooperation, and presumably, at least up to a point, social stability increases with higher degrees of willingness. One might add an epistemic twist to this argument: Since more favoured individuals in the real world do not necessarily *know* how much stability is enough, it is presumably in their interest to adopt distributive principles (like maximin) with *high degrees* of expectable stability. The epistemic point is that it is better for fallible individuals in their situation to 'err on the side' of stability, as it were, since giving up

---

[22] *TJ*, p. 87. Though Rawls is talking here in the context of 'background' institutions, he presumably would not consider the maximin principle itself to be satisfied either. One aspect of bad background conditions would presumably be inter-class 'visibility', explained below, which tends to *aggravate* the socially disruptive consequences of violating maximin.

[23] Once again I would like to thank Allan Gibbard for making this general suggestion to me in conversation. Certainly any suggestion here by Gibbard should be taken seriously, since Rawls himself credits Gibbard as the progenitor of the favoured-man argument, as we noted earlier (viz., n. 7). More specifically, Gibbard's suggestion corresponds to the interpretation attaching direct *moral* significance to the idea of 'willing' cooperation—as delineated and rejected below.

Again, since writing this essay, I note several related points in Gibbard's new book, *Wise Choices, Apt Feelings: A Theory of Normative Judgment*, Cambridge, Mass., 1990. On the one hand, there is similar reference in passing to the idea of '*glad* cooperation', p. 270 (italics added). On the other hand, there appear to be also psychological mechanisms which would make people 'willing to accept poor terms': cf. p. 298.

Moreover, Gibbard elsewhere insightfully observes that Rawls's sense of 'reasonable' is distinct from (Rawls's sense of) 'rational': ibid., p. 261, n. 6. But does this not imply that people may find it *rational* to accept and cooperate with even 'poor terms' which they regard as 'unreasonable'? If so, this appears to reinforce the problem of how the idea of 'glad' cooperation could help Rawls.

more than is necessary for stability is a lesser evil than coming up short.

These points may be amalgamated into one cohesive chain of reasoning. The ultimate objective is cooperation by the least favoured; but the best way to ensure the desired level of cooperation, in the long run, is to make sure that it is fully voluntary or 'willing'; and the best way to *ensure* willingness is to make sure that the least favoured *think* their circumstances are, at least, reasonable or fair, or even *more* than fair! Finally, then, the surest circumstances, and most stable in the long run, for bringing about any desired perception or *belief* is to make sure it is *true*. Consequently, even for those favoured in the real world with their own ideas about what is fair or just, it would be in their interest, according to this argument, to give the less favoured more than 'justice' requires. This generates what may be called a *quasi-moral* argument, for here the favoured are supposed to have moral views, but are still using morality instrumentally in service to an ultimately self-interested objective.

This souped-up argument to the favoured is nevertheless unconvincing, though these general contentions are not themselves implausible. There are several difficulties. First, as to the initial moral interpretation attaching intrinsic value to the idea of 'willing' cooperation, we have seen that any attempt to impute moral motivation to favoured individuals both weakens the forensic force of Rawls's argument, and thwarts its purpose in establishing a claim of 'reciprocity'. There is no reason why favoured individuals in the real world, or choosers in Rawls's choice model hypothetically contemplating this prospect, should have any *intrinsic* concern for making the cooperation of the less favoured 'willing'. Secondly, the epistemic point is uncompelling, again from either perspective. In Rawls's choice model, the choosers presumably should *know* 'general facts' about *how* stable the competing distributive principles are, and should not have to 'play it safe', by conceding to the less favoured *overly* stable principles like maximin. The postulated 'uncertainty' here (viz., about stability), if it exists anywhere, occurs at the wrong place to affect the hypothetical choice of principles in Rawls's choice model.[24] In any event, outside of the choice model, where admittedly there *is* uncertainty about distributive principles, their practical application or consequences, maximin would likewise appear to be excessive for an argument aimed only at stability. Here, the general links in the above chain of reasoning are not implausible—what has seemed implausible is the more specific nexus in (i)–(iii) mentioned earlier. The initial problem, then, is that the more

[24] In general, much of Rawls's argument against utilitarianism hinges on this same type of equivocation as to *where* 'uncertainty' exists. See my 'Uncertainty in Moral Theory: An Epistemic Defense of Rule–Utilitarian Liberties', 143 ff.

specific connections in moral psychology, linking stability specifically to the maximin principle, do not appear to be as tight as the argument to the favoured man requires.

There are two, perhaps still more serious, difficulties with the argument, again from a purely empirical point of view. These are most perspicuous in the third statement of the argument cited earlier in Section II, explicitly contrasting maximin with the principle of utility. There Rawls suggests that the more favoured 'value their situation relatively in comparison with others' and are presumably consoled by the thought (i) that under maximin they are still *more* favoured, and (ii) that *because* they are more favoured, they 'give up that much less'. The two main mistakes are: first, this argument seems to rest on a bogus sense of comparison. There does not seem to be any reason why the more favoured should think in terms of *this* comparison to begin with— viz., a comparison with (or contrast to) what the *less* favoured get under the *maximin* principle—rather than in terms of what they themselves, the *more* favoured, *could* get under other principles. We have just seen that there are plausibly other *stable* principles of distribution for them to consider. Thus, the point in (i) appears rather irrelevant, while the suggestion in (ii) appears false, if 'giving up less' means less than what the *more* favoured would give up under other principles, where they would be not only 'more favoured', but *favoured still more*. Nor, under maximin, does it appear true that the more favoured 'give up less' *than* do the less favoured. Thus, even assuming that proposed basis of comparison, the argument fails.

Secondly, the proposed basis of comparison is undermined by other elements of Rawlsian social theory. Thus, the effectiveness of this argument is further impaired by empirical circumstances which Rawls has suggested in connection with the problem of envy. Rawls's argument here, appealing to 'our tendency to evaluate our circumstances in relation to the circumstances of others', seems to be going against the grain of his solution to the problem of envy, according to which society is to be arranged precisely to prevent this kind of interpersonal comparison. *There* the argument was that, as a stability measure in order to keep envy from getting out of hand, society will be segmented 'into so many noncomparative groups' obstructing the 'visibility' of the holdings of other individuals, so that people are conditioned as much as possible not to perceive their holdings comparatively in relation to the holdings of others.[25] If we combine what Rawls says on the problem of envy, with what he says on the problem of the more favoured man, what emerges is a society characterized by a kind of unilateral 'visibility', or one-way window, through which the more favoured

[25] *TJ*, pp. 535 ff. For more detail and a critical analysis on the envy problem, see my 'Economic Equality: Rawls Versus Utilitarianism', 233–7.

enjoy the comparisons they make with those who have less—while the latter somehow do not make the same (invidious) comparisons with those who have more. It is difficult to imagine a social structure, or system of social conditioning, that could implement this arrangement, and such a system would surely pose a genuine problem of *stability*. Certainly in the real world, 'unilateral visibility' tends to operate in the opposite direction. As Kant once observed, the rich tend *not* to enjoy the comparisons they could make with those who have less; moreover, since wealth is typically acquired slowly, they tend not to compare their present holdings with the lesser holdings which even they themselves previously had![26] On the other hand, envious comparisons made by the poor would seem much more prevalent.

There is a final empirical difficulty associated with the preceding one. As we have seen, the third version of the favoured-man argument, invoking the idea of interpersonal comparisons, draws an explicit contrast with utilitarianism. The conclusion is that the maximin principle beats the principle of utility. A final difficulty, then, is raised by the prospect that, in *practice*, utilitarian theory yields a distributive *result* quite similar to maximin. Thus, it is generally plausible that the principle of utility (or the various forms of it that have been proposed) would in fact yield a high degree of socioeconomic *equality*.[27] In utilitarian theory, concern for the less favoured is generated, for instance, by the law of 'decreasing marginal utility', among other factors. At the same time, however, utilitarians cannot demand equality to a degree that would too severely depress incentives, among the more favoured, as needed for economic productivity. This begins to look much like the maximin principle, even though derived from very different ethical underpinnings. The difficulty, then, is that the maximin principle will *not* seem preferable on grounds of reciprocity if, as a matter of empirical fact, it yields essentially the same practical distributive results as the principle of utility.

Critics of utilitarianism have characteristically failed to show that utilitarianism will *in fact* yield objectionable distributive *inequality* in practice, and the present analysis suggests that this problem be focused more incisively on the issue of how closely utilitarianism

---

[26] In Kant's book on practical anthropology: Bk. 2, § 60, and Bk. 3, § 75. For page references in the German text: *Anthropologie in pragmatischer Hinsicht*, Philosophische Bibliothek, Bd. 44, Hamburg, 1980, pp. 155, 187. Kant adduces the example of a rich man angered when his servant breaks one of his rare glass goblets. Similarly, in his lectures on ethics, and again in the context of interpersonal comparisons, Kant observes that the beggar at the door is often happier than the king on his throne: *Eine Vorlesung Kants Über Ethik*, ed. Paul Menzer, Berlin, 1924, p. 182 (section entitled 'command of oneself').

[27] See Richard B. Brandt, 'Problems of Utilitarianism: Real and Alleged', in N. Bowie, ed., *Ethical Theory in the Last Quarter of the Twentieth Century*, Indianapolis, 1983, pp. 102 ff.

would approximate maximin.[28] This problem is exacerbated by the foregoing argument in this section. We have seen that the favoured-man argument relies on interpersonal comparisons, in which presumably the more favoured are substantially better off. (Other difficulties aside, how could this be 'visible' to them, and thereby the source of their being 'happy with their situation', if it were not true?) But then this suggests that maximin *allows* a substantial level of economic *in*equality, even if it remains 'egalitarian' relative to many other distributive principles (e.g., Nozick's). The question becomes, then, whether what utilitarianism yields in practice is any more *in*egalitarian.

VI. MAXIMAX AND THE MORAL ARGUMENT: A UTILITARIAN REJOINDER

We have seen that it is possible to criticize Rawls's favoured-man argument on purely empirical grounds, without appealing to any controversial moral intuitions about fairness or desert, as Nozick does. The rest of Nozick's argument, not covered by the analysis so far, is that what Rawls says to the favoured man is inadequate because it fails to distinguish maximin as uniquely attractive among other possible principles of economic distribution. Thus, as Nozick argues, Rawls's observation that 'cooperation is necessary for the well-being of all', and consequently that the more favoured must be concerned to secure the cooperation of the less favoured, could just as easily be used by the more favoured to support principles more advantageous to themselves. Nozick proposes the logically 'symmetrical' reasoning that the *less* favoured must also worry about getting cooperation from others, viz., the more favoured. In fact, Nozick goes much farther than to contend that this *symmetrical reasoning* could support principles merely 'more advantageous' to favoured individuals than maximin. He argues that it could, just as (im)plausibly as Rawls's argument, support the *opposite conclusion*: the principle of maximizing society's *maximum* economic shares, a 'maximax' principle.[29]

This is incorrect, for several reasons. First, Nozick's hypothetical *maximax* argument to the *less* favoured does not in fact have the same plausibility as Rawls's original *maximin* argument to the *more* favoured. There is the initial difference that the maximax principle, as

---

[28] I have argued for this approximation thesis, i.e., that both yield similar degrees of economic (in)equality, in my essay, 'Economic Equality: Rawls Versus Utilitarianism'. Cf. Rawls's casual assumption, cited at n. 13 above, that the more favoured will receive 'less' with maximin than with the utility principle.

[29] Nozick, *Anarchy, State, and Utopia*, pp. 195–6—although 'maximax' is not Nozick's term here. Nor does Nozick use the term 'maximin' to designate Rawls's difference principle; he denotes *that* principle as 'minimax': p. 190.

contrasted with maximin, requires increasing the well-being of those who are already the most well off, and alternatively, decreasing the welfare of those who are already worst off. Thus, we might say that maximax makes *two* demands on the less favoured: to accept having less than everybody else, and to consent to giving some other economic class as much as possible. By contrast, maximin makes only the latter demand of the more favoured. Surely, the *maximax* principle, then, makes a more 'extreme psychological demand' on the less favoured than Rawls's *maximin* makes on the more favoured. This can be explained by observing that, whatever the superficial *logical* 'symmetry' in Nozick's hypothetical maximax argument, there is nevertheless an important *psycho*logical *a*symmetry between the situations of more and less favoured individuals. Further, due to this asymmetry in the psychological strains of commitment, maxi*max* may in fact be so demanding as to pose a problem of social *stability*. One might attempt to obviate this problem by stressing the idea of maximax as giving those at the top 'as much *as possible*' — i.e., as much as allowed by the best *stable* system of cooperation. Thus, *un*stable goods for the more favoured are, in an important practical sense, 'impossible' (or at least not possible for long). Still, it is plausible that attempts to *implement* 'maximax' as one's conscious goal will, in *practice*, and especially when this aim is recognized by the less favoured, be socially disruptive. From a utilitarian standpoint, then, a maximaximizing economic system would seem, at the least, to lose significant amounts of social utility — a point whose ethical significance will become apparent in a moment.

For the above reason, Nozick's 'symmetry' argument is unsuccessful against Rawls, and his criticism must be sharply differentiated from the empirical criticism in the preceding section. As just seen, Nozick's point about symmetry appears to overlook the fundamental insight of Rawls's argument: that maximin offers the more favoured some consolation. We have just seen that maximax does not offer the less favoured any such consolation. Thus, the failure of Nozick's criticism may be taken as illustrating what is *right* with Rawls's favoured-man argument. There is nothing in the preceding section that denies Rawls's insight on this point. Admittedly, we *have* noted, along with Nozick, that the less favoured, too, must worry about getting the cooperation of others, but this observation does not warrant the conclusion that Nozick attempts to extract from it.

It should also be observed here that the argument against Rawls in the preceding section has also not relied upon any of the stronger *instability* charges against maximin that are suggested by much of Nozick's better-known intuitive argumentation. On the present view, Nozick certainly exaggerates when he alleges that maximin (in *practice?*) requires 'continuous interference' by the state in private economic exchanges (even the giving of gifts!) between consenting individuals, or requires 'redistributive' taxation which is (psychologically?) like *robbery* of the rich, i.e., 'on a par with *forced labour*'. The *pragmatic* rebuttal here is that a maximinimizing economic system does not *take away* (or redistribute) wealth from the wealthy (and certainly not by random violence 'on a par' with mugging!), but rather *prevents* its accumulation, as well as the expectations and comparisons which Nozick appears to assume.[30]

A second reason for rejecting Nozick's symmetry-argument here is that it fails to appreciate the force of Rawls's subsequent *moral* argument *from* reciprocity. As seen in Sections II and V, Rawls's concern with 'reciprocity', which the favoured-man argument is supposed to establish, is ultimately to score a moral point against utilitarianism. The idea is that Rawlsian justice, because it is 'reciprocally' beneficial to all, is supposed to be morally preferable in a contrast with utilitarian 'sacrifices', etc. This ethical *use* of the favoured-man argument is again explicit in the third version cited in Section II above. Thus, Nozick's observation about *symmetry*, even if correct, would not entirely refute Rawls's claim about *reciprocity*. On the other hand, Nozick's observation about symmetry is incorrect; maximin and maximax are psychologically asymmetrical, and this asymmetry indicates that maximin does indeed have a stronger claim to reciprocity than does maximax. Thus, the failure of Nozick's argument may in fact be used to strengthen Rawls's.

Nozick's directly moral criticism, to the effect that maximin is unfair or unreasonable, can be rebutted by a parallel analysis. Admittedly, Nozick appears to have a point when he observes that Rawls has not established the 'fairness' or 'reasonableness' of maximin. Like Nozick's point about symmetry, however, this objection is a *non sequitur*. It is irrelevant to Rawls's claim that maximin, even if not *'reasonable'* (to Lockeans or Nozickians) is nevertheless *reciprocal* in its distributed benefits. This claim, we have seen, is then used as part of a *moral*

[30] Ibid., esp. pp. 163, 169, 219–20. Cf. T. Nagel, 'Libertarianism Without Foundations', in J. Paul, ed., *Reading Nozick*, Oxford, 1982, p. 199, n. 13. Nozick's suggestion here that 'patterned' principles like Rawls's are generally *unstable* (cf. p. 164n.) is reminiscent of Rawls's own (in)stability charges against Nozickian principles (recall n. 21 above), and provides a good example of what we do *not* assume in the above 'visibility' argument (at n. 25 above). The basic pragmatic point about economic accumulation was well expressed by Rousseau in his 'Discourse on Political Economy'. The state is to prevent extreme economic inequality, not by removing treasures, but rather by removing all means of their accumulation; and the state protects the poor not by building hospitals, but by safeguarding citizens from *becoming* so poor: 'C'est donc une des plus importantes affaires du gouvernement de prévenir l'extrême inégalité des fortunes, non en enlevant les trésors à leurs possesseurs, mais en ôtant à tous les moyens d'en accumuler, ni en bâtissant des hôpitaux pour les pauvres, mais en garantissant les citoyens de le devenir.' This essay, 'Discours Sur L'Économie Politique', in *Du Contrat Social: ou principes du droit politique*, Paris, 1985, p. 236.

argument which Rawls directs not against Nozickians, but rather against utilitarians. On the other hand, apart from the problem of irrelevance, the maximin principle appears to be a good deal more 'reasonable' than Nozick suggests, certainly more so than maxi*max*, as indicated again by the failure of the symmetry argument.

Since Nozick's analysis has not properly interpreted or refuted Rawls's moral argument about reciprocity, the question arises as to what the proper rejoinder should be. Since the thrust of Rawls's argument, at this stage, is aimed at utilitarians, the pertinent question is what *utilitarians* should say. We recall that Rawls's express point is that 'if possible all [society's] members [should] be happy with their situation' and that 'the maximin criterion achieves this better than the principle of utility' (cited in Section II above). One line of utilitarian reply, then, would be the *empirical* criticism in the preceding section. Certainly Rawls's moral argument loses force insofar as it leans on implausible factual claims, about stability, the necessary conditions for cooperation, or the feasibility of interpersonal comparisons. Additionally, the proposed contrast is blurred insofar as the *practical result* of 'the principle of utility', in actual economic distributions, in fact tends to approximate maximin.

There may indeed be other psychological factors which give the principle of utility an edge in this competition. Plausibly, as argued earlier, utilitarianism (in some suitably sophisticated form) does at least *approximate* maximin in practice. Certainly it would be much closer to maxi*min* than to maxi*max*. Part of the argument for the statement just made (apart from decreasing marginal utility, etc.) would be the psychologically 'strenuous' character of maximax. On the other hand, while no doubt utilitarianism implies much sympathy for the disadvantaged, it is not obviously committed to the demand that their socioeconomic status be *max*imized, as required by maximin. Thus, while utilitarianism no doubt implies a generally 'egalitarian' approach to economic justice, it is plausibly somewhat more moderate than maximin. This claim of moderation may be viewed in two ways: First, the least favoured stratum in a utilitarian distribution may get somewhat less than the *maximum* amount *possible*! Secondly, even if the utilitarian distribution tends to approximate Rawls's maximin principle in *practice*, or under many socioeconomic conditions, there is perhaps a psychological advantage in not announcing this result as a rigid constraint in ethical *theory*. Certainly, one notable feature of utilitarianism here is that its *theoretical aim* is much more 'impersonal', since it aims at the maximum good of all, rather than the maximum well-being of any particular economic group or stratum. On the whole, then, and contrary to Rawls's contention, utilitarianism would seem in fact to be *less* 'psychologically demanding' than the maximin principle.

In the wake of these practical, psychological considerations, it is helpful to recall to mind the original purpose of the favoured-man argument.[31] The idea, observed in Section V above, was that maximin justice involves a *reciprocity* of advantages, between upper and lower economic classes—as contrasted with alleged utilitarian *sacrifices* of the less favoured. The point of the favoured-man argument is presumably to show that maximin does not do the same thing here in principle, merely to *more* favoured individuals, as utilitarianism is supposed characteristically to do to *less* favoured individuals. The alleged *moral* superiority of maximin, then, is not that its *un*reciprocal (or 'sacrificial') trade-offs of interests happen to be *just*, but rather that this *kind* of interpersonal treatment of interests, condoned under utilitarianism, is not exhibited under maximin at all.

This argument against utilitarianism is rendered ineffective by the analysis of the present section. One difficulty is that the putative contrast fails to the extent that both maximin and utilitarianism, in practice, yield similar distributive results. Even if utilitarian theory yields somewhat less economic equality than maximin, however, it remains heavily egalitarian (for anything that Rawls has argued), and therefore utilitarians can also claim to dispense 'reciprocal' advantages. Evidently, as suggested by the foregoing analysis, reciprocity is a matter of *degree*. This point could be extracted from Nozick's maximax argument, despite its flaws—for even maximax can claim a certain 'reciprocity', in the sense of an abstract symmetry. Surely utilitarianism yields much *more* reciprocity, and substantive equality, than maximax. Consequently, the sharp moral contrast which Rawls intends here between the principle of utility and the maximin principle is blurred, apart from the empirical implausibilities on which we have seen the favoured-man argument rests.

VII. CONCLUSION

We have seen that Rawls's argument is in the first instance an attempt

---

[31] It has been objected here that my treatment of Rawls's 'moral argument' in the preceding paragraphs overlooks that fact that Rawls has much more extensive moral argumentation for maximin and/or against utilitarianism. One must recall, however, that the present essay is concerned only with the 'moral argument' connected directly with the favoured-man argument, and in this context, the idea of reciprocity. (Recall specifically the opening paragraphs of Section IV above, where we delineated, and deferred discussion of, the 'moral phase' of the favoured-man/reciprocity argument until now.) This is a significant (and as I have argued, neglected) *part* of Rawls's overall moral argument, but it is certainly not intended that the present essay (or indeed any single essay) could deal with *all* of Rawls's argument. I have addressed other important strands of Rawls's anti-utilitarian argumentation in my essays cited above, esp. at note 1 above.

to contrast the 'reciprocal' character of maximin with the putative 'sacrificial' character of utilitarian theory. Nozick's criticism, then, misses the point. Nozick is trying to show that the argument fails to establish Rawls's liberal theory of justice to be morally compelling for 'favoured' individuals who are political conservatives. In this objection, as we saw earlier in Sections IV and V, Nozick misunderstands the pragmatic force of the reciprocity argument in terms of cooperation and stability; moreover, Nozick conflates this prudential appeal with a directly moral one. Thus, Rawls's reciprocity argument can be successfully defended from Nozick's critique. More accurately, the objection should be that Rawls's argument hinges on a too stark empirical claim about the need for maximin justice in order to stabilize a cooperative scheme. But there, too, Nozick's critique misses the mark, since the main problem is Rawls's failure to convince—not political conservatives with Nozickian moral intuitions, but rather— fellow liberals! As just seen in Section VI, Rawls does not establish maximin justice to be preferable for utilitarians, and it is in this context that Rawls is arguing maximin to be 'reciprocal' rather than 'sacrificial'. The general problem is that the empirical and pragmatic considerations on which that argument rests, however, do not plausibly establish *maximin* as superior in this respect to other *egalitarian* conceptions. i.e., do not make maximin *uniquely* attractive among other forms of liberalism. More specifically, then, since utilitarianism is historically both egalitarian and an important form of liberalism, the reciprocity argument against utilitarianism fails.

To keep the result of this essay in perspective, it is important also to bear in mind what we are *not* supposed to be concluding. In rejecting Rawls's reciprocity argument, we have been dealing primarily with 'pragmatic' concerns—in order to rebut the first phase of Rawls's argument. where he adduces empirical and prudential considerations in an (unsuccessful) attempt to prove that maximin justice *is* 'reciprocally' beneficial to higher and lower socioeconomic strata. Without this distinctive claim of reciprocity, Rawls cannot operate the second phase of his argument, contrasting the reciprocal advantages of maximin as *morally* preferable to the ostensibly *non*-reciprocal 'sacrifices' of utilitarian justice. This result should be a significant contribution to the case for utilitarian ethics, since the latter is often maligned nowadays for its alleged 'sacrificial' implications, and Rawls's reciprocity argument is a straightforward way to articulate and argue this popular objection. Certainly, in any case, the notion of reciprocity in the favoured-man argument figures prominently in Rawls's own 'moral' case against utilitarianism. Nevertheless, nothing in the present essay precludes the possibility of *other* such arguments; indeed, at the outset of this essay, we noted a variety of related lines of objection to utilitarianism. So one cannot conclude here that utilitarianism must escape *every* objection, nor could such a sweeping conclusion be drawn from any single essay at this stage in the literature. Still, it should be clear that Rawls's reciprocity argument to the 'favoured man' is important for anyone who attacks utilitarianism for perpetrating 'sacrifices' in distributive justice. After all, 'reciprocity' would seem to be the most obvious concept to contrast with 'sacrifice'. Consequently, the failure of Rawls's reciprocity argument should seriously impede *this* standard type of sacrifice objection to utilitarian ethical theory as inadequate on the topic of economic justice.

Another pertinent line of inquiry here would be to explore and elaborate Rawls's remark, injected above in the course of his favoured-man argument, that people do not 'deserve' their genetic assets. This is most obviously construed as a directly 'moral' judgement, but there are other interpretations which may pertain to the favoured-man argument. One might argue, for instance, the psychological thesis that the less favoured tend to *think* of natural assets as 'undeserved', and thus will tend to cooperate (willingly, etc.) only when the socioeconomic effects of such genetic (dis)advantages are minimized. Perhaps Rawls is suggesting that the 'more favoured man' understands at least that the less favoured feel this way, and/or that the more favoured themselves must also recognize this point about desert, and that this recognition will tend to make them more amenable to maximin. In view of the argument in this essay, it is empirically implausible that such psycho-social tendencies could make maximin necessary merely for stability. Finally, however, a Rawlsian might contend that additional philosophical argument about desert and genetic assets could induce such a *change* in beliefs about justice. In terms of our schema in Section IV, the suggestion is that further argument could *make* premise 6 true; however, even if the impact would not be so dramatic as to affect stability in this way, Rawlsians might contend that further reflection on 'justice and genetics' constitutes at any rate a substantial part of the *moral* argument for maximin.

We cannot pursue this prospect.[32] Once again, however, the argument of this essay indicates several important conclusions. Most significantly, Rawls's remark about desert and natural assets exacerbates his problem of contrasting maximin against utilitarianism, as argued in Section VI. Since both represent forms of political liberalism, *neither* rests socioeconomic distributions on the Lockean idea that individuals deserve their natural assets. Rather, Rawls's subsequent view here is that individual talents are to be treated as 'collective'

[32] I would like to thank a critical referee for detailed guidance in shortening this essay and delimiting the scope of my argument. As to what cannot be concluded or precluded here, please recall also notes 1 and 12 above.

assets owned by society as a whole, and this should make it all the more difficult for Rawlsian liberals to wage the usual objection, noted at the outset of this essay: that utilitarianism is supposed to be contrasted as 'sacrificing' individuals, by 'conflating' their interests or personal characteristics, etc. Since Rawls's reciprocity argument to the favoured man rests on an implausible stability claim, we can conclude here that maximin and utilitarian justice are similarly 'sacrificial'. On the other hand, we have also seen that maximin is considerably more 'reciprocal' and 'reasonable' than Nozick makes it seem, and this result should apply now to utilitarianism as well. If the argument in this essay has been correct, then, critics like Nozick have failed to refute Rawls, and both have failed to refute utilitarians.[33]

---

[33] In his new book (1993) which largely reiterates his essays, which we have taken into account, Rawls emphasizes a 'liberal' conception of what is 'reasonable' or 'reciprocal' as a matter of political compromise, or available consensus; however, this does not explicitly address Nozick, nor solve the general problem about 'sacrifice', etc., that has been argued in this essay. See my review of Rawls's book, to appear in this journal.

Kantian Constructivism in Ethics*

Thomas E. Hill, Jr.

A *Theory of Justice* has stimulated so much useful discussion in political theory, economics, legal philosophy, moral psychology, and other areas that one tends to forget the hopes it initially stirred among those of us seeking alternatives to utilitarianism in ethical theory.[1] At last, it seemed, we had a comprehensive, systematic model for nonutilitarian moral theory, rooted in the classics of the past but responsive to the best in modern thought. Its monumental scope, elevated sentiments, richness of detail, and optimistic tone easily tempted followers to overlook the carefully circumscribed nature of its project. Not surprisingly, then, Rawls's more recent papers have been disappointing to some sympathetic readers of his book, for these papers emphasize the limitations of Rawls's project and may seem to abandon earlier ambitions.[2] Critics of Rawls's book may read the later papers as a forced retreat and partial confession of failure, for, they may say, the theory of justice is now only a pragmatic compromise, designed for current political purposes, not even a working approximation to moral truth. Earlier suggestions that it could be expanded into a neo-Kantian comprehensive theory of right conduct seem to have been abandoned, or postponed, for the sake of the more modest aim of achieving an overlapping political consensus for our times.[3]

Although I am convinced of the immense importance of Rawls's project as he currently sees it, my concern here is not to defend that project or his contribution to it. Nor do I wish to enter the controversies about how far the recent papers deviate from the theory and ambitions of the book, though I suspect that the degree of change has been exaggerated. What I aim to do, instead, is to raise the question of whether

---

* I want to thank Richard Arneson, Bernard Boxill, and Geoffrey Sayre McCord for their helpful comments on an earlier version of this article.

1. My discussion will assume that the reader is familiar with John Rawls's *A Theory of Justice* (Cambridge, Mass.: Harvard University Press, 1971), hereafter referred to as *TJ*.

2. The papers by Rawls most relevant here are: "Kantian Constructivism in Moral Theory: The Dewey Lectures 1980," *Journal of Philosophy* 77 (1980): 515–72, "Justice as Fairness: Political not Metaphysical," *Philosophy and Public Affairs* 14 (1985): 223–51, and "The Idea of an Overlapping Consensus," *Oxford Journal of Legal Studies* 7 (1987): 1–25.

3. See, e.g., *TJ*, pp. 17, 111.

Ethics 99 (July 1989): 752–770

Rawls's work on justice offers a reasonable and workable model for ethical theory in areas apart from the special subject for which it was primarily designed. More specifically, does his particular version of Kantian Constructivism serve well the broader purposes of ethical theory when questions about the justice of basic political and economic institutions are not the central focus of attention? And, supposing the theory might be extended in this way, what modifications, if any, would be necessary or desirable?

These are large questions, and my comments on them will be admittedly quite incomplete and tentative. Since my discussion concerns the possible extension of Rawls's work, a road not taken by Rawls himself in recent papers, what I have to say is not to be construed as criticism of that work. Though my remarks will not presuppose that Rawls's theory is satisfactory even within its own domain, I do assume that the theory is richly suggestive of further extensions in ethical theory. At the same time, I sense the dangers of attempting to extend the theory uncritically. As will be evident, I take for granted some of Rawls's methodological assumptions: for example, that in moral philosophy we need for a time to deemphasize criticism and instead to work constructively to develop our alternative theories, painting at first with broad strokes, then filling in details, and only later assessing the comparative merits of the products as wholes. One-shot objections rarely demolish a moral theory, and premature demands for rigor of detail often impede progress. Any adequate ethical theory is likely to be complex and many-sided, and attempts to draw practical conclusions from a theory should be sensitive to its purpose and limitations.

My discussion will proceed as follows: first, I call attention to the explicit limits Rawls places on his project and the claims he makes for its results, but I also note widely appealing features of his theory that might encourage one to extend it beyond the purposes for which it was designed.

Second, I argue that, despite these attractive features, one cannot simply appropriate Rawls's theory, as it stands, for all purposes of moral decision making. Rawls's own reluctance to extend his theory suggests this conclusion, which becomes even more evident as we reflect on how the limited purpose of the original position has guided the selection of its defining features. Different moral questions call for different levels of reflection, and what features appropriately define a "moral point of view" for resolving a particular question depend importantly on the specific nature of that question. Rawls's original position is obviously not the appropriate stance for individuals facing immediate moral choices; and, I shall argue, it is also not a perspective from which we can justify and resolve disputes about our most basic moral values. If the original position is to be used to address ethical questions about matters beyond the justice of basic institutions, the only plausible alternative is to treat it as a perspective for reflecting about what intermediate-level moral principles would be suitable for certain ideal conditions. Even for this purpose, however, the original position, as currently defined, has serious drawbacks, which should at least lead constructivists to explore alternatives.

Third, for comparison, I sketch some features of an alternative "original position" drawn from Kant's idea of a kingdom of ends. Though incomplete and problematic in its own way, this Kantian perspective seems in some respects more appropriate than its Rawlsian counterpart when we go beyond Rawls's "primary subject" to raise questions about intermediate level moral principles for individuals.

I conclude with a reminder that both Rawls and Kant use thought experiments with an idealizing feature which creates a gap between what we can conclude from those reflections and what we need in order to make reasonable moral decisions about immediate problems in the real world.

EXTENDING THE THEORY: WARNINGS AND TEMPTATIONS

Despite his optimistic suggestions that the theory of justice might be expanded into a general theory of right conduct, Rawls never claims that one can resolve particular moral problems simply by putting the issues before deliberators in the original position. Nor does he claim that his two principles of justice, which he argues would be chosen in the original position, can be appropriately used to guide individual decisions about questions of justice in small groups. In *A Theory of Justice* he argues that certain principles of "natural duty" and "the principle of fairness," which apply to individual choices, would be adopted in the original position, and he suggests that this fact amounts to some kind of justification for them.[4] But these principles, as Rawls admits, are far from a comprehensive moral guide for individual choice; and, though Rawls speculates that his theory of justice might be extended into a general theory of right conduct, and even a theory of virtues, he does not develop these suggestions.[5]

Several papers written after *A Theory of Justice* make even more explicit and unmistakable Rawls's intention to limit his theory, as presented so far, to questions about the justice of the basic institutions of large-scale cooperative societies.[6] Insofar as he comments on the moral decisions of individuals, this is to draw out the implications of his conclusions about this primary subject, not to propose a comprehensive moral theory. The Dewey Lectures might seem to be an exception, but they are not.[7] In those lectures Rawls sketches a type of moral theory ("Kantian Constructivism") that he says Sidgwick, and most subsequent moral philosophers, have overlooked, and he cites his own theory of justice as an illustration.

4. Ibid., pp. 108–17, 333–50.
5. Ibid., pp. 17, 436–37.
6. See esp. John Rawls, "The Basic Structure as Subject," *American Philosophical Quarterly* 14 (1977): 159–65.
7. Rawls, "Kantian Constructivism in Moral Theory," esp. the third lecture, "Construction and Objectivity," pp. 554–74.

But careful readers will readily notice that, though certain formal features of a constructivist type of ethical theory are described, Rawls makes no pretensions of having offered a comprehensive theory of this type. His theory remains, as before, a theory about how reasonably to assess and order certain conflicting views about the justice of the basic institutions of society. This is an ambitious, and urgently needed, project, but it is not itself a *comprehensive* ethical theory of the "Kantian Constructivist" sort which, Rawls says, Sidgwick and others have overlooked.

Two more recent papers also show that Rawls's current intention is to offer his theory of justice as something less than a comprehensive moral guide.[8] Not only is the subject restricted to "the basic structure of society," but the aim is also limited to finding a reasonable basis for "overlapping consensus" among those whose values are deeply formed by certain Western democratic traditions. The results are not claimed to be timeless moral truths but rather a core of political principles that reasonable adherents of different moral perspectives can publicly agree upon. These restrictions on the subject, aims, and hopes for the theory, as currently developed, need not detract from its value; nor do they preclude extensions of the theory for broader purposes. Yet when tempted to use Rawls's theoretical framework for more far-reaching moral purposes, we should at least take warning from Rawls's own acknowledgments that a theory carefully constructed with compromises and simplifying assumptions suitable for his limited purposes may not serve as well our grander ambitions for a comprehensive moral theory.

The fact that Rawls himself does not extend his theory is, of course, no absolute bar against our doing so. Appeals to authority are out of place here, and we may attribute Rawls's restrictions to excessive modesty or caution. Initial hopes for extending Rawls's work should not be lightly abandoned, for important features of that work still have a powerful appeal to those dissatisfied with other traditional types of ethical theory. Moreover, some of those appealing features are independent of other controversial aspects of Rawls's methodology, which might deter some philosophers from trying to extend his theory.

Rawls's basic strategy is the attempt to determine the content and ranking of normative principles, and to justify them in some sense, by showing that these would be chosen in a specified hypothetical choice situation by persons conceived in a specified way. The choosers are not seen as seeking to *discover* a moral order, Platonic, natural, or divine, which exists independently of their reasoned choices; rather, we are to view principles as justifiable by virtue of their being what persons with the specified values would choose in the defined situation. Obviously the value of this general strategy depends upon the adequacy of the initial stipulations for the purpose at hand, and these purposes may vary.

8. Rawls, "Justice as Fairness," and "The Idea of an Overlapping Consensus."

"Kantian Constructivism," as Rawls presents it, uses this strategy in a way that gives a central role to a conception of persons as free, equal, and rational agents. Rawls's own theory is a particular version of Kantian Constructivism. Its "original position," in its final form, gives a specific interpretation of this Kantian conception of persons together with other features of the initial choice situation.[9] In addition, the Rawlsian theory is primarily focused on the justice of basic institutions, presupposes shared values in a public culture, uses a method of "reflective equilibrium,"[10] and claims only "reasonableness" in our times and not timeless "truth" for its results.

These additional features, I take it, are separable from Rawls's basic strategy and his Kantian conception of persons. The focus on the justice of basic institutions, for example, can be set aside in order to raise the question whether the original position can resolve moral questions *beyond justice*. One could use the basic strategy without the method of reflective equilibrium if one thought that a well-defined initial choice situation should not be modified to accommodate commonsense "intuitions" about particular cases. And less modest versions of Kantian Constructivism could attempt to derive principles from the will of free and rational agents without conceding that one must rely on shared values in a culture and forgo claims to "moral truth." Controversies about these matters, then, need not prevent us from trying to use Rawls's basic strategy in its Kantian form for moral theory generally.

The reason for wanting to do so is the hope that certain appealing features of Rawls's theory could be preserved in inquiries of more far-reaching scope. Among the aspects of Rawls's theory which readers have found attractive, the following are perhaps most relevant for our purposes. First, the theory develops in a more thorough and contemporary fashion a line of thought deeply embedded in our intellectual history, most prominently in the works of Rousseau, Kant, and other social contract theorists.

---

9. The features of Rawls's theory mentioned so far, in contrast to those that follow, are the main ones that I shall be considering as I raise doubts about "extending his theory" in ethics. It is important to note, however, that other features associated with his methodology, especially his holistic approach and rejection of "foundationalism," will be set aside. Rawls does not suppose that ethics can proceed by deducing specific principles from self-evident starting points. He grants both that alternative descriptions of the initial choice situation could be employed and that the best description is to be selected in part by considering how its results match our "considered judgments" about more specific principles. Nonetheless he does present and argue independently for a preferred specific description (which is what I shall subsequently refer to as "the original position"), and he uses this to guide decisions about the principles of justice, "natural duties," "the principle of fairness," etc. When I later refer to drawing "more specific principles" from "basic moral values," I have in mind this guiding function of his original position as finally specified, realizing that the values built into the original position are not for Rawls "basic" in the foundationalist sense of "unrevisable," "self-evident," or "warranted altogether independently of the acceptability of their applications."

10. *TJ*, pp. 20–21, 48–51.

Second, by attempting to justify principles from the hypothetical choices of idealized agents, Rawls offers hope of a kind of moral objectivity missing in familiar emotivist and prescriptivist theories, such as those of Stevenson and Hare, while avoiding the strong metaphysical commitments of "moral realist" theories of the sort advocated by Plato, Moore, and others. Rawls may stretch one's imagination about *possible* agents, but he seeks to avoid ontological commitment to the existence of values and principles apart from hypothetical choices. Third, whereas prior to Rawls's work utilitarian moral thinking was opposed primarily by intuitionist critics who relied upon refutation by counter-example, Rawls has developed and defended a competing way of thinking that offers hopes of making anti-utilitarian sentiments more systematic and deeply grounded.

A fourth feature of Rawls's theory which I believe is intuitively attractive to many is that it seeks to contribute to the resolution of important disputes about substantive principles by first adopting a more neutral point of view appropriate for the purpose. It asks us to picture an ideal perspective, reflecting the more formal commitments shared by people of diverse moral opinions, and then to use this as a heuristic device for adjudicating more particular disputes. Like Kant, Baier, ideal observer theorists, and some rule-utilitarians, Rawls seems to offer a model of the basic features of a "moral point of view" which can be recommended independently of one's position on specific moral controversies.[11] Such theories often attract or repel us, not so much by their results as by the way they envision the attitudes and procedures suitable for seeking specific moral conclusions. Though controversial in many respects, Rawls's model of the ideal choice situation seems to represent some of the most essential features of a widely shared moral point of view.

Our question, then, is whether the particular way Rawls works out the Kantian constructivist strategy can be extended for general moral theory without losing the appealing features just mentioned, even though Rawls himself has not taken this route. As a *first step* toward answering this question, I shall consider whether the original position *as currently defined* can serve this larger purpose. Later we can speculate about what alternative or modified perspective might be more suitable.

THE ORIGINAL POSITION AS A MORAL GUIDE?

Since we reflect on moral issues of different levels of generality, with appropriately different background assumptions, we need to sharpen

11. See, e.g., Immanuel Kant, *Groundwork of the Metaphysics of Morals*, trans. H. J. Paton (New York: Harper & Row, 1964); Kurt Baier, *The Moral Point of View* (Ithaca, N.Y.: Cornell University Press, 1958); Roderick Firth, "Ethical Absolutism and the Ideal Observer," *Philosophy and Phenomenological Research* 12 (1952): 317–45; R. M. Hare, *Moral Thinking* (Oxford: Clarendon, 1981); Richard Brandt, *Ethical Theory* (Englewood Cliffs, N.J.: Prentice-Hall, 1959), chaps. 10 and 15, and *A Theory of the Good and the Right* (Oxford: Clarendon, 1979), chap. 15; and William K. Frankena, *Ethics* (Englewood Cliffs, N.J.: Prentice-Hall, 1973), pp. 107–14.

our question by distinguishing different moral tasks which one might try to address from the original position.[12] Most important, we should separate (1) the problems faced by particular individuals trying to decide what they should do in a specific context, (2) philosophical inquiry into the nature and grounds of our most basic moral values, and (3) the attempt to determine from our most basic moral values what "intermediate level" principles of conduct are appropriate for ourselves and others who share a specified historical and cultural context. The question, then, will be: which, if any, of these tasks is appropriately addressed from the standpoint of Rawls's original position?

1. Consider, first, moral choices faced by particular moral agents in concrete situations, for example, my decision whether to lie to a friend, Carla, about the past infidelities of her recently deceased husband, Floyd. Here I may find it helpful to be guided by principles which I believe rational agents in some idealized situation might adopt. In doing so I would be making *indirect* use of the idea of an "original position," but only by first trying to derive general principles from that position. (I return to this option below, under 3.) What is clear and obvious, after the least reflection, is that I cannot reasonably address my problem *directly* from the perspective of the original position. Indeed, to attempt to do so would be unhelpful and morally perverse. Why? Taking up the perspective of the original position would mean trying to make a choice while behind a thick "veil of ignorance," focusing exclusively on "primary goods," and thinking only of my own (abstractly conceived) interests.[13] This means not only that I would need to put aside my sympathy and the intuitive urgings of conscience but also that I must ignore my most reflectively considered moral policies as well my particular commitments to my friend. I must disregard my knowledge of the special things we value as *ends* and count as relevant only how the choice would affect the distribution of *means* which I can reasonably expect everyone to want, whatever their conception of the good life. The "veil" would, of course, free me from bias in favor of my own special interests, but it would also blind me to potentially relevant facts about the personal relationships in the case, my ability to sustain the lie effectively, and the sincerity of my friend's professed desire to know the truth. Indeed, if I take the "veil" seriously, I cannot even pose my problem from the perspective of the

---

12. In referring to "levels of generality" here, and elsewhere, I oversimplify somewhat. Moral issues can be divided along several dimensions: e.g., scope of the moral values in question (all moral values vs. justice vs. charity); order of justification (basic vs. derivative); degree of acceptance or controversy (commonly agreed vs. disputed); and domain of reference (institutions vs. individuals, all persons vs. our contemporaries vs. that person here-now). When I refer to "extending" Rawls's strategy for ethics, I have in mind mainly expanding the scope and reference from the justice of the basic structure of society to nonpolitical moral questions for individuals; but in this section I am also concerned with other distinctions, as I hope the context will make clear.

13. *TJ*, pp. 17–22, 18–50.

original position, for to understand that problem presupposes that I know more facts about particulars than the veil allows me to consider. The problem refers to real individuals in a concrete context on the other side of the veil; and it calls for sympathy, respect, and sensitivity to detail, not blind disinterest or judicial "ignorance."

In the original position the members have vast general knowledge but do not know particulars. Before the "veil" is lifted, they are ignorant not only of their own place in history but also of the particular course of history. One might suggest, however, that the members could contemplate *possible* historical scenarios, described in full detail, without identifying actual individuals. Then, it might be thought, the members could pass judgment on the problem of people just like Carla and Floyd in a situation exactly like theirs. The problem with this suggestion, however, is that the motivational structure attributed to the members is obviously insufficient to enable us to pick out a solution on which all members would agree for such particular problems. The difficulties in demonstrating agreement on even the abstract principles of justice are all too familiar, and the motives that typically move us in judging concrete moral cases have been explicitly excluded in order to promote that higher order agreement. Moreover, as I argue later, even if their exclusive concern for "primary goods" could generate agreement on (possible) concrete cases, there is little reason to suppose that decisions reached on *that* basis would reflect all the morally relevant criteria.

When critics reject Rawls's theory as "too abstract" and "impartialist," they may sometimes do so because of a failure to appreciate fully the fact that it was never intended to be applied directly to concrete moral problems. Rawls, however, is quite clear on the point. Even in his restricted domain of political questions, Rawls insists that the results of the original position be applied in successive stages (constitutional, legislative, judicial), each lifting the "veil" appropriately for the task at hand;[14] and to do otherwise leads quickly to absurdity. If we want to extend Rawls's theory for broader ethical purposes, then, we need to consider whether the original position can be usefully extended in ethics at a higher level of abstraction, which might at least give us general guidelines relevant to concrete moral choices.

2. Will the original position serve, at the highest level, to settle disputes about our most basic moral values? Here too the original position, as Rawls defines it, is inadequate, but for a reason quite different from what we have considered so far. The problem is that many of our most fundamental moral convictions are already built into the description of the original position. As Rawls says, it is a point of view designed to represent widely accepted assumptions about a *fair* way to determine and rank competing guidelines for constitutional and legislative choices.[15]

14. Ibid., pp. 195–201.
15. Ibid., pp. 12–13; John Rawls, "Kantian Constructivism in Moral Theory," p. 522, "Fairness to Goodness," *Philosophical Review* 84 (1975): 536–40.

Its defining features were selected partly for moral reasons: that everyone's interests count, that he or she "deserves" his or her natural gifts, that conceptions of justice should be public, general, universal, and not tailored to special interests, that malicious envy should be discounted, that the welfare of future generations is important, and that procedural fairness, rather than particular visions of the good life, should provide the primary standard for our basic institutions.[16] These are not, of course, arguments that are supposed to move us once we have adopted the point of view of the original position, for the "members" are to reflect prudentially, not morally. However, as Rawls often acknowledges, shared basic moral assumptions are *represented* by the overall characterization of the parties together with their choice situation.[17] Moreover, the justificatory force of arguments from the original position to the principles of justice is largely dependent upon audience acceptance of those basic moral assumptions.

Though more evident in the book, these points are not incompatible with Rawls's later insistence on the political and pragmatic nature of his project. For even then the aim is "overlapping consensus," rather than a mere "modus vivendi," among those with diverse *moral* viewpoints.[18] Although the theory of justice is not itself a "general and comprehensive moral philosophy," and perhaps not even a core of moral truth in the overlap of such philosophies, its status as a reasonable political compromise for our times rests upon its appeal to the basic moral assumptions of the diverse groups that would make up the consensus.

3. The original position, then, is not and was never meant to be a morally neutral position from which our most basic moral assumptions can be justified. One consequence is that a familiar criticism, namely, that a rational amoralist could reject the original position, misses the point; arguments from the original position are meant to presuppose at least minimal moral commitments. The more relevant consequence for our purposes is that if the original position is to be of use in ethics it must be as a mediating device, enabling us to deliberate from our more basic, abstract, or uncontested moral values to more derivative, specific, or disputed principles. This is the only plausible use, and is suggested by Rawls's own procedures. The question remains, though, whether it is an appropriate use when we venture beyond Rawls's restricted subject. Does the original position adequately represent a "moral point of view" from which we can reasonably try to justify and order our moral guidelines for individual conduct, where the justice of basic institutions is not in question?

A thorough treatment of this question would require a critical examination of Rawls's arguments for "natural duties," and so on, in *A*

16. *TJ*, pp. 119–50.
17. Ibid., pp. 17–22, 120, 141, "Fairness to Goodness," p. 539, "The Basic Structure as Subject," p. 159, "Kantian Constructivism in Moral Theory," p. 529.
18. Rawls, "The Idea of an Overlapping Consensus," pp. 1–25.

Theory of Justice, a review of objections and replies in the subsequent literature, and a constructive effort to derive from the original position ethical principles beyond those that Rawls himself has discussed. This is more than I can attempt here, but I want nonetheless to mention several sources of doubt about the project of extending the original position, as currently defined, for ethical questions beyond its intended domain. These problems stem from a package of stipulations regarding the original position: that the members deliberate behind a thick "veil of ignorance," focus exclusively on social "primary goods," and are "mutually disinterested."

Consider, first, doubts concerning the *results* we may expect from extending the use of the original position (without modification). Will the original position give us *enough* guidance of the *right sort* when we raise ethical issues besides the justice of basic social institutions?

One consideration which raises doubts is that the thick veil excludes all knowledge, and even considered opinion, about what ultimate ends are most worth pursuing and what goods are in themselves most worth protecting. Members are supposed to focus exclusively on *social primary goods*, which are means or enabling conditions most directly influenced by basic political and economic institutions.[19] Within Rawls's project there are good reasons for this stipulation, but it is doubtful that those considerations justify the same stipulation for the broader moral task now under discussion.[20] For example, Rawls sets aside "natural" primary goods, such as health, because, he says, these are not so directly influenced by basic social institutions as are wealth, liberty, and the bases of self-respect.[21] One may question this judgment even for Rawls's purposes, but in any case it is clear that health, and other nonsocial goods, are often important concerns when we turn to moral questions about interpersonal relations within our social structure. Again, focus on primary goods instead of "happiness" or "intrinsic value" is a "simplifying device" warranted by the need for a publicly acknowledged "objective measure" in political processes on which we need agreement among people of widely divergent life-styles.[22] But for purposes of guiding our individual efforts to reach tenable moral policies, within a basically just social order, public agreement is less crucial and there is less need for such simplifying devices. The liberal aim of establishing a constitution and economic order that mutually respecting citizens can publicly affirm without judging one another's individual ways of life may be an admirable one; it does not follow, however, that one should try to establish one's moral guidelines for friendship, family, charity, personal integrity, and so forth from the same restricted point of view. Here one's concern for the shared values of one's

19. *TJ*, pp. 90–95.
20. Ibid., pp. 90–91, 142–43, 260, 433, 440, 447–48, "Fairness to Goodness," pp. 537–38, "Kantian Constructivism in Moral Theory," p. 526.
21. *TJ*, p. 62.
22. Ibid., p. 95.

community and one's best judgment regarding the most valuable ends of life may reasonably play a central role.

Another consideration that may encourage our doubts is that members of the original position are devoid of any moral commitment to protect and respect other persons. They are *mutually disinterested* and barred by the veil from consulting even their most basic moral values. Moral values have, of course, guided the construction of the original position. For example, though an impartial regard for others is not an attitude which the members have, it has been built into the constraints on their choices: they must choose principles that are universal, general, and final behind the veil of ignorance. Only superficial readers will infer that Rawls tries to justify his principles from egoistic premises, for this impartiality constraint, though indirectly represented, is crucial and severe. One may question, however, whether this constraint is sufficient, and of the right sort, for our extended moral purposes. The impartiality needed in assessing the most basic social institutions may not be the sort appropriate in reflecting on principles of charity, family responsibilities, and personal loyalties. And one may well doubt whether impartiality in the distribution of social primary goods is the only other-regarding moral value relevant to these matters.

Furthermore, despite Rawls's arguments to the contrary, it remains controversial whether original position members would opt for utilitarian principles, which ensure impartial regard only for preferences (or satisfactions) detached from the individuals who have them. In principle, as often noted, this allows the sacrifice of a few for the greater good of many. Whether to adopt such utilitarian principles, or even (by default) permissive egoism,[23] at least remains on the agenda for members of the original position. While this is entirely appropriate when one's project is to assess the relative merits of utilitarian and alternative principles of justice, one may reasonably doubt whether such questions should remain open when one is trying to characterize the appropriate moral point of view for applying basic moral values to more specific issues. For that purpose, more substantive moral commitments are in order, even if they are less widely shared than the assumptions of the original position.

Finally, any theory which throws a veil over information about historical and cultural information raises doubts about whether it can give adequate guidance that is sensitive to all morally relevant circumstances. Perhaps all conditions call for some sort of prohibitions against killing, bodily injury, infidelities, and so on as well as duties of aid, support of children, et cetera, but the practically important moral controversies about such

23. Ibid., p. 135–36. My intention here is not to imply that utilitarianism or egoism would be adopted in the original position but rather to suggest that these basic questions should be taken as settled once we turn to the sort of mediating task we have been considering, i.e., working from basic moral values to more specific principles. My point is just that the original position itself leaves open too many questions for our purposes; but this does not mean that modified versions or later "stages" of that position would do so as well.

matters arise because people disagree about how to make such principles specific. For example, what exceptions, if any, are allowed, how are the crucial terms to be interpreted, and to whom do the principles apply? Moral principles which specify answers to these questions are applications of more fundamental values to local circumstances, and the articulations of those principles may reasonably vary to some degree with historical and cultural conditions. Though moral principles are not simply whatever norms a community accepts, we cannot reasonably determine what should count as "infidelity" and "child neglect" while disregarding altogether the cultural context of the question. What one should regard as a justified killing may depend to some extent on the maturity and stability of the society, and even what is appropriately considered to be killing may vary with medical technology. The line between required and generous aid may depend upon the affluence of the community and alternative arrangements for meeting needs.

Now Rawls acknowledges the relevance of information about historical and cultural conditions even to questions of social justice, and he proposes a several stage sequence of deliberations in which the thick veil of ignorance is gradually lifted.[24] First we deliberate to the principles of justice in the original position behind the thick veil; next we reflect as members of a hypothetical constitutional convention to apply the principles of justice to our historical circumstances, broadly construed; then we assess laws from the point of view of an imaginary legislature with fuller knowledge of local conditions. The aim, Rawls says, is not to fix precisely one constitution and set of laws as just for a given society; it is rather to define a range of just institutions and legislative procedures so that further questions can be left to quasi-pure procedural justice and the ongoing processes of actual institutions.[25] For Rawls it is important that there is wide agreement on the terms of the original position and the general principles derived from it; but it is not so important, or expected, that the theory dictate specific policies for particular historical circumstances. Accordingly, it is appropriate for the moral constraints in the original position to be minimal and many specific applications to be underdetermined.

One may doubt, however, whether this same strategy would work if we leave the political realm. There are no real constitutional conventions and legislatures for moral decision making, though perhaps we can imagine moral analogues of these institutions. But can we reach adequate specific moral principles, sensitive to historical conditions, by imagining ourselves going from the original position through a sequence of deliberations, each with more information about our place and times? The problem with this approach in ethics is that the stages seem to serve no function. Since, unlike Rawls, we are not working out standards for criticism of

24. Ibid., pp. 195–201.
25. Ibid., p. 201.

actual constitutions and legislatures, we would simply be applying the basic moral values in our original position in the light of more and more historical information. Whether the original position provides the guidelines we need depends entirely on how richly it is endowed with morally appropriate assumptions. Since Rawls intentionally makes only the minimal moral assumptions for his purposes, it seems doubtful that it could guide us, even with historical information, to many of the more specific moral answers we seek. Also, since the original position was constructed primarily to address questions of social justice, it seems doubtful that the answers it does give would reflect the full range of moral values that are relevant.

The considerations reviewed above raise doubts about whether the original position, as currently defined, will lead to sufficient and adequate results when applied outside its intended domain. But we need also to consider how well the original position *represents* the moral point of view appropriate for deliberating about ethical issues beyond social justice; for, as I have suggested, part of the appeal of ideal models of deliberation in ethics lies in the heuristic value of the *way* they picture the moral deliberator, quite aside from any specific advice we derive from them. In this respect, too, the original position seems inadequate when extended beyond its primary subject.

The fact that members of the original position are concerned exclusively with social primary goods, and make no judgments about the relative importance of ends, tends to undermine its value as a general model for moral deliberators to emulate. Respectful acceptance of individual differences is an admirable trait, particularly when one is designing coercive institutions; but suspending all judgments about what is valuable, besides social primary goods, would not be admirable if one were working out moral policies, within the limits of just laws, for governing oneself and one's voluntary dealings with others. But the main problem stems, not from focus on primary goods, but from the fact that members of the original position are *mutually disinterested.*

This stipulation, that the parties take no interest in each other's interests, means that the deliberators in the original position have no other-regarding motives, moral or otherwise. It simplifies the decision process, and it does not prevent Rawls from representing the impartiality of justice, indirectly, in the constraints on members' choices (especially the veil). This way of representing impartiality admittedly has some advantages. For example, it enables Rawls to use decision theoretic principles for individual rational choice which allow theoretically neater arguments; and when such arguments run out, he is able to substitute "prudential intuition" for "moral intuition."[26] Some ideal observer theories represent the moral point of view as a position of full information with impartiality ensured by the observer's vicarious identification with the interests of each agent (and lack of other motives) but this simply encapsulates the

26. Ibid., pp. 44, 94, 152–58.

utilitarian perspective and makes agreement on specific principles unlikely.[27] Rawls also avoids the vagueness of the commonsense notion that
a proper moral perspective is *somewhat* other-regarding and impartial on
some matters but not all.

Despite these advantages, representing the agents of the original
position as mutually disinterested reduces its heuristic value as model
for the attitude one should try to approximate in deliberating about how
to specify (intermediate level) moral principles. Exclusive concern with
one's own welfare, even if severely constrained by limited knowledge, is
so deeply associated with common paradigms of amoral egoists that, I
suspect, the best intentions and most careful explanations cannot mold
it into an intuitive model of a general "moral point of view." The image
of "blind justice," weighing self-interested claims without knowledge of
whose claims they are, is a powerful and time-honored symbol, when the
only issue is *fairness;* but this is hardly an adequate general representation
of the proper position and attitude for those who would deliberate from
their more essential moral values to specific policies for a wide range of
interpersonal issues. Rawls does not claim that the original position is a
general representation of this sort; but for the broader purposes of constructivism in ethics it would be advantageous to have an alternative
model which represented the deliberative point of view in a more intuitively
appealing way.

Such an alternative, I imagine, would picture the ideal moral deliberator as more informed than Rawls's veil permits but still prepared to
disregard morally irrelevant considerations of gender, race, and social
status, as respectful of individual differences but not ready to ignore firm
convictions about the relative value of various human ends, and as committed to advancing the happiness of others but unwilling to merge all
interests into a pool for distribution by a utilitarian archangel. Kant
suggests a model of this sort, which I shall sketch for comparison.

AN ALTERNATIVE MODEL

One version of Kant's Categorical Imperative says that one must act as
if one were a legislating member in an ideal "kingdom of ends."[28] Kant
offers this principle as a combination of the main ideas expressed in
previous formulations of the Categorical Imperative. Thus the kingdom
of ends is meant to summarize certain basic moral values, for which he

27. See ibid., pp. 184 ff.; and Hare, esp. chap. 3. For a different sort of ideal observer
theory, see Firth.

28. Kant, *Groundwork of the Metaphysics of Morals*, pp. 100–102. Some of the points
summarized in the next few pages are discussed in my papers "The Kingdom of Ends,"
in *Proceedings of the Third International Kant Congress*, ed. Lewis White Beck (Dordrecht: D.
Reidel, 1972), pp. 307–15, and "Humanity as an End in Itself," *Ethics* 91 (1980): 84–99.
My discussion, it should be noted, follows Paton's rendering of "Reich" (in Kant's *Groundwork
of the Metaphysics of Morals*) as "kingdom" even though this has some unfortunate connotations.
"Realm" or "state" is perhaps a better translation, but Paton's has become the familiar one.

argues independently; it is not a morally neutral rational standpoint from which those values might be justified. Kant also suggests that the kingdom of ends is not the best stance for making everyday moral decisions, for he implies that the "universal law" formula is the stricter method for that purpose. It seems, then, that the "laws" one is to legislate in the kingdom are neither one's specific maxims nor the supreme moral principle itself. Thus it is natural to regard these "laws" as the sort of intermediate-level moral principles which we have been considering. On this reading, the kingdom would be a heuristic model of the appropriate moral attitude to take when deliberating from basic moral values to moderately specific principles. Kant does not himself follow through this suggestion when he works out his own system of moral principles in the *Metaphysics of Morals,* and in the *Groundwork* he implies that the main function of the kingdom is to make his abstract moral principles more intuitive. Nonetheless, it may be useful to compare this model with the original position.

The kingdom of ends, like the original position, is an "ideal," not a description of an actual state of affairs. Kant sometimes speaks of it as the ideal world that would result if everyone made *and followed* moral laws and if God arranged nature so that everyone's permissible ends would be satisfied. But Kant also speaks of the kingdom as an ideal moral legislature, a point of view for adopting principles one should follow regardless of what others may actually do.[29] This ideal, which is the one relevant here, is not offered for the purposes of assessing the basic structure of society but rather as an intuitive model of the morally appropriate attitude to take when reflecting on all but the most general "moral laws." As in Rawls's theory, normative conclusions follow from hypothetical choices: one *should* act according to the "laws" one *would* adopt if one were legislating in the kingdom.

The main features of this legislative point of view, reconstructed liberally, are these. The members are rational and autonomous; they "abstract from personal differences"; they make only "universal laws"; they are "ends in themselves," and presumably recognize each other as such; they are all both "authors" and "subjects" of the law (except God, the sovereign, who is not "subject"). Like Rousseau's citizens of an ideal state, they are bound only by laws they give themselves. Each of these conditions requires interpretation, but for present purposes it is best to focus on the most significant ways in which the model compares and contrasts with the original position.

---

29. Kant implies, I think, that members of the kingdom, as such, conscientiously obey its laws (*Groundwork of the Metaphysics of Morals,* pp. 100–101, 105–7). Thus, in legislating from the perspective of the kingdom, we are to imagine that we are making laws for perfect law-abiders, i.e., we assume "strict compliance." However, Kant also implies that once the "laws" are settled from this ideal perspective, we (as individuals in the real world) must follow those laws even if others do not. This gives rise to the problem I mention in my concluding paragraph.

Kant's idea of "rationality" is broader than Rawls's but also less clearly defined. It includes taking the necessary means to one's (rationally adopted) ends, and it also encompasses dispositions to preserve, develop, and respect oneself as a thinking agent. Rational beings, Kant says, necessarily view their "rational nature" as an "end in itself," which implies placing a stringent priority on realizing these dispositions over satisfying various contingent ends when these two values ("dignity" and "price") conflict. Kant also held that rational consistency demands the same priorities in dealing with others, but the other-regarding attitudes of kingdom members are also stipulated more directly, as I explain below, by the characterization of all the members as "ends in themselves."

Autonomy is a controversial notion but implies, I think, at least the following: the members view each other, for practical purposes, as able to make and follow rational principles which are not simply a product of their strongest desires and impulses. They are not causally or rationally constrained to adopt as their ultimate guide, "Do whatever most efficiently satisfies your desires." They are not under obligation to independent authorities; obedience to God is required only because God's commands are supposed to coincide with the voice of their own reason. They are principled, but they cannot "discover" moral principles in nature, custom, or social institutions. Apart from the values inherent in being a rational agent, they acknowledge no fixed "intrinsic value" in the nature of things. Particular ends, such as fame, power, and wealth, are "relative" to individual tastes; they are morally important only when and because autonomous agents choose to make them their ends. Even pleasure and avoidance of pain, which are natural concerns of all human beings, have value only to the degree that autonomous agents incorporate them into their (permissible) projects; and they are subordinate to the values implicit in acknowledging rational agency as an end in itself.

In thinking of the kingdom, Kant says, we "abstract from the differences" between rational agents as well as from the "content" of their particular ends. This is Kant's analogue of the "veil of ignorance," but how far does it extend? Clearly one is to disregard gender, race, social rank, special talents, degree of wealth, and the like, and we are not to think as music lovers, birdwatchers, or sports fans. Unlike Rawls, however, Kant does not specify fully what other sorts of considerations we must set aside. Since all rational agents are potential "members," it seems that "abstracting from the differences" may require us to ignore not only the special values of particular communities but also any other distinguishing historical conditions. If so, some of the doubts I raised about extending the original position would apply equally well to Kant's model, unless the latter contains some compensating feature. (I return to this problem shortly.)

The stipulation that the members make "universal laws" may be construed as similar to Rawls's idea that members adopt only principles that are general in spirit as well as in form. That is, they do not direct

117

orders to particular individuals, and they do not arbitrarily design their principles to ensure the outcomes they especially favor for their own immediate situation. Since members make "universal laws," which for Kant must be (practically) "necessary" as well as general in scope, we can infer that the members will not make laws without sufficient reason. They choose only what, given their situation, they see as rationally compelling.

The conditions so far tell us little about what would motivate members of the kingdom to select one principle over another. We need an analogue to the original position members' concern for social primary goods. This must be drawn from the idea that members of the kingdom acknowledge each other as "ends," with "dignity" above all "price." The idea is not simply that "everyone should be considered," still less that the moral legislators' task is to satisfy the maximal set of individual preferences when these are "impartially" pooled together. Nor is Kant's idea merely the empty formal notion that people should be granted all the rights and consideration that are morally due to them. In calling rational agents "ends in themselves," Kant implies at least three points, all imprecise but nonetheless important.[30]

First, the "humanity," or rational nature, of each person is a rational value that has strict priority over contingent ends. That is, preserving and respecting the rational agency of the members is a central aim of the kingdom's legislators, and this has a higher priority, in case of conflict, than promoting the various particular ends that the members may adopt. In Kant's terms, "dignity" is an unconditional value that always takes precedence over "price."

Second, the "dignity" of rational agents is a value that has *no* equivalent. That is, we not only must avoid subordinating this value to less essential ends (with mere "price"); we also cannot justify sacrificing one rational agent for others on the grounds, say, that two persons are worth twice as much as one. (This does not necessarily mean that hard choices cannot reasonably be made, but only that they cannot be based on comparisons of quantities of value.) Persons are not to be treated as "mere means," even to the preservation and rational development of other persons.

Third, regarding rational agents as ends in themselves, Kant says, implies some degree of commitment to furthering their contingent ends (within the other constraints of moral law). This is not because those ends, or their satisfaction, have intrinsic value as such but because one cannot ignore the concerns and projects of agents whom one respects and values. Kant never specifies the extent to which one must care for the ends of others, and his principles in the *Metaphysics of Morals* place the priority on promoting the liberty and mutual respect needed for rational agents to pursue their own ends.

---

30. For further references and applications, see my "Humanity as an End in Itself."

This sketch of Kant's legislative model is admittedly both incomplete and controversial, and the model itself raises serious problems. But, as my main purpose is not to explain or defend Kant, perhaps enough has been said to make way for some useful comparisons.

To review, the main sources of doubt about extending the original position beyond its domain were these stipulations: (1) that its members focus exclusively on primary social goods, (2) that they are mutually disinterested and so lack moral regard for others, and (3) that they are ignorant of historical circumstances and too thinly described to give us adequate guidelines for when the veil is lifted. On each of these points Kant's model provides an interesting contrast.

First, the Kantian legislators have values beyond social primary goods. Since they value rational nature as an end itself, they are committed to the value priorities that Kant thought essential to being rational: that is, preserving, developing, exercising, and respecting rational agency takes precedence over other (contingent) ends. These priorities hold for self-regarding as well as other-regarding policies.

Second, and most striking, the Kantian legislators are not mutually disinterested. To the contrary, they are viewed as committed to furthering the ends of others and as valuing, above all, the dignity of each rational agent. Significant moral values are thus built into the attitudes of the deliberators, not merely represented in the stipulated constraints on their choices. Because their motives are complex and not morally neutral, they do not reason prudentially, using (say) a maximin strategy. This no doubt makes it harder to argue that all members will agree on exactly the same principles. For Rawls's project it is important that original position members publicly agree on the same general standards for the basic institutions of a heterogeneous society. But that every deliberator reach the same moral policies is less important if one's aim is to model an ideal point of view for applying basic moral values to more specific circumstances. And for this purpose, as I have suggested, it is helpful to represent the ideal deliberators as morally committed and (to some degree) other-regarding.

Third, and finally, since the Kantian model abstracts from all differences between rational agents, its deliberators must initially disregard historical and cultural conditions; but this initial abstraction may not be as severe a problem with the Kantian model as with the original position (taken outside the political sphere). This is because the Kantian model (as represented here) itself reflects a fuller, less modestly described moral viewpoint. The moral commitments implicit in the Kantian conception lead rather directly to general moral guidelines that may be used in deliberations about more specific policies when historical circumstances are taken into account. For example, the stipulated attitudes of the kingdom members ensure that, even before they consider historical information, they would accept a strict principle of respect for persons, an indefinite principle of beneficence (enjoining us to make the ends of others to some extent our own), and principles forbidding the sacrifice of the lives and liberty of any rational agent merely for an increase in general welfare. These and perhaps other principles in Kant's *Metaphysics of Morals* are, as Kant suggests, implicit in his idea of humanity as an end in itself.[31] Though they may be disputed, they are not without practical import.

The price for building more value assumptions into a constructivist model is, of course, the risk of generating more controversy about the model itself. Many may reject the strong initial commitments in the Kantian model, for example, and even those who find that it expresses their moral viewpoint may well ask for independent justification. Kant himself was not unmindful of this demand and in fact devoted more attention to deeper issues of justification than to developing or applying his heuristic model of the kingdom of ends. These other aspects of Kant's moral philosophy, which I have ignored here, may also be construed as constructivist; but that is a topic for another time.

To conclude, my aim has been to explore some possible extensions of Rawls's basic strategy in ethics, not to defend Kant or to criticize Rawls. The doubts I have raised have concerned the extended use of Rawls's current version of the original position and not possible modifications of this. Other extensions may be more promising, and my remarks on both Kant and Rawls are regrettably abstract and inconclusive. One further point, however, should not go unmentioned. This is the fact that the thought experiments which Rawls and Kant suggest, for different purposes, presuppose that we are deliberating about principles for an ideal world of conscientious agents. In Rawls's terminology, we assume "strict compliance." But there is an important gap between the policies that we would make for such a world and the policies that may be morally best for the real world. This world, unfortunately, includes people who refuse to comply with just institutions and moral principles, no matter how well these are explained and defended; and this creates a situation in which rigorous adherence to the principles for an ideal world may prove disastrous. To his credit, Rawls seems well aware of this; but one cannot confidently say the same of Kant.

31. Kant, *Groundwork of the Metaphysics of Morals*, pp. 95–104. Kant's *Metaphysics of Morals* is published in English in two parts: *The Metaphysical Elements of Justice*, trans. John Ladd (Indianapolis: Bobbs-Merrill, 1965), and *The Doctrine of Virtue*, trans. Mary Gregor (New York: Harper & Row, 1964).

CHARLES R. BEITZ

Justice and
International Relations

> Current events have brought into sharp
> focus the realization that . . . there is a
> close inter-relationship between the pros-
> perity of the developed countries and the
> growth and development of the developing
> countries. . . . International cooperation
> for development is the shared goal and
> common duty of all countries.[1]

Do citizens of relatively affluent countries have obligations founded on justice to share their wealth with poorer people elsewhere? Certainly they have some redistributive obligations, founded on humanitarian principles requiring those who are able to help those who, without help, would surely perish. But obligations of justice might be thought to be more demanding than this, to require greater sacrifices on the part of the relatively well-off, and perhaps sacrifices of a different kind as well. Obligations of justice, unlike those of humanitarian aid, might also require efforts at large-scale institutional reform. The rhetoric of the United Nations General Assembly's "Declaration on the Establishment of a New International Economic Order" suggests that it is this sort of obligation which requires wealthy countries to substantially increase their contributions to less developed countries and to radically restructure the world economic system. Do such obligations exist?

This question does not pose special theoretical problems for the utilitarian, for whom the distinction between obligations of humanitarian aid and obligations of social justice is a second-order distinc-

I am grateful to Huntington Terrell, who stimulated my interest in questions of international ethics, for comments and criticisms on an earlier version and to Thomas Scanlon, Richard Falk, and Dennis Thompson, for many helpful discussions of earlier drafts.

1. "Declaration on the Establishment of a New International Economic Order," Resolution No. 3201 (S-VI), 1 May 1974, United Nations General Assembly, *Official Records: Sixth Special Session*, Supp. No. 1 (A/9559) (New York, 1974), p. 3.

tion. Since utility-maximizing calculations need not respect national boundaries, there is a method of decision available when different kinds of obligations conflict. Contractarian political theories, on the other hand, might be expected to encounter problems in application to questions of global distributive justice. Contractarian principles usually rest on the relations in which people stand in a national community united by common acceptance of a conception of justice. It is not obvious that contractarian principles with such a justification underwrite any redistributive obligations between persons situated in different national societies.

This feature of contractarian principles has motivated several criticisms of Rawls' theory of justice.[2] These criticisms hold, roughly, that it is wrong to take the nation-state as the foundation of contractarian principles, that, instead, such principles ought to apply globally.[3] I want to pursue this theme here, in part because it raises interesting problems for Rawls' theory, but also because it illuminates several important features of the question of global justice, a question to which too little attention has been paid by political philosophers. In view of increasingly visible global distributive inequalities, famine, and environmental deterioration, it can hardly be denied that this question poses a main political challenge for the foreseeable future.

My discussion has four parts. I begin by reviewing Rawls' brief remarks on international justice, and show that these make sense only on the empirical assumption that nation-states are self-sufficient. Even if this assumption is correct, I then claim, Rawls' discussion of international justice is importantly incomplete, for it neglects certain problems about natural resources. In part three, I go on to question the empirical foundation of the self-sufficiency assumption, and sketch the consequences for Rawlsian ideal theory of abandoning the assumption. In conclusion, I explore the relation of an ideal theory of

2. John Rawls, *A Theory of Justice* (Cambridge, Mass., 1972). Page references are given parenthetically in the text.

3. Such criticisms have appeared in several places. For example, Brian Barry, *The Liberal Theory of Justice* (Oxford, 1973), pp. 128–133; Peter Danielson, "Theories, Intuitions and the Problem of World-Wide Distributive Justice," *Philosophy of the Social Sciences* 3 (1973), pp. 331–340; Thomas M. Scanlon, Jr., "Rawls' Theory of Justice," *University of Pennsylvania Law Review* 121, no. 5 (May 1973), pp. 1066–1067.

international justice to some representative problems of politics in the nonideal world.

This is a large agenda, despite the absence of any extended consideration of the most familiar problems of international ethics, those concerning the morality of war, which I take up only briefly. While these are hardly insignificant questions, it seems to me that preoccupation with them has too often diverted attention from more pressing distributive issues. Inevitably, I must leave some problems undeveloped, and merely suggest some possible solutions for others. The question of global distributive justice is both complicated and new, and I have not been able to formulate my conclusions as a complete theory of global justice. My main concern has been to see what such a theory might involve.

I

Justice, Rawls says, is the first virtue of social institutions. Its "primary subject" is "the basic structure of society, or more exactly, the way in which the major social institutions distribute fundamental rights and duties and determine the division of advantages from social cooperation" (7). The central problem for a theory of justice is to identify principles by which the basic structure of society can be appraised.

Rawls' two principles characterize "a special case of the problem of justice." They do not characterize "the justice of the law of nations and of relations between states" (7–8) because they rest on morally significant features of an ongoing scheme of social cooperation. If national boundaries are thought to set off discrete schemes of social cooperation, as Rawls assumes (457), then the relations of persons situated in different nation-states cannot be regulated by principles of social justice. As Rawls develops the theory, it is only after principles of social justice and principles for individuals (the "natural duties") are chosen that principles for international relations are considered, and then only in the most perfunctory manner.

Rawls assumes that "the boundaries" of the cooperative schemes to which the two principles apply "are given by the notion of a self-contained national community" (457). This assumption "is not relaxed until the derivation of the principles of justice for the law of nations" (457). In other words, the assumption that national communities are self-contained is relaxed when international justice is considered. What does this mean? If the societies of the world are now to be conceived as open, fully interdependent systems, the world as a whole would fit the description of a scheme of social cooperation and the arguments for the two principles would apply, a fortiori, at the global level. The principles of justice for international politics would be the two principles for domestic society writ large, and their application would have a very radical result, given the tendency to equality of the difference principle. On the other hand, if societies are thought to be *entirely* self-contained—that is, if they are to have no relations of any kind with persons, groups, or societies beyond their borders—then why consider international justice at all? Principles of justice are supposed to regulate conduct, but if, ex hypothesi, there is no possibility of international conduct, it is difficult to see why principles of justice for the law of nations should be of any interest whatsoever. Rawls' discussion of justice among nations suggests that neither of these alternatives describes his intention in the passage quoted. Some intermediate assumption is required. Apparently, nation-states are now to be conceived as largely self-sufficient, but not entirely self-contained. Probably he imagines a world of nation-states which interact only in marginal ways; perhaps they maintain diplomatic relations, participate in a postal union, maintain limited cultural exchanges, and so on. Certainly the self-sufficiency assumption requires that societies have no significant trade or economic relations.

Why, in such a world, are principles of international justice of interest? Rawls says that the restriction to ideal theory has the consequence that each society's external behavior is controlled by its principles of justice and of individual right, which prevent unjust wars and interference with human rights abroad (379). So it cannot be the need to prohibit unjust wars that prompts his worries about the law of nations. The most plausible motivation for considering principles of justice for the law of nations is suggested by an aside regarding the difficulties of disarmament (336), in which Rawls suggests that state relations are inherently unstable despite each one's commitment to its own principles of justice. Agreement on regulative principles would then be a source of security for each state concerning each other's external behavior, and would represent the minimum conditions of peaceful coexistence.

For the purpose of justifying principles for nations, Rawls reinterprets the original position as a sort of international conference:

> One may extend the interpretation of the original position and think of the parties as representatives of different nations who must choose together the fundamental principles to adjudicate conflicting claims among states. Following out the conception of the initial situation, I assume that these representatives are deprived of various kinds of information. While they know that they represent different nations each living under the normal circumstances of human life, they know nothing about the particular circumstances of their own society. . . . Once again the contracting parties, in this case representatives of states, are allowed only enough knowledge to make a rational choice to protect their interests but not so much that the more fortunate among them can take advantage of their special situation. This original position is fair between nations; it nullifies the contingencies and biases of historical fate [378].

While he does not actually present arguments for any particular principles for nations, he claims that "there would be no surprises, since the principles chosen would, I think, be familiar ones" (378). The examples given are indeed familiar; they include principles of self-determination, nonintervention, the *pacta sunt servanda* rule, a principle of justifiable self-defense, and principles defining *jus ad bellum* and *jus in bello*.[4] These are supposed to be consequences of a basic principle of equality among nations, to which the parties in the reinterpreted original position would agree in order to protect and uphold their interests in successfully operating their respective societies and in securing compliance with the principles for individuals which protect human life (378, 115).

One objection to such reasoning might be that there is no guarantee that all of the world's states are internally just, or if they are, that they

---

4. These principles form the basis of traditional international law. See the discussion, on which Rawls relies, in J.L. Brierly, *The Law of Nations*, 6th ed. (New York, 1963), especially chaps. 3 and 4.

are just in the sense specified by the two principles. If some societies are unjust according to the two principles, some familiar and serious problems arise. In a world including South Africa or Chile, for example, one can easily imagine situations in which the principle of non-intervention would prevent other nations from intervening in support of an oppressed minority fighting to establish a more just regime, and this might seem implausible. More generally, one might ask why a principle which defends a state's ability to pursue an immoral end is to count as a moral principle imposing a requirement of justice on other states.

Such an objection, while indicating a serious problem in the real world, would be inappropriate in this context because the law of nations, in Rawls, applies to a world of just states. Nothing in Rawls' theory specifically requires this assumption, but it seems consonant with the restriction to ideal theory and parallels the assumption of "strict compliance" which plays a role in arguments for the two principles in domestic societies. It is important to see, however, that the suggested justification of these traditional rules of international law rests on an ideal assumption not present in most discussions of this subject. It does not self-evidently follow that these rules ought to hold in the nonideal world; at a minimum, an additional condition would be required, limiting the scope of the traditional rules to cases in which their observance would promote the development of just institutions in presently unjust societies while observing the basic protections of human rights expressed by the natural duties and preserving a stable international order in which just societies can exist.

Someone might think that other principles would be acknowledged, for example, regarding population control and regulation of the environment. Or perhaps, as Barry suggests, the parties would agree to form some sort of permanent international organization with consultative, diplomatic, and even collective security functions.[5] However, there is no obvious reason why such agreements would emerge from an international original position, at least so long as the constituent societies are assumed to be largely self-sufficient. Probably the parties, if confronted with these possibilities, would reason that fundamental questions of justice are not raised by them, and such issues of policy

5. Barry, *The Liberal Theory of Justice*, p. 132.

as arise from time to time in the real world could be handled with traditional treaty mechanisms underwritten by the rule, already acknowledged, that treaties are to be observed. Other issues that are today subjects of international negotiation—those relating to international regulation of common areas such as the sea and outer space—are of a different sort. They call for a kind of regulation that requires substantive cooperation among peoples in the use of areas not presently within the boundaries of any society. A cooperative scheme must be evolved which would create new wealth to which no national society could have a legitimate claim. These issues would be excluded from consideration on the ground that the parties are assumed not to be concerned with devising such a scheme. As representatives of separate social schemes, their attention is turned inward, not outward. In coming together in an international original position, they are moved by considerations of equality between "independent peoples organized as states" (378). Their main interest is in providing conditions in which just domestic social orders might flourish.

II

Thus far, the ideal theory of international justice bears a striking resemblance to that proposed in the Definitive Articles of Kant's *Perpetual Peace.*[6] Accepting for the time being the assumption of national self-sufficiency, Rawls' choice of principles seems unexceptionable. But would this list of principles exhaust those to which the parties would agree? Probably not. At least one kind of consideration, involving natural resources, might give rise to moral conflict among states and thus be a matter of concern in the international original position. The principles given so far do not take account of these considerations.

We can appreciate the moral importance of conflicting resource claims by distinguishing two elements which contribute to the material advancement of societies. One is human cooperative activity itself, which can be thought of as the human component of material advancement. The other is what Sidgwick called "the utilities derived from any portion of the earth's surface," the natural component.[7]

6. Trans. and ed. Lewis White Beck (Indianapolis, 1957), pp. 10–23.
7. Henry Sidgwick, *The Elements of Politics* (London, 1891), p. 242; quoted in S.I. Benn and R.S. Peters, *The Principles of Political Thought* (New York,

While the first is the subject of the domestic principles of justice, the second is morally relevant even in the absence of a functioning scheme of international social cooperation. The parties to the international original position would know that natural resources are distributed unevenly over the earth's surface. Some areas are rich in resources, and societies established in such areas can be expected to exploit their natural riches and to prosper. Other societies do not fare so well, and despite the best efforts of their members, they may attain only a meager level of well-being due to resource scarcities.

The parties would view the distribution of resources much as Rawls says the parties to the domestic original position deliberations view the distribution of natural talents. In that context, he says that natural endowments are "neither just nor unjust; nor is it unjust that men are born into society at any particular position. These are simply natural facts. What is just or unjust is the way that institutions deal with these facts" (102). A caste society, for example, is unjust because it distributes the benefits of social cooperation according to a rule that rests on morally arbitrary factors. Rawls' objection is that those who are less advantaged for reasons beyond their control cannot be asked to suffer the pains of inequality when their sacrifices cannot be shown to advance their position in comparison with an initial position of equality.

Reasoning analogously, the parties to the international original position, viewing the natural distribution of resources as morally arbitrary, would think that they should be subject to redistribution under a resource redistribution principle. This view is subject to the immediate objection that Rawls' treatment of natural talents is troublesome. It seems vulnerable in at least two ways. First, it is not clear what it means to say that the distribution of talents is "arbitrary from a moral point of view" (72). While the distribution of natural talents is arbitrary in the sense that one cannot deserve to be born with the capacity, say, to play like Rubinstein, it does not obviously follow that the possession of such a talent needs any justification. On the contrary, simply having a talent seems to furnish prima facie warrant for making use of it in ways that are, for the possessor, possible and

---

1959), p. 430. Sidgwick's entire discussion of putative national rights to land and resources is relevant here—see *Elements*, pp. 239–244.

desirable. A person need not justify his possession of talents, despite the fact that he cannot be said to deserve them, because they are already *his*; the prima facie right to use and control talents is fixed by natural fact.

The other point of vulnerability is that natural capacities are parts of the self, in the development of which a person might take a special kind of pride. A person's decision to develop one talent, not to develop another, as well as his choice as to how the talent is to be formed and the uses to which it is to be put, are likely to be important elements of his effort to shape an identity. The complex of developed talents might even be said to constitute the self; their exercise is a principal form of self-expression. Because the development of talents is so closely linked with the shaping of personal identity, it might seem that one's claim to one's talents is protected by considerations of personal liberty. To interfere with the development and use of talents is to interfere with a self. Or so, at least, it might be argued.

While I believe that Rawls' discussion of talents can be defended against objections like these, that is not my concern here. I want to argue only that objections of this sort do not apply to the parallel claim that the distribution of natural resources is similarly arbitrary. Like talents, resource endowments are arbitrary in the sense that they are not deserved. But unlike talents, resources are not naturally attached to persons. Resources are found "out there," available to the first taker. Resources must be appropriated before they can be used, whereas, in the talents case, the "appropriation" is a fait accompli of nature over which persons have no direct control. Thus, while we feel that the possession of talents confers a right to control and benefit from their use, we may feel differently about resources. Appropriation may not always need a justification; if the resources taken are of limited value, or if, as Locke imagined, their appropriation leaves "enough and as good" for everyone else, justification may not present a problem. In a world of scarcity, however, the situation is different. The appropriation of valuable resources by some will leave others comparatively, and perhaps fatally, disadvantaged. Those deprived without justification of scarce resources needed to sustain and enhance their lives might well press claims to equitable shares.

Furthermore, resources do not stand in the same relation to personal identity as do talents. It would be inappropriate to take the sort of pride in the diamond deposits in one's back yard that one takes in the ability to play the *Appassionata*. This is because natural resources come into the development of personality (when they come in at all) in a more casual way than do talents. As I have said, talents, in some sense, are what the self is; they help constitute personality. The resources under one's feet, because they lack this natural connection with the self, seem to be more contingent than necessary elements of the development of personality. Like talents, resources are used in this process; they are worked on, shaped, and benefited from. But they are not there, as parts of the self, to begin with. They must first be appropriated, and prior to their appropriation, no one has any special natural claim on them. Considerations of personal liberty do not protect a right to appropriate and use resources in the same way as they protect the right to develop and use talents as one sees fit. There is no parallel, initial presumption against interference with the use of resources, since no one is initially placed in a naturally privileged relationship with them.

I conclude that the natural distribution of resources is a purer case of something's being "arbitrary from a moral point of view" than the distribution of talents. Not only can one not be said to deserve the resources under one's feet; the other grounds on which one might assert an initial claim to talents are absent in the case of resources, as well.

The fact that national societies are assumed to be self-sufficient does not make the distribution of natural resources any less arbitrary. Citizens of a nation which finds itself on top of a gold mine do not gain a right to the wealth that might be derived from it *simply* because their nation is self-sufficient. But someone might argue that self-sufficiency, nevertheless, removes any possible grounds on which citizens of other nations might press claims to equitable shares. A possible view is that no justification for resource appropriation is necessary in the global state of nature. If, so to speak, social cooperation is the root of all social obligations, as it is on some versions of contract theory, then the view is correct. All rights would be "special rights" applying only when certain conditions of cooperation obtain.[8]

I believe that this is wrong. It seems plausible in most discussions of distributive justice because their subject is the distribution of the benefits of social cooperation. Appropriate distributive principles compensate those who are relatively disadvantaged by the cooperative scheme for their participation in it. Where there is no social cooperation, there are no benefits of cooperation, and hence no problem of compensation for relative disadvantage. (This is why a world of self-sufficient national societies is not subject to something like a global difference principle.) But there is nothing in this reasoning to suggest that our *only* moral ties are to those with whom we share membership in a cooperative scheme. It is possible that other sorts of considerations might come into the justification of moral principles. Rawls himself recognizes this in the case of the natural duties, which are said to "apply to us without regard to our voluntary acts" (114) and, apparently, without regard to our institutional memberships.

In the case of natural resources, the parties to the international original position would know that resources are unevenly distributed with respect to population, that adequate access to resources is a prerequisite for successful operation of (domestic) cooperative schemes, and that resource supplies are scarce. They would view the natural distribution of resources as arbitrary in the sense that no one has a natural prima facie claim to the resources that happen to be under his feet. The appropriation of scarce resources by some requires a justification against the competing claims of others and the needs of future generations. Not knowing the resource endowments of their own societies, the parties would agree on a resource redistribution principle which would give each national society a fair chance to develop just political institutions and an economy capable of satisfying its members' basic needs.

There is no intuitively obvious standard of equity for such matters; perhaps the standard would be population size, or perhaps it would be more complicated, rewarding nations for their efforts in extracting resources and taking account of the differential resource needs of

8. William N. Nelson construes Rawlsian rights in this way in "Special Rights, General Rights, and Social Justice," *Philosophy & Public Affairs* 3, no. 4 (Summer 1974): 410–430.

nations with differing economies. The underlying principle is that each person has an equal prima facie claim to a share of the total available resources, but departures from this initial standard could be justified (analogously to the operation of the difference principle) if the resulting inequalities were to the greatest benefit of those least advantaged by the inequality (cf. 151). In any event, the resource redistribution principle would function in international society as the difference principle functions in domestic society. It provides assurance to resource-poor nations that their adverse fate will not prevent them from realizing economic conditions sufficient to support just social institutions and to protect human rights guaranteed by the principles for individuals. In the absence of this assurance, these nations might resort to war as a means of securing the resources necessary to establish domestic justice, and it is not obvious that wars fought for this purpose would be unjust.[9]

Before turning to other issues, I must note two complications of which I cannot give a fully satisfactory account. The international original position parties are prevented by the veil of ignorance from knowing their generation; they would be concerned to minimize the risk that, when the veil is lifted, they might find themselves living in a world where resource supplies have been largely depleted. Thus, part of the resource redistribution principle would set some standard for conservation against this possibility. The difficulties in formulating a standard of conservation are at least as formidable as those of defining the "just savings rate" in Rawls' discussion of justifiable rates of capital accumulation. I shall not pursue them here, except to point

9. On this account, United Nations General Assembly Resolution 1803 (XVII), which purports to establish "permanent sovereignty over natural resources," would be prima facie unjust. However, there are important mitigating factors. This resolution, as the text and the debates make clear, was adopted to defend developing nations against resource exploitation by foreign-owned businesses, and to underwrite a national right of expropriation (with compensation) of foreign-owned mining and processing facilities in some circumstances. While the "permanent sovereignty" doctrine may be extreme, sovereignty-for-the-time-being might not be, if it can be shown (as I think it can) that resource-consuming nations have taken more than their fair share without returning adequate compensation. United Nations General Assembly, *Official Records: Seventeenth Session*, Supp. No. 17 (A/5217) (New York, 1963), pp. 15–16.

out that some provision for conservation as a matter of justice to future generations would be necessary (cf. 284–293).

The other complication concerns the definition of "natural resources." To what extent is food to be considered a resource? Social factors enter into the production of food in a way that they do not in the extraction of raw resources, so it may be that no plausible resource principle would require redistribution of food. A nation might claim that it deserves its abundant food supplies because of its large investments in agriculture or the high productivity of its farmers. On the other hand, arable land is a precondition of food production and a nation's supply of good land seems to be as morally arbitrary as its supply of, say, oil.[10] A further complication is that arable land, unlike iron ore or oil, cannot be physically redistributed to those nations with insufficient land, while food grown on the land is easily transportable. These dilemmas might be resolved by requiring redistribution of a portion of a country's food production depending on the ratio of its arable land to its total production; but the calculations involved would be complex and probably controversial. In the absence of a broader agreement to regard international society as a unified scheme of social cooperation, formulation of an acceptable food redistribution rule might prove impossible.

In failing to recognize resource problems, Rawls follows other writers who have extended the social contract idea to international relations.[11] Perhaps this is because they have attributed a greater symmetry to the domestic and international contracts than is in fact appropriate. Resource problems do not arise as distinct questions in the domestic case because their distribution and conservation are implicitly covered by the difference principle and the just savings principle. When the scope of social cooperation is coextensive with the territorial boundaries of a society, it is unnecessary to distinguish natural and social contributions to the society's level of well-being.

10. This statement needs qualification. After a certain point in economic development, a society could make good much of its apparently nonarable land, e.g. by clearing and draining or irrigating. So we ought not regard the total amount of arable land as fixed in the same sense as the total of other resources like oil. This was pointed out to me by Huntington Terrell.

11. Two classical examples are Pufendorf and Wolff. See Walter Schiffer, *The Legal Community of Mankind* (New York, 1954), pp. 49–79.

But when justice is considered internationally, we must face the likelihood of moral claims being pressed by members of the various social schemes which are arbitrarily placed with respect to the natural distribution of resources. My suggestion of a resource redistribution principle recognizes the fundamental character of these claims viewed from the perspective of the parties' interests in securing fair conditions for the development of their respective schemes.

III

Everything that I have said so far is consistent with the assumption that nations are self-sufficient cooperative schemes. However, there are strong empirical reasons for thinking that this assumption is no longer valid. As Kant notes in the concluding pages of *The Metaphysical Elements of Justice*, international economic cooperation creates a new basis for international morality.[12]

The main features of contemporary international interdependence relevant to questions of justice are the result of the progressive removal of restrictions on international trade and investment. Capital surpluses are no longer confined to reinvestment in the societies where they are produced, but instead are reinvested wherever conditions promise the highest yield without unacceptable risks. It is well known, for example, that large American corporations have systematically transferred significant portions of their capitalization to European, Latin American, and East Asian societies where labor costs are lower, markets are better, and profits are higher. A related development is the rise of an international division of labor whereby products are manufactured in areas having cheap, unorganized labor and are marketed in more affluent areas. Because multinational businesses, rather than the producing countries themselves, play the leading role in setting prices and wages, the international division of labor results in a system of world trade in which value created in one society (usually poor) is used to benefit members of other societies (usually rich).[13] It is also important to note that the world economy

12. Trans. John Ladd (Indianapolis, 1965), pp. 125ff.
13. Cf. Richard J. Barnet and Ronald E. Müller, *Global Reach* (New York, 1975), chaps. 2, 6, and passim. See also Stephen Hymer, "The Multinational Corporation and the Law of Uneven Development," in *Economics and World Order*, ed. J.N. Bhagwati (New York, 1972), pp. 113–141.

has evolved its own financial and monetary institutions that set exchange rates, regulate the money supply, influence capital flows, and enforce rules of international economic conduct.

The system of interdependence imposes burdens on poor and economically weak countries that they cannot practically avoid. Industrial economies have become reliant on raw materials that can only be obtained in sufficient quantities from developing countries. In the present structure of world prices, poor countries are often forced by adverse balances of payments to sell resources to more wealthy countries when those resources could be more efficiently used to promote development of the poor countries' domestic economies.[14] Also, private foreign investment imposes on poor countries patterns of political and economic development that may not be optimal from the point of view of the poor countries themselves. Participation in the global economy on the only terms available involves a loss of political autonomy.[15] Third, the global monetary system allows disturbances (e.g. price inflation) in some national economies to be exported to others that may be less able to cope with their potentially disastrous effects.[16]

Economic interdependence, then, involves a pattern of relationships which are largely nonvoluntary from the point of view of the worse-off participants, and which produce benefits for some while imposing burdens on others. These facts, by now part of the conventional wisdom of international relations, describe a world in which national boundaries can no longer be regarded as the outer limits of social cooperation. Note that this conclusion does not require that national societies should have become entirely superfluous or that the global economy should be completely integrated.[17] It is enough, for setting

14. Suzanne Bodenheimer gives an account of the role of foreign investment in exploiting the resources of Latin American countries in "Dependency and Imperialism: The Roots of Latin American Underdevelopment," *Politics and Society* 1 (1971): 327–357.

15. Peter B. Evans, "National Autonomy and Economic Development," in *Transnational Relations and World Politics*, ed. Robert O. Keohane and Joseph S. Nye (Cambridge, Mass., 1972), pp. 325–342.

16. See Richard N. Cooper, "Economic Interdependence and Foreign Policy in the Seventies," *World Politics* 24, no. 2 (January 1972): 159–181.

17. This conclusion would hold even if it were true that wealthy nations such as the United States continue to be economically self-sufficient, as Kenneth

the limits of cooperative schemes, that some societies are able to increase their level of well-being via global trade and investment while others with whom they have economic relations continue to exist at low levels of development.[18]

In view of these empirical considerations, Rawls' passing concern for the law of nations seems to miss the point of international justice altogether. In an interdependent world, confining principles of social justice to national societies has the effect of taxing poor nations so that others may benefit from living in "just" regimes. The two principles, so construed, might justify a wealthy nation's denying aid to needy peoples if the aid could be used domestically to promote a more nearly just regime. If the self-sufficiency assumption were empirically acceptable, such a result might be plausible, if controversial on other

---

Waltz has (mistakenly, I think) argued. A nation might be self-sufficient in the sense that its income from trade is marginal compared with total national income, and yet still participate in economic relations with less developed countries which impose great burdens on the latter. (See fn. 18, below.) To refute the claim I make in the text, it would be necessary to show that all, or almost all, nations are self-sufficient in the sense given above. This, plainly, is not the case. Waltz argues his view in "The Myth of National Interdependence," *The International Corporation*, ed. Charles P. Kindleberger (Cambridge, Mass., 1970), pp. 205–226; he is effectively refuted by Richard Cooper, "Economic Interdependence . . ." and Edward L. Morse, "Transnational Economic Processes," in *Transnational Relations and World Politics*, pp. 23–47.

18. The situation is probably worse than this. A more plausible view is that the poor countries' economic relations with the rich have actually worsened economic conditions among the poor. Global trade widens rather than narrows the rich-poor gap, and harms rather than aids the poor countries' efforts at economic development. See André Gunder Frank, "The Development of Underdevelopment," in James D. Cockcroft et al., *Dependence and Underdevelopment* (Garden City, N.Y., 1972), pp. 3–18. This raises the question of whether interdependence must actually benefit everyone involved to give rise to questions of justice. I think the answer is clearly negative; countries A and B are involved in social cooperation even if A (a rich country) could get along without B (a poor country), but instead exploits it, while B gets nothing out of its "cooperation" but exacerbated class divisions and Coca-Cola factories. If this is true, then Rawls' characterization of a society as "a cooperative venture for mutual advantage" (4) may be misleading, since everyone need not be advantaged by the cooperative scheme in order for requirements of justice to apply. It would be better to say that such requirements apply to systems of economic and social interaction which are nonvoluntary from the point of view of those least advantaged (or most disadvantaged) by them, and in which some benefit as a result of the relative or absolute sacrifices of others.

grounds.[19] But if participation in economic relations with the needy society has contributed to the wealth of the "nearly just" regime, its domestic "justice" seems to lose moral significance. In such situations, the principles of domestic "justice" will be genuine principles of justice only if they are consistent with principles of justice for the entire global scheme of social cooperation.

How should we formulate global principles? As several others have suggested, Rawls' own two principles, suitably reinterpreted, could themselves be applied globally.[20] The reasoning is as follows: if evidence of global economic and political interdependence shows the existence of a global scheme of social cooperation, we should not view national boundaries as having fundamental moral significance. Since boundaries are not coextensive with the scope of social cooperation, they do not mark the limits of social obligations. Thus, the parties to the original position cannot be assumed to know that they are members of a particular national society, choosing principles of justice primarily for that society. The veil of ignorance must extend to all matters of national citizenship. As Barry points out, a global interpretation of the original position is insensitive to the choice of principles.[21] Assuming that the arguments for the two principles are successful as set out in Rawls' book, there is no reason to think that the content of the principles would change as a result of enlarging the scope of the original position so that the principles would apply to the world as a whole.[22]

Rawls' two principles are a special case of the "general conception" of social justice.[23] The two principles hold when a cooperative scheme

19. For example, on utilitarian grounds. See Peter Singer, "Famine, Affluence, and Morality," *Philosophy & Public Affairs* 1, no. 3 (Spring 1972): 229–243.

20. For example, Barry, *The Liberal Theory of Justice*, pp. 128–133; and Scanlon, "Rawls' Theory of Justice," pp. 1066–1067.

21. Barry, *The Liberal Theory of Justice*, p. 129.

22. David Richards also argues that the principles apply globally. But he fails to notice the relationship between distributive justice and the morally relevant features of social cooperation on which its requirements rest. It is this relationship, and not the simpler, blanket assertion that the original position parties are ignorant of their nationalities, which explains why Rawlsian principles of social justice should be thought to apply globally. See David A.J. Richards, *A Theory of Reasons for Action* (Oxford, 1971), pp. 137–141.

23. The general conception reads as follows: "All social primary goods— liberty and opportunity, income and wealth, and the bases of self-respect—are to

has reached a level of material well-being at which everyone's basic needs can be met. The world, conceived as a single cooperative scheme, probably has not yet reached this threshold. Assuming that this is the case, on Rawls' reasoning, we should take the general conception, which does not differentiate the basic liberties from other primary goods, as the relevant standard for assessing global economic institutions. In conditions of underdevelopment or low-average levels of well-being, he argues, rational people might opt for a principle allowing rapid growth at the expense of some personal liberties, provided that the benefits of growth and the sacrifices of liberty are fairly shared and that the bases of self-respect relevant to such background conditions are not undermined (see 152, 298–303). The argument is that the prospects of the least advantaged would be less advanced, all things considered, by observing the lexical priority of liberty than by following the general conception of social justice.[24]

The globalization of the two principles (or of the general conception, if appropriate) has the consequence that principles of justice for national societies can no longer be viewed as ultimate. The basic structure of national societies continues to be governed by the two principles (or by the general conception), but their application is derivative and hence their requirements are not absolute. A possible view is that the global principles and the principles applied to national societies are to be satisfied in lexical order. But this view has the consequence, which one might find implausible, that national policies which maximize the welfare of the least-advantaged group within the society cannot be justified if other policies would be more optimal

---

be distributed equally unless an unequal distribution of any or all of these goods is to the advantage of the least favored" (303).

24. It must be noted that the question whether the general conception is more appropriate to developing societies turns heavily on empirical considerations. In particular, it needs to be shown that sacrifices of liberty, equally shared, really do promote more rapid advances in average levels of well-being than any other possible development strategy not involving such sacrifices. After considering the evidence, it might seem that an altogether different conception of justice is more appropriate to such societies than either of Rawls' conceptions. Perhaps, in the end, the general conception will turn out to be the best that can be advanced, but it would be interesting to canvass the alternatives. See Norman Bowie's attempt to do this in *Towards a New Theory of Distributive Justice* (Amherst, Mass., 1971), pp. 114ff.

from the point of view of the lesser advantaged elsewhere. Furthermore, no society could justify the additional costs involved in moving from the general to the special conception (for example, in reduced productivity) until every society had, at least, attained a level of well-being sufficient to sustain the general conception.

These features of the global interpretation of Rawlsian principles suggest that its implications are quite radical—considerably more so even than their application to national societies. While I am not now prepared to argue positively that the best theory of global justice consists simply of Rawls' principles interpreted globally, it seems to me that the most obvious objections to such a theory are not valid. In the remainder of this section, I consider what is perhaps the leading type of objection and suggest some difficulties in giving it theoretically compelling form.

Objections of the type I have in mind hold that considerations of social cooperation at the national level justify distributive claims capable of overriding the requirements of a global difference principle. Typically, members of a wealthy nation might claim that they deserve a larger share than that provided by a global difference principle because of their superior technology, economic organization, and efficiency.

Objections of this general sort might take several forms. First, it might be argued that even in an interdependent world, national society remains the primary locus of one's political identifications. If one is moved to contribute to aggregate social welfare at any level, this level is most likely to be the national level. Therefore, differential rates of national contribution to the global welfare ought to be rewarded proportionally. This is a plausible form of the objection; the problem is that, in this form, it may not be an objection at all. The difference principle itself recognizes the probability that differential rates of reward may be needed as incentives for contribution; it requires only that distributive inequalities which arise in such a system be to the greatest benefit of the world's least-advantaged group. To the extent that incentives of the kind demanded by this version of the objection actually do raise the economic expectations of the least advantaged without harming them in other ways, they would not be inconsistent with the difference principle.

Such objections count against a global difference principle only if they hold that a relatively wealthy nation could claim more than its share under the difference principle. That is, the objection must hold that some distributive inequalities are justified even though they are not to the greatest benefit of the world's least-advantaged group. How could such claims be justified? One justification is on grounds of personal merit, appealing to the intuition that value created by someone's unaided labor is properly his, assuming that the initial distribution was just.[25] This sort of argument yields an extreme form of the objection. It holds that a nation is entitled to its relative wealth because each of its citizens has complied with the relevant rules of justice in acquiring raw materials and transforming them into products of value. These rules might require, respectively, that an equitable resource redistribution principle has been implemented and that no one's rights have been violated (for example, by imperial plunder) in the process of acquisition and production leading to a nation's current economic position. (Note that my arguments for a resource principle are not touched by this sort of objection and would impose some global distributive obligations even if the personal merit view were correct in ruling out broader global principles.)

This interpretation of the objection is strictly analogous to the conception of distributive justice which Rawls calls the "system of natural liberty." He objects to such views that they allow people to compete for available positions on the basis of their talents, making no attempt to compensate for deprivations that some suffer due to natural chance and social contingency. These things, as I have said, are held to be morally arbitrary and hence unacceptable as standards for distribution (cf. 66–72). I shall not rehearse this argument further here. But two things should be noted. First, the argument seems even more plausible from the global point of view since the disparity of possible starting points in world society is so much greater. The balance between "arbitrary" and "personal" contributions to my present well-being seems decisively tipped toward the "arbitrary" ones by the realization that, no matter what my talents, education, life goals, etc., I would have been virtually precluded from attaining my present level

25. This, roughly, is Robert Nozick's view in *Anarchy, State, and Utopia* (New York, 1974), chap. 7.

of well-being if I had been born in a less developed society. Second, if Rawls' counterargument counts against natural liberty views in the domestic case, then it defeats the objection to a global difference principle as well. A nation cannot base its claim to a larger distributive share than that warranted by the difference principle on factors which are morally arbitrary.

A third, and probably the most plausible, form of this objection holds that a wealthy nation may retain more than its share under a global difference principle, provided that some compensation for the benefits of global social cooperation is paid to less fortunate nations, and that the amount retained by the producing nation is used to promote domestic justice, for example, by increasing the prospects of the nation's own least favored group. The underlying intuition is that citizens owe some sort of special obligation to the less fortunate members of their own society that is capable of overriding their general obligation to improve the prospects of lesser advantaged groups elsewhere. This intuition is distinct from the intuition in the personal desert case, for it does not refer to any putative individual right to the value created by one's labor. Instead, we are concerned here with supposedly conflicting rights and obligations that arise from membership in overlapping schemes of social cooperation, one embedded in the other.

An argument along these lines needs an account of how obligations to the sectional association arise. One might say that the greater degree or extent of social cooperation in national societies (compared with that in international society) underwrites stronger intranational principles of justice. To see this objection in its strongest form, imagine a world of two self-sufficient and internally just societies, A and B. Assume that this world satisfies the appropriate resource redistribution principle. Imagine also that the least-advantaged representative person in society A is considerably better off than his counterpart in society B. While the members of A may owe duties of mutual aid to the members of B, it is clear that they do not have parallel duties of justice, because the two societies, being individually self-sufficient, do not share membership in a cooperative scheme. Now suppose that the walls of self-sufficiency are breached very slightly; A trades its apples for *B*'s pears. Does this mean that the difference principle suddenly applies to the world which comprises *A* and *B*, requiring *A* to share all of its wealth with *B*, even though almost all of its wealth is attributable to economic interaction within *A*? It seems not; one might say that an international difference principle can only command redistribution of the benefits derived from international social cooperation or economic interaction. It cannot touch the benefits of domestic cooperation.

It may be that some such objection will turn out to produce modifications on a global difference principle. But there are reasons for doubting this. Roughly, it seems that there is a threshold of interdependence above which distributive requirements such as a global difference principle are valid, but below which significantly weaker principles hold. I cannot give a systematic account of this view here, but perhaps some intuitive considerations will demonstrate its force.

Consider another hypothetical case. Suppose that, *within* a society, there are closely-knit local regions with higher levels of internal cooperation than the level of cooperation in society as a whole. Certainly there are many such regions within a society such as the United States. The argument rehearsed above, applied to closely-knit localities within national societies, would seem to give members of the localities special claims on portions of their wealth. This seems implausible, especially since such closely-knit enclaves might well turn out to contain disproportionate numbers of the society's most advantaged classes. Why does this conclusion seem less plausible than that in the apples and pears case? It seems to me that the answer has to do with the fact that the apples and pears case looks like a case of voluntary, free-market bargaining that has only a marginal effect on the welfare of the members of each society, whereas we assume in the intranational case that there is a nonvoluntary society-wide system of economic institutions which defines starting positions and assigns economic rights and duties. It is these institutions—what Rawls calls "the basic structure" (7–11)—that stand in need of justification, because, by defining the terms of cooperation, they have such deep and pervasive effects on the welfare of people to whom they apply regardless of consent.

The apples and pears case, of course, is hardly a faithful model of the contemporary world economy. Suppose that we add to the story to make it resemble the real world more closely. As my review of the current situation (above, pp. 373–375) makes clear, we would have to add just those features of the contemporary world economy that find their domestic analogues in the basic structure to which principles of justice apply. As the web of transactions grows more complex, the resulting structure of economic and political institutions acquires great influence over the welfare of the participants, regardless of the extent to which any particular one makes use of the institutions. These features make the real world situation seem more like the case of subnational, closely-knit regions.

These considerations suggest that the amount of social and economic interaction in a cooperative scheme does not provide a straightforward index of the strength of the distributive principle appropriate to it. The existence of a powerful, nonvoluntary institutional structure, and its pervasive effects on the welfare of the cooperators, seems to provide a better indication of the strength of the appropriate distributive requirements. This sort of consideration would not necessarily support a global difference principle in the apples and pears case; but it does explain why, above a threshold measure of social cooperation, the full force of the difference principle may come into play despite regional variations in the amount of cooperation.[26]

Proponents of this objection to a global difference principle might have one last resort. They might appeal to noneconomic features of national societies to justify the special obligations that citizens owe to the less fortunate members of their own societies. On this basis, they could claim that the difference principle applies to national societies despite regional variations in cooperation but not to international society. Probably the plausibility of this sort of argument will depend on the degree to which it psychologizes the ties that bind

26. I do not claim to have resolved the problem which underlies this objection, although I believe that my remarks point in the right direction. It should be noticed, however, that what is at issue here is really a general problem for any theory which addresses itself to institutional structures rather than to particular transactions. One can always ask why institutional requirements should apply in full force to persons who make minimal use of the institutions they find themselves in. This point emerged from discussions I have had with Thomas Scanlon.

the members of social institutions.[27] There are problems, however. First, it needs to be shown that psychological ties such as national loyalty are of sufficient moral importance to balance the international economic ties that underwrite a global difference principle. Second, even if this could be persuasively argued, any account of how institutional obligations arise that is sufficiently psychological to make plausible a general conflict of global and sectional loyalties will probably be too psychological to apply to the large modern state (cf. 477).

Perhaps this line of objection can be made good in some way other than those canvassed here. If this could be done, it would not follow that there are no global distributive obligations but only that some portion of a nation's gross product would be exempt from the requirements of the global standard provided that it were used domestically in appropriate ways. The question would not be whether there are global distributive obligations founded on justice, but rather to what extent considerations relevant to the special features of cooperation within national societies modify the egalitarian tendencies of the global standard.

IV

We have now reached two main conclusions. First, assuming national self-sufficiency, Rawls' derivation of the principles of justice for the law of nations is correct but incomplete. He importantly neglects resource redistribution, a subject that would surely be on the minds of the parties to the international original position. But second, the self-sufficiency assumption, upon which Rawls' entire consideration of the law of nations rests, is not justified by the facts of contemporary international relations. The state-centered image of the world has lost its normative relevance because of the rise of global economic interdependence. Hence, principles of distributive justice must apply in the first instance to the world as a whole, then derivatively to nation-states. The appropriate global principle is probably something like Rawls' general conception of justice, perhaps modified by some provision for intranational redistribution in rela-

27. For a suggestive account of a similar problem, see Michael Walzer, "The Obligation to Disobey," *Obligations: Essays on Disobedience, War, and Citizenship* (Cambridge, Mass., 1970), pp. 3–23.

tively wealthy states once a threshold level of international redistributive obligations has been met. Rawls' two principles become more relevant as global distributive inequalities are reduced and a higher average level of well-being is attained. In conclusion, I would like to consider the implications of this ideal theory for international politics and global change in the nonideal world. In what respects does this interpretation of the social contract doctrine shed light on problems of world order change?

We might begin by asking, in general, what relevance social ideals have for politics in the real world. Their most obvious function is to describe a goal toward which efforts at political change should aim. In Rawls' theory, a very important natural duty is the natural duty of justice, which "requires us to support and to comply with just institutions that exist and . . . constrains us to further just arrangements not yet established, at least if this can be done without too much cost to ourselves" (115). By supplying a description of the nature and aims of a just world order, ideal theory "provides . . . the only basis for the systematic grasp of these more pressing problems" (9). Ideal theory, then, supplies a set of criteria for the formulation and criticism of strategies of political action in the nonideal world, at least when the consequences of political action can be predicted with sufficient confidence to establish their relationship to the social ideal. Clearly, this task would not be easy, given the complexities of social change and the uncertainties of prediction in political affairs. There is the additional complication that social change is often wrongly conceived as a progressive approximation of actual institutions to ideal prescriptions in which people's welfare steadily improves. An adequate social theory must avoid the pitfalls of a false incrementalism as well as what economists call the problem of the second best.[28] But a coherent social ideal is a necessary condition of any attempt to conquer these difficulties.

Ideal justice, in other words, comes into nonideal politics by way of the natural duty to secure just institutions where none presently exist. The moral problem posed by distinguishing ideal from nonideal theory is that, in the nonideal world, the natural duty of justice is like-

28. On the problem of the second best, see Brian Barry, *Political Argument* (London, 1965), pp. 261–262.

ly to conflict with other natural duties, while the theory provides no mechanism for resolving such conflicts. For example, it is possible that a political decision which is likely to make institutions more just is equally likely to involve violations of other natural duties, such as the duty of mutual aid or the duty not to harm the innocent. Perhaps reforming some unjust institution will require us to disappoint legitimate expectations formed under the old order. The principles of natural duty in the nonideal world are relatively unsystematic, and we have no way of knowing which should win out in case of conflict. Rawls recognizes the inevitability of irresolvable conflicts in some situations (303), but, as Feinberg has suggested, he underestimates the role that an intuitive balancing of conflicting duties must play in nonideal circumstances.[29] Rawls says that problems of political change in radically unjust situations must rely on a utilitarian calculation of costs and benefits (352–353). If this is true, then political change in conditions of great injustice marks one kind of limit of the contract doctrine, for in these cases the principles of justice collapse into utilitarianism. It seems to me, however, that this conclusion is too broad. At least in some cases of global justice, nonideal theory, while teleological, is not utilitarian. I shall try to show this briefly with respect to questions of food and development aid, the principle of nonintervention, and the obligation to participate in war on behalf of a nation-state.

The duty to secure just institutions where none exist endows certain political claims made in the nonideal world with a moral seriousness which does not derive merely from the obligations that bind people regardless of the existence of cooperative ties. When the contract doctrine is interpreted globally, the claims of the less advantaged in today's nonideal world—claims principally for food aid, development assistance, and world monetary and trade reform—rest on principles of global justice as well as on the weaker duty of mutual aid. Those who are in a position to respond to these claims, despite the absence of effective global political mechanisms, must take account of the stronger reasons provided by the principles of justice in weighing their response. Furthermore, by interpreting the principles

29. Joel Feinberg, "Duty and Obligation in the Nonideal World," *Journal of Philosophy* 70 (10 May 1973): 263–275.

globally, we remove a major source of justifying reasons for not responding more fully to such claims. These reasons derive from statist concerns, for example, a supposed right to reinvest domestic surpluses in national societies that are already relatively favored from a global point of view. The natural duties still require us to help members of our own society who are in need, and a wealthy nation would be justified on this account in using some of its resources to support domestic welfare programs. What cannot be argued is that a wealthy nation's general right to retain its domestic product always overrides its obligation to advance the welfare of lesser-advantaged groups elsewhere.

An ideal theory of global justice has implications for traditional doctrines of international law as well. Consider, as a representative example, the rule of nonintervention. It is often remarked that this rule, which is prominently displayed in a number of recent authoritative documents of international law, seems inconsistent with the international community's growing rhetorical commitment to the protection of human rights, which is also prominently displayed in many of the same documents.[30] The conflict can be illustrated with reference to South Africa: the doctrine of nonintervention seems to prevent other states from giving aid to local insurgent forces explicitly committed to attaining recognition of basic human rights for the vast bulk of the South African population. Ordinarily, such conflicts are regarded as simple matters of utilitarian balancing, but the global interpretation of social contract theory shows that more can be said. The global interpretation introduces an asymmetry into the justification of the rules of international law. These rules impose different obligations depending on whether their observance in particular cases would contribute to or detract from a movement toward more just institutions.

The nonintervention rule is to be interpreted in this light. When it would demonstrably operate to advance or protect just arrange-

30. For example, the U. N. Charter, articles 2(4) and 1(3), and article 1 of the "Declaration of Principles of International Cooperation . . . ," approved by the General Assembly on 24 October 1970. Both are reprinted in *Basic Documents in International Law*, ed. Ian Brownlie, 2nd ed. (Oxford, 1972), pp. 1–31 and 32–40.

ments, it furnishes a strong reason not to intervene. In the absence of compelling reasons to the contrary, it imposes a duty to comply. This is typically the case when intervention would interfere with a people's right of self-determination, a right which protects the fair exercise of political liberty. Thus, American intervention in Allende's Chile certainly violated a basic requirement of global justice. But sometimes, as in South Africa, observing the nonintervention rule cannot be justified in this way. Rather than resting on considerations of justice, which give strong reasons for compliance, it rests on considerations of natural duty—such as protection of the innocent against harms that might be suffered if large-scale military intervention occurred—and of international stability. These are certainly not negligible reasons for nonintervention, but, from the standpoint of global justice, they are weaker reasons than those provided by global justice itself. Obviously, peaceful resolution of cases such as that of South Africa is to be preferred. But when this goal cannot be attained, or when insurgent forces fighting for human rights request foreign assistance, intervention cannot be opposed as a matter of justice (as it could be on the traditional interpretation of this international rule, preserved in Rawls' own brief discussion), for its effect would be to help secure rights, including the right of self-determination, protected by the global principles. Again, in the absence of compelling reasons to the contrary (of which, certainly, a great number can be imagined), there might be an international duty to intervene in support of insurgent forces. I say that there may be an *international* duty because it seems clear that unilateral intervention can almost always be successfully opposed on grounds of international stability. But a decision by the international community to enforce principles of justice would be less susceptible to this sort of objection. Here I note what has too often been overlooked (except, perhaps, by American multinationals), that intervention in another country's internal affairs can take many nonviolent forms, including economic blockades, nonmilitary aid to insurgent forces, diplomatic pressure, etc. While such forms of intervention obviously carry no guarantee of success, it is fair to say that their potential effectiveness has been widely underestimated.[31]

31. See Gene Sharp, *The Politics of Non-violent Action* (Boston, 1973).

Finally, what are the implications of global justice for participation in a nation's military forces? From what I have said thus far, it should be clear that the global interpretation supplies reasons for acting or not acting which are capable of overriding the reasons provided by traditional rules of international law. These reasons are also capable of overriding the rule that demands compliance with internally just domestic regimes. One important consequence is that conscientious refusal to participate in a nation's armed forces would have far broader possible justifications than on the account given in Rawls (cf. 377–382), assuming for the moment that, given the great destructiveness of modern weapons and war strategies, participation in national armed forces could ever be justified at all. For instance, in some circumstances, a war of self-defense fought by an affluent nation against a poorer nation pressing legitimate claims under the global principles (for example, for increased food aid) might be unjustifiable, giving rise to a justified refusal to participate in the affluent nation's armed forces.

These three examples show that the contract doctrine, despite limitations noted here, sheds light on the distinctive normative problems of the shift from statist to global images of world order. The extension of economic and cultural relationships beyond national borders has often been thought to undermine the moral legitimacy of the state; the extension of the contract doctrine gives a systematic account of why this is so, and of its consequences for problems of justice in the nonideal world, by emphasizing the role of social cooperation as the foundation of just social arrangements. When, as now, national boundaries do not set off discrete, self-sufficient societies, we may not regard them as morally decisive features of the earth's social geography. For purposes of moral choice, we must, instead, regard the world from the perspective of an original position from which matters of national citizenship are excluded by an extended veil of ignorance.

I do not believe that Rawls' failure to take account of these questions marks a pivotal weakness of his theory; on the contrary, the theory provides a way of determining the consequences of changing empirical circumstances (such as the assumption of national self-sufficiency) for the concept of justice. The global interpretation is the result of recognizing an important empirical change in the structure of world political and social life. In this way the theory allows us to apply generalizations derived from our considered judgments regarding familiar situations to situations which are new and which demand that we form intelligent moral views and act on them when action is possible and appropriate. This is no small achievement for a moral theory. Some might think, however, that our moral intuitions are too weak or unreliable to support such an extension of the theory. I doubt that this is true; rather, it often seems to be a convenient way to beg off from unpleasant moral requirements. But if I am wrong about this—if we cannot expect moral theory to provide a firm guide for action in new situations—one might wonder whether moral theory has any practical point at all.

THOMAS W. POGGE   An Egalitarian Law of Peoples

Expanding on a brief sketch of over twenty years ago, Rawls has recently offered a more detailed extension of his theory of justice to the international domain.[1] Like that first sketch, the "law of peoples" he now proposes has no egalitarian distributive component. In my own extension of Rawls's frame-work, I had argued that a criterion of global justice must be sensitive to international social and economic inequalities.[2] Here I take another look at this issue in light of Rawls's new and more elaborate deliberations about it.

There are three components of Rawls's conception of domestic justice that, in his view (LP, p. 51), qualify it for the predicate "egalitarian":

(1) His first principle of justice requires that institutions maintain the fair value of the political liberties, so that persons similarly motivated and endowed have, irrespective of their economic and social class, roughly equal chances to gain political office and to influence the political decisions that shape their lives (cf. *TJ*, p. 225).

(2) His second principle of justice requires that institutions maintain

Work on this paper was supported by a Laurance S. Rockefeller fellowship at the Princeton University Center for Human Values. Written for a conference on "the Ethics of Nationalism" at the University of Illinois at Urbana-Champaign, it was also presented to audiences at Princeton, Harvard, New York, Stanford, and Oxford Universities. I am grateful for the barrage of forceful criticisms I have received—in particular from Alyssa Bernstein, Brian Barry, Lea Brilmayer, Anthony Coady, John Cooper, Roger Crisp, Peter de Marneffe, Alan Houston, Frances Kamm, Elizabeth Kiss, Christine Korsgaard, Ling Tong, Stuart White, and the editors of *Philosophy & Public Affairs*.

1. John Rawls, "The Law of Peoples," in *On Human Rights*, ed. Stephen Shute and Susan Hurley (New York: Basic Books, 1993), pp. 41–82, 220–30. Page numbers preceded by "LP" refer to this lecture. The earlier sketch is on pp. 378f of *A Theory of Justice* (Cambridge, Mass.: Harvard University Press, 1971); henceforth *TJ*.

2. See Chapter 6 of *Realizing Rawls* (Ithaca: Cornell University Press 1989); henceforth *RR*.

fair equality of opportunity, so that equally talented and motivated persons have roughly equal chances to obtain a good education and professional position irrespective of their initial social class (cp. *TJ*, pp. 73, 301).

(3) His second principle also requires that, insofar as they generate social or economic inequalities, social institutions must be designed to the maximum benefit of those at the bottom of these inequalities (the difference principle—cf. *TJ*, pp. 76f).

Each of these egalitarian components furnishes separate grounds on which the current basic structure of the United States can be criticized for producing excessive inequalities.

Analogous points can be made about our current world order:

(1) It fails to give members of different peoples roughly equal chances to influence the transnational political decisions that shape their lives.

(2) It fails to give equally talented and motivated persons roughly equal chances to obtain a good education and professional position irrespective of the society into which they were born.

(3) It also generates international social and economic inequalities that are not to the maximum benefit of the world's worst-off persons.

These observations are certainly true. The question is: Do they show faults in the existing global order?

Rawls's law of peoples contains no egalitarian distributive principle of any sort; and he seems then to be committed to the view that none of the three analogous criticisms is valid, even though he explicitly attacks only the analogue to his third egalitarian concern: the proposal of a global difference principle. My own view still is that all three of the analogous egalitarian concerns are valid in a world characterized by the significant political and economic interdependencies that exist today and will in all likelihood persist into the indefinite future. Here I will, however, defend against Rawls a much weaker claim: A plausible conception of global justice must be sensitive to international social and economic inequalities.

My focus on this one disagreement should not obscure the fact that I agree with much in this Amnesty Lecture—both substantively and methodologically. Substantively, I agree with his view that a just world order can contain societies governed by a conception of justice that differs from his own political liberalism by being nonpolitical, nonliberal, or both (*LP*, pp. 42f, 46); and that a main demand to make upon how their institutions work domestically is that they secure human rights (LP, pp. 61–63, 68–71). Methodologically, I agree that it is too early to tell how his idea of the original position—initially devised to deal with a closed, self-contained society (*TJ*, pp. 4, 8, 457)—should best be adapted to the complexities of our interdependent world (LP, pp. 50, 65f). Various possibilities should be worked out in some detail. One main strategy is Rawls's: Apply the two principles to the basic structure of a national society, and then reconvene the parties for a second session to deal with the relations among such societies. Another main strategy is to start with a global original position that deals with the world at large, even asking, as Rawls puts it (somewhat incredulously?), "whether, and in what form, there should be states, or peoples, at all" (LP, p. 50). Variants of this second strategy have been entertained by David Richards, Thomas Scanlon, Brian Barry, Charles Beitz, and myself. I can leave aside this second strategy here, because international egalitarian concerns can easily be accommodated within the first strategy; as we shall see, Rawls simply decides against doing so.

My focus on one disagreement should also not obscure the fact that there are others. Two of these are relevant here. First, I do not believe that the notion of "a people" is clear enough and significant enough in the human world to play the conceptual role and to have the moral significance that Rawls assigns to it. In many parts of the globe, official borders do not correlate with the main characteristics that are normally held to identify a people or a nation—such as a common ethnicity, language, culture, history, tradition. Moreover, whether some group does or does not constitute a people would seem, in important ways, to be a matter of more-or-less rather than either-or. I have suggested that these complexities might be better accommodated by a multilayered institutional scheme in which the powers of sovereignty are vertically dispersed rather than heavily concentrated on the single level of states.[3] But I will set aside this topic as well. Let us assume that there really is a clear-cut distinction between peoples and other kinds of groupings, that every person belongs to exactly one people, and that each national territory really does, nearly enough, contain all and only the members of a single people. In this highly idealized case, egalitarian concerns would seem to be least pressing. Hence, if I can make them plausible for this case, they should be plausible for more realistic scenarios as well.

3. "Cosmopolitanism and Sovereignty," *Ethics* 103 (1992):48–75.

Second, I do not believe that Rawls has an adequate response to the historical arbitrariness of national borders—to the fact that most borders have come about through violence and coercion. He writes:

> From the fact that boundaries are historically arbitrary it does not follow that their role in the law of peoples cannot be justified. To wit: that the boundaries between the several states of the United States are historically arbitrary does not argue to the elimination of our federal system, one way or the other. To fix on their arbitrariness is to fix on the wrong thing. The right question concerns the political values served by the several states in a federal system as compared with the values served by a central system. The answer is given by states' function and role: by the political values they serve as subunits, and whether their boundaries can be, or need to be, redrawn, and much else. (LP, p. 223 n16)

Let us suppose that the mere fact of historical arbitrariness is indeed no argument against the status quo, that a forwardlooking justification suffices. What such a justification should be able to justify is threefold: that there should be boundaries at all, that they should be where they are now, and that they should have the institutional significance they currently have. I am not interested in the first two issues: Let there be national borders and let them be just where they are today. The issue I am raising is the third: How can Rawls justify the enormous distributional significance national borders now have, and in a Rawlsian ideal world would continue to have, for determining the life prospects of persons born into different states? How can he justify that boundaries are, and would continue to be, associated with ownership of, full control over, and exclusive entitlement to all benefits from, land, natural resources, and capital stock? It is revealing that, in the midst of discussing national borders, Rawls switches to considering state borders within the U.S., which have virtually no distributional significance. It does not really matter whether one is born in Kansas or in Iowa, and so there is not much to justify, as it were. On the other hand, it matters a great deal whether one is born a Mexican or a U.S. citizen, and so we do need to justify to a Mexican why we should be entitled to life prospects that are so much superior to hers merely because we were born on the other side of some line—a difference that, on the face of it, is no less morally arbitrary than differences in sex, in skin color, or in the affluence of one's parents. Justifying this is more difficult when national borders are historically arbitrary or, to put it more descriptively, when the present distribution of national territories is indelibly tainted with past unjust conquest, genocide, colonialism, and enslavement. But let me set aside this difficulty as well and focus on moral rather than historical arbitrariness. Let us assume that peoples have come to be matched up with territories in the morally most benign way one can conceive.

My defense, against Rawls, of an egalitarian law of peoples labors then under a self-imposed triple handicap: I accept Rawls's stipulation that global justice is addressed in a second session of the original position, featuring representatives of peoples who take the nation state system as a given; I accept Rawls's fantasy that the world's population neatly divides into peoples cleanly separated by national borders; and I waive any support my egalitarian view could draw from the role that massive past crimes have played in the emergence of current national borders. I make these concessions strictly for the sake of the argument of Sections I–V and otherwise stand by my earlier contrary positions.

I. A GLOBAL RESOURCES TAX

Some of the arguments Rawls advances against incorporating an egalitarian component into the law of peoples are pragmatic, mainly having to do with inadequate administrative capabilities and the dangers of a world government. To make it easier for you to assess these worries, I want to put before you a reasonably clear and specific institutional proposal and thereby give our central disagreement a concrete institutional form. I lack the space, however, to develop and defend a complete criterion of global justice and to show what specific institutional arrangements would be favored by this criterion. I will therefore employ a little shortcut. I will make an institutional proposal that virtually any plausible egalitarian conception of global justice would judge to be at least a step in the right direction. Rawls's law of peoples, by contrast, would not call for such a step. It would permit the step among consenting peoples, but would not view it as required or suggested by justice.

When sketching how a property-owning democracy might satisfy the difference principle, Rawls entertains a proportional income or consumption tax with a fixed exemption. The tax rate and exempt amount are to be set so as maximally to benefit the lowest economic position in the present and future generations. Focusing on one such (as he says) instrument "frees us from having to consider the difference principle on every question of policy."[4]

I have proposed a similar instrument to control international inequality: a global resources tax, or GRT.[5] The basic idea is that, while each people owns and fully controls all resources within its national territory,[6] it must pay a tax on any resources it chooses to extract. The Saudi people, for example, would not be required to extract crude oil or to allow others to do so. But if they chose to do so nonetheless, they would be required to pay a proportional tax on any crude extracted, whether it be for their own use or for sale abroad. This tax could be extended, along the same lines, to reusable resources: to land used in agriculture and ranching, for example, and, especially, to air and water used for the discharging of pollutants.

The burdens of the GRT would not be borne by the owners of resources alone. The tax would lead to higher prices for crude oil, minerals, and so forth. Therefore, some of the GRT on oil would ultimately fall upon the Japanese (who have no oil of their own, but import a good bit), even while the tax would be actually paid by the peoples who own oil reserves and choose to extract them. This point significantly mitigates the concern that the GRT proposal might be arbitrarily biased against some rich peoples, the resource-rich, and in favor of others. This concern is further mitigated by the GRT's pollution component.

The GRT is then a tax on consumption. But it taxes different kinds of consumption differentially. The cost of gasoline will contain a much higher portion of GRT than the cost of a ticket to an art museum. The tax falls on goods and services roughly in proportion to their resource content: in proportion to how much value each takes from our planet. The GRT can therefore be motivated not only forwardlookingly, in consequentialist and contractualist terms, but also backwardlookingly: as a proviso on unilateral appropriation, which requires compensation to those excluded thereby. Nations (or persons) may appropriate and use resources, but humankind at large still retains a kind of minority stake, which, somewhat like pre-

4. John Rawls, "Justice as Fairness: Revisited, Revised, Recast," 1992, typescript, p. 136.
5. *RR*, pp. 256n18, 264f. See also "An Institutional Approach to Humanitarian Intervention," *Public Affairs Quarterly* 6 (1992):89–103, p. 96.
6. This accommodates Rawls's remark that "unless a definite agent is given responsibility for maintaining an asset and bears the loss of not doing so, that asset tends to deteriorate" (LP, p. 57).

ferred stock, confers no control but a share of the material benefits. In this picture, my proposal can be presented as a global resources dividend, which operates as a modern Lockean proviso. It differs from Locke's own proviso by giving up the vague and unwieldy[7] condition of "leaving enough and as good for others": One may use unlimited amounts, but one must share some of the economic benefit. It is nevertheless similar enough to the original so that even such notoriously antiegalitarian thinkers as Locke and Nozick might find it plausible.[8]

National governments would be responsible for paying the GRT, and, with each society free to raise the requisite funds in any way it likes, no new administrative capabilities would need to be developed. Since extraction and pollution activities are relatively easy to quantify, the assurance problem would be manageable and total collection costs could be negligible.

Proceeds from the GRT are to be used toward the emancipation of the present and future global poor: toward assuring that all have access to education, health care, means of production (land) and/or jobs to a sufficient extent to be able to meet their own basic needs with dignity and to represent their rights and interests effectively against the rest of humankind: compatriots and foreigners. In an ideal world of reasonably just and well-ordered societies, GRT payments could be made directly to the governments of the poorest societies, based on their per capita income (converted through purchasing power parities) and population size. These data are readily available and easy to monitor—reliable and comprehensive data are currently being collected by the United Nations, the World Bank, the IMF, and various other organizations.[9]

GRT payments would enable the governments of the poorer peoples to maintain lower tax rates, higher tax exemptions and/or higher domestic spending for education, health care, microloans, infrastructure, etc. than

7. Consider: Must we leave enough and as good for future generations? For how many? Are air and water pollution ruled out entirely because the air and water left behind is not as good?

8. Cf. John Locke, *Second Treatise*, §§27, 33; Robert Nozick, *Anarchy, State, and Utopia* (New York: Basic Books 1974), pp. 175–77 and Chapter 4.

9. One may think that domestic income distribution should be taken into account as well. Even if two states have the same per capita income, the poor in the one may still be much worse off than the poor in the other. The problem with taking account of this fact is that it may provide a perverse incentive to governments to neglect their domestic poor in order to receive larger GRT payments. This incentive is bad, because governments might act on it, and also because governments might, wrongly, be thought to act or be accused of acting on it (appearance and assurance problems).

would otherwise be possible. Insofar as they would actually do this, the whole GRT scheme would require no central bureaucracy and certainly nothing like a world government, as governments would simply transfer the GRT amounts to one another through some facilitating organization, such as the World Bank, perhaps, or the UN. The differences to traditional development aid are: Payments would be a matter of entitlement rather than charity and—there being no matching of "donors" and recipients— would not be conditional upon rendering political or economic favors to a donor or upon adopting a donor's favored political or economic institutions.[10] Acceptance of GRT payments would of course be voluntary: A just society may certainly shun greater affluence if it, democratically, chooses to do so.

In a nonideal world like ours, corrupt governments in the poorer states pose a significant problem. Such governments may be inclined, for example, to use GRT funds to underwrite indispensable services while diverting any domestic tax revenue saved to the rulers' personal use. A government that behaves in this way may be cut off from GRT funds.[11] In such cases it may still be possible to administer meaningful development programs through existing UN agencies (World Food Program, WHO, UNICEF, etc.) or through suitable nongovernmental organizations (Oxfam). If GRT funds cannot be used effectively to improve the position of the poor in a particular country, then there is no reason to spend them there. They should rather be spent where they can make more of a difference in reducing poverty and disadvantage.

There are then three possibilities with regard to any country that is poor enough in aggregate to be eligible for GRT funds: Its poorer citizens may benefit through their government, they may benefit from development programs run by some other agency, or they may not benefit at all. Mixtures are, of course, also possible. (A country might receive 60 percent of the GRT funds it is eligible for, one third of this through the government and two thirds of it through other channels.) How are these matters to be decided? And by whom? The decisions are to be made by the facilitating

10. For a detailed account of how the latter feature renders current aid highly inefficient, if not useless, see the cover story "Why Aid Is an Empty Promise," *The Economist* 331/7862 (May 7, 1994), pp. 13–14, 21–24.

11. For a contrary conception, see Brian Barry, "Humanity and Justice in Global Perspective," in NOMOS XXIV, *Ethics, Economics, and the Law*, ed. J. R. Pennock and J. W. Chapman (New York: New York Univ. Press, 1982), pp. 219–52. Barry holds that the governments of poor societies should receive funds regardless of their domestic policies.

organization, but pursuant to clear and straightforward general rules. These rules are to be designed, and possibly revised, by an international group of economists and international lawyers. Its task is to devise the rules so that the entire GRT scheme has the maximum possible positive impact on the world's poorest persons—the poorest quintile, say—in the long run. The qualification "in the long run" indicates that incentive effects must be taken into account. Governments and also the wealthier strata of a people stand to gain from GRT spending in various ways ("trickle-up") and therefore have an incentive to ensure that GRT funds are not cut off. The rules should be designed to take advantage of this incentive. They must make it clear to members of the political and economic elite of GRT-eligible countries that, if they want their society to receive GRT funds, they must cooperate in making these funds effective toward enhancing the opportunities and the standard of living of the domestic poor.[12]

Specifying how GRT funds should best be raised poses some complex problems, among them the following four: First, setting tax rates too high may significantly dampen economic activity—in extreme cases so much that revenues overall would decline. It must be noted, however, that the funds raised through the GRT scheme do not disappear: They are spent by, and for the benefit of, the global poor and thereby generate effective market demand that spurs economic activity. Second, imposing any GRT on land use for cultivation of basic commodities (grains, beans, cotton, etc.) might increase their prices and thereby have a deleterious effect on the position of the globally worst-off. Hence it may make sense to confine any GRT on land to land used in other ways (e.g. to raise cattle or to grow tobacco, coffee, cocoa, or flowers). Third, the setting of tax rates should also take into account the interests of the future globally worst-off. The GRT should target the extraction of nonrenewable resources liable to run out within a few decades in preference to that of resources of which we have an abundant supply; it should target the discharging of pollutants that will persist for centuries in preference to the discharging of pollutants that decay more quickly. Finally, while designing the GRT is inevitably difficult and complicated, the tax itself should be easy to understand and to apply. It should, for example, be based on resources and pollutants whose extraction or dis-

---

12. In some GRT-eligible countries there may well be factions of the ruling elite for whom these incentives would be outweighed by their interest in keeping the poor uneducated, impotent, and dependent. Still, the incentives will shift the balance of forces in the direction of reform.

charge is reasonably easy to monitor or estimate, in order to ensure that every people is paying its fair share and also to assure every people that this is so.

The general point behind these brief remarks is that GRT liabilities should be targeted so as to optimize their collateral effects. What is perhaps surprising is that these effects may on the whole be positive, on account of the GRT's considerable benefits for environmental protection and conservation. These benefits are hard to secure in a less concerted way because of familiar collective-action problems ("tragedy of the commons").

What about the overall magnitude of the GRT? In light of today's vast global social and economic inequalities, one may think that a massive GRT scheme would be necessary to support global background justice. But I do not think this is so. Current inequalities are the cumulative result of decades and centuries in which the more-developed peoples used their advantages in capital and knowledge to expand these advantages ever further. They show the power of long-term compounding rather than overwhelmingly powerful centrifugal tendencies of our global market system. Even a rather small GRT may then be sufficient continuously to balance these ordinary centrifugal tendencies of market systems enough to prevent the development of excessive inequalities and to maintain in equilibrium a rough global distributional profile that preserves global background justice.

I cannot here work through all the complexities involved in determining the appropriate magnitude of the GRT scheme. To achieve some concreteness nevertheless, let us, somewhat arbitrarily, settle for a GRT of up to 1 percent of world product—less than 1 percent if a smaller amount would better advance the interests of the globally worst-off in the long run. Almost any egalitarian conception of global justice would probably recognize this proposal as an improvement over the status quo. A 1 percent GRT would currently raise revenues of roughly $270 billion per annum. This amount is quite large relative to the total income of the world's poorest one billion persons and, if well targeted and effectively spent, would make a phenomenal difference to them even within a few years. On the other hand, the amount is rather small for the rest of us: not only less than the annual defense budget of the U.S. alone, but also a good bit less than the market price of the current annual crude oil production, which is in the neighborhood of $400 billion (ca. 60 million barrels per day at about $18 per barrel). Thus the entire revenue target could be raised by taxing a small number of resource uses—ones whose discouragement seems especially desirable for the sake of future generations. A \$2-per-barrel GRT on crude oil extraction, for example, would raise about one sixth of the overall revenue target—while increasing the price of petroleum products by about 5¢ a gallon. It would have some substitution effects, welcome in terms of conservation and environmental protection; and, if it had any dampening effect on overall economic activity at all, this effect would be quite slight.

Having tried to show that introducing a 1 percent GRT would be an instantly feasible and morally attractive institutional reform of the existing global order,[13] let me now focus on its plausibility as a piece of ideal theory. To do this, we append my GRT proposal to Rawls's law of peoples.[14] The resulting alternative to Rawls is not my considered position on global justice. Its point is rather to allow us to focus sharply on the topic of international inequality. Egalitarian concerns will be vindicated, if it can be shown that the amended law of peoples is morally more plausible than Rawls's original—and especially so, if this can be shown on Rawlsian grounds.

II. RAWLS'S POSITION ON INTERNATIONAL DISTRIBUTIVE JUSTICE

In his initial sketch, Rawls's brief discussion of international justice was characterized by a tension between three views:

(1) He speaks of the second session of the original position as featuring *persons* from the various societies who make a rational choice of principles so as best to protect their interests while "they know nothing about the particular circumstances of their own society, its power and strength in

13. This is a bit of an exaggeration: I have not yet given you any reason not to dismiss my GRT proposal as unfeasible in the political sense. This I hope to do in the final section.

14. Rawls characterizes this law of peoples by the following list of principles (LP, p. 55): "(1) Peoples (as organized by their government) are free and independent and their freedom and independence is to be respected by other peoples. (2) Peoples are equal and parties to their own agreements. (3) Peoples have the right of self-defense but no right to war. (4) Peoples are to observe a duty of nonintervention. (5) Peoples are to observe treaties and undertakings. (6) Peoples are to observe certain specified restrictions on the conduct of war (assumed to be in self-defense). (7) Peoples are to honor human rights." Though this list is not meant to be complete (ibid.), the complete list would not contain an egalitarian distributive principle (LP, pp. 75f). Throughout Rawls makes no attempt to show that representatives of peoples would, in his second session of the original position, adopt these principles. The presentation is far less rigorous than the one he had offered in support of his two principles of domestic justice. My response in this essay is then not so much a critique of Rawls as a detailed and, I hope, constructive invitation to defend his conclusions.

comparison with other nations, *nor do they know their place in their own society*" (*TJ*, p. 378, my emphasis). I called this reading R₁ (*RR*, pp. 242ff).

(2) On the same page, Rawls also speaks of this second session as featuring "representatives of *states* [who are] to make a rational choice to protect their interests" (*TJ*, p. 378, my emphasis). Here, "the national interest of a just state is defined by the principles of justice that have already been acknowledged. Therefore such a nation will aim above all to maintain and to preserve its just institutions and the conditions that make them possible" (*TJ*, p. 379). I called this reading R₂ (*RR*, pp. 243ff).

(3) Rawls also wanted to endorse the traditional (pre–World War II) principles of international law as outlined by James Brierly.

I have tried to show (*RR*, §21) that no two of these views are compatible.

Rawls has now fully resolved the tension by clearly and consistently endorsing the second view, R₂—without, however, offering any reasons for favoring it over R₁. He stipulates that the parties "are representatives of peoples" (LP, p. 48) and "subject to a veil of ignorance: They do not know, for example, the size of the territory, or the population, or the relative strength of the people whose fundamental interests they represent. Although they know that reasonably favorable conditions obtain that make democracy possible, they do not know the extent of their natural resources, or level of their economic development, or other such related information" (LP, p. 54).

And what are those fundamental interests of a people? As in his initial account of R₂, Rawls takes each people to have only one such fundamental interest: that its domestic institutions satisfy its conception of justice (LP, pp. 54, 64). And while the parties to the first session of the original position do not know the particular conceptions of the good of the persons they represent, Rawls assumes, without justifying the disanalogy, that each party to the second session does know what conception of domestic justice "her" people subscribes to. It would seem that the various delegates would then favor different versions of the law of peoples, each one especially hospitable to a particular conception of domestic justice.[15] Rawls claims, however, that within a certain range of conceptions of domestic justice the

---

15. I say that any global (session of the) original position features *delegates* rather than parties or representatives. This is my expression, not Rawls's. Its sole purpose is to make more perspicuous that the reference is to deliberators about global rather than domestic institutions.

interests of peoples regarding the law of peoples coincide: Delegates of peoples whose conception of domestic justice is either *liberal* or *hierarchical* would all favor exactly the same law of peoples (LP, p. 60). This is then the law of peoples that we, as members of a society with a liberal conception of justice, should endorse: It is hospitable to liberal regimes and to the more palatable nonliberal regimes as well. The regimes it does not accommodate are "outlaw regimes" of various sorts or else committed to an expansionist foreign policy (LP, pp. 72f). Rawls's law of peoples cannot be justified to them as being (behind the veil of ignorance) in their interest as well. But this fact cannot count against it from our point of view—which, after all, is the one to which we seek to give systematic expression.

Given this structure of his account, Rawls decides to run the second session twice: Once to show that delegates of peoples with any liberal conception of domestic justice would favor his law of peoples and then to show that delegates of peoples with any hierarchical conception of domestic justice would do so as well.[16] He does not actually perform either of these two runs in any detail, and I am quite unclear as to how the second is supposed to go.

In the next two sections, I shall focus exclusively on the liberal run, in which "the parties deliberate among available principles for the law of peoples by reference to the fundamental interests of democratic societies in accordance with, or as presupposed by, the liberal principles of domestic justice" (LP, p. 54). A *liberal* conception of justice is defined (LP, p. 51) as one that

—demands that certain rights, liberties, and opportunities be secure for all citizens

—gives this demand a high priority vis-à-vis other values and interests, and

—demands that all citizens should have adequate means to take advantage of their rights, freedoms, and opportunities.

Liberal conceptions of justice may differ from Rawls's by being comprehensive rather than political, for example, or by lacking some or all of the three egalitarian components he incorporates.

16. See LP, pp. 52 and 60 for Rawls's distinction of these two steps, as he calls them, of his account of international ideal theory.

Rawls makes each delegate assume that her people is interested exclusively in being constituted as a just liberal society and he asserts that delegates with this sole interest would adopt his law of peoples, which lacks any egalitarian component. I will now argue against his stipulation that the delegates have only this one interest (Section III) and then against his claim that delegates with this sole interest would adopt his law of peoples (Section IV). If only one of my two arguments succeeds, Rawls's account is in trouble.

III. AGAINST RAWLS'S STIPULATION

An obvious alternative to the stipulation is this: Each delegate assumes that her people has an ultimate interest not only in the justice of its domestic institutions, but also in the well-being of its members (beyond the minimum necessary for just domestic institutions). Each delegate assumes, that is, that her people would, other things equal, prefer to have a higher rather than a lower average standard of living.[17]

Delegates so described would favor the GRT amendment. This is clearly true if, like the parties to the domestic session, they deliberate according to the maximin rule. But it is also true if they focus on average expectations: The GRT amendment would benefit all peoples by reducing pollution and environmental degradation. It is unclear whether it would have a positive or negative effect on per capita income for the world at large. But it would keep national per capita incomes closer together and thereby, given the decreasing marginal significance of income for well-being, raise the average standard of living as anticipated in the original position. An increase in national per capita income at the bottom matters more than an equal decrease in national per capita income at the top—in terms of a people's ability to structure its social world and national territory in accordance with its collective values and preferences, for example, and also in terms of its members' quality of life.

We need not stipulate that a people's interest in well-being is strong relative to its interest in domestic justice. For suppose we have each delegate assume that her people's interest in well-being is very slight and subordinate to the interest in domestic justice. Then the delegate will care

17. Rawls makes the analogous stipulation for the domestic session of the original position, remarking that it cannot hurt a person to have greater means at her disposal: One can always give them away or forego their use (*TJ*, pp. 142f).

relatively little about what her people would gain through the amendment in case it would otherwise be poorer. But then she will also care little about what it would lose through the amendment in case it would otherwise be more affluent. She would care little both ways, and therefore would still have reason to adopt the amendment if, as I have argued, the gains outweigh the losses.

I conclude that, if a delegate assumes her people to have an interest in well-being, and be it ever so slight, then she will favor my amendment—regardless of whether she seeks to maximize her people's average or worst-case expectations. Rawls must therefore posit the opposite: Each delegate assumes that her people has no interest at all in its standard of living (beyond its interest in the minimum necessary for just domestic institutions). This is, of course, precisely what his stipulation entails. But why should we find this stipulation plausible once we see what it excludes?

There are several reasons to find it *im*plausible. There are, for one thing, variants of liberalism that—unlike Rawls's own—are committed to continued economic growth and progress; and a people committed to one of them should be presumed to want to avoid economic stagnation and decline. There are also cosmopolitan variants of liberalism which extend the egalitarian concerns that Rawls confines to the domestic case to all human beings worldwide; and a people committed to one of them should be presumed to want to avoid relative deprivation for itself as well as for others.

The stipulation also has implausible side effects. In explicating the outcome of the liberal run of his second session, Rawls writes: "There should be certain provisions for mutual assistance between peoples in times of famine and drought and, were it feasible, as it should be, provisions for ensuring that in all reasonably developed liberal societies people's basic needs are met" (LP, p. 56). Does he really mean what this sentence suggests: that provisions are called for to meet basic needs only in reasonably developed societies? His account may well leave him no other choice. In his second session, each delegate cares solely about her people's achieving domestic justice. However, helping a people meet their basic needs may not enable them to achieve domestic justice, if their society is still quite undeveloped. Hence aid to members of such societies is not a requirement of global justice on Rawls's stipulation. His law of peoples requires basic food aid, say, only to peoples who but for their poverty would be able to maintain just domestic institutions.

Now it would be outrageous to suggest that Rawls deems it a matter of moral indifference whether members of undeveloped societies are starving or not. But, given his stipulation, he would have to say that such aid is an ethical duty, which we might discharge individually, or collectively through our government. International *justice* requires institutions designed to meet basic needs in societies where this contributes to domestic justice, but not in societies where it does not. Yet this looks counterintuitive: Why, after all, do liberals want the law of peoples to be supportive of the internal justice of all societies, if not for the sake of the persons living in them? And if our concern for the domestic justice of societies is ultimately a concern for their individual members, then why should we focus so narrowly on how well a law of peoples accommodates their interest in living under just domestic institutions and not also, more broadly, on how well it accommodates their underlying and indisputable interest in secure access to food, clothing, shelter, education, and health care, even where a reasonably developed liberal society is still out of the question?

The danger here is not merely moral implausibility, but also philosophical incoherence between Rawls's conceptions of domestic and of global justice. According to the latter, a just domestic regime is an end in itself. According to the former, however, it is not an end in itself, but rather something we ought to realize for the sake of individual human persons, who are the ultimate units of moral concern. Our natural duty to create and uphold just domestic institutions is a duty owed to them (*TJ*, p. 115). Their well-being is the *point* of social institutions and therefore, through the first session of the original position, gives content to Rawls's conception of domestic justice.

The incoherence might be displayed as follows. Suppose the parties to the first, domestic session knew that the persons they represent are the members of one society among a plurality of interdependent societies; and suppose they also knew that a delegate will represent this society in a subsequent international session, in which a law of peoples is to be adopted. How would they describe to this delegate the fundamental interests of their society? Of course they would want her to push for a law of peoples that is supportive of the kind of national institutions favored by the two principles of justice which, according to Rawls, they have adopted for the domestic case. But their concern for such domestic institutions is derivative on their concern for the higher-order interests of the individual human persons they themselves represent in the domestic original position. Therefore, they would want the delegate to push for the law of peoples that best accommodates, on the whole, those higher-order interests of individuals.[18] They would want her to consider not only how alternative proposals for a law of peoples would affect their clients' prospects to live under just domestic institutions, but also how these proposals would affect their clients' life prospects in other ways—for example through the affluence of their society. This point, by the way, strongly suggests that those committed to a Rawlsian (or, indeed, any other liberal) conception of domestic justice should want the delegates to any global original position to be conceived as representatives of persons rather than peoples.

I suspect that Rawls wants his second session of the original position to be informed by the interests of peoples, conceived as irreducible to the interests of persons, because the latter would inject an individualistic element that he deems unacceptable to hierarchical societies. The problem he sees is real enough, but his solution accommodates the hierarchicals at the expense of not being able to accommodate the liberals. I will return to this point in Section V.

IV. AGAINST RAWLS'S REASONING

The foregoing arguments notwithstanding, let us now allow the stipulation. Let us assume that each people really does have only the one interest in the justice of its own domestic institutions, and that its delegate to the second session of the original position is instructed accordingly. Would such delegates prefer Rawls's law of peoples over my more egalitarian alternative? The answer, clearly, is NO: They would at most be indifferent between the two proposals. I don't know why Rawls thinks otherwise. But he may have been misled by an unrecognized presumption that a laissez-faire global economic order is the natural or neutral benchmark which the delegates would endorse unless they have definite reasons to depart from it.

This presumption would explain his discussion of a global difference principle, which is peculiar in two respects. First, Rawls considers such a principle only in regard to one part of nonideal theory: coping with unfavorable conditions (LP, p. 75), although it has generally, if not always, been proposed as an analogue to the domestic difference principle, which is

18. For Rawls's account of the three higher-order interests of the persons whom the parties to the first, domestic session represent, see his *Political Liberalism* (New York: Columbia Univ. Press 1993), pp. 74f, 106.

169

used primarily to design the ideal basic structure.[19] Second, the tenor of his remarks throughout is that a global difference principle is too strong for the international case, that it demands too much from hierarchical societies (e.g., LP, p. 75). This suggests a view of the difference principle as a principle of *re*distribution, which takes from some to give to others: The more it redistributes, the more demanding is the principle. But this view of the difference principle loses an insight that is crucial to understanding Rawls's own, domestic difference principle: There is no prior distribution, no natural baseline or neutral way of arranging the economy, relative to which the difference principle could be seen to make *re*distributive modifications. Rather, there are countless ways of designing economic institutions, none initially privileged, of which one and only one will be implemented. The difference principle selects the scheme that ought to be chosen. The selected economic ground rules, whatever their content, do not *re*distribute, but rather govern how economic benefits and burdens get distributed in the first place.

This point is crucial for Rawls's reply to Nozick's critique. Nozick wants to make it appear that laissez-faire institutions are natural and define the baseline distribution which Rawls then seeks to revise *ex post* through redistributive transfers. Nozick views the first option as natural and the second as making great demands upon the diligent and the gifted. He allows that, with unanimous consent, people can make the switch to the second scheme; but, if some object, we must stick to the first.[20] Rawls can respond that a libertarian basic structure and his own more egalitarian liberal-democratic alternative are options on the same footing: the second is, in a sense, demanding on the gifted, if they would do better under the first—but then the first is, in the same sense and symmetrically, demanding on the less gifted, who would do much better under the second scheme.

In his discussion of the global difference principle, Rawls's presentation of the issue is the analogue to Nozick's in the domestic case. It is somehow natural or neutral to arrange the world economy so that each society has absolute control over, and unlimited ownership of, all natural resources within its territory. Any departures from this baseline, such as my GRT proposal, are demanding and, it turns out, too demanding on some soci-

19. In the penultimate draft of "The Law of Peoples," Rawls did argue also against the global difference principle as a proposal for ideal theory, but he has deleted those arguments.
20. See *Anarchy, State, and Utopia*, pp. 167–74, 198–204, 280–92.

eties. I want to give the analogue to the Rawlsian domestic response: Yes, egalitarian institutions are demanding upon naturally and historically favored societies, as they would do better in a scheme with unlimited ownership rights. But then, symmetrically, a scheme with unlimited ownership rights is at least equally demanding upon naturally and historically disfavored societies, since they and their members would do much better under a more egalitarian global basic structure.

I have argued that Rawls has given no reason why the delegates—even if each of them cares solely about her people's prospects to live under just domestic institutions—should prefer his inegalitarian law of peoples over more egalitarian alternatives. Might they have a reason for the opposite preference? I believe that they do. In a world with large international inequalities, the domestic institutions of the poorer societies are vulnerable to being corrupted by powerful political and economic interests abroad. This is something we see all around us: politicians and business people from the rich nations self-servingly manipulating and interfering with the internal political, judicial, and economic processes of third-world societies.

Rawls is presumably aware of this phenomenon, but he fails to see its roots in gross international inequality: In poorer societies, he writes, "the problem is commonly the nature of the public political culture and the religious and philosophical traditions that underlie its institutions. The great social evils in poorer societies are likely to be oppressive government and corrupt elites" (LP, p. 77). Now Rawls is surely right that many poor countries have corrupt institutions and ruling elites, which do not serve the interests of the people and contribute to their poverty. But the inverse is certainly true as well: Relative poverty breeds corruptibility and corruption. Powerful foreign governments support their favorite faction of the local elite and often manage to keep or install it in power—through financial and organizational help for winning elections, if possible, or through support for security forces, coups d'état, or "revolutions" otherwise. Third-world politicians are bribed or pressured by firms from the rich societies to cater to their sex tourism business, to accept their hazardous wastes and industrial facilities, and to buy useless products at government expense. Agribusinesses, promising foreign exchange earnings that can be used for luxury imports, manage to get land use converted from staple foods to export crops: Wealthy foreigners get coffee and flowers year-round, while many locals cannot afford the higher prices for basic foodstuffs. Examples could be multiplied; but I think it is indisputable that the oppression and corruption in the poorer countries, which Rawls rightly deplores, is by no means entirely homegrown. So it is true, but not the whole truth, that governments and institutions of poor countries are often corrupt: They are actively being corrupted, continually and very significantly, by private and official agents from vastly more wealthy societies. It is entirely unrealistic to expect that such foreign-sponsored corruption can be eradicated without reducing the enormous differentials in per capita GNP.

So long as the delegates to Rawls's second session are merely presumed to know that large international inequalities *may* have a negative impact upon the domestic justice of the poorer societies, they have a tie-breaking reason to favor a more egalitarian law of peoples over Rawls's.[21]

V. Another Way of Understanding Rawls's Liberal Delegates

If only one of my two arguments is sound, then delegates of liberal societies would prefer a more egalitarian law of peoples over Rawls's inegalitarian alternative. I suppose Rawls would regret this fact, if it destroys the desired coincidence between the law of peoples adopted by delegates of liberal societies (at step 1 of his second session) and the law of peoples adopted by delegates of hierarchical societies (at step 2). But this coincidence fails, in any case, on account of human rights.

Rawls claims that both sets of delegates would adopt precisely the same law of peoples (LP, p. 60), which includes a list of human rights (LP, pp. 62f, 68, 70) featuring minimum rights to life (means of subsistence and security), to liberty (freedom from slavery, serfdom, and forced occupations), to personal property, to "a measure" (LP, p. 63) of liberty of conscience and freedom of thought and "a certain" (LP, p. 68) freedom of association (compatible with an established religion), to emigration, and to the rule of law and formal equality as expressed by the rules of natural justice (for example that similar cases be treated similarly). He gives no reason, and I can see none, historical or philosophical, for believing that

---

21. While the delegates to an R_2-type second session would view my modification as an improvement, they would presumably like even better the addition of a more statist egalitarian component, such as Brian Barry's proposal cited in note 11. This does not worry me, because it was only for the sake of the argument that I have here accepted Rawls's R_2 set-up, which treats peoples, not persons, as ultimate units of moral concern. I am confident that a more plausible construal of a global original position—G, for example, as defended in *RR* §§22–23—would support something very much like the GRT as an essential part of a fully just law of peoples.

hierarchical societies, as such, would incorporate these human rights into their favored law of peoples. Perhaps many such societies can honor these rights while retaining their hierarchical, nonliberal character, as Rawls suggests (LP, p. 70); but this hardly shows that they would choose to be bound by them. Human rights are not essential to hierarchical societies, as they are essential to liberal ones.

Not only is it highly doubtful that delegates of hierarchical societies would choose to commit themselves to so much; it is also quite unclear why delegates of liberal societies would not want to incorporate more than Rawls's list, which specifically excludes freedom of speech (LP, p. 62), democratic political rights (LP, pp. 62, 69f), and equal liberty of conscience and freedom of thought (LP, pp. 63, 65).

Rawls's quest for a "politically neutral" (LP, p. 69) law of peoples—one that liberals and hierarchicals would independently favor on the basis of their respective values and interests—thus holds little promise: Those who are really committed to a liberal conception of justice will envision a law of peoples which demands that persons everywhere enjoy the protection of the full list of human rights as well as adequate opportunities and material means that are not radically unequal. The friends of hierarchical societies will prefer a world order that is much less protective of the basic interests of persons as individuals. The former will want the interests of persons to be represented in the second session of the original position. The latter will care only about the interests of peoples.

Occasionally, Rawls suggests a different picture, which jettisons the claim to political neutrality. On this picture, the law of peoples he proposes is not what liberals would ideally want, but rather is affected by the existence of hierarchical societies. The alleged coincidence of the results of the two runs of the second session is then not luck, but design. It comes about because good liberals seek to accommodate hierarchical societies by adjusting their ideal of global justice so as to "express liberalism's own principle of toleration for other reasonable ways of ordering society" (LP, p. 43).[22] Just as Rawls himself may be expressing this desire by conceiving the second session of the original position in nonindividualistic terms, he may conceive of his liberal delegates as having a similar desire to adopt a law of peoples acceptable to hierarchical societies. This could explain their—

22. Another, related reason might be, as Rawls remarks in another context, that "all principles and standards proposed for the law of peoples must, to be feasible, prove acceptable to the considered and reflective public opinion of peoples and their governments" (LP, p. 50).

otherwise incredible—decisions against certain human rights (precisely those most offensive to the hierarchicals) and against any egalitarian principle.

This picture is not at all that of a negotiated compromise in which the liberal delegates agree to surrender their egalitarian concerns and some human rights in exchange for the hierarchical delegates accepting the remainder. Such a bargaining model is quite un-Rawlsian and also does not fit with his account, on which the two groups of delegates deliberate in mutual isolation. The toleration model is more noble than this: The liberal delegates, informed that their societies share a world with many hierarchical societies, seek to design a law of peoples that hierarchical societies, on the basis of their values and interests as such, can reasonably accept. Yet, for all its nobility, the toleration model has a drawback that the bargaining model avoids: It is rather one-sided. The hierarchicals, unencumbered by any principle of toleration, get their favorite law of peoples, while the liberals, "to express liberalism's own principle of toleration," surrender their egalitarian concerns and some important human rights.[23] This fits the witty definition of a liberal as someone who will not take her own side in any disagreement.

What goes wrong here is that Rawls, insofar as he is committed to this picture, does not clearly distinguish two views, and hence is prone to accept the second with the first:

(1) Liberalism involves a commitment to tolerance and diversity that extends beyond the family of liberal conceptions: A liberal world order will therefore leave room for certain kinds of nonliberal national regimes.

(2) Liberalism involves a commitment to tolerance and diversity that extends beyond the family of liberal conceptions: It would thus be illiberal to impose a liberal global order on a world that contains many peoples who do not share our liberal values.

By acknowledging (1), we are not compromising our liberal convictions. To the contrary: We would be compromising our liberal convictions if we did not envision a liberal world order in this way. A world order would not be genuinely liberal if it did not leave room for certain nonliberal national regimes. Those who acknowledge (2), by contrast, *are* compromising their

23. And probably some additional human rights as well, if I was right to argue that the hierarchical delegates would not adopt even the truncated list that Rawls incorporates into his law of peoples.

liberal convictions for the sake of accommodating those who do not share them. Liberals should then accept (1) and reject (2).

This reasoning is the analogue to what Rawls himself would say about the domestic case. Consider:

(1') A liberal society must leave room for certain nonliberal communities and lifestyles.

(2') It would be illiberal to impose liberal institutions on a society that contains many persons who do not share our liberal values.

Rawls would clearly accept (1') and reject (2'). He could give the following rationale for this: While our society can contain many different kinds of communities, associations, and conceptions of the good, some liberal in character and others not, it can be structured or organized in only one way. If my neighbor wants to be a Catholic and I an atheist, we can both have our way, can both lead the life each deems best. But if my neighbor wants the U.S. to be organized like the Catholic Church and I want it to be a liberal state, we can *not* both have our way. There is no room for accommodation here, and, if I really believe in egalitarian liberal principles, I should politically support them and the institutions they favor against their opponents. These institutions will not vary with the shifting political strength of groups advocating various religious, moral, or philosophical doctrines.[24]

My rationale is the analogue to this: While the world can contain societies that are structured in a variety of ways, some liberal and some not, it cannot itself be structured in a variety of ways. If the Algerians want their society to be organized as a religious state consistent with a just global order and we want ours to be a liberal democracy, we can both have our way. But if the Algerians want the world to be organized according to the Koran, and we want it to accord with liberal principles, then we can *not* both have our way. There is no room for accommodation here, and, if we really believe in egalitarian liberal principles—in every person's equal claim to freedom and dignity—then we should politically support these principles, and the global institutions they favor, against their opponents. These institutions

24. In supporting his view that our conception of justice should not, in the manner of (2'), be sensitive to what competing views happen to be prevalent among our compatriots, Rawls also stresses that such sensitivity would render this conception "political in the wrong way," thus leading to some of the problems associated with institutions that reflect a *modus vivendi*. (See *Political Liberalism*, Lecture IV, esp. pp. 141–48.) This concern, too, has an analogue on the global plane (see *RR*, Chapter 5).

will not vary with the shifting political strength of states committed to various conceptions of domestic justice.

I conclude that Rawls has failed to show that the law of peoples liberals would favor and the law of peoples favored by hierarchicals either coincide by sheer luck or can be made to coincide by morally plausible design. We should then work toward a global order that—though tolerant of certain nonliberal regimes, just as a liberal society is tolerant of certain nonliberal sects and movements—is itself decidedly liberal in character, for example by conceiving of individual persons and of them alone as ultimate units of equal moral concern. This quest will put us at odds with many hierarchical societies whose ideal of a fully just world order will be different from ours.

It may seem then that my more assertive liberalism will lead to greater international conflict. And this may well be so in the area of human rights. But it may not be so in the area here at issue: international inequality. Rawls rejects all egalitarian distributive principles of international justice on the ground (among others) that they are inseparable from liberal values and therefore unacceptable to hierarchical societies (LP, p. 75).[25] But in the real world, the chief opponents of proposals along the lines of my GRT are the affluent liberal societies. We are, after all, also the wealthy ones and account for a vastly disproportionate share of global resource depletion and pollution. If we submitted the GRT proposal to the rest of the world, I believe it would be accepted by most societies with some enthusiasm.[26]

Given that institutional progress is politically possible, it would be perverse to oppose it by saying to the rest of the world: "We care deeply about equality, and we would very much like it to be the case that you are not so much worse off than we are. But, unfortunately, we do not believe that you ultimately care about equality the way we do. Therefore we feel entitled to refuse any global institutional reforms that would lead to greater international equality." One reason this would be perverse is that those touting hierarchical values and those suffering most from global inequality are rarely the same. Those whose lot a GRT would do most to improve—poor women and rural laborers in the third world, for example—rarely give the

25. I believe, to the contrary, that rather a lot could be said to support the GRT scheme in terms of nonliberal values prevalent in many hierarchical societies today, though I cannot undertake this task here.

26. Witness the debates during the 1970s, in UNCTAD and the General Assembly of the United Nations, about a new international economic order.

hierarchical values of their rulers and oppressors their considered and reflective endorsement.[27]

VI. THE PROBLEM OF STABILITY

Delegates of liberal societies might *prefer* an egalitarian law of peoples and yet *adopt* Rawls's inegalitarian alternative.[28] For they might believe that a scheme like the GRT would simply not work: The moral motives ("sense of justice") that a just world order would engender in peoples and their governments would not be strong enough to ensure compliance. There would always be some wealthy peoples refusing to pay their fair share, and this in turn would undermine others' willingness to participate. In short: The GRT scheme is practicable only if backed by sanctions.[29] And sanctions presuppose a world government, which the delegates have abundant reasons to reject.

In response, I accept the claim that the GRT scheme would have to be backed by sanctions. But sanctions do not require a world government. They could work as follows: Once the agency facilitating the flow of GRT payments reports that a country has not met its obligations under the scheme, all other countries are required to impose duties on imports from, and perhaps also similar levies on exports to, this country to raise funds equivalent to its GRT obligations plus the cost of these enforcement measures. Such decentralized sanctions stand a very good chance of discouraging *small*-scale defections. Our world is now, and is likely to remain, highly interdependent economically; most countries export and import between 10 percent and 50 percent of their gross domestic product. None of them would benefit from shutting down foreign trade for the sake of avoiding a GRT obligation of around 1 percent of GDP. And each would have reasons to meet its GRT obligation voluntarily: to retain full control

27. Should I apologize for my liberal bias here, for being concerned with endorsement by individual persons rather than by whole peoples (as expressed, presumably, by their governments and "elites")?

28. The problem I try to deal with in this final section is not one raised by Rawls, who holds that the delegates would even *prefer* his law of peoples. So nothing I say in response to the problem is meant to be critical of him.

29. One might justify including this claim among the general knowledge available to the delegates by pointing to how lax many states have been about paying their much smaller membership dues to the UN.

over how the funds are raised, to avoid paying for enforcement measures in
addition, and to avoid the negative publicity associated with noncompliance.

This leaves the problem of *large*-scale defections, and the related problem of getting most of the more affluent societies to agree to something like
the GRT scheme in the first place. This scheme could not work in our world
without the willing cooperation of most of the wealthier countries. You may
be tempted to look at the world as it is and conclude that the hope for such
willing cooperation is not realistic. So you would have the delegates to any
global original position choose Rawls's law of peoples after all. And you
might then give the following speech to the global poor: "We care deeply
about equality, and we would very much like it to be the case that you are
not so much worse off than we are. But, unfortunately, it is not realistic to
expect that we would actually comply with more egalitarian global institutions. Since no one would benefit from a futile attempt to maintain imprac-
ticable institutions, we should all just rest content with the global inequalities of the status quo."

This little speech is not quite as nefarious as I have made it sound,
because the "we" in the first sentence denotes a significantly smaller group
than the "we" in the second, which refers to the entire population of the
first world. Still, if it is true that reflection on our (wide sense) liberal values
would support a preference for more egalitarian global economic institutions, then we (narrow sense) should at least try to stimulate such reflection in our compatriots before declaring such institutions to be impractica-
ble. We should seek to make it become widely recognized among citizens of
the developed West that such institutions are required by justice. I have
already suggested one reason for believing that this may be a feasible
undertaking—a scheme like the GRT can be justified by appeal to different
(and perhaps incompatible) values prominent in Western moral thought:

(a) It can be supported by libertarian arguments as a global resources
dividend that satisfies a modern Lockean proviso on unilateral appropriation (cf. pp. 200f, above).[30]

30. Cp. the far more radical idea that on a Lockean account "each individual has a right to
an equal share of the basic nonhuman means of production" (i.e., means of production other
than labor which are not themselves produced: resources in the sense of my GRT), as presented in Hillel Steiner, "The Natural Right to the Means of Production," *Philosophical
Quarterly* 27 (1977):41–49, p. 49; and further developed in G. A. Cohen, "Self-Ownership,
World Ownership, and Equality: Part II," *Social Philosophy and Policy* 3 (1986):77–96,
pp. 87–95.

(b) It can be supported as a general way of mitigating the effects of grievous historical wrongs (see pp. 198f, above) that cannot be mitigated in any more specific fashion.[31]

(c) It is also supported by forwardlooking considerations as exemplified in the hypothetical-contract (Rawls) and consequentialist traditions.

These rationales are not unassailable. For one thing, they all hinge upon empirical facts of interdependence:

(a) Peoples must share the same planet with its limited resources.

(b) The common history that has produced peoples and national territories as they now exist and will continue to exist in the forseeable future is replete with massive wrongs and injustices.

(c) Existing peoples interact within a single global framework of political and economic institutions which tends to produce and reproduce rather stable patterns of inequalities and deprivations.

To undermine those rationales and the moral conclusion they support, first-worlders often downplay these interdependencies and think of real societies as "self-sufficient" (*TJ*, p. 4), "closed," "isolated" (*TJ*, p. 8), and "self-contained" (*TJ*, p. 457).[32] Like the closely related notion that the causes of third-world poverty are indigenous (cf. pp. 213f above), this fiction is a severe distortion of the truth—most clearly in the especially relevant case of today's most unfortunate societies, which are still reeling from the effects of slavery and colonial oppression and exploitation and are also highly vulnerable to global market forces and destabilization from abroad.

The three rationales are also frequently confronted with notions of national partiality: It is perfectly permissible for us and our government, in a spirit of patriotic fellow-feeling, to concentrate on promoting the interests of our own society and compatriots, even if foreigners are much worse off. I need not deny this claim, only to qualify it: Partiality is legitimate only in the context of a *fair* competition. This idea is familiar and widely accepted in the domestic case: It is perfectly all right for persons to concentrate on promoting the interests of themselves and their relatives, provided they do

31. Nozick entertains this backwardlooking rationale for the difference principle: If we cannot disentangle and surgically neutralize the effects of past wrongs, then implementing Rawls's difference principle may be the best way of satisfying Nozick's principle of rectification at least approximately. See *Anarchy, State, and Utopia*, p. 231.

32. Rawls describes societies in this way only for purposes of a "first approximation." See *Political Liberalism*, p. 272.

so on a "level playing field" whose substantive fairness is continually preserved. Partiality toward one's family is decidedly not acceptable when we, *qua* citizens, face political decisions in which that level playing field itself is at stake. It would be morally wrong, for example, even (or perhaps especially) if one's children are white boys, to use one's political influence to oppose equal access to higher education for women or blacks. Most citizens in the developed West understand and accept this point without question. It should not be all that hard to make them understand that for closely analogous reasons national partiality is morally acceptable only on condition that the fairness of international competition is continually preserved, and that it is morally wrong in just the same way for the rich Western states to use their vastly superior bargaining power to impose upon the poor societies a global economic order that tends to perpetuate and perhaps aggravate their inferiority.[33]

If the three rationales can be properly developed and defended against these and other challenges, a moral commitment to something like the GRT scheme may gradually emerge and become widespread in the developed West. Even if this were to occur, however, there would still be the further question whether our governments could be moved to introduce and comply with such institutions. I think that an affirmative answer to this question can be supported by some historical evidence. Perhaps the most dramatic such evidence is provided by the suppression of the slave trade in the nineteenth century. Great Britain was in the forefront of these efforts, actively enforcing a ban on the entire maritime slave trade irrespective of a vessel's ownership, registration, port of origin, or destination. Britain bore the entire cost of its enforcement efforts and could not hope to gain significant benefits from it—in fact, Britain bore additional opportunity costs in the form of lost trade, especially with Latin America. States do sometimes act for moral reasons.[34]

It should also be said that institutional reforms establishing a GRT need not go against the national interest of the developed states. I have already

33. For a different argument, to the effect that unqualified partiality constitutes a loophole, see my "Loopholes in Moralities," *Journal of Philosophy* 89 (1992):79–98, pp. 84–98.

34. I owe this example to W. Ben Hunt. Obviously, much more could and should be said about the various similarities and dissimilarities between this nineteenth-century case and our current global situation. I mention the case here mainly as a preliminary, but I think powerful, empirical obstacle to the claim that governments never act contrary to what they take to be in their own, or their society's, best interest. There are, I believe, many other less dramatic, but also more recent, counterexamples to this claim.

said that the GRT would slow pollution and resource depletion and thereby benefit all peoples in the long run. Let me now add that the fiction of mutual independence, and the cult of state sovereignty associated with it, have become highly dangerous in the modern world. Technological progress offers rapidly expanding possibilities of major devastations, of which those associated with nuclear, chemical, or biological weapons and accidents are only the most dramatic and the most obvious. If responsibility for guarding against such possibilities remains territorially divided over some two hundred national governments, the chances of avoiding them in the long run are slim. No state or group of states can protect itself against all externally induced gradual or catastrophic deteriorations of its environment. The present geopolitical constellation offers a unique opportunity for bringing the more dangerous technologies under central international control. If the most powerful states were to try to mandate such control unilaterally, they would likely encounter determined resistance and would have to resort to force. It would seem more promising to pursue the same goal in a multilateral fashion, by relaxing the idea of state sovereignty in a more balanced way: We, the first world, give up the notion that all our great affluence is ours alone, fit to be brought to bear in our bargaining with the rest of the world so as to entrench and expand our advantage. They, the rest, give up the notion that each society has a sovereign right to develop and control by itself all the technological capacities we already possess.

This scenario shows another reason for believing that it may be possible for a commitment to the GRT scheme to become and remain widespread among our compatriots in the first world: We, too, like the global poor, have a strong interest in a gradual erosion of the doctrine of absolute state sovereignty through a strengthening concern for the welfare of humankind at large,[35] though our interest is a more long-term one than theirs. It may seem that a commitment motivated along these lines would be excessively prudential. But then our concern to protect our environment is not merely prudential, but also moral: We do care about the victims of Bhopal and Chernobyl, as well as about future generations. And once the new institutions begin to take hold and to draw the members of different societies closer together, the commitment would in any case tend gradually to assume a more moral character.

35. Note the success of recent programs under which third-world governments are forgiven some of their foreign debts in exchange for their undertaking certain environmental initiatives in their territory.

I conclude that there is no convincing reason to believe that a widespread moral commitment on the part of the more affluent peoples and governments to a scheme like the GRT could not be sustained in the world as we know it. Delegates of liberal societies as Rawls conceives them would therefore not merely *prefer*, but would *choose*, my more egalitarian law of peoples over his inegalitarian alternative. In doing so, they would also envision a more democratic world order, a greater role for central organizations, and, in this sense, more world government than we have at present—though nothing like *a* world government on the model of current national governments.

"The politician," Rawls writes, "looks to the next election, the statesman to the next generation, and philosophy to the indefinite future."[36] Our task as philosophers requires that we try to imagine new, better political structures and different, better moral sentiments. Yes, we must be realistic, but not to the point of presenting to the parties in the original position the essentials of the status quo as unalterable facts.

36. "The Idea of an Overlapping Consensus," *Oxford Journal of Legal Studies* 7 (1987): 1–25, p. 24.

DUTY AND OBLIGATION IN THE NON–IDEAL WORLD

THERE is no need to summarize the argument of this philosophical epic. In its basic outline it is sufficiently well known to the readers of this journal from Rawls's articles over the last twenty years. In this book Rawls has filled in gaps in the argument, answered numerous critical objections, applied his theory to problems of justice in politics, economics, education, and other important areas, and buttressed it with a theory of moral psychology and other argumentative reinforcement. The result is a remarkably thorough treatise which well deserves to be called a philosophical classic.

Rawls's primary aim, he tells us, is to provide a "workable and systematic moral conception" (viii) to oppose utilitarianism. Until now, the opponents of utilitarianism have been unable to provide an equally systematic alternative of their own, and have contented themselves with a series of *ad hoc* amendments and restrictions to utilitarianism designed to bring it into closer harmony with our spontaneous moral sentiments, at whatever cost in theoretical tidiness. They are likely to concede that *one* of the prime duties of social policy makers is to promote social utility, but then insist that one may not properly pursue that commendable goal by grinding the faces of the poor, framing and punishing the innocent, falsifying history, and so on. On the level of personal ethics, such moralists as W. D. Ross admit utilitarian duties of beneficence and non-maleficence, but supplement them with quite nonutilitarian duties of veracity, fidelity, and the like, and there is no way of telling in advance which duty must trump the others when circumstances

183

seem to bring them into conflict. Similarly, on the level of social policy, such theorists as Brian Barry (*Political Argument*) and Nicholas Rescher (*Distributive Justice*) endorse utilitarian "aggregative principles" but insist that they be supplemented or limited by equally valid equalitarian "distributive principles," and when circumstances bring the principles of utility and equality into opposition, there is no higher-order criterion to settle the conflict or to provide in advance one uniquely correct set of weightings to the conflicting principles. All pluralistic theories that do not provide rigid "priority rules" among principles require us to balance conflicting considerations against one another on the particular occasions of their conflict and "simply strike a balance by intuition, by what seems to us most nearly right" (34). Rawls calls all theories of this type "intuitionistic."

Rawls's main objection to intuitionism is its modesty. It doesn't even try to provide us with a rigorously rational method of settling hard problems in ethics; in cases of close conflict there are no demonstrably correct results, and "the means of rational discussion have come to an end" (41). Perhaps no theory can do better, Rawls concedes, but that is no reason why theorists shouldn't try; for a pluralistic theory without rigid priority rules is but "half a theory." Many intuitionists, however, will be inclined to reply, at this early stage of the argument, that "half-theories" are the only kind that can fit the facts of moral experience. Difficult moral decisions and judgments often (if not always) require balancing of conflicting claims, deciding and choosing rather than calculating and applying rules, committing oneself and legislating for others, taking "existential leaps" in situations of "tragic surdity," and so on. To most persons who have struggled with moral dilemmas, I submit, the suggestion that Reason can provide a ready-made set of priority rules is astonishing. Still, this observation is question-begging if intended as criticism. The question for the critic is whether Rawls's theory itself has been able to dispense (convincingly) with the balancing of coordinate considerations. If it has, it is an extraordinary triumph over what would initially appear to be common sense.

Rawls's objection to his other leading rival, utilitarianism, is the familiar one that the theory in all its forms would justify too much, in particular that it can justify sacrificing the interests of a few for the sake of the greater total good shared by many. The complaint is not new, of course, but Rawls makes it with unexcelled elegance and persuasiveness. Utilitarianism, however, is a slippery target, and it is sometimes not clear whether arguments fatal to one of its forms have been aimed by Rawls at another form that has a relative immunity to them. There is some confusion, for example, between a utilitarian *analysis* of justice, as found, for example, in the final chapter of J. S. Mill's *Utilitarianism*, and a normative utilitarian theory of on-balance justification which can admit that utility is one thing and justice another, even admit that Rawls's analysis of justice is correct, and yet hold that, when they conflict, social utility has an invariant moral priority. A utilitarian *analysis* of justice will entail that justice, being "the name for certain social utilities which are vastly more important . . . than any others" [1] can never conflict with social utility. That implausible thesis is an easy target for Rawls. The utilitarian who will allow conceivable, though perhaps rare, conflicts between social utility (conceived in a sophisticated way) and justice, but stubbornly insists that social utility must win out in those cases, is a harder target, and the intuitionist who refuses to legislate in advance for all conceivable cases of conflict, a harder target still.

Rawls calls his own theory (the third horse in the race) "contractarianism," or "the contract theory," and traces its ancestry to the traditional theory of the social contract "as found, say, in Locke, Rousseau, and Kant" (11). This is a bit puzzling, for that part of Rawls's theory which is a direct rival to utilitarianism and intuitionism does not employ the idea of a *contract* at all. Depending on how the rival theories are interpreted, they are either statements of the ultimate principle (or principles) of right conduct generally or of social justice in particular. The principle Rawls proposes in opposition to them he takes to be a general test for the truth of specific principles (including priority rules) of social justice. A specific principle is correct, he argues, provided it would be chosen over any alternative that could be proposed to a hypothetical group of normally self-interested rational persons, each wearing an appropriate "veil of ignorance," gathered together in a state of nature for the specific purpose of designing afresh the institutions that will regulate their future lives. *That* criterion is neither utilitarian nor pluralistic, but neither does it make any reference to a "contract." Rawls holds that *any* rational person in the circumstances he describes would choose one definite set of principles over all others as the basic ground rules of the society he is to join, and that a collection of such persons, therefore, would choose those rules *unanimously*. In that case, in applying Rawls's ultimate cri-

[1] J. S. Mill, *Utilitarianism*, chapter v, final paragraph.

terion (that is, in employing his method for testing proposed principles of justice) we need consider only the reasoning processes of *one* hypothetical rational chooser. The concept of a conditional agreement sworn to by a number of parties and binding upon each on condition of promised performance or *quid pro quo* by the others does not enter the argument at all (at least at this stage). The traditional social-contract doctrine, as I understand it, was an answer to a different question from that answered by Rawls's "contractarianism." In its Hobbesian and Lockean forms, for example, it is not so much a general criterion for the truth of principles of social justice as a statement of the grounds and limits of *political obligation*; and the concept of a contract—tacitly actual or hypothetical, among subjects or between subjects and a sovereign—was essential to it. I shall discuss Rawls's own theory of political obligation, and the limited role that contract plays in it, below.

The "contract theory" as Rawls develops it, then, is a poorly named but genuine alternative to utilitarian and intuitionistic systems of ultimate justification (or "justicization," as the case may be). Like utilitarianism, contractarianism can be applied primarily to individual acts and policies or primarily to more general rules and institutions. Rawls did so much to clarify the distinction between acts and rules and to emphasize its importance in his famous early discussion of utilitarianism [2] that for several years he was thought by some to be working toward a rule-utilitarian theory himself. Instead, he was apparently setting the stage for his own rule-oriented brand of "contractarianism." "The primary subject of justice," as Rawls sees it, "is the basic structure of society" (7). By this he means that the principles of justice he has derived by the contractarian method are to be applied directly to the design or criticism of the major institutions—a political constitution, an economic system, and such basic social forms as the monogamous family. Institutions are defined by their constitutive rules which create offices and roles, regulate procedures, and assign rights and duties. Ultimately, then, the principles of justice apply to those rules, and only indirectly or derivatively to the acts and states of affairs that fall under the rules. A given pattern of wealth distribution is just, for example, whatever it be like, provided only it follows from the fair operation of a just economic practice as determined by the procedural rules of that practice. Distributive justice, in Rawls's own terminology, is an instance of "pure procedural

[2] John Rawls, "Two Concepts of Rules," *Philosophical Review*, LXIV, 1 January 1955): 3–32.

justice," insofar as there is no criterion of a just result independent of the fairness of the procedures followed to reach the result. The procedural rules themselves are part of the basic structure, which can be justified only by the principles of justice derived from the contractarian method.

As for the justice of particular economic transactions—"It is a mistake to . . . require that every change, considered as a single transaction viewed in isolation, be in itself just" (87/8). Rawls is not so much expressing his tolerance here for a certain amount of distributive injustice (despite his wording) as denying that a criterion of just arrangements can be found apart from the fairness of the procedures followed to reach them. (Note the parallel contention that could be made by a rule-utilitarian: "It is a mistake to require that every act considered in isolation from the practice that gives it its meaning be socially useful; it is sufficient that the rule-defined practice of which it is a part be socially useful.") The same point is made about legislation in a somewhat modified way: "Thus on many questions of social and economic policy we must fall back upon a notion of quasi-pure procedural justice: laws and policies are just provided that they lie within the allowed range, and the legislature, in ways authorized by a just constitution, has in fact enacted them" (201). The justice of a particular statute, then, is several steps removed from Rawls's initial contractarian criterion: the choice of hypothetical rational persons determines the basic principles of justice, which in turn determine the justice of a political constitution, which in turn determines the proper law-making procedures, which in turn partly determine the justice of a particular legislative outcome. At each stage, the fairness of a procedure (hypothetical or actual) largely determines the justice of a result. This general priority of fair procedures to just outcomes (in particular at the stage at which basic principles are chosen) leads Rawls to label his whole conception "Justice as Fairness."

Rawls makes one further qualification that is essential to an understanding of his theory. His book is an essay in what he calls "ideal theory" (as opposed to "non-ideal theory") or more specifically, "strict-compliance theory" (as opposed to "partial-compliance theory"). He presumes that his original choosers are to select principles that will regulate a "well-ordered society," that is, a society in which every one always acts justly, all laws are just, and all citizens always comply with them. (It is apparently also a society in which no one ever acts negligently and there are no automobile collisions, since Rawls consigns questions about compensatory justice to nonideal theory.) Rawls admits that the really pressing and important problems about justice belong to partial-compliance theory (e.g., questions in the theory of criminal justice, in tort law, in the theory of civil disobedience, and justice between nations) but "assumes" that the question of ideal theory is more fundamental since its answer will provide direction to our inquiries in non-ideal theory, and will be "the only basis for the systematic grasp of these more pressing problems" (8).

One of the ways the ideal theory helps with the real-life problems of the non-ideal world, according to Rawls, is by mediating our "natural duty" to promote just institutions. Insofar as our actual institutions depart from Rawls's basic principles of justice, we have a duty, he says, to work toward their reform. But in our actual imperfect world things are rarely that straightforward. For example, Sidgwick's paradox of "conservative justice" confronts us at every turn. Every reform of an imperfect practice or institution is likely to be unfair to someone or other. To change the rules in the middle of the game, even when those rules were not altogether fair, will disappoint the honest expectations of those whose prior commitments and life plans were made in genuine reliance on the continuance of the old rules. The propriety of changing the rules in a given case depends upon (*inter alia*) the degree of unfairness of the old rules and the extent and degree of the reliance placed upon them. Very often, when we consider reform, we must weigh quite legitimate incompatible claims against each other in circumstances such that whichever judgment is reached it will be unfair to someone or other. Rawls admits that intuitive balancing is unavoidable in dealing with problems of non-ideal theory, but I find very little acknowledgment (if any) that justice can be in *both* pans of the balance beam when claims are weighed. By and large, however, Rawls, in talking about non-ideal theory, makes large concessions to the skeptical intuitionist who insists on the necessity of claim-balancing. His sensitive treatment of the duty to obey an unjust law and its limits (350–355) is a good example of this. So is his grudging admission (on page 303) that in the more "extreme and tangled instances of nonideal theory" there will be a point where his rigid priority rules designed for ideal theory will fail, and there may be "no satisfactory answer at all."

Rawls's chapter devoted to civil disobedience and conscientious refusal is the one place in the book where political ties are analyzed, and so the one place where "social-contract theory," in a strict and traditional sense, might come into play. It is also worth discussing here since it provides a usefully illustrative problem for the clash between rule-contractarianism and act-contractarianism.

The problem of civil disobedience is primarily a problem in individual ethics. To ask under what conditions, if any, an individual citizen is morally justified in engaging in a "public, non-violent, conscientious yet political act contrary to law" (63) is to ask a question very much like those about when an individual is morally justified in telling lies, breaking promises, inflicting pain, or otherwise acting contrary to normally binding moral rules. That is because there is normally a presumption against disobeying the law in a just, or near-just, society—not an unconditional moral prohibition, but a kind of standing case that must be overridden in a given instance by sufficient reasons. [Rawls does *not* hold the discredited view, effectively attacked by Hugo Bedau, that there is such a presumption in favor of obedience to "*any* law, however instituted and enforced, whatever its provisions, and no matter what would be the consequences of universal unswerving compliance with it." [3] His whole discussion of civil disobedience assumes the special context of a near-just society with "legitimately established democratic authority" (63).] To solve the problem, it is not sufficient to have a set of principles for determining the justice of the basic structure of society; rather we need supplementary principles to guide the individual conscience in a society already assumed to have more or less just institutions.

Rawls derives his principles for individuals in the same rationalistic way he derived his principles of social justice. Once again, the "contractarian method" is employed, and we must ask ourselves which principles of right conduct would be chosen unanimously by the rational and self-interested parties in the original position *after* they have chosen the principles of social justice. These form a relatively untidy miscellany, and as Rawls enumerates and clarifies them, the reader is naturally reminded of Hobbes's "Laws of Nature or Dictates of Reason." The main distinction Rawls draws among them is between those which impose "natural duties" and those which impose "obligations." Obligations arise from voluntary acts, e.g., express or tacit promises, or accepting benefits; their content derives in part from the specifications of institutional rules; they are owed to definite individuals, namely, those "cooperating together to maintain the arrangement in question" (113). On the other hand, such natural duties as the duty not to be cruel and the

[3] Hugo Bedau, review of Carl Cohen, *Civil Disobedience: Conscience, Taxes, and the Law*, this JOURNAL, LXIX, 7 (April 6, 1972): 179–186, p. 185.

duty to help others in need "apply to us without regard to our voluntary acts . . . have no necessary connection with institutions or social practices . . . and hold between persons irrespective of their institutional relationships" (114 f). The principles imposing natural duties are irreducibly diverse, but all obligations ultimately are derived from a single principle which Rawls calls the "principle of fairness." This expresses the requirement that an individual "do his part as defined by the rules of an institution when . . . (1) the institution is just . . . and (2) one has voluntarily accepted the benefits of the arrangement or taken advantage of its opportunities" (111 f).

Insofar as the presumption in favor of obedience to law is grounded in the principle of fairness in Rawls's philosophy, his theory of political obligation falls squarely within the (or a) social-contract tradition. (Indeed, that interpretation of his theory is reminiscent of Socrates in his jail cell.) In fact, however, Rawls does not use the principle of fairness to provide much support for the presumption in favor of obedience. "There is . . . no political obligation strictly speaking," he says, "for citizens generally" (114). Those members of society whose "equal liberties" are worth very little because of economic deprivation, social discrimination, and exclusion from powerful offices (even under just and enlightened rules) and those whose "consent" to the governing institutional rules has been coerced by a kind of "extortion" are free of any genuine *obligation* to obey the law even in a society whose *institutions* (as opposed to policies and practices) are just. Society is not a "mutually advantageous venture" (343) for these citizens, and they do not "voluntarily" restrict their liberties under law in it. The principle of fairness, then, does not establish even the presumption of an obligation of obedience for them: "only the more favored members of society are likely to have a clear political obligation as opposed to a political duty" (376). Since the principles of natural duty "do not presuppose any act of consent, express or tacit, or indeed any voluntary act, in order to apply" (115), even this part of Rawls's system is not a "social-contract theory" except in a watered-down and untraditional sense.

The principle of natural duty that *does* account for the general presumption in favor of obedience in a just society is the principle imposing what Rawls calls the "duty to uphold justice." That principle, which Rawls argues would be acknowledged in the original position and is in that sense "derived from reason," requires individuals to "support and comply with" already existing just institutions and help bring about new just arrangements (115). It is *this* principle that binds people generally to their political institutions, and it is a "contractarian principle" only in the sense that it is derived by Rawls's so-called contractarian method.

Under what conditions can the presumption in favor of obedience be overridden? The problem of justifying civil disobedience, as Rawls conceives it, is a problem for individual choice, and "the difficulty is one of a conflict of [natural] duties": "At what point does the duty to comply with laws enacted by a legislative majority (or executive acts supported by such a majority) cease to be binding in view of . . . the duty to oppose injustice?" (363) (The latter, presumably, is another of the "natural duties.") If I understand Rawls correctly, the "intuitionism" that he rejected in his account of social principles is re-introduced here in his discussion of conflicting individual duties (though Rawls denies that he resorts to intuitionism even here). Intuitionism, as I understand Rawls's use of the term, is the view that there are no rigid priority rules assigning weights to normative principles that can conflict. Yet in his discussion of the conflict of duties that makes the problem of civil disobedience difficult, he cautions us that "Precise principles that straightway decide actual cases are clearly out of the question" (364). He modestly claims for his own discussion only that "it identifies the relevant considerations and helps us to assign them their correct weights in the more important instances," thus "clearing our vision" generally (364).

Rawls then lists a number of conditions whose satisfaction usually or generally (he calls them mere "presumptions") makes civil disobedience reasonable. First, it should be limited to the protest of wrongs that are "instances of substantial and clear injustice," in effect to "serious infringements of the principle of equal liberty" (373), that is to say, to denials of the basic political rights of citizenship. (It is worth noting in passing that this condition is not satisfied by civilly disobedient protests against cutting down sycamore trees to widen a city road, against busing pupils, over-severe marijuana laws, failure to install a traffic light at an intersection that is unsafe for children, or excessive air pollution. The weight Rawls assigns to the presumption for obedience is not easily outbalanced.) Second, civil disobedience is justified as, but only as, a last resort after legal means of redress have failed. Third, the case for civil disobedience weakens in proportion to the extent to which others have recently resorted to it or have as good a case for resorting to it, for "there is a limit to which civil disobedience can be engaged in without leading to a breakdown in the respect for law and the constitution" (374).

The question that divides both utilitarian and contractarian theories into "act" and "rule" varieties is the following: In choosing and justifying our actions, when may we appeal *directly* to an ethical first principle and when (if ever) must our appeal stop at some subordinate rule, itself justified by an ethical first principle? The act-utilitarian permits (indeed requires) each of us always to do the act that promises to produce the greatest gain in net utility. He admits, of course, that often (even usually) we can best maximize utility by conforming to rules and regulations that summarize the experience of many generations that acts of certain kinds tend to have bad consequences. He might even agree with G. E. Moore that some moral rules should be taken as absolutely binding, but only because the chances of a given murder, say, being optimific are always less than the chances that our predictions of optimificity are mistaken. Still he will hold, at least in principle, that we ought to violate any moral or legal rule whenever doing so will produce consequences that are better on the whole than the consequences of our obeying it. On the other hand, the philosopher who holds the view suggested by Rawls's "Two Concepts of Rules," which I have elsewhere called "Actual-Rule Utilitarianism," [4] will interpret our duties much more strictly. He may admit that some "moral rules" are mere "summaries," or rules of thumb, to be violated whenever the expected consequences of doing so are better than those of conformity (most "rules" of sexual ethics can be interpreted that way), but he will insist that valid legal rules and legal-like rules governing such practices as promising and punishing cannot rightly be broken merely to achieve a small gain in utility, but only to avoid a disastrous *loss* in utility. And he will support his strict legalism, paradoxically, by a kind of appeal of his own to utility. He will point out that it is conducive to social utility to have some rules (e.g., those pertaining to promising) that deprive persons, under certain conditions, of the right to appeal directly to the principle of utility in deciding what to do.

At first sight, it is not easy to see how a similar act-rule division would apply to contractarian theories, partly because it is difficult to say what corresponds to an "ethical first principle" in Rawls's system. It is implausible, I think, to take Rawls's statement of the contractarian method itself to fill the same role in his theory as

---

[4] "The Forms and Limits of Utilitarianism," *Philosophical Review*, LXXVI, 3 (July 1967): 368–381, p. 378.

the principle of utility does in utilitarianism. The principle that moral principles are correct if and only if they would be chosen by the parties in the original position is not itself an ultimate moral principle so much as a test of truth for proposed ultimate principles. The principles of social justice, though several in number, do have sufficient cohesion to play the role of a single ultimate principle in virtue of the strict priority rules that govern their application, but they are principles for the design of institutions and practices, not principles for individual actions. The most plausible candidate for a rival to the principle of utility as a standard of right conduct is the whole collection of principles assigning "natural duties" and obligations. However, these are *not* ordered by rigid priority rules and, thus, they lack the unity of their utilitarian counterpart. Still, the principle that imposes the "duty to uphold justice," directing us to obey the rules of established just practices and institutions, is very stringent and fundamental among these. So, for the sake of simplifying this discussion, we could consider *it* to be "the ethical first principle" for individuals in Rawls's system, at least for actions that fall within the ambit of already established near-just institutions. But we would have to remember that there are other natural duties that can conflict with the "duty to uphold justice" even for clearly rule-governed conduct. Some of these might very well have included the word 'justice' in *their* names; for surely the duties not to harm the innocent, not to disappoint reasonable expectations, not to assign arbitrarily heavy burdens, etc. have as much to do with justice as the duty to uphold just institutions has.

Now, one way of interpreting Rawls's rule-contractarianism is as follows. Normally we have the discretion, morally speaking, to appeal directly to the principles of natural duty in deciding what would be the right thing to do. Some actions, for example, are seen to be ineligible for our choice since they would violate the natural duty not to inflict harm upon the innocent. But when we are to act in our role as citizens in a fairly functioning democracy, when obedience to law is at issue, or when we occupy a special office such as juryman in a just institution, then we forfeit our right to appeal directly to the (other) first principles of natural duty, and the duty to uphold just institutions will normally trump. Thus, when the evidence establishes beyond a reasonable doubt that the defendant committed the crime with which he is charged, then we must find him guilty even though he is a morally innocent and admirable person charged under an odious but valid law. The example is an instance of "quasi-pure procedural justice," but it has elements of imperfect procedural justice too, since the fair procedures of a just institution, fairly followed, lead to a result which is unjust by a criterion that is independent of the institution itself. In a society whose basic structure is itself unjust or in an otherwise just society where a law has been created without proper regard to constitutionally specified procedures, the juryman's normal duty might be canceled. But the example in question is a case where there is a duty to perform an act (voting "guilty") that will have an unjust result. As such it is exactly parallel to the case under rule-utilitarianism where a person has a duty to perform an action with less than optimific consequences simply because he promised to perform that act and thus forfeited his right to appeal directly to considerations of utility in deciding what to do.

But suppose now that you are on a jury and the evidence establishes beyond a reasonable doubt that the ten-year-old defendant did steal turnips as charged and thereby committed a capital felony under duly established law. In this case the duty to uphold just institutions would have you commit not merely an unfortunate but routine injustice; rather it would have you become a party to a monstrous perversion of natural justice, a result so disastrously severe that the normally trumping effect of the duty to uphold just institutions would be nullified in this case. This example is exactly parallel to the case under rule-utilitarianism where a person must deliberately break his promise not because the net consequences of so doing are likely to be somewhat better on the whole than the consequences of keeping the promise (rule-utilitarianism would not permit that) but rather because breaking the promise is necessary to prevent some *severe* harm to third parties. The rules of promising themselves, having utilitarian grounding, would permit *that* kind of breach.

Violating one's oath as a juryman is an example more like conscientious refusal than like civil disobedience, but the principle involved is much the same. In both cases the natural duty to uphold just institutions conflicts with what can be called "the natural duty to oppose unjust laws, policies, and actions" (the latter a summary of all other natural duties that could well include the term 'justice' in their names). When the conflict is close, our natural duty on balance will be to try somehow to support just institutions and oppose injustice both, and civil disobedience, as Rawls conceives it, is a way of doing both these things at one stroke, since it is a way of "expressing disobedience to law within the limits of fidelity to law, although it is at the outer edge thereof" (366). In a nearly just society where the sense of justice is deeply entrenched, justified civil disobedience actually functions as "a final device to maintain the stability of a just constitution" (384). This is a welcome and ingenious idea, but one wonders whether an ideally just constitution will itself make some reference to civil disobedience and the conditions of its permissibility. If not, why not? If so, in what sense is civil disobedience "illegal"?

Rawls's theory of civil disobedience may well be the nearest thing we have yet to an adequate account of these subtle matters, but, for the reasons given above, I think that Rawls overestimates the role that contract and "pure procedural justice" play in it and in his theory of justice generally, and underestimates the extent of his own intuitionism.

JOEL FEINBERG

The Rockefeller University

Justice and the Treatment of Animals:
A Critique of Rawls

Michael S. Pritchard and Wade L. Robison*

Although the participants in the initial situation of justice in John Rawls' *Theory of Justice* choose principles of justice only, their choices have implications for other moral concerns. The only check on the self-interest of the participants is that there be unanimous acceptance of the principles. But, since animals are not participants, it is possible that principles will be adopted which conflict with what Rawls calls "duties of compassion and humanity" toward animals. This is a consequence of the initial situation's assumption that principles of justice can be determined independently of other moral considerations. We question this assumption, and show that satisfactory modifications of Rawls' initial situation undermine its contractarian basis and require the rejection of exclusively self-interested participants.

As Rawls himself points out, his theory of justice is not a complete moral theory. It concerns justice only, and justice is owed only to beings with a capacity for a sense of justice.[1] It says nothing about our moral duties to creatures lacking that capacity, except that we do not owe them justice. Of course, Rawls says:

It does not follow that there are no requirements at all in regard to them, nor in our relations with the natural order. Certainly it is wrong to be cruel to animals and the destruction of a whole species can be a great evil. The capacity for

---

* Michael S. Pritchard, Department of Philosophy, Western Michigan University, Kalamazoo, MI 49008; Wade L. Robison, Department of Philosophy, Kalamazoo College, Kalamazoo, MI 49001. Pritchard and Robison co-chair an interinstitutional committee on environmental ethics composed of faculty from Kalamazoo College and Western Michigan University, including such disciplines as philosophy, biology, political science, physics and religion. The authors thank Holly Goldman for helpful comments on an earlier draft of this paper.
[1] Rawls says this explicitly in "The Sense of Justice," *Philosophical Review* 72 (1963): esp. 281, 302–5. His position in *A Theory of Justice* (Cambridge: Harvard University Press, 1972) is not so clear. In section 77 he explicitly refuses to maintain "that the capacity for a sense of justice is necessary in order to be owed the duties of justice," but he finishes the same sentence by saying that "it does seem that we are not required to give strict justice anyway to creatures lacking this capacity" (p. 512). As he pointed out in "The Sense of Justice," "something must account for animals not being owed the duty of justice" (p. 303), and it is difficult to understand his hesitation in *A Theory of Justice*, section 77. This is particularly so because he says that "we use the characterization of the persons in the original position to single out the kind of beings to whom the principles chosen apply," and because he commits himself to the claim that the parties in the original position are capable of a sense of justice (*A Theory of Justice*, pp. 505 and 145 respectively). There are, in addition, good reasons for his making that capacity a necessary condition for being owed the duty of justice (see n. 4), and we shall thus assume that it is.

feelings of pleasure and pain and for the forms of life of which animals are capable clearly impose duties of compassion and humanity in their case.[2]

However, as Rawls adds, the "initial situation" of justice cannot account for such duties. Only a metaphysical theory determining our place in the natural order can do this. So, Rawls says:

> I shall not attempt to explain these considered beliefs. They are outside the scope of the theory of justice, and it does not seem possible to extend the contract doctrine so as to include them in a natural way. (p. 512)

Rawls' approach thus sharply contrasts with that of a utilitarian. A utilitarian proceeds from the consideration of the widest possible moral perspective to the principles of justice derived from that perspective. There can be no attempt to develop a utilitarian theory of justice independently of other moral considerations, since everything is supposed to be derived from the principle of utility. In contrast, Rawls assumes that it is possible to develop part of a moral theory, a theory of justice, independently of other moral concerns. Our contention is that if this is done as Rawls does it, the resulting institutional arrangements can very well involve unnecessary and undesirable conflicts between justice and duties of compassion and humanity to animals. Such conflicts, we believe, should not arise in an acceptable theory of justice. While no theory of justice can be expected to avoid the possibility of some conflict with duties to animals, there is reason to be concerned about the circumstances in which it is reasonable to say that these conflicts arise. Our contention is that, from the standpoint of Rawls' contractarian approach to justice, justice and duties to animals can be pitted against one another in circumstances in which such conflicts should not arise. We argue that the reason why Rawls cannot prevent these conflicts from arising is that there are serious defects in his initial situation.

We begin by presenting three essential features of the initial situation. First, the participants in that situation choose on the assumption that whatever society they may be in, "the condition of moderate scarcity" will obtain (pp. 127–28). Indeed, this is an objective condition that makes a theory of justice necessary, since, according to Rawls, without scarcity, every participant could have what is wanted, and there would be no need for a theory of distribution. Second, "the parties take no interest in one another's interests" (p. 127), only in their *own* interests. Rawls does not want to call them egoists because he thinks that implies they have specific interests, "say in wealth, prestige, and domination" (p. 13; see also p. 129), but they are self-interested because each is concerned with advancing his own interests. They "are not willing to have

---

[2] Rawls, *A Theory of Justice,* p. 512. Subsequent references to *A Theory of Justice* are placed within the body of the text.

their interests sacrificed to the others" (p. 129), and, indeed, "it is rational for (them) to suppose that they . . . want a larger share" of social goods (p. 143). We are thus supposed to assume them to be *so* self-interested that, if they could, they would not simply ignore, but hurt the interests of others for the sake of their own. But, third, no participant is able to do this to the other participants because unanimity in the selection of a theory of justice is required.[3] With that requirement, "it is not reasonable for (a participant) to expect more than an equal share in the division of social goods, (though it is) not rational for him to agree to less . . ." (p. 150). The check on the self-interest of a participant is the presence of other equally self-interested participants.

There is no check at all provided by those who are not participants. They are not parties to the initial contractual situation, and those who are parties are thus not required to take their interests into account in deciding upon a theory of justice: the principle of unanimity does not range over nonparticipants—and, indeed, it cannot, for one of the conditions of the contract is the requirement that those who are party to it be capable of living up to its conditions (p. 145). But nonparticipants are nonparticipants precisely because they are not capable of living up to its conditions: they lack the necessary capacity for a sense of justice. They thus cannot take part in deliberations about how benefits and burdens ought to be distributed in a just society.

Since those who can take part are presumed to be exclusively self-interested, they cannot consider the interests of nonparticipants except insofar as it is in their self-interest to do so. But they are choosing under conditions of moderate scarcity and cannot therefore treat animals, for example, in any other way than as resources. Self-interest requires that, for if "it is rational for (them) to suppose that they . . . want a larger share" of social goods, it is certainly not rational for them to accede to a lesser amount by, say, granting a right to life to nonparticipant sentient beings who have no right to have their interest in such a right taken into account. Like other natural resources, animals are simply there to be used.[4]

That many seem to have just this attitude towards animals is no consolation for Rawls. Since he morally objects to the cruelties and abuses inflicted on animals by those with this attitude, it should increase his worries. Even if one concedes that the contract doctrine does not imply the needless cruelty that so often accompanies the conception of animals as resources, it is consistent with it. Suppose that the participants agree upon a theory whose application

---

[3] This issue and its consequences have been explored in a paper by Wade Robison on "Rawls' Contractarianism." A version was presented at the American Philosophical Association Eastern Division Meeting, 1973.

[4] The implications of this point in regard to problems of the environment are explored in a paper by Wade Robison entitled "Rawls and Other Beings," in *Ecology and the Law*, ed. Eugene E. Dais (Buffalo: Wm. S. Hein & Co., 1978), pp. 205–16. That paper contains arguments for Rawls' commitment in *A Theory of Justice* to the capacity for a sense of justice being a necessary condition for being owed the duty of justice.

involves such needless cruelty. This undoubtedly would betray a lack of compassion and humanity for animals. But there is nothing in the initial situation to prohibit, or even discourage, this: self-interest checked only by other equally self-interested human beings is no check at all against perverse moral principles regarding other sentient beings.

A simple hypothetical example may help clarify this point and bring out another, more important, one. Imagine that four persons, Adams, Baker, Clark, and Davis, and a dog are left on an island for a month. Although the island itself can provide no food, they have been left with a moderate amount for their stay. No one can have all that he wants, but each can have enough to survive in relative comfort. The four persons now try to decide what a just distribution of the food would be. Having read Rawls' *Theory of Justice,* they try to simulate the deliberations of the participants in the initial situation (see p. 139). Eventually they agree that no inequality in the distribution of goods would be to the advantage of all of them and so decide that a just distribution of the food would be one-fourth each. Each is now assured of enough food to survive and can complain on grounds of justice if some inequality occurs.

So far there is no mention of the dog. In fact, as far as the theory of justice is concerned, the dog can be left to starve. Since "justice is the first virtue of social institutions" (p. 3), committing one's self to Rawls' theory of justice means committing one's self to treating certain other beings in ways that respect their sense of dignity of themselves as equals. But this commitment is consistent with perverse moral principles in regard to the rest of the sentient world. That is why there is no necessity for those on the island to feed the dog: having settled upon what is just, they are free to do what they will with the dog—insofar as justice is concerned.

But this objection, as stated, is a weak one, easily met by the counter argument that we should settle things one at a time. If Rawls' theory of justice is only consistent with perverse moral principles, there is no reason to suppose it inconsistent with laudable ones. Although each person on the island can claim that he has a just claim to his full share, there is nothing to prevent each from giving the dog some food if he wants to. In fact, each might act from a sense of duty toward the dog. Giving up a part of one's share under these circumstances does not seem to constitute an injustice to anyone. Although compassion and a sense of duty toward animals are not a part of the initial situation, once the veil of ignorance is lifted, it is quite possible for the participants to find themselves having these qualities.

But let us introduce a variation on the above. Suppose that everyone but Davis thinks that the dog should have some food, too. Now, if Davis is unwilling to give some food to the dog, the other three are faced with a dilemma. Either they allow Davis to keep all his food and they provide the dog with food only from their shares, or they try to make Davis give up some of his food, too. (This is assuming that they will not refuse to give the dog food simply so their shares remain the same as that of Davis.) On either alternative, Rawls' theory creates the real possibility of a moral conflict between justice and duties toward animals that an acceptable theory of justice should not allow.

If they choose the first alternative, they have a right to complain that, because of Davis' refusal to give up some of his share, they are suffering an injustice. After all, they agreed to equal shares, but now it turns out that Davis will have more than the rest and, if only he would do his part for the dog, Adams, Baker, and Clark would each have more for themselves (but no more than Davis). By their doing their duty, and Davis not doing his, they are making up out of their share what ought to be given by Davis, and thus, they complain, they are giving more than their fair share. Having recognized a duty towards animals, they now have a new problem of justice, one they could not have anticipated from the initial situation because, from that vantage point, there are no duties towards other sentient beings. In short, questions of justice cannot be separated from questions concerning how the rest of the sentient world should be treated. That they *ought* not to be separated is shown by the second alternative.

On this alternative, rather than suffer an injustice at Davis' hands, the others decide to try to make Davis give up some of his food. Of course, there are serious questions about how this might appropriately be done, but let us consider only the moral arguments that might be raised. Adams, Baker, and Clark claim that if only they feed the dog, Davis will be gaining unjustly at their expense. However, since Davis does not agree that he has a duty to help feed the dog, he will be unmoved. He might well reply: " "Look, if you want to feed the dog, that's your business. I couldn't care less what you do with your shares. But I want all of mine for myself."

One might be tempted to reply to Davis that he has a duty to give the dog some food whether he recognizes it or not; and, therefore, he has no moral complaint against some of his food being taken to feed the dog. Unfortunately, the initial situation prevents this reply from being adequate. It will be recalled that the initial situation yielded the result that each of the four persons has a just claim to one-fourth of the food. Now, although we need not hold that considerations of justice always outweigh other moral considerations, it cannot be denied that for Rawls just claims carry great moral weight. Even if it can be argued that Davis has a duty to help feed the dog, this duty must be pitted against Davis' claim, in the name of justice, that he is entitled to keep his full share.

Regardless of which way the argument ultimately swings, it cannot be denied that the initial situation gives *some* moral weight to Davis' position. Such a consequence is not simply bizarre; it is dangerous as well. It is dangerous because it gives moral weight to matters that should not be taken seriously at all, let alone as considerations of justice, for it presents us with the problem of having to choose between treating persons with full justice or treating animals without compassion or humanity. Unfortunately, this adds *moral* weight to the perspective of those already prepared to do the latter. There could be circumstances in which there is such a shortage of resources that one might have to face up to such a moral choice, but the example under consideration, not to speak of many others of a similar nature, is not one of them.

Our objection is not that treating animals cruelly is unjust, but rather that the domain of just concerns ought to be restricted from the very outset in light of other moral considerations. There is no good reason to suppose that the range of resources to which human beings might claim they are justly entitled is not limited by other moral considerations. This is perfectly compatible with animals not being owed duties of justice. It does not follow from the fact that animals are not owed duties of justice that the scope of possibly just claims should not be affected by other kinds of duties we have toward them.

Rawls' contract doctrine seems unable to incorporate such a restriction, for there seem to be only two ways to modify the initial situation to bring about the required result, and neither preserves contractarianism. The first modification would be to lower the veil of ignorance so that the participants might end up, for all they could know, being animals once the veil is removed. As a practical matter, this would enormously complicate calculations. (For example, the primary good, self-esteem, would be inapplicable to animals, so any presumption of initial equality with respect to it would be pointless.) But, apart from this, it would conflate the derivation of Rawls' theory of justice with the derivation of morality in general. The participants would not be determining simply what is just. They would be asking the far more general question of what kind of moral world there should be. This is no longer merely a matter of reciprocity among moral persons, and the concept of a contract simply disappears. If it is an essential condition of a contract for Rawls that those who make it be able to keep it, and if a condition of keeping it is that one have the capacity for a sense of justice, then there can be no contract among participants, some of whom may become sentient beings without the capacity for a sense of justice. Perhaps this is why Rawls says that "it does not seem possible to extend the contract doctrine ... in a natural way" to include duties of compassion and humanity (p. 512).

The other modification would be to impose another condition on the participants, *viz.*, that they accept the notion that animals should be humanely treated. But, if this modification is made, the participants are no longer contracting only in their own behalf, and the mutual acknowledgement of those in whose behalf they are acting (animals) is not being sought. There is no longer any point in supposing that the participants are mutually and exclusively self-interested. It is more appropriate to suppose the participants compassionate and humane; and it would be arbitrary to have their compassion and humanity extend only to animals and not to their fellow humans as well.

But this supposition effectively destroys one of the most powerful features of Rawls' contractarian justification of his theory: that a strongly egalitarian theory is chosen by self-interested persons. This feature serves to buttress his theory in a powerful way, for if self-interested persons choose it, certainly, it seems, anyone else would. Yet, given concerns about the rest of the sentient world, conceiving of the participants as compassionate is more acceptable morally than conceiving of them as exclusively self-interested. In fact, it would seem that Rawls should conceive of them as compassionate. He characterizes those in the original position as moral persons (e.g., p. 19), and of moral persons he says that "they are capable *(and are assumed to acquire)* a sense of justice" (p. 505, emphasis added). But in his account of the development of moral personality in part three of his book, by the time a person has a sense of justice he or she already has considerable fellow-feeling: the latter is presented as a psychologically necessary condition for the former (see sections 70–75). To ask such persons to leave their compassion at the gate when considering principles of justice is to ask for an unrealistic splintering of moral personality as well as for a distortion of their sense of justice, for it is a distortion to suggest that those with a sense of justice feel any *moral conflict* between humane treatment of animals and the requirements of justice in the kind of circumstances we have discussed.

An Extension of Rawls' Theory of Justice to Environmental Ethics

Brent A. Singer*

By combining and augmenting recent arguments that have appeared in the literature, I show how a modified Rawlsian theory of justice generates a strong environmental and animal rights ethic. These modifications include significant changes in the conditions of the contract situation vis-à-vis *A Theory of Justice*, but I argue that these modifications are in fact more consistent with Rawls' basic assumptions about the functions of a veil of ignorance and a thin theory of the good.

I

My overall goal in this paper is to show how a modified Rawlsian theory of justice generates a relatively strong environmental and animal rights ethic. I combine, and, in many cases, sharpen the focus of arguments that have appeared in recent literature on the subject, and, in addition, I develop some insights of my own.

I speak of "a Rawlsian theory of justice" because although the modifications herein advocated significantly alter the conditions of the contract situation vis-à-vis *A Theory of Justice,* this modified theory still proceeds according to the idea of self-interested participants in an original position selecting principles of justice according to a thin theory of primary goods.[1]

That these ideas are conceived within a Rawlsian framework does not imply that such a framework is the only one, nor even the best one, within which a satisfactory environmental and animal rights ethic can be formulated. Nor does it imply that (environmental and animal rights issues aside) a Rawlsian theory of justice is generally superior to all the rest. I do believe that one of the virtues of a Rawlsian approach is that within such a framework one is able to develop and to evaluate various contents. In this way I sympathize with the concerns of those who criticize various parts of the content of Rawls' theory. At the same time, however, I remain unconvinced that there is something essentially pernicious

* Department of Philosophy, The Maples, University of Maine, Orono, ME 04469. Singer's primary interest is the history of modern philosophy, with special emphasis on practical and political issues and on phenomenology. He has previously published papers on the practical philosophies of Kant and Spinoza.
[1] John Rawls, *A Theory of Justice* (Cambridge: Harvard University Press, 1972). All page numbers in the text refer to this work.

about the very way that a Rawlsian sort of social contract theorist must pose the issues from the outset.

This paper is divided hereafter into three mostly independent sections followed by a brief and general conclusion. The first section deals with issues in the conservation of air, land, and water; the second deals with the rights of nonhuman animals with interests; and the third deals with the preservation of natural settings on behalf of securing the liberty of conscience (religious and spiritual freedoms) for members of a just society.

II

According to Rawls, primary goods are those things that a rational man is supposed to want, whatever else he wants (pp. 66, 92, 411).[2] "The preference for primary goods is derived," says Rawls, "from only the most general assumptions about rationality and the conditions of human life" (p.293). Rawls assumes that the reasoners behind the veil of ignorance all accept the same list of primary goods, and it is this "thin" conception of the good that enables them to choose principles of justice on a rational basis (p. 397).

Within the category of primary goods, Rawls distinguishes between *social* and *natural* primary goods (p. 62). The former are "at the disposition of society," whereas the latter are "not so directly" under the control of the basic structure of society (p. 62). Rawls lists rights and liberties, power and opportunities, income and wealth, and self-respect, as examples of social primary goods, and he lists health, vigor, intelligence, and imagination as examples of natural primary goods (p. 62).

Among primary social goods Rawls draws a further distinction between basic liberties on the one hand, and economic and social gains on the other (p. 63). Rawls lists as basic liberties the right to vote and to be eligible for public office, freedom of speech and assembly, liberty of conscience, the right to hold personal property, and freedom from arbitrary arrest and seizure (p. 61). Together these basic liberties form the basis for self-respect, which is also a primary social good. Rawls argues that reasoners behind the veil of ignorance would select principles of justice such that exchanges between basic liberties and economic/social gains would not be allowed—that is, it would be unjust to trade the basic liberties of some for the economic/social gains of others (p.63). Thus, on behalf of Rawls, I distinguish between *higher* primary social goods and *lower* primary

---

[2] Except for one larger and two smaller modifications, the reasoning in this section parallels that found in Russ Manning, "Environmental Ethics and Rawls' Theory of Justice," *Environmental Ethics* 3 (1981): 155–66.

social goods, where the former include basic liberties and self-respect, and the latter include such things as power, opportunities, income, and wealth.[3]

Now, supposing (with Rawls) that whatever else rational human beings desire, they desire, for example, the right to vote, it is also true that whatever else rational human beings desire, they desire, on the whole, regular access to potable water, shelter from freezing temperatures, uncontaminated food supplies, and safe air to breathe. Although it may be true (following Rawls) that it is not rational for human beings to sacrifice higher social primary goods (such as the right to vote) for various social and economic privileges, it is also not rational for human beings to sacrifice potable water and safe air to breathe for various social and economic privileges *if* such privileges, whatever they are, are had at the expense of potable water and safe air to breathe. That is, it is at least as rational for human beings *not to trade* safe air and potable water for social and economic privileges, as it is rational for human beings *not to trade* the right to vote for social and economic privileges. The question thus arises, "Why does Rawls not include from the start such things as regular access to safe air and potable water in his list of higher primary goods?"

The answer is that Rawls assumes from the start that the reasoners behind the veil of ignorance know that whatever else is the particular circumstances of their lives, they will, in any case, find themselves living under "conditions of moderate scarcity" (p. 127). Although Rawls is not very precise about what this means, it is fair to assume (on the basis of what he says) that a "condition of moderate scarcity" can be taken as a condition where there are no unalterable natural circumstances such that, no matter the basic structure of society, some persons *must* do without regular access to potable water, uncontaminated food, shelter from freezing temperatures, and safe air to breathe. In other words, Rawls takes it for granted, albeit indirectly, that the lower social primary goods (i.e., various economic and social gains) are luxury items compared with regular access to potable water, uncontaminated food, and safe air to breathe, and that these latter goods, on the whole, rank just as highly in order of rational preference as do the higher primary social goods.[4]

---

[3] Manning appears to be mistaken in his explication of Rawls' account of primary goods. In terms of the distinctions just made, Manning appears to conflate lower primary social goods with the category of primary social goods in general, and he places self-respect in this lower category rather than among the higher primary social goods as Rawls suggests (Manning, "Environmental Ethics and Rawls' Theory of Justice," p. 157). This change does not, however, adversely affect Manning's overall thesis.

[4] One might wonder whether such things as regular access to potable water and safe air to breathe are "natural" or "social" primary goods. Because they are "bodily," one might list them as "natural." Yet the water that flows from my tap depends on an extensive public works program, and the quality of air that I breathe depends greatly on the principal economic, social, educational, and legal arrangements of my society, which, in Rawls' terms, amounts to the "basic structure of society" (Rawls, *A Theory of Justice*, p. 7).

My position, therefore, is that principles of justice ought to stipulate directly that just as it is wrong to trade the right to vote and liberty of conscience of some for the social and economic privileges of others, so too it is wrong to trade the food and water of some for the social and economic privileges of others. If it were to turn out that there are *no* unalterable natural circumstances such that some people *must* do without regular access to potable water, uncontaminated food, and so forth, then the satisfaction of primary desires of rational beings for these goods would be assured in a just society—that is, *if* there were people who did lack these goods, our principles of justice would direct us explicitly to resolve the situation as expediently as possible.[5]

It is important to emphasize the ramifications here not just in terms of duties toward those living in abject poverty, but also in terms of duties toward persons currently of economic and social privilege. For given conditions as they are today, it would not take much by way of certain industrial developments—or nuclear accidents—to create conditions of severe scarcity in which it would be physically impossible for some—even many—to satisfy their primary desires for regular access to potable water, uncontaminated food supplies, and so forth. Thus the principles of justice that I am considering would forbid institutional and social developments that risk putting us into conditions of severe scarcity, and the force of these injunctions would be even stronger—in fact, far stronger—if such principles required that we also take into account the primary interests of future generations as well. Rawls argues that they do, and I agree, but not for the same reason.[6]

Rawls asserts that participants behind the veil of ignorance do not know to which generation they belong; they do not know the economic or political situation of their society, and they do not know the form of its culture or civilization (p. 137). But they do know that, whatever their generation, they all belong to the same one (p. 292). The question is, "What prevents them from selecting principles of justice which would permit their generation to use up all of

---

[5] Manning argues that health, which is a natural primary good according to Rawls, is actually a social primary good and he then draws the obvious connection between health and the requisite air, land, and water ("Environmental Ethics and Rawls' Theory of Justice," pp. 158–60). Although this approach succeeds, it is not necessary to be this indirect, and moreover, one might want to challenge the rationale for making the distinction between natural and social primary goods in the first place.

[6] Manning also argues that Rawls is open to criticism on this point and that a different approach is needed. I am uncertain, however, that Manning's solution ultimately stands up to his objection. That is, Manning argues that Rawls' assumption that participants in the original position are self-interested, and mutually disinterested, contradicts Rawls' further assumption that they represent continuing lines of claims and care for their immediate descendants. Manning's solution is to treat future generations analogously to children, which is to say, as potential participants in a just society ("Environmental Ethics and Rawls' Theory of Justice," pp. 161–65). But accepting Manning's premise that the participants' self-interest and mutual disinterest precludes their caring about their continuing lines of descent, why should it not also preclude their caring for the rights of future potential participants as well?

the available water, air, and soil as long as barely enough remains until they die?"

Rawls' response is that participants in the original position know that they represent family lines with ties of sentiment for their immediate descendants (p. 292). The problem with this (besides appearing somewhat gratuitous) is that it also assumes, indirectly at least, that having children is part of every rational plan of life.[7] My spouse and I, however, have thought the matter through, and we are not planning to have any children. I believe that in our case this is consistent with a rational plan of life, and, in any event, it would be easy to conceive of other cases in which this is more clearly the case. It therefore makes more sense to assume that the parties behind the veil of ignorance do not know to which generation they belong *in the stronger sense* that they may turn out to belong to the current generation, or they may turn out to belong to any one of several future generations. In this case, participants would not pick principles that permitted the current generation to use up all of the air, land, and water, since participants might find themselves belonging to a future generation. This is more in keeping with the purpose of the veil of ignorance, which is to ensure that principles are not chosen which favor the particular circumstances of any one person or group of persons.[8]

Thus by supplementing Rawls' list of primary goods to include directly such things as regular access to potable water and safe air to breathe, and by taking into account the interests of future generations as I have just suggested, strong principles of environmental conservation follow from a Rawlsian theory of justice.

III

Consider the following line of reasoning which I shall refer to as the "Van-DeVeer thesis."[9] (1) In a Rawlsian theory of justice, the purpose of the veil of

---

[7] The point is that, according to Rawls, all participants in the original position find themselves in the same position, namely, caring for their immediate descendants. This means that even if one interprets "immediate descendants" to include adopted children (which makes good sense) or nieces and nephews (which may be stretching it), *all* participants in the original position know that they either have children or siblings with children. Since every rational plan of life is built first of all upon the theory of the good entertained in the original position, it follows that not having children (or siblings with children) is inconsistent with a thoroughly rational plan of life.

[8] Rawls considers the alternative I suggest, and he rejects it (*A Theory of Justice*, p. 292). The only apparent reason that he gives is that to include the interests of future generations in this way is too hard to intuit (p. 139). Yet by insisting that participants in the original position take into account their continuing lines of descent, Rawls basically asks them to intuit the same thing that they would following my suggestion. That is, in both cases they are to intuit the interests of future generations as if these interests are their own. My alternative is more direct, less gratuitous, and it does not assume that every rational plan of life involves having children.

[9] See Donald VanDeVeer, "Of Beasts, Persons, and the Original Position," *The Monist* 62 (1979): 368–77. The line of reasoning that I present is a reconstruction of VanDeVeer's basic argument. It

ignorance is to ensure that self-interested reasoners, whose task it is to select principles of justice under which they will live, decide impartially in the sense that they will not favor their own interests over the interests of others, on the basis of natural contingencies and social accidents.[10]

(2) Thus, in a Rawlsian theory of justice, the veil of ignorance does not allow the reasoners in the original position to know anything about the natural contingencies and social accidents that play a role in their particular cases.

(3) It is therefore "not contrary to the presuppositions of Rawls' heuristic device to think of the participants in the original position as yet-to-be-embodied or yet-to-be-born souls at least temporarily having the sophisticated capacities to rationally consider alternatives, the subtleties of a just-savings principle, and maximax and maximin decision principles."[11]

(4) By (2), such yet-to-be-embodied reasoners are ignorant of the natural contingencies and social accidents of their embodiment. For all they know, their embodiment might be as anencephalic infants, Tay-Sachs children, or serious psychotics.[12]

(5) By (4), reasoners in the original position ought to take into account the interests of *nonmoral beings with interests* (see note 12), and this accords with

---

does not exhaust his treatment, and in places, with malice of forethought, I have altered his emphasis and terminology. One finds similar arguments, though not as fully developed, in Tom Regan, "Duties to Animals: Rawls' Dilemma," *Ethics and Animals* 2 (1981): 76–81; Robert Elliot, "Rawlsian Justice and Non-Human Animals," *Journal of Applied Philosophy* 1 (1984): 95–106. All three authors consider possible objections to this line of reasoning, and all three argue that these objections fail. I consider three such objections below.

[10] VanDeVeer nowhere asserts this all at once, though it is strongly implied at various points in his article. There is current debate over the precise function of the veil of ignorance in Rawls' theory of justice, and one objection that has been raised against the VanDeVeer thesis is that it does not correctly conceive the role of the veil of ignorance. See Alan E. Fuchs, "Duties to Animals: Rawls' Alleged Dilemma," *Ethics and Animals* 2 (1981): 83–87. Fuchs argues that the primary function of the veil of ignorance is not "to ensure the impartiality of the chosen principles," but "to model the Kantian idea of a *categorical imperative*, a principle that would be autonomously chosen by free and equal rational beings who merely regard themselves as such and who seek to express that nature in their choices" (Fuchs, "Duties to Animals," p. 85). I consider this objection later in this section in terms of the question of the nature of the self-interest of rationality.

[11] Donald VanDeVeer, "Of Beasts, Persons, and the Original Position," p. 369.

[12] I do not think that Rawls would agree that their embodiment might be as serious psychotics, Tay-Sachs children, etc., and a weakness of VanDeVeer's article is that he appears to assume that Rawls does hold such a position (VanDeVeer, "Of Beasts, Persons, and the Original Position," p. 371). The important issue here is whether the reasoners behind the veil of ignorance know that they will turn out to be *moral beings,* where moral beings are understood as beings whose capacity to reason is sufficient for developing a sense of justice and a sense of their own good in terms of a rational plan for living (Rawls, *A Theory of Justice,* pp. 506–12; VanDeVeer, "Of Beasts, Persons, and the Original Position," pp. 369–70). VanDeVeer's point is that the people alluded to in (4) are plausible candidates for beings who do not meet this minimum level of rationality, and yet who still possess interests in the sense that they still can feel better and worse. I hereafter refer to the desires and interests of such "nonmoral" beings as "nonrational desires and interests." I also assume that such "nonrational" desires need not be "irrational"—that is, they need not come into conflict with reason, although, in some cases, they might.

the purpose of the veil of ignorance, which is to ensure that self-interested reasoners do not favor their own interests over the interests of others on the basis of natural contingencies and social accidents.

(6) Like anencephalic children, Tay-Sachs children, and serious psychotics, many animals also have interests in how they are treated. Such animals can suffer and feel better and worse, and if the natural contingencies of reasoners in the original position include the possibility that they might turn out to be extreme psychotics, etc., it is arbitrary to insist that they cannot turn out to be healthy pandas, llamas, seals, whales, lions, horses, gorillas, otters, or any other animal with interests.

(7) Therefore, by (6), reasoners in the original position ought to take into account the interests not only of moral and nonmoral humans, but of many species of animals as well. This accords with the purpose of the veil of ignorance, which is to ensure that self-interested reasoners do not favor their own interests on the basis of natural contingencies and social accidents. Not to include many animals in this thought experiment, the aim of which is to develop sound principles of justice, would be to prejudice the question of the just treatment of animals in favor of human beings from the outset.

Let's consider three objections to the VanDeVeer thesis.[13] The first is that to allow that reasoners in the original position may turn out to be nonhuman animals "enormously complicate[s] calculations."[14]

One response to this objection is that to argue that something is difficult—even extremely difficult—is no argument against it being morally right.[15] A second response, however, is that there are reasons to think that calculations would not be more difficult than they would be with only humans to worry about, and that, in some instances, the calculations might even be simpler.[16] That is, we regularly make comparative judgments about the well-being of different animals since it is easy to see, for example, that this bear is probably very healthy, whereas that otter is living a miserable life. Indeed, it is often (though clearly not always) easier to judge that nonhuman animals suffer, and why, than it is to judge that humans suffer, and why, for, on the whole, the primary interests of nonhuman animals are often more straightforward than the primary interests of human

---

[13] The first objection is contained explicitly in Michael S. Pritchard and Wade L. Robinson, "Justice and the Treatment of Animals: A Critique of Rawls," *Environmental Ethics* 3 (1981): 55–61. Robert Elliot responds to this objection in "Rawlsian Justice and Non-Human Animals," pp. 95–106. The second objection is also contained explicitly in Pritchard and Robinson, "Justice and the Treatment of Animals," as well as implicitly in Alan E. Fuchs, "Duties to Animals: Rawls' Alleged Dilemma," *Ethics and Animals* 2 (1981): 83–87. Elliot responds to this objection, but not as sharply as he could. The third objection, in its strongest form, is not found explicitly in any of these works, although it is anticipated by Fuchs, Pritchard and Robinson, and, to some degree, even Rawls.

[14] Pritchard and Robinson, "Justice and the Treatment of Animals," p. 60.

[15] Elliot, "Rawlsian Justice and Non-Human Animals," p. 103.

[16] Ibid., pp. 103–04.

beings, even though the ecological factors which sustain a healthy environment for humans and nonhumans alike are very subtle and complex.[17] In addiction, it is unnecessary (and unreasonable) to pick principles of justice that require fine distinctions between the comparative well-being of, say, an ox (well treated) on the farm and an otter in the wild. Rawls himself purposely avoids putting people in the position of having to make fine numerical distinctions between the relative well-being of different individuals, and there is no reason why this level of generality could not be applied to various species of animals as well.[18]

The second objection to the VanDeVeer thesis is that for a contract to be binding those who make the contract must be able to keep it. Because only moral beings with a sense of justice can keep contracts, nonmoral beings with interests cannot be included as the VanDeVeer thesis requires.[19]

The response to this objection is that it misunderstands the VanDeVeer thesis. The VanDeVeer thesis does not require that any being make a contract who cannot keep it. The only beings who make the contract (which is purely hypothetical anyway) are rational beings—reasoners behind the veil of ignorance. Since there are no nonmoral beings *behind* the veil of ignorance, all beings who are party to the "contract" are also beings who can keep the contract.[20]

---

[17] For example, Gerald Doppelt has recently argued that Rawls misunderstands the material bases for peoples' self-respect, and that this mistake tends to undermine Rawls' entire system. See Gerald Doppelt, "Rawls' System of Justice: A Critique from the Left," *Nous* 15 (1981): 259–308. My point is not that Doppelt is actually correct or incorrect, but that his objection is plausible, and, apparently, not easily resolved. The case with regard to primary goods for many species of nonhuman animals does not appear to be so complex. To be sure, certain species of whales or apes (for example) may well be able to suffer serious spiritual or psychological discomfort even if they have safe food and water supplies in an open range that can support their populations, and we should remain open to this possibility in light of any tendency to underestimate the intellect and feelings of animals; nevertheless, similar claims on behalf of numerous other species (for example, otters, deer, alligators, and ducks), claims that they too can suffer serious spiritual or psychological discomfort when there is adequate open range, etc., do not appear very reasonable on the basis of some of what we already know from neurology, evolutionary biology, and empirical psychology.

[18] Since Rawls defines primary goods as those things which a rational *man* wants, whatever else he wants, the VanDeVeer thesis also requires some modifications in Rawls' account of primary goods. Elliot raises this issue, but his most substantive remarks are devoted to trying to show how income and wealth can be reinterpreted as primary goods for nonhuman animals ("Rawlsian Justice and Non-Human Animals," pp. 102–03). In section two, I argued that Rawls' account of primary goods ought to be supplemented regardless of the VanDeVeer thesis, and it should be apparent that the changes suggested therein already go some way toward making Rawls' theory of primary goods applicable to nonhuman animals as well (i.e., human and nonhuman animals alike have primary interests in regular access to safe air, food, and water).

[19] Pritchard and Robinson, "Justice and the Treatment of Animals," p. 60.

[20] Thus Fuchs is mistaken when he interprets the VanDeVeer thesis as entailing that we "entertain the thought of parties in the original position who are not rational beings" ("Duties to Animals," p. 86). Elliot also does not see this as clearly as he might since his response is not that the VanDeVeer thesis does not require nonmoral beings behind the veil of ignorance, but that it is false that a sense of justice is required by all parties to a contract in order that the contract be binding ("Rawlsian Justice and Non-Human Animals," p. 105).

The second objection, however, does anticipate the third and most serious objection. This objection, as it is formulated by Pritchard, Robinson, and Fuchs, is that to include animals within the scope of the principles chosen behind the veil of ignorance is to choose principles that can no longer be principles of *justice*. Justice is a matter of reciprocity among moral beings only. Nonmoral beings fall outside the sphere of justice.[21]

Elliot's only response to this objection is that the VanDeVeer thesis merely widens the scope of justice to include animals.[22] From the objectors' position (including Rawls', pp. 251–57), however, this not only begs the question, but it covers up a deeper issue (at least as I understand it). To follow the line of reasoning of the objectors, we are to think of the principles chosen behind the veil of ignorance as legislation *for* a kingdom of ends.[23] That is, the veil of ignorance is designed to model a situation in which rational beings are legislating for—that is, in the interest of—*rational beings*. Such rational beings are to choose principles that best manifest *their* freedom (p. 255), and hence principles of justice are *self*-interested principles, where the "self" involved is a *rational* self.

The issue, therefore, is not just a terminological dispute in which Fuchs wants to restrict the use of the term *justice* and Elliot does not; rather, the dispute centers on the nature of the *self*-interestedness of rationality. If we want to maintain (as VanDeVeer does) that we are looking for principles that would be chosen on behalf of *self-interest alone,* we are open to the following objection: the VanDeVeer thesis claims that natural contingencies allow that a reasoner behind the veil of ignorance might become, for example, an otter. Reasoners in the original position, in contrast, consider the matter only in terms of the self-interest of a self that is rational, and this rational self, which is the object of their self-interest, is necessarily different from nonrational otter selves. Hence, reasoners in the original position cannot, on the basis of self-interest alone, determine any principle that would be directly in the interest of otters (or any other nonrational beings).

Consider two responses to this objection. First, on what basis has it been shown that it is not the nature of reason itself, as a ruling principle, to take into direct account nonrational interests? To recall a theme from book one of the *Republic,* it is the nature of a ruling principle not to look out for itself, but to look out for whatever it is that it rules. The implication is that, contrary to the view of Thrasymachos, justice is not following the laws of rulers who legislate for their own advantage only, but rather, justice is following the laws of genuine rulers

---

[21] Pritchard and Robinson, "Justice and the Treatment of Animals," p. 60; Fuchs, "Duties to Animals," p. 86.

[22] Elliot, "Rawlsian Justice and Non-Human Animals," pp. 104–05.

[23] Rawls, *A Theory of Justice,* p. 252; Fuchs, "Duties to Animals," p. 86.

who legislate for the good of their subjects as well. This is not to say that the genuine ruler (and the ultimate ruler, for Socrates, is reason) gets sacrificed in the process, but that the genuine ruler makes laws that bind, *in harmony*, the nonrational with the rational. Thus, reason is not a tyrant that perceives its own good in the disadvantage of its subjects, but a sovereign that conceives its own good in the advantage of rational and nonrational alike.[24]

Second, reasoners behind the veil of ignorance *do* have a direct interest, albeit a *partial* one, in the satisfaction of nonrational desires, since reasoners in the original position and nonrational beings *share* certain primary goods. That is, the self that reasons *behind* the veil of ignorance is a self that includes, even according to Rawls, an interest in health as a living being, and this interest only makes sense in terms of concomitant interests in potable water, safe air to breathe, and so forth, interests that are the typical interests of nonrational beings as well.

Thus, the self that is *behind* the veil of ignorance is a self that includes nonrational (though not irrational) interests. When reasoners behind the veil of ignorance consider the interests of nonrational animals, they are not considering wholly alien interests. On the contrary, *behind* the veil of ignorance, reasoners know that *parts of themselves* (their nonrational parts) are *the same* as parts of what might be otter selves, and hence, out of a *complete* self-interest—that is, out of an interest for *all parts* of themselves, rational and nonrational alike— reasoners must take into account the nonrational interests of otters as well. In other words, even though certain rational parts of themselves would be missing should they turn out to be otter selves, parts of themselves would still be there (for example, parts that experience pain due to poisoned air or water, or due to highly traumatic situations), and it is these latter parts that need to be taken into account if the reasoners are to be completely self-interested, which is to say, interested in *all parts* of themselves, including those nonrational parts with interests that could be incarnated as various animals.

The third objection is correct in pointing out that the rational self, which is the object of the self-interest of reasoners in the original position, is different from, for example, a nonrational otter self. But the objection is wrong to infer from this that the reasoners in the original position cannot, on the basis of self-interest alone, determine any principle that would be directly in the interest of an otter self (or some other nonrational self), for the objection fails to realize that being different does not in this case entail being completely other. Even though part of the rational self behind the veil of ignorance is different from an otter self, part of it is also the same, and a complete (or perfect) regard for the former entails a regard for the latter as well.

---

[24] One may disagree that this is a lesson from the *Republic;* the important point is only that regardless of where the idea comes from, its relevance for the VanDeVeer thesis is clear.

IV

We have seen that a Rawlsian theory of justice can be extended so that it requires strong legislation for the conservation of water, air, and land. We also have seen that such a theory can be extended to include the rights of nonrational animals with interests. Yet this extension tends to leave out a concern for the environment, which has more to do with the aesthetic and spiritual dimension of our intercourse with nature than with satisfying our primary desires for safe air, water, and food. That is, can a Rawlsian theory of justice be extended to require legislation to protect, for example, stretches of wilderness, or places of great natural beauty, even if the preservation of these locations is not vital for securing regular access to safe air, potable water, and so forth?

To begin with, insofar as we are required to take into account the interests of nonhuman animals, not just of this, but of future generations as well (as I have argued in sections two and three), it is very likely that legislation protecting the integrity of many natural habitats and wilderness areas has to be, as a matter of course, forthcoming. We can go somewhat further, however, by taking into fuller consideration Rawls' ideas about liberty of conscience (pp. 205–21), for in Rawls' theory of justice (and I assume that he is correct about this), liberty of conscience is a basic liberty. This means that it is unjust to sacrifice the religious and moral freedom of some for the lower social primary goods of others (p. 206). Moreover, the right to practice one's religion does not depend on what religion it happens to be (unless it violates the basic liberties of others). In other words, for all they know, reasoners behind the veil of ignorance could turn out to be Catholic, Anglican, Jewish, Taoist, Hopi, Cherokee, Mbuti, or *caboclos* (an aboriginal Amazonian tribe). Although it is sometimes overlooked, many religions (probably most) have material bases such that in the absence of these, the practice of that religion is rendered very difficult, if not impossible. In addition, it is often the case that these material bases include land formations, forests, lakes, mountains, streams, and caves as these natural phenomena exist for the most part untouched by human hands—or, if touched, left as much as possible undisturbed. Thus, to safeguard religious freedoms in practice, and not in name only, such sacred sites must be protected by law from various forms of industrial and commercial development.[25]

In the United States, for example, some American Indian tribes have recently filed lawsuits pleading that their first amendment rights are (or shortly will be) violated by certain industrial expansions, most of which (in terms of the categories set forth in this paper) clearly pertain to the satisfaction of the lower primary

---

[25] For example, the destruction of some parts of the Amazon forest has been at least temporarily halted because of the religious beliefs of the *caboclos* who hold that the forest is a home for all sorts of vital spirits. See Nigel Smith, "Enchanted Forest," *Natural History* 92, no. 8 (1983): 14–20.

social desires of a few.[26] Typical of such cases is a case in which the expansion of a ski resort in North Central Arizona would destroy the "Home of the Kachinas."[27] As a chairman of the Hopi Indian Tribal Council testified:

> . . . in the long run if the expansion is permitted, we will not be able successfully to teach our people that this is a sacred place. If the ski resort remains or is expanded, our people will not accept the view that this is the sacred Home of the Kachinas. . . . This will have a direct and negative impact upon our religious practices. The destruction of these practices will also destroy our present way of life and culture.[28]

In this court action, and four out of five similar cases, the Indians lost. In general, authors seem to agree that part of the problem is a kind of implicit religious preference that inhabits the federal court system.[29] Here the predominant ideology perceives religion as a segment of a life that can be clearly documented, neatly set apart, and transported at will from place to place. Religion in this sense is primarily "in the head" and "otherworldly."[30] From this perspective, religions that are not set down in writing, or that are inextricably interwoven with daily practices and natural phenomena, are "primitive," perhaps not "genuine religions" at all, and, in any event, not to be taken as seriously. Thus the American legal system, as Gordan puts it,

> has generally failed to recognize that physical locations within its own jurisdiction may be of vital significance to site-specific religions. It does not acknowledge that a sense of spiritual immediacy and of awe for places that have witnessed momentous spiritual events, similar to that felt by many Jews and Christians only in the "Holy Land," is felt by Native Americans for sites that may seem unremarkable or of mere natural beauty to non-Indian observers.[31]

---

[26] See Sarah B. Gordan, "Indian Religious Freedom and Governmental Development of Public Lands," *Yale Law Journal* 94 (1985): 1447–71; Robert S. Michaelsen, "American Indian Religious Freedom Litigation: Promises and Perils," *Journal of Law & Religion* 3 (1985): 47–76.

[27] Michaelsen, "American Indian Religious Freedom Litigation," p. 47; Gordan, "Indian Religious Freedom," p. 1448. The case is *Wilson* v. *Block*, 708 F.2d 735 (D.C. Cir. 1983), *cert. denied*, 104 S. Ct. 371 (1983). The Kachinas are spirits who are intermediaries between people and the creator.

[28] *Wilson* v. *Block*, at 740, note 2.

[29] Michaelson, "American Indian Religious Freedom Litigation," pp. 58–64; Gordan, "Indian Religious Freedom," p. 1464.

[30] Marx also thought that religion is primarily "otherworldly" (although he did think that this aspect of religion tends to express itself most completely in a liberal democracy). Thus, he wrote, "For what in fact is [the religious spirit] but the unwordly form of a stage in the development of the human mind. . . . The religious and theological consciousness itself is heightened and accentuated under a completed democracy, because it is apparently without political significance, without earthly aims . . . because it is a really other-wordly life." See Karl Marx, "On the Jewish Question," in *Selected Essays of Karl Marx*, trans. H. Stenning (London: Leonard Parsons, 1926), pp. 66–67.

[31] Gordan, "Indian Religious Freedom and Governmental Development of Public Lands," p. 1451.

In a Rawlsian theory of justice such cultural prejudices are (ideally) wiped away behind the veil of ignorance. Not only are legislation and institutions derived from the principles chosen from the original position highly sensitive to the real diversity of religious practices, but, in addition, liberty of conscience is conceived broadly by Rawls as a liberty to pursue the perfection of the human spirit, however this perfection is conceived. This, in effect, grants security for many practices that are associated with people who simply have a great reverence for nature, regardless of the peculiarities of their metaphysics. Included herein, are the practices associated with such people as Aldo Leopold, Thoreau, certain romantic poets and artists, as well as "nature freaks" in general.

The point, of course, is not that liberty of conscience ought now to ride roughshod over every other concern of justice. On the contrary, conflicts naturally occur between protecting the liberty of conscience of some and securing the basic liberties of others. For example, the Seminole Indians in Florida are currently arguing in federal court that it is part of their religion to hunt panthers (which are now protected under the Endangered Species Act). In terms of what I am suggesting, however, a judgment about whether such hunting practices are just has to be formulated in light not only of securing the religious freedom of the Seminoles, but of the VanDeVeer thesis as well. In terms of the latter, it is doubtful that hunting panthers would be allowed (unless the overall quality of life of the panthers of this and future generations would not be adversely affected by the type of hunting in question). In such a case, the panthers' right to certain primary goods would be given priority over the religious freedom of others, and, in general, such issues would get formulated more closely (than it is our custom today) in terms of an analogy with a religion that claims for itself a right to hunt certain types of human beings.

A more legitimate concern is whether the extension of the notion of liberty of conscience to include fully religious practices that acknowledge considerable material bases might put, in the end, too great a strain on the very notion of liberty of conscience itself. For example, suppose someone were to claim that his religion is to ski, and that he can only obtain that "sacred consciousness" by skiing with the aid of lifts or helicopters on that mountain over there where the Indians want to pray (for it is only there that the "Big Powder Spirit" speaks). In such a case it would seem contrary to the spirit of the notion of liberty of conscience to demand that other people share this skier's religion in order for his religion to be recognized, and it would seem out of place for the courts to decide whether his (or the Indians') feelings are "sacred," or "mere sensations of profane pleasure" (just as it is out of place for the courts to decide whether Jesus or the Kachinas were really sent by God).[32]

---

[32] In this sense I believe that Rawls is incorrect when he vaguely alludes to a class of larger metaphysical issues, the solution of which takes priority over a theory of justice in that the latter have

In cases in which there is a stalemate between claims to spiritual freedom the courts have to decide by appealing to other interests of justice. For example, it may turn out that a decision for one side will tend to promote the primary interests of other beings of this or of future generations, the rule of law, or some type of desirable equality of economic opportunity.[33] The principle of liberty of conscience, in effect, will be of no use in deciding such cases. If such cases were to multiply rapidly, the viability of such a principle in its legal context would wither away. But as long as this latter is not the case, decisions can be made within a Rawlsian framework that have the effect of preserving places of great natural beauty in the name of securing the liberty of conscience for members of a just society. In cases where the practices of those who, for example, experience nature as the "living garment of God" do not interfere with the basic liberties of others, those who argue for the security of such practices will actually have *higher* ground to stand on, within a Rawlsian framework, than those who encourage economic expansions that do not aim at promoting higher primary goods.

V

In a Rawlsian system of justice, when the principles chosen in the original position do not lead to legislation that matches our considered judgments about what is just we can either modify the original position, or, if our interpretation of the original position appears sound, we can "bite the bullet," as it were, and recognize that what we took to be our considered judgments in fact reflect certain arbitrary prejudices. Although little work has been done in specifying which

---

to be modified to fit the former metaphysical world view, whatever this world view turns out to be (*A Theory of Justice*, p. 512). On the contrary, a theory of justice needs to ensure that the members of a just society are at liberty to determine their metaphysical world views as they see fit, under the constraint that such metaphysical world views do not unjustly interfere with the liberties of others. This is not to say that a theory of justice can ever be made completely metaphysically neutral, but that ideally it should be as "thin" on metaphysics as possible (hence the so-called "thin" theory of the good). In fairness to Rawls, he generally recognizes this point, but he seems to overlook it in this instance where he labors under (what I take to be) an incorrect assumption about the relation between metaphysics and modern natural science. This assumption is born out of an otherwise healthy respect for the successes of modern science and the role of empirical data in making considered practical judgments. The assumption is that modern natural science can somehow also generate an accompanying metaphysical world view that is rationally superior in contrast to other possibilities, and that this "correct" metaphysics ought to inform an overall theory of justice (Rawls, *A Theory of Justice*, p. 512). But this amounts to a subversion of what I interpret as the "primacy of the practical." To put the matter more concretely, even though I think that it is theoretically absurd to believe, for example, in reincarnation, I do not think that a system of justice ought to discourage such beliefs, if they do not interfere with the good of others.

[33] Notice that the collateral interests of justice in maintaining supplies of safe air, land, and water tend indirectly to favor religions that are similarly conserving (not because such religions are essentially "correct," but simply because they happen to harmonize better with the thin theory of the good that operates behind the veil of ignorance).

principles would be forthcoming from the modified original position herein advocated, it is clear that in the light of the principles that would be forthcoming, far more of what human beings have done, are doing, and are likely to do would be marked as unjust, than is customarily the case. Thus, many common ways of dealing with the environment, and with nonhuman animals, would be marked as unjust, and many would be called upon to relinquish, in the name of justice, various lower social primary goods to which they are now accustomed (and this often in the name of securing the rights of nonhuman animals of current and future generations). It is therefore safe to assume that the considered judgments of many people today are contrary to the principles that are forthcoming from the modified original position herein advocated.

On behalf of the judgments of such people, not only could one argue that the modified original position herein advocated is to blame, but, within a Rawlsian framework, one could also raise the problem of relative stability. That is, part of the grounds (though not the principal grounds) for evaluating a Rawlsian theory of justice is the degree to which one can expect that people will identify with the laws of the land so that the laws of the land, and popular moral sentiments, will be mutually reinforcing (pp. 496–504). The point is that no matter how righteous a law might be, if, on the whole, people do not feel the need to live up to it, or break it regularly without remorse, then the overall stability of society is thereby put into jeopardy. Here justice is better served without such a law, and reason persuades us to be content with the lesser of two evils. In particular, it is unrealistic to expect that many people today will be content to give up their motor boats, fancy foods, fine clothing, and so forth in order to secure the rights of nonhuman animals (many of whom have yet to be born). Thus, one could argue that the modifications in Rawls' theory herein advocated (and particularly the VanDeVeer thesis) must be rejected, even if they are ideally correct.

This objection fails, however, to appreciate a distinction among what might be called *philosophers, politicians,* and *political philosophers,* for it ought not to surprise *philosophers* if "what is" falls far shorter of "what ought to be" than most would care to imagine. But it is not the job of philosophers to shy away from rational ideals, and thus the challenge to philosophers is not to worry that regular life styles will be disrupted, but to demonstrate how the modified original position herein advocated is unreasonable, if in fact it is. On the other hand, it is *politicians* (including nonelected but politically influential people) who actually manage states, and if certain state laws protecting animals or the environment, however righteous, so conflict with current customs that more harm than good will come from them, then it is the job of *political philosophers* (elected or otherwise), through compromise, not to lose sight of the ideal of justice toward which they nevertheless seek gradually to lead society at every level of its operation.

The Pursuit of Equality

ROBERT NISBET

IT is evident that, barring major physical catastrophe, war, or some other massive cause of deflection of current social interests, the idea of equality will be sovereign for the rest of this century in just about all circles concerned with the philosophical bases of public policy. One would have to go back to certain other ages in history to find a unifying theme among intellectuals possessed of the intensity and universality we find today with respect to equality. In the past, unifying ideas tended to be religious in substance. There are certainly signs that equality is taking on a sacred aspect among many minds today, that it is rapidly acquiring dogmatic status, at least among a great many philosophers and social scientists.

Equality has all the requisites for becoming a religious—a providential—idea in our affluent age. It is simple, at least in immediate conception; it is capable of extension or application to the whole of a population, even to all mankind; it can be made to seem the very purpose of modern social and political experience, indeed a purpose contained in the bone and marrow of Western history. Finally, there is in the idea of equality that essence of permanent revolution we find in so many religious values—at least those of universal religions such as Christianity, Islam, and Buddhism at the moments of their founding—when they are counterposed to the traditions and laws surrounding them.

Equality, not freedom, is, as Tocqueville emphasized, the *vis creatrix* of most modern social movements. Even when freedom is extolled by such movements, it is characteristically freedom to have equal shares of something—usually political power, but also, increasingly, other social, cultural, and intellectual goods. Certainly, this has been true in the West since the fateful writings of Rousseau. It is noteworthy that in our own time conceptions of freedom resting on autonomy, on personal and associational immunity from supposedly popular opinion, and on the capacity for creativeness, in whatever sphere, are being pushed aside more and more by conceptions in which freedom is little more than a total social experience in which all citizens are to have equal shares.

More than any other single value, equality is the mainspring of

221

radicalism. No other value serves so efficiently in the work of distinguishing among the varied ideologies of the present and, for that matter, of the past couple of centuries. What one's attitude is toward equality in the whole complex of social, cultural, and economic goods tells us almost perfectly whether one is radical, liberal, or conservative. Preoccupation with equality has indeed been the constant mark of the radical in the West for a long time. The passion for equality, first vivid at the time of the Puritan Revolution, has been the essential mark of every major revolution in the West (with the possible and mixed exception of the American) and has carried with it, often in millennial degree, the urge among its more ardent votaries to undermine, topple, and destroy wherever inequality can be found.

As Tocqueville noted, equality arouses passions, at least in modern times, denied even to freedom. In substantial part, this role of equality as a motivating value is the product of the growth of large populations; the erosion of local and regional boundaries which could once conceal inequalities, or render innocuous those that had been noticed; the rise of large, legally undiversified electoral masses; and, above all, a constantly accelerating political centralization that, by its very nature, has dissolved ancient identities and made people increasingly aware of themselves as more or less identical units. There is nothing strange, really, in the ascendant place the value of equality has in our society. "When inequality of conditions is the common law of society, the most marked inequalities do not strike the eye; when everything is nearly on the same level, the slightest are marked enough to hurt it. Hence the desire for equality always becomes more insatiable in proportion as equality is more complete."

There is truth, of course, in Tocqueville's words. It is not certain, though, exactly how far this truth applies in American society at the present time. That the desire for equality as keystone of national social policy is great, even insatiable, among substantial numbers of intellectuals is evident enough. But among the people at large? Individuals at all levels may at times burn with the sense of injustice, may feel and struggle against the sense of dispossession, may crave more than they have, but it is far from certain that a majority, if given the clear choice, would wish for a generalized policy of equality, whether of income or anything else. There is something, after all, that appeals to the imagination, to the risk-taking sensibility, to the ever present hope of "hitting it big," in a non-equalitarian society where channels of mobility are at least reasonably open. Beyond this, hierarchy and inequality are key elements of the social bond. We become used to these elements in nearly all forms of association, starting with family. And there is, finally, the seemingly ineradicable American respect for merit, and for goods and statuses arrived at (or which appear to have been arrived at) through merit.

There is, in sum, undoubted truth in Tocqueville's words on the place of equality, as a value, in modern populations. It does indeed bulk large, especially during times of revolutionary or near-revolutionary crisis. And yet, the element of truth notwithstanding, it would be hard to validate the proposition in general terms through a polling of the American people today. All evidence suggests that a very large number of Americans are indifferent, if not actually hostile, to any idea for national social policy that has substantial equalitarianism behind it.

THIS fact, this seeming indifference among the multitudes regarding inequality as such, cannot fail to have much the same effect upon our contemporary lay priests of equalitarianism that similar indifference among pagan multitudes regarding Christian values must have had upon early missionaries. If certain crucial practices are *not* regarded as sins, if indeed there is widespread stubbornness among people in this respect, and if there is a deeply rooted reluctance to accept the new god as the sole or sovereign god, then only steps of the most heroic nature can be usefully contemplated. Thought must be given to social surgery of the most radical kind. How will it otherwise be possible to penetrate to the innermost depths of moral belief and of social tradition?

Something of this is beginning to be realized by intellectuals today, and no doubt such realization will spread widely among intellectuals during the years just ahead. Christopher Jencks, with a candor that is still somewhat rare, tells us in the final pages of his *Inequality:* "The crucial problem today is that relatively few people view income inequality as a serious problem." Precisely. Or any other kind of inequality. What is desired is not so much equality of any kind as freedom, whether individual or collective, to pursue chosen ends to the limit of capacity and desire. But such freedom, even when granted by law and convention to a degree not yet attained in America, will not satisfy our intellectuals, our priests in service to the god of equality (God is not dead; God is Equality; and this is rapidly becoming as much the case within organized Christianity as it is among descendants of Rousseau and his fellow *philosophes*). One remembers the hard-shelled missionary in Maugham's *Rain* saying of his South Sea parishioners: "The trouble with these people is that they will not believe in sin even when it is shown to them." So it is with Professor Jencks' parishioners, the hungry sheep for whom he has assumed responsibility. If we want substantial redistribution, Jencks writes (in a chapter reminiscently and excitingly titled "What Is to Be Done?"), "We will not only have to politicize the question of income inequality but alter people's basic assumptions about the extent to which they are responsible for their neighbors and their neighbors for them." How true. So reflected St. Paul, and after him a long succession of Christian missionaries, right down to the Berrigans. So reflected Rousseau, no Christian, but no less the messianic apostle of the only true good—which in his case, as in the case of our contemporary *hommes de zèle,* was equality, no less, no more.

The problem, though, is a formidable one: convincing a population against its conscious will that it is in fact living in immorality and injustice, that its true good lies elsewhere. Left to ordinary processes of decision, even—as Jencks has shown in some detail—when these processes are based upon free public education that is more or less constantly bombarded by the equalitarian views of intellectuals able to make their way to the fore, the people still cannot be counted on to adore equality as the first of the social virtues. Respect for equality before the law, yes, though with reservations and few illusions; and respect also for reasonable equality of opportunity in education and in getting jobs suited to one's talents and desires. But for the overwhelming majority, that is about it. On the evidence of polls and surveys there is little respect for the kind of equalitarianism that matters most to intellectuals: equalitarianism that would by design sweep away the built-in inequalities of family, of inheritance, of luck, and of individual ability and aptitude. To most people legitimate equality is epitomized by equality of *opportunity* for the great diversity of tastes, talents, strengths, and aspirations to be found in a population. But to a rising number of intellectuals this is the worst kind of *inequality*, for it produces, it is said, a meritocracy, which is in its own way as evil as any of the historic forms of aristocratic privilege.

Majority will, the historic foundation of democracy, cannot, then, be counted on to inaugurate the regime of equality that is desired by intellectuals. Does this have implications for the future of democracy? May we look forward to the growth of a political theory that is rooted not in majority will but instead in virtue and justice (these terms meaning, for intellectuals, equality)? The politics of virtue, from Plato to Rousseau, has rarely coincided in the past with anything easily describable as democracy.

We shall see. Present disaffection with politics, spreading alienation from the ideal of the political community and its values, and widening rents in the social fabric might easily produce a situation within the near future whereby majority will would be jettisoned along with a few other historic marks of political democracy. True, in such circumstances it would by no means follow that power in the hands of equality-oriented intellectuals would result. It might be —and on the evidence of history probably would be—power of a very different sort, power that might use the rhetoric of equality as window-dressing, as Augustus, Torquemada, Napoleon, and even Hitler did, but that would surely have its mind on something else. Still, hope springs eternal in the intellectual breast.

THE recent work that can certainly be counted on to keep hope buoyant so far as realization of the City of Equality is concerned is John Rawls' *A Theory of Justice*. I do not recall in my lifetime a book in philosophy greeted with as much praise as has been accorded this book. On both sides of the Atlantic, Rawls (who is Professor of Philosophy at Harvard University and Chairman of the Department of Philosophy there) has been hailed as author of the greatest work in ethics since Sidgwick's *The Methods of Ethics,* certainly, and quite possibly since Kant's writings on moral theory. I rather imagine that among circles of professional, genuinely informed philosophers, much of this enthusiasm for the book will shortly wane. Although it is indubitably a learned work in its way, with incontestable evidences of the author's ingenuity of argument, second and more sober readings of the book will surely come up with judgments less rapturous than those I have seen by philosophers in, say, lead reviews in the (London) *Times Literary Supplement* and the *New York Times Book Review.* But such rumination here has to do only with appreciation of the book as the work of a philosopher. It has nothing to do with the kind of appreciation that will, I am convinced, remain unabated among equality-oriented intellectuals, among those for whom *A Theory of Justice* can be regarded as the long-awaited successor to Rousseau's *Social Contract,* and as the rock on which the Church of Equality can properly be founded in our time.[1]

The essential point is, I think, that there are really two books given us under the title of *A Theory of Justice.* One is by John Rawls, philosopher. The other is by John Rawls, *philosophe.* There is, as we know, a great difference between philosophers as such and *philosophes.* It is not necessary to idealize either group to say that whereas philosophers have as their first and overriding goal inquiry into the nature of things—of the good, the true, the beautiful—*philosophes* have as *their* goal radical critique of a social order united with a vision of social utopia. Admittedly, *philosophes* use the works and ideas of philosophy, but they use them as handmaidens in the work of outlining the City of God while destroying the City of Man. *Philosophes* may even resemble philosophers—just as philosophers may now and then indulge in *philosophe* activity. But the difference, as is known to all intellectual historians, is very great. Whatever else the *philosophes* of the late 18th century in France were, they were not philosophers. To have been called philosophers would no doubt have seemed the unkindest cut of all to Rousseau, Diderot, Condorcet, and the others. Merely read what Rousseau thought of the "herds of textbook authors" in his day, or note the purposes of the *Encyclopedia.*

I do not for a moment dispute Professor Rawls' claim to be a philosopher or to have written a book in philosophy. I merely suggest, on the evidence of *A Theory of Justice,* that he is also a *philosophe,* with aims and interests which would have equipped him well for the salons of 18th-century Paris. We live, quite evidently,

---

[1] Professor Rawls declares that his book is grounded in Kant's moral theory. I understand I am not alone in being very skeptical of this. For every teaspoon of Kant, my own reading suggests, there are whole cupfuls of Rousseau. Strangely, though, little is said of Rousseau in *A Theory of Justice,* even though one might infer a great deal from a single remark (p. 256): "Kant's main aim is to deepen and to justify Rousseau's idea that liberty is acting in accordance with a law that we give to ourselves."

in an age of *philosophes;* they are as honored by our upper class
as ever they were in the 18th century. *Philosophes* do not like revolutions any more than wars; too many things get broken or threatened.
But they love dealing with issues likely to result in revolutions and
wars—issues characterized by perceptions of crisis, by conflicts of
mighty abstractions, and, above all, by indictments of society united
with visions of utopia. To read *philosophes* is to read about a surrounding *ancien régime* by definition rooted in corruption, inauthen-
ticity, and tyranny, about major institutions powerless to effect
reform, and about the principles of the lastingly, incorruptibly good:
the social good—that is, utopia. There is a great deal of all this in
Rawls. He is, without question, a lineal descendant of Rousseau.

Not, I hasten to say, in style. Rousseau may have his faults, but
it would be hard to improve upon the style he adopted for his principal moral-political writings, given their objectives. He had not
read much, but what he read he distilled into an oracularity that is
never less than exciting to read, no matter how much one may dis-
trust its content. With Professor Rawls it is very different. I do not
know when I have read a book so dense in its rhetoric, so thicket-
like in the form of its argument. One has the feeling that the book
was not so much written as accumulated over the years, like some
of the old mansions of the South. There is so much backing and
filling, adding and subtracting of premises, introduction of assumptions where none before were necessary, and so much use of the
first person pronoun (the book must set an all-time record in this
respect in the history of philosophy) that one has the feeling of
Rawls as a *deus ex machina.* Books are supposed to write themselves, and the best ones do. Here the person of the author is constantly intruding, redesigning the architecture, rearranging the fur-
niture.

I**N** some respects, too, the book is like a palimpsest. What first hits
the eye is the vast number of propositions of a more or less technical kind, along with innumerable references to other philosophical
works. But if we look carefully through all of this we shall see the
clear outline of another work, one not by any means separate from
the first but nevertheless different, one that is in direct descent from
the tracts written in the 18th century by the French *philosophes.*
This is the work I shall largely be concerned with in what follows.

"Justice is the first virtue of social institutions, as truth is of systems of thought." That is the electrifying sentence the book opens
with, after briefest preface. Its rhetorical affinity with the celebrated
opening of Rousseau's *Social Contract* will be lost to few readers.
And with good reason. Just as Rousseau's exclamation about man
being born free but being everywhere in chains is the axiom from
which he derives an entire republic of virtue, total in its dedication
to equality, so Rawls' sentence may be seen as the rock on which
he builds his own community of virtue—that is, justice, itself defined as equality of the most thoroughgoing kind. The whole of *A*

Theory of Justice is no more than an extension of that opening theme:

> Each person possesses an inviolability founded on justice that even the welfare of society as a whole cannot override. For this reason justice denies that the loss of freedom for some is made right by a greater good shared by others. It does not allow that the sacrifices imposed on a few are outweighed by the larger sum of advantages enjoyed by the many. Therefore in a just society the liberties of equal citizenship are taken as settled; the rights secured by justice are not subject to political bargaining or to the calculus of social interests. The only thing that permits us to acquiesce in an erroneous theory is the lack of a better one; analogously, an injustice is tolerable only when it is necessary to avoid an even greater injustice. Being first virtues of human activities, truth and justice are uncomprimising (pp. 3-4).

Now that is an astonishing passage and deserves to be ranked as at least a major footnote to any of the opening sections of the *Social Contract*. I dare say it would have been gladly accepted by most of the *philosophes* of 18th-century France, for it contains the thrilling and oracular rhetoric they loved, of devotion to the absolute individual and to the equally absolute moral community within which alone the ideal individual could realize himself without interference from intermediate institutions—institutions born merely out of history, convention, and ordinary use and wont. There is also the cherished depreciation of the merely political and pragmatic in human affairs. Justice, we are told, is not a matter for those mechanisms of compromise that have been humanity's chief means of reconciling the antinomies of moral abstraction throughout history. Justice demands that the "liberties of equal citizenship" be taken as antecedent and settled once and for all. The "rights secured by justice" are "not subject to political bargaining," which presumably takes care of political processes endemic in all known forms of democracy.

In fact, of course, we have no real repudiation of politics here; only of conventional politics in favor of the politics of virtue, which is, as we know, never a relative politics but always absolute. Rare indeed is the statement of political authoritarianism in Western literature that is not built around the premise of virtue or justice— each, naturally, declared absolute, non-negotiable, and superior to all ordinary processes of "political bargaining." Seldom, from the time of Plato's *Republic,* has absolute authority been presented in its own name. Almost always it is authority clothed in the garments of justice, or of freedom, or of rights, with the welfare of "the individual" held sacrosanct. I do not charge Professor Rawls with political authoritarianism; only with a Delphic intensity in the name of an absolute justice that can hardly help but suggest to many minds the sanctity of any form of power that might fulfill such justice—defined, as we shall see, as equality. It is the ineffaceable mark of every philosophy of moral absolutism to despise "political bargaining" and to see this as necessarily inimical to the good and just society.

To return to Professor Rawls' propositions: They express, he writes, "our intuitive conviction of the primacy of justice." But whose conviction? There, as I have suggested, is the rub. For there is no evidence, either in our own time or in the past, that justice defined as equalitarianism would be regarded by most people, intuitively, as "the first virtue of social institutions." Any more than most people, either in Rousseau's or in our time, would think of themselves as born free but living in chains.

As a historian and social scientist I would not wish, myself, to declare any single virtue sovereign over all others, and capable of being intuitively arrived at. But if I were to speculate on what the majority of us would come up with "intuitively" along these lines, I think it would not be justice, however defined. More likely it would be *protection* or *security*, followed closely by *conservation* (in the sense of perpetuation of norms and ways of life). No doubt even our remotest ancestors had, and may have occasionally snarled or fought over, rude conceptions of justice considered as fairness. And I am willing to concede that few persons, today or in the past, are likely to express a positive preference for *injustice*, once this particular value is set before them and suitably described. But to declare, as the opening line of argument in a 600-page book on morality, that justice is the virtue that will be intuitively arrived at by all human beings as primary for social institutions is to fly in the face of history and also, I would judge, in the face of sentiments regarding both security and conservation in our own day.

Now, how does Professor Rawls support his contention that justice—meaning "fairness," meaning in turn equality—is the first virtue? Through comparative history, psychology, social science? Indeed not. Here we come to the *philosophe* heart of the book, the methodology through which Rawls reaches confirmation of what is for him primary and intuitive. I am going to devote most of what remains in this review to precisely this, the book's by now celebrated method of proof and of demonstration; for we have Rawls' own word for the fact that the greater part of the rest of his book, including propositions of the most radical and sweeping kind concerning social institutions, is rooted in this method, a method epitomized by what Rawls calls "the original position" and "the veil of ignorance."

Before describing Rawls' method, though, I want to offer a little background for it by turning briefly to *philosophe* thought in 18th-century France. No reviewer I have chanced to read thus far seems to be aware of the true nature of Rawls' method of proof, a commentary no doubt on the sad decline of the history of philosophy in our time. Much is said in the reviews about Rawls' return to "social contract" theory as the means of refuting the utilitarianism that has (on Rawls' testimony, at least) dominated moral philosophy for a century or more. But while description of Rawls' method as "contractarianism" is perhaps not erroneous, it is far from sufficient and does not get at what is essential.

When the *philosophes* in the 18th century wished to "prove" the rightness of a given value or set of values, in their larger work of annihilating the values and structures they found around them, they availed themselves of a technique widely known then as *histoire raisonnée* or, variously, "conjectural," "hypothetical," or "speculative" history. This was set in sharpest contrast to the more conventional kind of history that concerned itself with actual persons, places, nations, and events in the annals of mankind. Such conventional history was largely repugnant to the *philosophes*, though one or two of them did it reasonably well on occasion; for, plainly, it was not the kind of investigation from which first principles and first virtues could easily be derived by those dedicated to reformation of a social order. "Hypothetical" history was a means of dealing with the nature and history of man as though he were liberated from all the "corrupting" and "distorting" influences that normally go into socialization. It was a means of contriving—to use Professor Rawls' words—an "original position" and a "veil of ignorance" for man which would then make it possible to uncover the "real" elements of man's mind and morality, and to build on these in the construction of a utopia.

Conceivably, honest and forthright critics of a social order might have said simply: "These are the values we approve of and these are the values we intend to see woven into the fabric of the social order. All else will be obliterated." But such forthrightness is alien to the mind of the true *philosophe*. He must always give the semblance of dealing with the roots of human nature, of demonstrating what would in fact be in force if it were not for a false consciousness that has been generated in men's minds by the corruptions, inauthenticities, tyrannies, and above all, inequalities, of a given social order.

Obviously, in such an enterprise the ordinary factual materials of history, social science, and experience are useless. For how is one to extract first principles and "first virtues" from the chronicles of Egyptians, Romans, and Greeks, and from tedious annals of who ruled where and when? It is Man and Mankind, not peoples and individuals of record, that we must go to if we would reach the roots of justice or find moral levers with which to move whole worlds. And for this exciting work, as the *philosophes* knew well, there was no substitute for an imagination equipped with all the desired answers in advance and capable of "proving" its intuitive correctness through use of a *histoire raisonnée* that would discard as irrelevant all recorded experiences of human beings and fix attention solely upon what could be cleverly assigned to a supposedly "original position" by the *philosophe* concerned. It was precisely in this light that Rousseau, in a frequently misunderstood and often maligned sentence at the beginning of his momentous *Discourse on the Origin of Inequality,* wrote: "Let us begin, then, by laying facts aside, as they do not affect the question." Rousseau was only candidly admitting a practice followed by all *philosophes* from his day to ours.

Fundamentally, this *philosophe* strategy is the real core of Professor Rawls' book. He too is playing the exciting game of imagining that through use of what he calls "the original position" (read: state of nature) he is entering on a mode of reality denied those of us who live in the caves of contemporary social science, history, and experience. He too is, in the precise sense of Rousseau's words, laying the facts aside on the ground that they do not affect the question—which indeed they do not, given the nature of the question posed by Rawls. And finally, Professor Rawls, like any sophisticated *philosophe* of two centuries ago, can say: "We want to define the original position so that we get the desired solution" (p. 141). Naturally. That is the very essence of the *philosophe* mentality. One must never lose sight of the desired, the "intuitive," solution, no matter what else one carries in the way of ethnological tidbits, alleged principles of psychology, apothegms of moral philosophy, even citations from Scripture, to supply ballast.[2]

LET us move now from method to conclusion, bearing in mind, of course, that no conclusion can be other than what has been directed by the method of inquiry. "It seems reasonable to suppose," writes Rawls, "that the parties in the original position are equal" (p.19). Well, yes, but then again it doesn't—at least when one thinks of the findings of ethnology and physical anthropology in the study of human behavior. Never mind, though. We are dealing here, not with facts, which have been laid aside in appropriate *philosophe* manner, but with an "original position" so contrived as to reveal to us what human beings *would* be, *would* think, *would* do and contract for, *if* they are imagined as having been liberated from identities conferred through processes of ordinary socialization. "The original

---

[2] There is, though, one major difference between what Professor Rawls does and what his illustrious forerunners in the 18th century did (that is, apart from ballast; Rawls favors game theory and tidbits from free market economics over ethnology, etc.). The French *philosophes* were drawing upon the best, or at least the commonly accepted social science and psychology of their day. Professor Rawls most assuredly is not. Taking refuge in something termed an "original position" and using a "veil of ignorance" is as far from scientific procedure as anything I can think of. Rawls seems at times to conceive of himself in the role of social scientist; there are enough references to economic theory alone to suggest this. But there is a broad gulf between what Rawls is doing in his rather simplistic use of *philosophe* method and what econometrists are involved in today in their very careful and rigorous analyses of the free market or the firm. The same has to be said of Rawls' numerous references to game theory. I am afraid the kind of game Professor Rawls is playing with imagined motivations in a hypothetical "original position" is much more like the games philosophers might give each other for Christmas than anything easily found today in the higher reaches of mathematics and economic theory.

position," we are told, "is the appropriate initial status quo which insures that the fundamental agreements reached in it are fair. This fact yields 'justice as fairness'" (p. 17). Indeed it does. We need add only that such a "fact" will yield just about anything one desires.

It is not possible to understand the "original position" without reference to what Professor Rawls calls "the veil of ignorance." What does this veil consist of?

> First of all no one knows his place in society, his class position or social status; nor does he know his fortune in the distribution of natural assets and abilities, his intelligence and the like. Nor, again, does anyone know his conception of the good, the particulars of his rational plan of life, or even the special features of his psychology such as his aversion to risk or liability to optimism or pessimism. More than this, I assume that the parties do not know the particular circumstances of their own society. That is, they do not know its economic or political situation, or the level of civilization and culture it has been able to achieve. The persons in the original position have no information as to which generation they belong (p. 137).

In sum, they don't know much of anything—anything, that is, that we are justified by contemporary psychology in deeming requisite to thought and knowledge of any kind whatever. Nevertheless, Professor Rawls is shortly going to put his happy primitives through feats of cerebration that even the gods might envy. Out of the minds of his homunculi, these epistemological zombies who don't know their names, families, races, generations, or societies of origin, are going to come principles of justice and society so vast in implication as to throw all present human societies into a philosopher's limbo.

This must be said, though: Despite the parties' abysmal ignorance of the things which alone make thought possible, they are not wholly bereft. Professor Rawls assures us that his primitives in the "original position" do know "the general facts about human society." He goes on: "They understand political affairs and the principles of economic theory; they know the basis of social organization and the laws of human psychology. Indeed, the parties are presumed to know whatever general facts affect the choice of the principles of justice" (p. 137). There are those who would say they sound like certain academic intellectuals of today. There are others who would say they sound exactly like the confined neurasthenics Proust described in *Remembrance of Things Past*: able endlessly to discuss and debate monumental abstractions, but helpless when it came to the simplest duties of ordinary existence.

Such is the "original position" and such is the "veil of ignorance." One's first thought is to say: Welcome to the 18th century! In a footnote (p. 137) Rawls seems uneasily aware that *someone* besides himself must have thought somewhere, sometime, of this device— but he can think of no one but J. C. Harsanyi, who, I infer, drew from

231

it the wrong conclusions, inasmuch as they are pronounced utilitarian. I know nothing about the Harsanyi article referred to, but I can assure Professor Rawls that he would find much company in Parisian salons of the 18th century, where conceptualized primitives often strolled, in aristocrats' or *philosophes'* dress, discussing from the vantage point of the "veil of ignorance" and the "original position" principles of the ideal society so profound and so noble in purpose as to make surrounding culture seem base, misdirected, and obsolete.

I WILL not go into a detailed account of the principles of a just society that Professor Rawls extracts from the mouths of his happy and omniscient primitives. Those principles have been described profusely by reviewers and other admirers of the book. It will suffice to say that foremost among them are what Rawls calls his "two principles of justice for social institutions." According to the first of these momentous principles, "each person must have an equal right to the most extensive total system of equal basic liberties compatible with a similar system of liberty for all" (p. 302). That is, the principle of liberty is made prior to all else, even equality. Ostensibly, at any rate, it is made prior. A second reading of the passage just quoted might suggest that it is not so much liberty that Rawls has in mind there as equal shares in a vast, homogenized structure *called* liberty.

Prior or no, however, the first principle is utterly outweighed in mass and use by the second principle, which is that "social and economic inequalities are to be arranged so that they are both (a) to the greatest benefit of the least advantaged, consistent with the just savings principle, and (b) attached to offices and positions open to all under conditions of fair equality of opportunity" (p. 303). And here, of course, we are out of the suburbs and in the City itself. For the book is consecrated to as radical a form of equalitarianism as may be found anywhere outside the pages of the *Social Contract*. Liberty, yes, but liberty carefully defined as a monolithic, total, practically identical experience for the entire population, something in which, by definition, people have equal shares—or else it does not exist. It was Rousseau who first perfected the technique of defining liberty in the rhetoric of equality, so as to make liberty and equality indeed virtually synonymous. Rousseau's pages abound in use of the words "freedom" and "liberty." But no one with scantest acquaintance with these pages can doubt that the words have been forged on the anvil of equality—an equality that will be total, permeating, and made to reach the depths of human consciousness.

Equality is assuredly total in Rawls. From his two fundamental principles of justice—themselves derived, it must always be remembered, from the cerebrations of his conceptualized primitives in the state of nature—Professor Rawls deduces something portentously called "the difference principle," under which "all social primary goods" must be distributed equally throughout a society unless an unequal distribution of any of these goods is to the advantage of the least favored. By social primary goods Rawls means not only wealth and income but such things as liberty, opportunity, and even "bases of self-respect."

Nor is it the familiar liberal concept of a merit system that Rawls proposes. Meritocracy comes in for repudiation on the ground that equality—given thrust by the two principles of justice and by the powerful and sweeping "difference principle"—would be undermined. For obviously there are differences of strength, acuity, temperament, and, inevitably, of motivation and aspiration in any group of human beings. A merit system, one based upon equal opportunity for talents and desires, would inevitably destroy that homogeneity of life Rawls seems to prize above all else. In this respect too Rawls is the child of Jean-Jacques who, directing himself precisely to the same point in the *Social Contract,* declared that the social compact (read: original position) demands that we substitute "for such physical inequality as nature may have set up between men, an equality that is moral and legitimate, and that men, who may be unequal in strength or intelligence, become every one equal by convention and legal right." Elsewhere in the *Social Contract* Rousseau tells us: "It is precisely because the force of circumstances tends continually to destroy equality that the force of legislation should always tend toward its maintenance."

That civil law should protect the weak from the strong, should, that is, guard their right to existence from arbitrary invasion or violence, goes without saying. It is, however, a very different thing to see the function of law as making equal the diversity of strengths and talents in all fields that is but a part of the human condition. I do not know how the absurd myth got started in modern thought that Rousseau urged a "return to nature." Nothing could be farther from the truth. He did indeed start with the concept of nature, but this was only to give even greater emphasis to his desire to create a social system so powerful, so minute and penetrating in its grasp of individuals, that a monolith of artificial equality and of equal shares of membership in an all-benign, all-knowing, and omnipotent General Will would become the basis for all life and thought.

No doubt when Professor Rawls urges upon us his revolutionary "difference principle" he wishes us to think primarily of money and property differences. If only it were possible to limit such a principle to such matters! After all, Rawls refers in the statement of his principle to "all social primary goods," and as one reflects on the matter, the real and far-reaching impact of the principle would be less in the sphere of money than in the world of the mind, of intellectual and cultural achievement, and in all the subtle but potent gradations of status in life which follow directly from differential achievement. On the evidence, it is not monetary differentiation—much as equalitarians like to dwell upon it—that galls and occasionally humiliates; it is rather the type of differentiation that comes from unequal intellectual and moral strengths, unequal applications of resolve and aspiration, and unequal benefactions of luck. What can we assume but that the effect of Rawls' "difference principle" would be greatest in these respects?

I cannot help thinking that the closest we come at the present time to a manifestation of Rawls' "difference principle" is in respect to Open Admissions and Affirmative Action in the college and university world. In each of these the ostensible and declared function is that of helping the disadvantaged on their way up in life. In both, however, what we see in fact is simultaneous destruction of standards of performance and of the hopes of those individuals *within the disadvantaged groups* whose talents and aspirations put them above the lowest common denominator of their groups. How, we are constrained to ask, is the long-run rise of any group in society helped by a principle—and, in the cases of the two programs I have just mentioned, by ongoing policies—that gives protection not so much to the least advantaged groups in the social order as to the least able, least qualified, and least motivated individuals among the least advantaged groups?

To be sure, Professor Rawls, writing in glittering abstraction from his Ivy League fastness, can point to, can take philosopher's refuge in, the fine-print clause that says "unless an unequal distribution of any of these goods is to the advantage of the least favored." How ingenious! But "advantage" by whose judgment? Aye, that is the question. We will probably not go wrong if we bet that the controlling judgment will emanate from intellectuals in the world of government, foundations, and academy. At least it has been that way in all other revolutions!

J OHN RAWLS is clearly a learned mind, and the sources, references, and allusions in his book reflect a wide diversity of reading. Even so, the omissions are massive, not to say staggering. In a work that makes liberty and equality the two sovereign virtues of social institutions, that indeed sees them intertwined in a theory of justice, the author might have thought it incumbent upon him to consider in some detail the long tradition in Western thought, beginning with Aristotle's criticism of Plato and continuing down to such minds as Tocqueville, Henry Maine, and James Fitzjames Stephens, among others, that has made the *conflict between liberty and equality* its theme. There is little if any such consideration in A *Theory of Justice*, however, and one can only conclude that in this as in other respects, *philosophe* conquered philosopher, with principles reached *in scrinio pectoris* deemed sufficient unto the purpose.

So might one also expect consideration of the problem of the *contexts* of liberty in society. I refer to the kinds of contexts which a large number of historians, social scientists, and philosophers have thought vital to the nourishing and reinforcement of any spirit of liberty. Professor Rawls' dedication to freedom is unimpeachable; he declares it prior in importance and lexical order even to equality. But oracularity and repetition of principle are never proper substitutes for genuine consideration of relevant circumstances and conditions. There is a long and impressive body of writings in the West which tells us that freedom needs to have roots in social differentiation, cultural pluralism, conflict of institutions, balance of power among strong social interests, and deeply based traditions—economic, religious, ethnic, and other. It is difficult to see how application of Rawls' "difference principle" could take place without destruction or substantial erosion of these—a result allowable enough if equality alone is the desired end of life, but not if equality is declared secondary to liberty, as it is so declared by Rawls. Principles are very important; but principles have consequences, and we are surely entitled in a book of this length to the author's views on both contexts and consequences.

I think most readers will find Rawls far better in his elaboration of equality, of justice as fairness, than in what he writes at great length about freedom. I believe the book would have been a better one if he had frankly abandoned his first principle of liberty, so called, and concerned himself entirely with developing the theme of equality. As I suggested above, much of the difficulty with Rawls' treatment of liberty lies in the fact that he repeatedly presents it as an overall system in which abstract individuals are to have "equal shares." It is impossible to conquer the belief that in Rawls as in Rousseau there is far more interest in the equal sharing of liberty than in the nature of liberty itself. I do not doubt that there are types of liberty in which equal shares may be decreed. This would appear to be as true of totalitarian governments as democratic ones. But there is a large and historically indispensable sphere of liberty—that relating to the pragmatic capacity of individuals and groups to express their essence, to fulfil chosen objectives, *to initiate, to create, and to do*—in which the thought of equal shares is plainly absurd. In *this* sphere we are forever dependent upon the talents, strengths, interests, and aspirations we are in some part born with and in probably larger part recipients of during the crucial early period of socialization. Plainly, chance, contingency, luck play a great role in liberty understood in this sense. Equality is nonexistent here.

When one thinks of the implications for liberty, in the sense in which it has been known by most people for a very long time in the West, of Rawls' "difference principle" (with its binding requirement that all "social primary goods" must be distributed equally or, if there must be unequal distribution, in a way that it is to the advantage of the least favored), one can only confess bewilderment as to what liberty would actually consist of in Rawls' just society. I can conceive of even a despot, especially of the Napoleonic type, approving of liberty of the kind that may be parcelled out in "equal shares." It is, on the historical record, the kind of liberty that is *not* divisible into equal shares, that is always found in the very unequal proportions in which initiative, creativity, and motivation are to be found, that has proved troubling to despots and the bureaucracies they administer.

As I say, we must take Professor Rawls at his word that he loves liberty and wants it to be primary in his just society. But he is not thereby absolved from the responsibility of letting us know what the difference is between liberty in a society *not* founded upon his rigorous equalitarianism and liberty in the society where all "social primary goods," including opportunity and "bases of self-respect," as well as income and property, must be equal or arranged to favor the underprivileged. Incessantly repeated incantations about the "inviolability" of the person and about the absolute necessity of "liberty of conscience" will not suffice.

There is much about liberty of conscience in *A Theory of Justice.* So is there, *mutatis mutandis*, in Plato's *Republic*, in Hobbes' *Leviathan*, and in Rousseau's *Social Contract*. Rawls shows no real awareness that *mere liberty of conscience or belief is compatible with systems of extraordinary repressiveness*. I repeat, what despotic governments have immemorially feared is not anything as private and secluded as conscience or belief, but rather those expressions of action and organization which must by their nature always exist in highly unequal shares in any population, based as they are on unequal motivations and strengths. Rousseau's well-known antagonism toward the arts springs less, I judge, from any genuine "puritanism" in his makeup than from the hopelessness of trying to maintain an iron equality, or justice defined as equality, in arts, letters, and science.

Rousseau grants an absolute freedom of opinion and belief to his citizens in the very chapter of the Social Contract where he prescribes the death penalty for those who act as if they do not believe in the tenets of the Civil Religion. Of course, nothing so harsh is to be found in *A Theory of Justice*. It does come as a slight shock, though, when Rawls, following a number of pages on the sanctity of freedom of conscience (extending, *inter alia*, to civil disobedience, draft evasion, and the like), concludes with the statement: "Furthermore liberty of conscience is to be limited only when there is reasonable expectation that not doing so will damage the public order which the government should maintain" (p. 213). True, he goes on to say that such limitation must be restricted to instances where the expectation will "be based on evidence and ways of reasoning acceptable to all." But in large nations with excellent communications systems in the hands of their governments, that should not be a difficult matter. In fairness to Professor Rawls, he makes no Rousseauan reference to such limitation upon liberty as a means whereby individuals are "forced to be free." But it is worth a thought!

So is Rousseau's General Will worth a thought in any subsequent edition of *A Theory of Justice,* Rawls seems to have great trouble with the concept of majority will. One has the feeling he doesn't particularly like it—nor should he, given the outrageous preferences that democratic majorities invariably express for a social system based upon merit and achievement—but that he doesn't know quite what to do with it. What Rawls winds up doing is dissociating majority will from any of his principles of justice. That is, whatever else this deeply

236

embedded principle of democracy rests on, it does *not* rest on justice, as it is defined and elaborated in *A Theory of Justice*. He writes: "It is evident from the preceding remarks that the procedure of majority rule, however it is defined, and circumscribed, has a subordinate place as a procedural device. The justification for it rests squarely on the political ends that the constitution is designed to achieve, and therefore on the two principles of justice" (p. 356). Such a statement, quite apart from whatever may lie in Professor Rawls' hopes and dreams, can serve as the basis for some tantalizing *philosophe* visions of "What Is To Be Done" when one becomes overpowered by the thought of the discrepancies between true justice and all the foibles, tastes, and whims of extant majorities. No doubt, in the years ahead, it will to serve. But if so, I recommend the powerful Rousseauan distinction between the General Will *(volonté générale)*, which is always and invariably right and may not at all coincide with a numerical majority, and the mere Will of All (*volonté de tous*) that is the product of a still uninstructed, wrong-thinking, and untreated mass formed by the accidents of history. Near the beginning of the *Discourse on Political Economy* Rousseau even provides us with some helpful instructions on how the General Will may be ascertained in a population without bothering with voting at all.

But as Rousseau was well aware, you can't hope to achieve authentic consciousness in a people—the basis of the General Will—without taking some very radical steps. Foremost among these is eradication of the family as the unit of the social order. I have always found treatment of the family to be an excellent indicator of the degree of zeal and authoritarianism, overt or latent, in a moral philosopher or political theorist. Basically, there have been two traditions in Western thought here. In one, reaching from Plato to Rousseau, the family is regarded as an insurmountable barrier to the achievement of absolute virtue or justice in a social order and therefore is to be obliterated. In the other, reaching from Aristotle to Burke and Tocqueville, the family is declared vital to the achievement and preservation of freedom and order alike in society.

Where does Professor Rawls stand? He is well aware of the social and psychological importance of the family, and refers to it in a number of places. Let us take his final reference (p. 511) as indicative. He writes: "The consistent application of the principle of fair opportunity requires us to view persons independently from the influences of their social position. But how far should this tendency be carried? It seems that when fair opportunity (as it has been defined) is satisfied, the family will lead to unequal chances between individuals. Is the family to be abolished then? Taken by itself and given a certain primacy, the idea of equal opportunity inclines in this direction. But within the context of the theory of justice as a whole there is much less urgency to take this course."

I am afraid that most readers will take that last as quite unsatisfactory, even as a form of flinching. After all, "theory of justice as a whole" notwithstanding, there is abundant evidence that the family is among the most powerful generators and reinforcers of inequality in a social order. Rawls knows this very well. He has already proclaimed his willingness to see the factors of motivation, chance, and merit reduced to nullity in behalf of his cherished principle of equality. Can he, in all consistency, long neglect the family, given its demonstrable relation to inequality? Rousseau, in his *Discourse on Political Economy*, was bold and consistent where Rawls is diffident. If the young are to be brought up in the bosom of equality, "early accustomed to regard their own individuality only in its relation to the body of the State, to be aware, so to speak, of their own existence merely as part of that of the State," then they must be saved from what Rousseau refers to as "the intelligence and prejudices of fathers." Public authority must supplant domestic authority; the molecule of the family must be broken. But this, Rousseau suggests with characteristic ingenuity, should occasion no alarm, for the father "would only be changing his title and would have in common, under the name of *citizen,* the same authority over his children as he was exercising separately under the name of *father.*"

Will Professor Rawls in due time find his way to this piece of radical surgery? We can only surmise that he will. Our surmise in this respect is encouraged by the final paragraph of *A Theory of Justice,* where we are urged to think, not merely big, but *"sub specie aeternitatis,"* and to "regard the human situation not only from all social but also from all temporal points of view." And in a final sentence that arouses visions of Rousseau's legislator, Professor Rawls writes: "Purity of heart, if one could attain it, would be to act with grace and self-command from this point of view." Rousseau put the matter better: "This sublime reason [he is writing about his philosopher-legislator], far above the range of the common herd, is that whose decisions the legislator puts into the mouth of the immortals, in order to constrain by divine authority those whom human prudence could not move. The great soul of the legislator is the only miracle that can prove his mission."

Phil. Soc. Sci. 3 (1973) 341–347 *Printed in Great Britain*

Rawls's Models of Man and Society

Now that Rawls's theory is presented in a fully integrated form, one naturally looks for enlightenment about features of his theory which had been puzzling, or which had seemed unsatisfactory, in the earlier, partial versions. I shall confine my attention to two such features, which will take us to some of his basic assumptions about the nature of man and of human society. The first is the curious fact that a theory of justice which starts from egalitarian premises should be mainly concerned with enquiring what justifies an inequality of life prospects as between members of different social classes. The second is the uncertainty as to how far his well-ordered society requires a capitalist market system and a bourgeois model of man. How far has he read back, into the nature of society and of man, the Hobbes-to-Bentham model of each?

I

The central concern of *A Theory of Justice* remains the justification of unequal life prospects for members of different social classes. The reason for this is that these inequalities are 'presumably inevitable in the basic structure of any society' (p. 7). Or, as he says,

consider the distribution of income among social classes. . . . those starting out as members of the entrepreneurial class in property-owning democracy, say, have a better prospect than those who begin in the class of unskilled labourers. It seems likely that this will be true even when the social injustices which now exist are removed. What, then, can possibly justify this kind of initial inequality in life prospects? (p. 78).

What does justify it, Rawls says, is 'the difference principle', which is the crucial part of his second principle of justice, and which may be said to be the outstanding novelty in Rawls's theory. The principle is that 'the higher expectations of those better situated are just if and only if they work as part of a scheme which improves the expectations of the least advantaged members of society' (p. 75), or more fully: 'Social and economic inequalities are to be arranged so that they are both (a) to the greatest benefit of the least advantaged and (b) attached to offices and positions open to all under conditions of fair equality of opportunity' (p. 83). The 'general conception of justice . . . is simply the difference principle applied to all primary goods including liberty and opportunity . . .' (p. 83).

Now clearly this principle makes sense if social and economic inequalities as between classes, amounting to inequality in life prospects, are presumed to be 'inevitable' or even 'likely' to persist even when existing social injustices have been removed. The question then is, why should this be presumed? Is a classless society unthinkable? Is it, that is to say, impossible to envisage a society in which, even if there are perceptibly different levels of income and authority, the occupancy of a higher level is neither the result nor the means of exploiting others (in the strict sense of exploitation, i.e. transferring to oneself for one's own benefit some of the powers of others)? I do not think so. But I see a possible reason why Rawls is unable to envisage it, namely that he does not see that class division in any society, not least in his free market society, is based on such continuous transfer: the transfer is the means and the result of class division.[1] (Oddly enough, in one footnote Rawls points out that 'Marxian exploitation is compatible with perfect competition, since it is the outcome of a certain structure of property relations' (p. 309, n. 35), but he does not avail himself of this insight any further.) Having thus abstracted from exploitation, Rawls is able to conceive 'the social injustices which now exist' as due to such present phenomena as monopolistic restrictions and absence of equality of opportunities (including educational opportunities), all of which are held to be remediable by the regulative welfare state. Their being remedied would indeed, as he says, leave natural differences of ability: it would also leave the transfer of powers, which permits, and in a market society requires, the more able to extract some of the others' powers, and so reproduces class differences.

It may be thought that the vision of a society without exploitive classes takes the visionary beyond the realm of justice. Rawls, perhaps anticipating the objection that his justice is too confined to class societies, makes a point which at first sight is sufficient: a society in which there is no conflict of interests is beyond justice. 'A society in which all can achieve their complete good, or in which there are no conflicting demands and the wants of all fit together in a harmonious plan of activity, is a society in a certain sense beyond justice. It has eliminated the occasions when the appeal to the principles of right and justice is necessary' (p. 281). Fair enough: a treatise on justice cannot be required to deal with a society where there would be no occasion for a principle of justice. And Rawls is scrupulous in setting out the circumstances in which alone a principle of justice is required. In this he follows Hume (p. 126, n. 3). His summary statement is that 'the circumstances of justice obtain whenever mutually disinterested persons put forward conflicting claims to the division of social advantages under conditions of moderate scarcity. Unless these conditions existed there would be no occasion for the virtue of justice ...' (p. 128). Again, fair enough.

But there is a further proposition: 'a human society [unlike an association of saints] is characterized by the circumstances of justice' (pp. 129–30). In other words, it is the inevitable human condition that there is a scarcity of 'natural and social resources' such that individuals, all of whom have their own plans of life or conceptions of the good and hence 'different ends and purposes', 'make conflicting claims on the natural and social resources available' (p. 127). The basic postulates here are (1) the inevitability of scarcity of natural and social resources in relation to (2) inevitably conflicting individual goals. No grounds are offered for either postulate, though one might think that nowadays, as compared with Hume's day, the postulate of moderate scarcity might need some defence; and without real scarcity it is not apparent why *different* individual goals must be *conflicting*.

It is true that if one assumes that human beings are *infinitely* desirous of goods, both material and immaterial—i.e. Rawls's 'primary goods' which include 'rights and liberties, powers and opportunities, income and wealth' (p. 92), and, 'perhaps the most important', self-respect or self-esteem (pp. 440, 178), then by definition there will always be scarcity of them. It is not entirely clear whether Rawls is assuming that these desires are without limit. When he discusses primary goods in general he says that since they are 'necessary means' to every individual's achieving his ends or plan of life, it may be assumed that all individuals 'prefer more rather than less primary goods' (p. 93). But later he points out that a just and good society need not wait upon a high material standard of life. What men want is meaningful work in free association with others, these associations regulating their relations to one another within a framework of just basic institutions. To achieve this state of things great wealth is not required. In fact, beyond some point it is more likely to be a positive hindrance, a meaningless distraction at best if not a temptation to indulgence and emptiness (p. 290).

And later still, in his endorsement of 'the Aristotelian principle' (pp. 426 ff), he strongly implies that he sees man as essentially a doer, an exerter and enjoyer of the exercise of his capacities, rather than as an infinite consumer.

Which, then, is Rawls's man? I shall return to this question after looking at his models of society. Meanwhile we need only note that, granting that individual ends are very diverse, and even for the sake of argument granting that the myriad individual ends make *conflicting* demands on scarce resources, this does not in the nature of things necessarily set up *class* differences. Hence there seems no warrant for treating justice as a principle for justifying (some types of) class inequalities.

II

A second uncertainty left over from the earlier, partial presentations of Rawls's theory is how far his conceptions of (a good) society and of man in society are drawn from capitalist market society and man. The ambiguity about this is more apparent in the fuller version.

The structure of social, economic and political institutions which best meets Rawls's criteria of a just society is the one he calls 'democratic equality', which is more than and different from some liberal societies ('the system of natural liberty' and 'liberal equality'), but which like them assumes 'that the economy is roughly a free market system, although the means of production may or may not be privately owned' (pp. 65–6). Again, the complex of institutions 'which we think of as establishing social justice in the modern state' is set out as follows:

Suppose that law and government act effectively to keep markets competitive, resources fully employed, property and wealth (especially if private ownership of the means of production is allowed) widely distributed by the appropriate forms of taxation, or whatever, and to guarantee a reasonable social minimum. Assume also that there is fair equality of opportunity underwritten by education for all; and that the other equal liberties are secured. Then it would appear that the resulting distribution of income and the pattern of expectations will tend to satisfy the difference principle. . . . the advantages of the better situated improve the condition of the least favoured. Or when they do not, they can be adjusted to do so, for example, by setting the social minimum at the appropriate level. As these institutions presently exist they are riddled with grave injustices. But there presumably are ways of running them compatible with their basic design and intention so that the difference principle is satisfied consistent with the demands of liberty and fair equality of opportunity (p. 87).

These descriptions of the basic institutions required for a just society are, except for one qualification Rawls inserts, in essence an advanced version of the current capitalist welfare and regulatory state. The state intervenes to keep markets competitive, but the motor of the economy is the entrepreneur moved by incentives of gain. This is the classic capitalist welfare state. But we are given pause by Rawls's repeated qualification that this system does not require private ownership of the means of production. There seems to be an extraordinary confusion here, and the confusion increases when Rawls elaborates his notion of market society (in Part Two, especially §§ 42–3).

He begins with a distinction 'between a private property economy and socialism' and accepts what he calls the classical distinction, which rests on the ownership of the means of production (though he puts the classical distinction very loosely, as a matter of the proportion publicly and privately owned: 'the size of the public sector under socialism . . . is much larger' (p. 266)). He then points out that the use of markets is not a distinguishing feature, since both systems commonly use them, but he sees a distinction in how the two systems use them. A socialist regime will use the market to ration out the consumption goods actually produced, but not to determine the direction of production, which will be done by planners or collective decisions; a private-property system, now also called 'a free market system' uses markets for both. It is unfortunate that Rawls does not adhere to a consistent definition of a 'free market system'. Here it is clearly the opposite of socialism: elsewhere he can speak of an economy as 'roughly a free market system, although the means of production may or may not be privately owned' (p. 66), and can say that 'there is no essential tie between the use of free markets and private ownership of the instruments of production' (p. 271).

The advantages of a market system on the grounds of efficiency and of consistency with equal liberties and fair equality of opportunity are pointed out, and a fully free market system with perfect competition is set up as 'an ideal conception [which] may then be used to appraise existing arrangements and as a framework for identifying the changes that should be undertaken' (p. 272). But in fact, 'the ideal scheme sketched in the next several sections' is not a regime of perfectly competitive free markets: it is merely one which 'makes considerable use of market arrangements' (p. 274). Since both socialist and private-property systems use markets, this seems to leave open the question which is preferable, and indeed Rawls says, 'which of these systems and the many intermediate forms most fully answers to the requirements of justice cannot, I think, be determined in advance' (p. 274). He will start his sketch of the ideal scheme on the assumption that it is a private-property system 'since this case is likely to be better known' (p. 274), but insists that 'this is not intended to prejudge the choice of regime in particular cases', and says that 'modifications for the case of a socialist regime will be considered briefly later' (p. 275).

The sketch of a just society that follows is an elaborated version of a capitalist welfare state, with an extensive set of regulators designed to ensure equality of opportunity, prevent monopolistic restrictions, guarantee a social minimum of real income, correct for 'the failure of prices to measure accurately social benefits and costs' (p. 276), bring about reasonably full employment, prevent inequalities of wealth exceeding the limit at which they would jeopardize equality of opportunity and political liberties, and prevent one fairly small sector controlling the preponderance of productive resources.

This would meet the requirements of the two principles of justice as well as they can be met given the assumption of self-interested individuals with definitely limited social and altruistic motivation (pp. 280–1). The 'modifications' for the case of a socialist regime are simply that 'a liberal socialist regime' can also meet the requirements of justice if it uses markets.

We have only to suppose that the means of production are publicly owned and that firms are managed by workers' councils, say, or by agents appointed by them. Collective decisions made democratically under the constitution determine the general features of the economy, such as the rate of saving and the proportion of society's production devoted to essential public goods. Given the resulting economic environment, firms regulated by market forces conduct themselves much as before (p. 280).

What is most notable about this model of socialism is its reliance on 'market forces' which are said to induce the firms to behave 'much' as under capitalism. What is omitted is any consideration of the absence, in any model of socialism, of *capitalist* market forces, the force of which derives from the desire of entrepreneurs and firms to increase their capital, and their ability to do so by virtue of the property institutions which facilitate and require exploitation (in the strict sense defined earlier).

It is not difficult to show, as Rawls does, that a socialist system can meet the requirements of his principles of justice. But it can do so not as a 'modification' of the capitalist market system, but by its rejection of exploitive property institutions. Rawls, however, does not see exploitive relations inherent in capitalism, so it does not occur to him that there is any more difficulty arranging for justice in capitalism, however much regulated, than in socialism. He takes for granted that 'there exists an ideal property-owning system that would be just' while pointing out that this 'does not imply that historical forms are just, or even tolerable' (p. 274). After his very brief excursion into socialism he returns to the private property model for the discussion of such other problems as that of justice between generations.

Thus, as far as his use of models of society is concerned, Rawls relies mainly on a reformed capitalist model and is able to treat a socialist model as an allowable modification because his socialist model embodies a considerable element of normal capitalist motivations. Can we say that his model of the well-ordered or just society is what it is because his model of man is a bourgeois model? We are brought back to the question of his model of man.

At first sight this is not a specifically bourgeois model. True, the rational individual is a maximizer: he wants more rather than less 'primary goods', including income and wealth; and 'the concept of rationality must be interpreted as far as possible in the narrow sense, standard in economic theory, of taking the most effective means to given ends' (p. 14). But the rational man wants to maximize his primary goods as means to ends which are far from bourgeois. He wants them as means to realize his plan of life or concepts of the good, to develop his capacities to their fullest. Moreover, the rational man

does not suffer from envy ... He is not downcast by the knowledge or perception that others have a larger index of primary social goods. Or at least this is true as long as the differences between himself and others do not exceed certain limits, and he does not believe that the existing inequalities are founded on injustice or are the result of letting chance work itself out for no compensating social purpose (p. 143).

And Rawls's men are not infinite material desirers. The 'desire for an absolute increase in economic advantages declines' (p. 543) as the general level of primary goods rises. And 'men's concern for their relative place in the distribution of wealth' is too weak to make them seek ever more goods, since by hypothesis 'they are not much affected by envy and jealousy' (pp. 543–4). All this is a far cry from bourgeois man.

Yet this rational man is, after all, required to operate by the incentive of material gain: 'in a well-ordered society . . . the distribution of material means is left to take care of itself in accordance with the idea of pure procedural justice' (p. 545), which requires that there be a just system of institutions (pp. 86–7) the only model of which is a competitive market system either in Rawls's revised capitalist version or in his socialist version in which 'firms' behave in much the same way as in capitalism. In either version, not only distribution but presumably also production relies on the material-maximizing behaviour of the rational man.

The ambiguity in Rawls's model of man thus goes deep. He seems to be using two contradictory models. But in fact, there is no contradiction. For his rational moral man, the man with his own plan of life and concept of the good, who is apparently so unbourgeois (and who, it may be noticed, much resembles T. H. Green's moral man) bears the very hallmark of bourgeois man: he *both* puts a high value on individual liberty *and* accepts as inevitable a class-divided society in which class determines life prospects. Surely none but bourgeois man exhibits both those characteristics.

A similar ambiguity pervades Rawls's model of the just or well-ordered society. Its competitive market orientation we have already seen, and we have seen the case for this to be based on the explicit postulate that different individuals' ends or plans make conflicting claims on scarce goods. We have now to notice that in his extensive treatment of ends (in Part Three, especially from section 67 on) he develops a model of a well-ordered society which is so fundamentally harmonious that it seems to contradict the postulate of conflicting ends. People's plans can be 'both rational and complementary' (p. 441). 'Human beings have various talents and abilities the totality of which is unrealizable by any one person or group of persons. Thus we not only benefit from the complementary nature of our developed inclinations but we take pleasure in one another's activities. It is as if others were bringing forth a part of ourselves that we have not been able to cultivate' (p. 448). 'We need one another as partners in ways of life that are engaged in for their own sake, and the successes and enjoyments of others are necessary for and complimentary [sic] to our own good' (pp. 522–3). 'Human beings have a desire to express their nature as free and equal moral persons' (p. 528). '. . . in a well-ordered society this unity ['the essential unity of the self'] is the same for all; everyone's conception of the good as given by his rational plan is a subplan of the larger comprehensive plan that regulates the community as a social union of social unions' (p. 563). '. . . as shown by the notion of society as a social union of social unions, the members of a community participate in one another's nature: we appreciate what others do as things we might have done but which they do for us, and what we do is similarly done for them . . . the self is realized in the activities of many selves . . .' (p. 565).

All this is very different from the model of the market society used in the first part of his argument. Are the two models inconsistent? Rawls believes not, for he believes that his just market system would, while retaining classes with different life prospects, reduce the class disparities, and soften the consciousness of them: 'both the absolute and relative differences allowed in a well-ordered society are probably less than those that have often prevailed . . . Moreover, the plurality of associations in a well-ordered society, with their own secure internal life, tends to reduce the visibility, or at least the painful visibility, of variations in men's prospects' (p. 536).

The resemblance of Rawls's model of a harmonious society (and of his model of the rational moral individual) to the models of T. H. Green is not surprising. For

Rawls, like Green, wants the harmonious moral model yet assumes that a competitive conflict model is, at least in some modified form, unavoidable. Each writer wants the liberal market freedoms *and* the moral values of community. Yet each has failed to see the inconsistency between these, because each has overlooked the inherently exploitive nature of liberal market freedoms.

Nevertheless, Rawls has done a new service to political theory by sketching the lineaments of a harmonious society of fully human beings. If his theory is deficient in its grasp of class and power, it yet has the substantial merit of taking us beyond the warmed-up utilitariansim of much current liberal theory while avoiding the gross idealism that tempts or afflicts anti-utilitarians of the centre and right. It thus opens the way for, one hopes, an immediately consequent generation of liberal scholars to move towards a still more realistic humanist political theory.

University of Toronto   C. B. MACPHERSON

NOTE

1 The transfer of powers is discussed in my *Democratic Theory : Essays in Retrieval*, Oxford, 1973.

24

RAWLS AND LEFT CRITICISM

ARTHUR DiQUATTRO
Reed College

IS RAWLS an "unreconstructed Gladstonian liberal"?[1] Does Rawls's theory of justice sanction class-divided societies?[2] Is Rawls an inegalitarian utilitarian, despite all appearances to the contrary?[3] Does Rawls's defense of market arrangements entail support of bourgeois norms of distribution?[4] Do Rawls's principles of justice stand in antagonistic relation to the value of community?[5]

Left critics of Rawls respond affirmatively to one or more of these questions. I want to defend Rawls against the interpretations on which these responses depend, showing them to be misconceived or mistaken. I maintain that Rawls's theory of justice, though in need of some friendly amendments, is essentially compatible with socialist, including Marxist, ideas of social justice. Since my defense proceeds from a socialist standpoint, my argument should be considered an immanent critique of the objections of some socialists to Rawls's theory. It is immanent also because it attempts to trace out the egalitarian implications of the difference principle. I seek to bring out these implications in more explicit terms than Rawls employs by focusing on the concepts of class and market and the place they occupy in the difference principle. While I specifically refrain from enjoining the argument that Rawlsian justice is necessarily socialist, I do interpret the difference principle as ruling out capitalism as just while admitting the possibility of a just socialism.

In what follows, I argue that Rawls does not allow for class-divided societies, given the Marxist conception of class; that the difference principle is not open to a utilitarian interpretation; that Rawls's theory

AUTHOR'S NOTE: An earlier version of this article was presented at the Philosophy Department Colloquium, University of Washington, and at the annual meetings of the American Political Science Association, Washington, D.C., September 1979. Thanks go to Milton Fisk and Lawrence Joseph for commenting on a previous draft.

POLITICAL THEORY, Vol. 11 No 1, February 1983 53-78
© 1983 Sage Publications, Inc.

0090-5917 83 010053-26$2.85

is not wedded to a defense of capitalist market society, as Marxists understand capitalism, and, indeed, dismisses it as inherently unjust; that Rawls's insistence on market devices is quite compatible with, and required by, the Marxian sense of socialist justice; and, finally, that if there is a tension between the concepts of justice and community in Rawls's theory, the problem is not peculiar to his theory and can be located also in the Marxist theory of transition from capitalism to communism.

CLASS INEQUALITY AND
THE DIFFERENCE PRINCIPLE

C. B. Macpherson is curious about the "fact that a theory of justice which starts out from egalitarian premises should be mainly concerned with enquiring what justifies an inequality of life prospects as between members of different social classes."[6] I take it that what strikes up Macpherson's curiosity is not the fact that Rawls spends considerable time in laying out what is involved in the difference principle. Conservative caricatures of egalitarian thought notwithstanding, egalitarian theorists (among whom I number Rawls) have never called for equal distribution of most goods; what they have instead required is an ethical justification for any deviation from equality, though as egalitarians they have sought to set limits on the extent of permissible differentials. So it is not unusual that Rawls should accord a central place in his theory to an explication of the nature and degree of *just* inequalities. Macpherson's concern, then, must stem from Rawls's talk of differences in life prospects of members of different social *classes,* suggesting as it does to Macpherson that the difference principle can be put to use in justifying inequalities not ordinarily countenanced in the egalitarian tradition.

It is not surprising that Macpherson is troubled by mention of class inequality. Macpherson means by "class" what Marxists mean by it. "Class is understood . . . in terms of property: a class is taken to consist of those who stand in the same relation of ownership or non-ownership of productive land and/or capital."[7] Further, class division in any society is based on exploitation; the transfer of powers or the product of those powers from some to others for their own benefit "is the means and the result of class division."[8] If Rawls meant by "class" what Marxists mean, who wouldn't share Macpherson's befuddlement over

Rawls's presumed attempt to reconcile an egalitarian theory of justice with class divisions and their inherent exploitative mechanisms? But does Rawls employ the Marxist conception of class? I think not. First, he could not consistently claim that the existence of social classes is compatible with a theory of justice if he believed that class division entailed exploitation of one class by another. "Justice" and "exploitation" express mutually exclusive concepts. It is unlikely that Rawls would commit a logical mistake of this magnitude. Second, as another socialist critic of Rawls points out, "Rawls largely ignores [the Marxian] conception and generally talks about classes in the way most bourgeois social scientists do, where 'class' and 'strata' are roughly interchangeable terms."[9]

Nielsen is right that Rawls disregards the Marxist criterion, but it does not follow that he substitutes for it the picture of social stratification drawn by most bourgeois sociologists. According to a predominant strain in bourgeois theory, "Each has a status which is defined by others . . . and social status or class is only one among several discriminations determined essentially by psychological phenomena."[10] In contrast to this definition, which "regards the psychology of individuals . . . as the essence of the phenomena [of social stratification],"[11] Rawls identifies classes in terms of their members' share of primary social goods. This provides Rawls a way "to find some objective grounds" for comparison of social positions; subjective preferences give way to judgments of welfare as measured by indices of primary social goods.[12] So Rawls's social classes are objectively defined in light of their constituents possessing proximate amounts of "rights and liberties, opportunities and powers, income and wealth."[13] Indeed, Rawls goes so far as to omit altogether "social status" from his list of basic goods subject to differential distribution in a well ordered society.[14] The fact that Rawls correlates income and wealth with power and authority is also significant because it sets off his conception of class from the radically pluralist component of bourgeois theories of stratification. The Rawlsian account of class fails to separate systems of power, wealth, and property, after the fashion of pluralist theory, and instead combines them to create "relevant social positions."[15]

These "relevant social positions" are Rawls's classes, and they fit neither Marxist nor bourgeois conceptions. The "representative citizens" who constitute these classes "stand for various levels of well-being," and there are as many classes as there are discernible differences in wealth, income, and occupation. At one point, Rawls defines classes solely in terms of wealth and income, suggesting that "all persons with less than half of the median of income and wealth be taken as the least advantaged segment."[16] "Segment," "group," "level of well-being"— Rawls's theory of class is not very complex and consists of little more than a breakdown of the population into differential levels of well-being.

There are, then, class divisions in Rawls's well-ordered society, but they are not the kind that Marxists have in mind. All that Marxists can claim legitimately is that, given their conception of class, Rawls allows for a "one-class" society, or something approximating it. Macpherson writes: "Different from [both classless and class-divided societies] is the idea of a society where there is individual ownership of productive land and capital and where everyone owns, or is in a position to own, such property: this we call a *one-class* society."[17] While noting that a decentralized socialist system can meet the requirements of his principles of justice, Rawls chooses to elaborate a regime of "property-owning democracy."[18] In this regime, "land and capital are widely though not equally held. Society is not so divided that one fairly small sector controls the preponderance of productive resources," and a distribution branch of government functions to support those institutions that perpetuate widespread private ownership of capital.[19] Nielsen remarks that "talk of 'people's capitalism' is at best fanciful," but, fanciful or not, Rawls entertains something like it, and it resembles Macpherson's one-class society.[20] Rawls does not include classes, in the Marxian sense, in his just society. Strictly speaking, Rawls's property-owning democracy is not a capitalist market system at all, and it is for good reason that Rawls never refers to his ideal political economy as capitalism. The word "capitalism" appears not once in *A Theory of Justice*. Rawls borrows the phrase "property-owning democracy" from James Meade, whose thesis turns on making a radical distinction between property-owning democracies and capitalist welfare systems. A welfare state presupposes extreme inequalities in property ownership and involves taxation of the incomes of the rich to subsidize directly or indirectly the incomes of the poor; a property-owning democracy involves widespread distribution of property ownership (pooled through insurance firms, investment trusts, and so on) so that each citizen receives a part of his or her income from property.[21] This distinction is more than simply verbal; it is conceptual and empirical since the terms identify different phenomena. The class divisions that Marx took to be the central feature of capitalism are nowhere to be found in the idea of property-owning democracy. Many interpreters of

Rawls have rushed to judgment in characterizing his property-owning democracy as a capitalist welfare system.[22]

Since the class divisions peculiar to capitalism are absent in a property-owning democracy, the exploitation specific to capitalism must also be absent. There is no small class that, because it monopolizes ownership and control of the means of production, can extort a surplus from a working class owning nothing productive but its power to labor. This does not entail an absence of exploitation of a different kind. Even in a society in which productive resources are widely owned (either privately or socially), significant differences of income, wealth, and power may persist, and it may be that these differences are spawned by exploitative institutions and morally unjustified. Whether the institutions sanctioned by Rawls's principles are the exploitative I will consider in the next section. For now, I want to note the stringent limits the difference principle sets on the justificatory basis for and the extent of permissible differentials.

Rawls views his well-ordered society as a cooperative social union in which everyone who is able is expected to live up to a social obligation.[23] This view finds expression in the difference principle in its requirement that members of the most advantaged stratum must contribute to the common good, which, thanks to the "chain-connectedness" assumption, Rawls interprets as improving the well-being of the least advantaged segment. The principle is one of "mutual benefit" and those who are better situated deserve their position only if their productive effort benefits others. It is precisely because the principle establishes a connection between the distribution of rewards and the discharge of social obligation that it differs radically from bourgeois conceptions of distributive justice. According to the latter, the distribution of benefits is determined by "[property] rights [that] are not deducible from the discharge of function and these rights are anterior to, and independent of, any service which [an individual] may render."[24] In bourgeois society, ownership of market-scarce productive factors or commodities yields rewards, and ownership need not be accompanied by productive service on the part of the owners. Bourgeois theorists, such as Hayek and Friedman, argue explicitly, as most neoclassicist theorists imply, that "luck" determines largely who gets (and should get) what in capitalist market society, so that if one is fortunate enough to be born into a wealthy family, or to have oil discovered on one's land, or to be born with certain characteristics that fetch high market prices, or to make profitable investments, then one qualifies for disproportionate rewards. In bourgeois society, no one who is lucky enough to own a commodity in great demand need make any productive effort to cash in on the public store. All one need do is *own* something and, as Joan Robinson phrases it in her contribution to the "Cambridge controversies" in the theory of capital, "ownership is not a productive activity."[25]

For Friedman, "Despite the lip service that we all pay to 'merit' as compared to 'chance,' market distribution is akin to a game or lottery which everyone agrees to enter with the anticipation of winning a jackpot prize." "Most differences of status or position or wealth can be regarded as the product of chance at a far enough remove," and redistribution of these goods after people play the game of economic life is "equivalent to denying them the opportunity to enter the lottery."[26] Hayek's acceptance of this view prompts him to wonder whether "we ought to encourage in the young the belief that when they really try they will succeed, or rather emphasize that inevitably some unworthy will succeed and some worthy will fail."[27] Friedman and Hayek would leave it to natural and social contingencies to arrive at an appropriate distribution of benefits and burdens. Coming to the marketplace with whatever resources they "happen" to own, individuals engage in exchange (which bourgeois theorists like to call "voluntary") and, aware that the initial distribution of resources affects the outcome of exchange, accept the resulting distributive configuration as "just." "Our only moral title to what the market gives us, we have earned by submitting to those rules which make the formation of the market order possible."[28] This is market "justice."

In contrast to market principles of distribution, the difference principle "does not weight men's share in the benefits and burdens of social cooperation according to their social fortune or their luck in the natural lottery."[29] "No one deserves his greater natural capacity nor merits a more favorable starting place in society" and "the naturally advantaged are not to gain merely because they are more gifted."[30] Instead, those who gain from their good fortune must work to improve the circumstances of those who have lost out, and their greater rewards constitute a kind of compensation for the costs incurred in the fulfillment of their social obligation. I will say more about the compensatory character of the difference principle; for now, it suffices to show how, by ruling out natural and social contingencies as a basis for distribution, so "arbitrary from a moral point of view,"[31] the difference principle can work to narrow the range of differentials. It excludes rewards not tied to the performance of social function and, in this way, undermines the claims of those who derive their wealth and power on the basis of mere ownership of productive factors.[32]

In addition to challenging one basis for differentials, the difference principle establishes a limit to their size by seeking to secure "equality of opportunities." Macpherson fails to see this. He calls Rawls on his admission of "inequalities in life prospects as between members of different social classes." In the passages cited by Macpherson, however, Rawls admits no such thing.[33] He speaks only of *initial* inequalities in life prospects and individuals *starting out* as members of different classes, that is, strata. The supplementary principle of fair, as opposed to formal, equality of opportunity is then introduced to whittle away preliminary inequalities by ensuring a similarity of social and economic circumstances for all, "regardless of their initial place in the social system, irrespective of the income class into which they are born."[34] Rawls assigns a not inconsiderable role to the state in providing practical equality of opportunity.

> Free market arrangements must be set within a framework of political and legal institutions which regulate the overall trends of economic events and preserves the social conditions for fair equality of opportunity. The elements of this framework are familiar enough, though it may be worthwhile to recall the importance of preventing excessive accumulations of property and wealth and of maintaining equal opportunities of education for all. Chances to acquire cultural knowledge and skills should not depend upon one's class position, and so the school system should be designed to even out class barriers.[35]

The point is that fair equality of opportunity presupposes a system of stratification that does not contain vast inequalities in the initial distribution of opportunities. The practical realization of the principle requires a setting of limited inequality. But might not the successful pursuit of fair equality of opportunity policies result in a meritocracy, that is, a society stratified according to the natural distribution of abilities and talents?[36] Rawls is sensitive to this problem and he rejects a meritocratic interpretation of the idea of equality of opportunity. Because a meritocratic system attaches so much wealth, income, power, and status to roles occupied by individuals of proven ability and so little of these goods to those who "fail," it tends to undermine the self-respect of the "failures." Self-respect is one primary social good that is equally distributed in a society the organization of which corresponds to Rawls's principles of justice. "It follows that the confident sense of their own worth should be sought for the least favored and this limits the forms of hierarchy and the degrees of inequality that justice permits."[37]

Rawls is not a meritocrat in the strong sense because he disallows rewarding differentially merit that is the result of the natural lottery. He *is* a meritocrat in the weak sense that abilities and talents are to be matched with certain roles or jobs. His argument appears to require this matching for two reasons: (a) the performance of tasks by those most qualified provides some insurance that recipients of their service will benefit, and (b) those with the requisite skills should have the opportunity to cultivate them, enabling them to experience "the realization of self which comes from a skillful and devoted exercise of social duties."[38] This does not mean that individuals need be confined to the performance of singular tasks. The aim is to provide equality of opportunity for individuals to develop and realize the capacities they possess; meritocratic job placement in no way rules out the holding of multiple roles.[39] It is true, as Daniels notes, that the natural lottery still determines access to jobs, so that some people will be excluded from the pursuit of certain occupations as their life's work.[40] This may seem morally problematical, as it limits liberty, but it would expect that, in line with the Aristotelian Principle, greater satisfaction is derived from engaging in those activities at which one is skilled than in facing up to the frustration involved in the unsuccessful pursuit of endeavors resulting in repeated failure. If meritocratic job placement limits liberty, it is a liberty the regulation of which works to protect the interests of both the frustrated aspirant and those who might be treated to his or her incompetence. To sum up: Far from denying individuals opportunities to actualize capacities, meritocratic role assignment (in what I have called the "weak sense") facilitates this process, and it does so in a way that does not permit the distribution of wealth and status to be settled by the distribution of natural assets.

UTILITARIANISM AND
THE DIFFERENCE PRINCIPLE

Rawls's main objection to utilitarian theory is the standard one that its application may occasion the violation of individual integrity, rights, and liberty. In particular, utilitarians aim to derive principles of justice from the singular end of attaining the maximum sum of satisfaction among individuals, so that it is a matter of secondary importance how this sum of satisfaction gets distributed among individuals.[41] As Rawls reads utilitarian theory:

> There is no reason in principle why the greater gains of some should not compensate for the lesser losses of others; or more importantly, why the violation of the liberty of a few might not be made right by the greater good shared by many.[42]

Rawls argues that rational, self-interested individuals in the original position, not prone to risk taking, would bypass a utilitarian interpretation of justice because it offers no guarantee for the protection of individual interests, broadly defined. By subordinating distributive principles to aggregative ones, utilitarian theory rides roughshod over distributive claims not grounded on the paramount principle of happiness maximization. The difference principle, in contrast, ensures a certain (I have argued, egalitarian) distribution irrespective of its consequences for the achievement of aggregate satisfaction.

Given Rawls's explicit rejection of utilitarian versions of distributive justice, Kai Nielsen's characterization of the difference principle as "plainly utilitarian" prompts some consternation.[43] The difference principle, on first reading, permits inequalities in the distribution of most goods if the productive effort of members of the most advantaged stratum redounds to the benefit of members of the least advantaged stratum, the inequalities providing incentives to attract individuals into socially necessary positions and to encourage efficient performance. Nielsen detects some "utilitarian reasoning" at work here and maintains that only "utilitarian considerations" can sustain a plausible justification for the difference principle.[44] He acknowledges the contribution of members of the top stratum to the material betterment of members of the lower stratum, generally increasing the aggregate amount of primary social goods available for distribution, but suggests that there is a sense in which the former gain *at the expense of* the latter. Nielsen complains that the improvement in the absolute position of the disadvantaged fails to compensate for the worsening of their relative position. In Rawls's stratified society, the advantaged exploit the disadvantaged in the sense that inequalities introduced as incentives create differential life prospects for those born into different strata, denying equality of opportunity for all to realize their human capacities or plans for the good life. For Nielsen, the primary values from which any theory of justice finds its derivation are those of equal self-respect and moral autonomy, and these values supersede the claims of the most advantaged to differential shares, which, to echo Macpherson, are the cause and means of class division and exploitation. Nielsen calls for equal distribution of income and wealth with adjustments for differences in need. Equal distribution sets the stage for a classless society, and it is only in such a society that equality of opportunity to realize life plans, equality of self-respect, and equal moral autonomy can flourish.

What of Nielsen's argument? I have already countered construals of the difference principle as allowing for significant differentials. Nielsen fails altogether in making good on his reading of Rawls in respect to this matter. However, the principle does tolerate—indeed, requires—limited differentials, and even after state activity takes its toll in narrowing initial class inequalities, there may remain disparities of life prospects among members of different classes sufficient to raise doubts about the justice of such an arrangement. Even slight differentials, combined with the institution of the family, can hamper the implementation of the egalitarian values embraced by Nielsen and assumed by Rawls as the foundation of his theory of justice. Though Nielsen exaggerates to the point of distortion the extent to which this problem afflicts Rawls's theory, he raises an issue that requires treatment.

The main thing to notice, in handling this problem, is that the difference principle does *not* justify greater rewards for the more advantaged solely on the basis of their greater contribution benefiting the less advantaged. We have already seen that Rawls discounts natural and social contingencies as grounds for desert. When Rawls speaks of some *earning*[45] greater benefits he cannot have in mind their receiving more just because they have contributed disproportionately, since their contribution may have resulted from their natural or social fortune. Rawls's justification proceeds along different lines: The advantaged merit a larger share because they undergo disproportionate disutility in the course of contributing to the common advantage; their greater benefits constitute compensation for greater costs incurred in the performance of socially necessary labor; the greater expectations associated with this kind of labor count as *just* incentives because they accord with the compensatory aspect of the difference principle adopted unanimously in the original position. The compensatory nature of the difference principle is often overlooked because Rawls fails uncharacteristically to set out the idea very persistently, but there do appear statements that offer support for this interpretation. For example:

> The naturally advantaged are not to gain merely because they are more gifted, but only to cover the costs of training and education and for using their endowments in ways that help the less fortunate as well.[46]

The function of unequal distributive shares is to cover the costs of training and education, to attract individuals to places and associations where they are most needed from a social point of view, and so on.[47]

Rawls takes the position that a "perfectly competitive market" set against the background of just institutions tends to satisfy the compensatory requirement of the difference principle. Such a market rewards individuals according to the marginal product of their factors of production, and since the implementation of fair equality of opportunity policies removes barriers of entry into different jobs and reduces imperfections in the market for loans or subsidies for education and training, there will be a strong tendency for differences in unequal returns to be equalized. This is because marginal return depends, in part, on the supply of resources or labor-power available for different markets. "Thus the precept to each according to his training and education is weighted less [in a competitive market plus state-regulated equality of opportunity policies] than in [a competitive market operating in a highly stratified society] and the precept to each according to his effort is weighted more."[48] A justly ordered society, in which there is freedom of employment, would no doubt have to award greater benefits to individuals who undertake activities involving "uncertain or unstable employment, or which are performed under hazardous and unpleasantly strenuous conditions. . . . Otherwise men cannot be found to fill them. From this circumstance arise such precepts as to each according to his effort or the risks he bears."[49] In this way, the market works to compensate individuals in proportion to the disutility undergone in satisfying social want. And in a market economy regulated by fair equality of opportunity policies and other egalitarian measures, the shortage of individuals prepared to offer their services in unenjoyable and risky activities would ensure them a higher marginal rate of return, in contrast to those enjoyable activities (which in present capitalist societies pay high rates because of the imperfections sustained by acute class inequalities and consequent structured lack of equality of opportunity) that would pay less because of the greater supply of labor.[50]

None of this is to say that Rawls advocates a market mode of distribution. While a "perfectly competitive market" provides a mechanism to compensate individuals according to their marginal disutility, distribution is determined ultimately by the state through its taxing and redistributive policies, its provision for need, its supply of public goods, and so on. The state sets limits on the extent of permissible inequalities, relying on the market only as it *happens* to meet the requirements of just principles. In Nozick's words, Rawls's principles are somewhat "patterned."[51] They are patterned even though they leave it to particular institutions, such as the market, to assist in determining particular distributions. The difference principle does not enjoin regular interference by the state with the immediate distributional effects of specific market transactions. The subject of justice is not the particular distributions themselves but rather the "basic structure" or organization of the background institutions that set the stage for particular distributions. It is still fitting, however, to characterize the difference principle as patterned, since the particular distributions would be different if it were not for the presence and operation of the background institutions. It is worth noting how Rawls's distinction between the basic structure and specific distributions works to immunize his theory against the libertarian criticism of Nozick, Hayek, et al., who conjure up the specter of the just state administered by legions of bureaucratic meddlers regulating the distributive result of each and every transaction among individuals. In Rawls's theory, the market, when set against the right basic structure, tends to yield automatically an overall distributive outcome consistent with social justice. It allows for freedom of employment and provides a way of objectively measuring degrees of disutility attached to productive contributions. No need, then, for government officials to regulate the job market by "assigning" jobs or to establish an incomes policy according to their "subjective" or "arbitrary" estimates of disutility. The place accorded to the market in the difference principle goes some distance in severing the "necessary" connection claimed to exist by libertarian theorists between the important role of the state in securing substantive justice and the "road to serfdom."

This brief excursion into the compensatory character of the difference principle should show why it is a mistake to interpret the principle as utilitarian, as well as why it would be unfair to award equal incomes to all individuals. Some people get more not only because they contribute to the satisfaction of consumer demand, but also because their contribution involves sacrifice, and to fail to compensate for the sacrificial component of the contribution would be to commit an injustice. I assume that people in the original position would readily acknowledge the fairness of unequal distribution in light of unequal burdens, especially if everyone benefits as a consequence of the disutility borne by some. Only if workers who bear greater burdens receive greater compensation can other workers avoid the charge that they are exploiting their harder-working comrades. The difference principle is one of mutual compensation, compensating the most advantaged when it can be reasonably expected that their contribution compensates the least advantaged for their shortfall in the distribution of natural and social fortune.

But might not differential rewards, combined with the institution of the family, lead to differential life prospects for members born into different classes? Yes. I think it not terribly problematical, given the egalitarian measures effected by the state, but short of abolishing the family and the cultural and material inheritances that are a part of it, unequal life prospects will be an occasional outcome of the slightly structured inequalities permitted by the difference principle. "The principle of fair equality of opportunity can only be imperfectly carried out, at least as long as the institution of the family exists."[52] The justificatory basis for inheritance is the difference principle and the fair equality of opportunity proviso sets limits on its size, but it is plain that Rawls's defense of inheritance is also grounded in his acceptance of the family. Does Rawls's defense of inheritance call into question the compensatory interpretation of the difference principle? Can it be said that people who inherit wealth are receiving compensation for productive contribution? The latter question misses the point and that is why the first question can be answered negatively. The focus should be placed on the parents, not on their offspring. Giving parents the liberty to benefit their children is a part of *their* compensation for *their* contributions; passing on inheritance counts as one way in which parents can spend their earned income, not to mention the multiplicity of ways in which parents seek to pass on immaterial assets while parenting.

But does not equal distribution of wealth and income violate our strong feeling that individuals whose activity involves greater disutility should receive extra compensation? Again, the answer is yes. We are faced here with conflicting intuitive feelings, both rooted in a belief in intrinsic human equality, and the conflict requires resolution. Rawls, I suggest, presents an acceptable compromise: The difference principle provides for unequal compensation to compensate those contributions involving disproportionate disutility, but it sets limits on the extent of tolerable inequalities, thus interfering with the claim of contributors to unrestricted access to primary social goods; at the same time, the principle ensures approximately equal circumstances for all, so as to radically, though not completely, exclude differential life chances among people starting out in different strata, thus interfering with the claim of individuals to unfettered equality of opportunities. Where conflicting claims are equally pressing and equally just, and where scarcity precludes the equal satisfaction of these claims (thus the conflict), the difference principle permits a resolution through compromise. There is no alternative solution that qualifies as fair.

THE MARKET AND THE DIFFERENCE PRINCIPLE

Since a "property-owning democracy" is not a capitalist system, as Marxists understand capitalism, it is not at all evident that "Rawls believes that a capitalist society can be a well-ordered, perfectly just society."[53] In fact, capitalist institutions fail to pass the Rawlsian muster. If Marxists are right about how capitalism works (and I think they are), capitalists derive an income (profit) and occupy positions of control independently of their performing any productive service. Capitalists are parasitic drones, as Marx has it, and because they do nothing that contributes to the well-being of the least advantaged, they cannot appeal to the difference principle to justify their privileged standing. This is not to say that capital is not productive, or that capital is not necessary to make labor productive, but it is to assert that *owning* capital is not a productive activity. Capitalist institutions allow owners of capital to charge a price (profit) to workers in order for the latter to gain access to the means of making a living. In this way, capitalists reap benefits minus any personal contribution to production. They live off a bribe.

There is another sense, not usually dwelled upon by Marxists, in which a capitalist market provides a mechanism for exploitation. Macpherson captures what is involved when he refers to a capitalist market system as requiring "the more able to extract some of the powers of the less able," where ability is measured by market indicators.[54] To employ a bit of neoclassical terminology, a capitalist market permits those who own an ample supply of "human capital" (what Marxists call "labor-power") to tax those who seek access to that "capital." Just as ownership of the "means of production," in the Marxian conception, allows owners to collect rewards (profit), so ownership of talents, abilities, or natural characteristics that happen to be in market demand yield differential rewards (wages). This mode of distribution, of course, allows individuals to cash in on natural or social fortune and, accordingly, runs up against the requirements of the difference principle. So on neither the traditional Marxian idea of capital nor the neoclassical conception of "human capital" does the second principle of justice authorize market distribution set against the institutional background of the structured inequalities characteristic of capitalist society.

At this point in my argument, some skeptics might object that even if I am right in distinguishing between a property-owning democracy and a capitalist market system, this shows only that Rawls does not rule in the latter as satisfying the difference principle. The question remains: Does he rule it out? How capitalism fares under the difference principle depends on Rawls's distinction between ideal and nonideal normative theory and, equally important, on his commitment to "generally shared ways" of ascertaining the truth or falsity of beliefs about matters of fact or what it is "reasonable to expect."[55]

By way of getting clear about this, consider what Rawls says about the institutions of slavery and serfdom. At one point, Rawls describes circumstances in which the institution of slavery qualifies as "tolerable" or "defensible" on the condition that it can be shown to be "less unjust" than available options.[56] For example, if the only alternative to putting war prisoners to death is their enslavement, slavery counts as tolerable. Presumably, if at a certain historical juncture there were no viable alternatives to serfdom (that is, it was not reasonable to anticipate the successful replacement—revolutionary or otherwise—of serfdom by more just arrangements), serfdom would have to do. Though at considerable distance from the ideal conception of justice, it is less unjust than feasible electives and, accordingly, defensible.

> Viewing the theory of justice as a whole, the ideal part presents a conception of a just society that we are able to achieve *if we can*. Existing institutions are to be judged to the extent that they depart from it *without sufficient reason*.[57]

One of the reasons that serfdom or a caste system deviates from ideal theory is that the "belief is not true" that a fixed natural order sanctions a hierarchical society.[58] "Our problem is how society should be arranged if it is to conform to principles that rational persons with true general beliefs would acknowledge in the original position."[59] Rawls's account of the requisite criteria for assessing the truth of general beliefs is overly brief and disappointing, but contained in his call to settle controversies about competing beliefs is an appeal to common experience and "plain facts accessible to all." Since Rawls characterizes as "dogma" sets of belief based on supernatural fiat or faith, where "no argument is possible," I assume that, despite his claim that he intends to "imply no particular metaphysical doctrine or theory of knowledge," the "sufficient reaons" he mentions in the passage cited above are generated by a critical attitude that bears some connection to the rational or scientific mode of inquiry. Indeed, in one place Rawls asserts that we "must rely upon current knowledge as recognized by common sense and the existing scientific consensus."[60]

Whether, and to what degree, actual institutions satisfy the requirements of ideal thory, then, depends in part on the truth of general beliefs about those institutions. Further, whether actual institutions (such as slavery or serfdom) that are less than just qualify as tolerable or defensible depends on the truth of general beliefs about the probability of ushering into existence viable alternatives conforming more closely to the ideal. Because the theory of justice entertains historical realities that may unavoidably constrain the implementation of its principles in their pure form, the theory is not utopian in the sense described by Marx.[61] While it is true that Rawls (deliberately) lacks a theory of historical development, it is also true that, unlike the utopian ideologies castigated by Marx, Rawls's theory does not overlook historical circumstances as either barriers to or facilitators of the realization of moral principles. Rawls does not work with the illusionary idea that the implementation of just principles can proceed independently of empirical plausibility or reasonable expectations about historical contingencies.

So does the difference principle rule out capitalism as just? For reasons I have laid out, capitalism falls far short of the ideal conception; it involves too great inequalities and systematically rewards individuals on the basis of natural and social fortune and irrespective of their performing a social function. But might not it be a system less unjust than available options and therefore tolerable or defensible? The answer to this question turns, in a decisive way, on settling controversies about relevant evidence and reasonable expectations. If Marxists are right in their empirical rendering of the nature of capitalism and if, as Marxists believe, historical circumstances make capitalism ripe for a transition to a more justly ordered society (socialism), then the principles of justice exclude capitalism. To nonsocialists, these are big "ifs," and a good part of the gulf separating socialist from nonsocialist thought consists of contested evidence. Disputes about matters of fact and what it is reasonable to expect constitute an important ingredient in the radically different assessments of the implications that Rawls's theory of justice has for different social systems. These disputes, as much as the abstractness of the theory, contribute to the view that the theory suffers from an indeterminancy allowing for a broad range of equally compatible interpretations. But this is hardly a weakness, unless it is thought that substantive (empirical) social theories have no bearing on the worth of normative theories. If they do have a bearing, as they must, only those interpretations resting on the more valid empirical theories merit acceptance or, at least, serious consideration. My aim in this essay is not to detail the truth or falsity of any particular social theory, including the Marxian account of capitalism, but rather to make good on the project initiated in the introductory section: An immanent treatment of aspects of Marxist and Rawlsian thought shows how Rawlsian justice rules out capitalism as just. The principles of justice (and the entire argument backing them) *plus* the truth of the Marxian account rule out capitalism as just. Schweikart makes this point: "If one holds, as Rawls appears to, that a theory of justice includes a greater-likelihood principle, then his theory is not neutral, especially when interpreted as embracing virtues of social institutions."[62] The two principles, plus empirical likelihoods about the structure and operation of economic systems, exclude capitalism, while allowing, at least, for socialism and property-owning democracy.[63]

If the difference principle fails to justify capitalist property, it does accord an indispensable place to the market as an allocative device. Following Meade, Rawls draws a distinction between the allocative and distributive functions of market prices and in this way calls attention to the compatability of free markets and public ownership of economic resources. Under socialism, the market might be used to *allocate* resources efficiently but never to *distribute* income, wealth, or power in proportion to the distribution of privately held capital. In either market socialist or property-owning democratic systems, distribution is determined politically in accord with the principles of justice.[64] Rawls recommends the use of markets because of the advantage of allocative efficiency and because he feels that comprehensive planning tends to interfere with equal liberties and fair equality of opportunity, that is, market devices decentralize economic power and enhance free choice of occupation. But there is another, more important reason for Rawls's insistence on markets. And he does *insist:* "The ideal scheme sketched . . . makes considerable use of market arrangements. It is *only* in this way, I believe, that the problem of distribution can be handled as a case of pure procedural justice."[65]

Besides distinguishing between private property and socialist economies, Rawls discriminates between private and public goods, pointing out that the quantity of public goods a society produces is a matter decided independently of the form of ownership of the means of production. Public goods are characterized by their indivisibility and publicness, that is, they are goods that cannot be, or would not be, packaged separately or parceled out to individuals for purchase according to personal preference scales. Instead, they can be, or would be, made available to relevant publics without limits placed on quantities enjoyed by particular individuals. Rawls offers as an example the polar case of national defense against unjustified foreign attack. Other examples would include clean air, public safety, lighthouses, and the like. Indeed, just about every good could be included theoretically in the public goods sector by having the state, through collective financing, provide the goods without rationing or charging consumers on an individual basis.

This is, in fact, the distributive goal set by Marxists in their vision of communist society. There is no market for goods in communist society, the market having been phased out during the transition period separating communism from capitalism. During the transitional interval, people consent to the gradual substitution of the collective provision of goods for their individual purchase in a market. This substitution would be piecemeal. Beginning with basic necessities, prices would be lowered slowly while the government notes the reaction of demand to price changes. If demand is fairly inelastic and goods nonsubstitutable, prices can be lowered to zero. The reduction of prices and their eventual disappearance would be paid for by lowering the money wages paid to individuals in exchange for their work, by substituting a social wage for an individual wage. For example instead of a worker receiving $25 daily, he might receive $20, but his bread, fish, and salt would be "free" for the taking at consumer goods outlets. Under communism, all costs would be socialized and all goods would become public.

The Marxian strategy runs head on against the requirements of the difference principle, and this conflict between communist and Rawlsian distributive principles brings out sharply why it is that Rawls considers markets an intricate component of his theory of justice. Justice requires the market because of the distributional consequences of its allocative function. I have already argued that the compensatory aspect of the difference principle calls for rewards proportional to the duration, intensity, difficulty, unenjoyability, hazardous nature, and so on of different jobs. The difficulty with the extension of the public goods sector is that it impinges upon this system of proportional reward under circumstances (moderate scarcity) that demand its continued application. The increased provision of public goods interferes with giving each his or her due, as prescribed by the distributional criterion of the difference principle, and compels some individuals to subsidize the unwanted benefits desired by others while necessarily subtracting from the range of want-satisfaction available to the former. This is why "all regimes will [must] normally use markets to ration out the consumption goods actually produced" such that "the output of commodities is guided as to kind and and quantity by the preferences of households as shown by their purchases on the market."[66] It follows, I think, that Rawlsian justice requires a market in production goods as well, since consumer preferences would of necessity play a large part in determining the direction of production. Rawls says that "there is no necessity for comprehensive direct planning" under socialism, but the context of his remark makes it clear that comprehensive "planning" that does not take its cue from market indicators violates the difference principle.[67] If the market is not used to allocate resources, individuals would be denied the opportunity to expend their merited incomes freely according to their preferences. Distribution patterned on the criterion "to each according to want and need" contrasts with distribution governed by the difference principle, that is, it violates justice.

Rawls, of course, does permit the production of public goods in a well-ordered society, but the difference principle circumscribes their nature and quantity. An exchange branch of government "arranges for public goods and services where the market breaks down," that is, in cases in which collective provision can be shown to be more Pareto-optimal than private consumption. A transfer branch of government may also provide public goods to ensure the satisfaction of basic needs of those who may not fare sufficiently well from market distribution. "But once a suitable minimum is provided by transfers, it may be perfectly fair that the rest of total income be settled by the price system," assuming that it is efficient, competitive, and set against the background of institutions conducive to equal liberty and fair equality of opportunity.[68] Rawls is careful to place limits on the provision of public goods and renders it difficult for the exchange branch to trade private for public goods. He accepts Wicksell's "unanimity criterion," which calls for near-unanimous approval of all citizens (or their representatives) on the public financing of collective goods. He points up that the criterion assumes the justice of existing distributions of income and property rights, and insists that when the latter condition is satisfied, "there is no more justification for using the state apparatus to compel some citizens to pay for unwanted benefits that others desire than there is to force them to reimburse others for their private expenses."[69]

When Rawls denies the justifiability of extending the public goods sector beyond a certain point, he must have in mind justification in light of just principles. It is, after all, possible to justify enlargement of that sector by appealing to moral principles other than justice. It might be argued, and Barry is open to this interpretation, that the value of community or social integration may contrast with that of distributive justice, and, in the event of conflict, should be accorded a place prior to justice.[70] If it could be shown (empirically) that a private goods sector of any appreciable size fosters competitiveness, acquisitiveness, and isolation, as Marxists claim;[71] that goods intended for common enjoyment "make for neighborliness and a sense of roots . . . remind us we are one with other generations, and . . . give us peace in surroundings that keep the spirit whole;"[72] and that the value of altruistic collaboration presupposed by a predominant public goods sector cannot long survive in a private goods economy governed by justice;[73] then we may decide to subordinate on moral grounds the value of justice to what may be taken to be the morally superior ideal of common enjoyment or social integration. It is precisely considerations such as these that are responsible for the Marxist distaste of market arrangements and the strategy designed to move society beyond justice to communist community.

Rawls believes that he can elude potential conflicts of this kind by embodying in his principles of justice the value of fraternity and the idea of mutual benefit. Further, the state's accounting for basic needs outside the market is supposed to constitute an expression of community at the highest social level. Rawls sees no necessary conflict emerging between the practice of justice, which includes the right of individuals to pursue their chosen life plans (as circumscribed by just principles) and the value of community. He only wants to leave it to individuals to decide whether, within the framework of just principles collectively adopted and enforced by the polity, they wish to realize whatever additional communitarian aims they may have. Though Rawls's principles are not morally neutral, in a way that tolerates the cultivation and satisfaction of any and all individual ends, they do provide a defense for a pluralistic organization of society.

> Other socially collective ends may well exist besides that of being a well-ordered society; but these ends cannot be upheld by the coercive apparatus of the state. If socially collective communitarian aims could survive in no other way, why should we regret their demise, and consider the original position unfair and arbitrarily biased against them?[74]

Rawls attempts to face up to communitarian objections to justice in a way similar to defenders of the practice of rights, a somewhat more encompassing concept and one presupposed by the practice of justice. Richard Flathman has addressed the "recurrent strain in communitarian thinking . . . that an emphasis on individual rights fragments human relationships in a manner and degree that renders genuine community impossible,"[75] and, like Rawls, is sensitive to ways in which certain interpretations of "community" stand in antagonistic relation to "rights" and "justice." Flathman endeavors to bring out the compatibility of individual rights with communitarian relationships: The practice of rights presupposes shared rules and judgments, enmeshes individuals in a network of social interaction, involves the acceptance of a common authority, and connects individuals through a series of mutual obligations. "In all these ways the practice of rights involves participants in patterned interrelationships and interdependencies."[76]

I doubt whether this way of alleviating the tension between the practice of rights (a practice whose utility stems from protecting individuals from each other) and community will satisfy those communitarian theorists who object to the kind of pluralistic or "liberal" society made possible, in part, by such a practice. Similarly, Rawls's view that "justice as fairness has a central place for the value of community,"[77] has not found a sympathetic audience in his critics, who persist in directing their fire at the individualistic or contractarian foundation of his well-ordered society.[78] I do not wish to rehearse these criticisms here, but since they often stem from theorists of Marxist predilections, I should like to conclude by noting that the tension between community and justice is present not only in "liberal" theory, but also in the Marxist conception of socialist justice. Marx prescribes as a distributive principle for the transition period from capitalism to communism "to each according to the duration and intensity of work, from each according to ability."[79] It should be apparent, for reasons I have already

267

supplied,[80] that this principle—just like the difference principle—requires the market. The main difference between Marx and Rawls is that the former is fully prepared to sacrifice justice and the market to community, whereas the latter believes that the two modes of life can peacefully coexist. Rawls, however, recognizes more clearly than Marx the conceptual difficulties involved in moving beyond justice to communist society under circumstances (moderate scarcity) that require (even for Marx) the application of just principles. If there is a tension among justice, the market, and community, Marx's theory of transition fails to offer a resolution clear of internal difficulties.[81] In this respect, Rawls is at least consistent.

NOTES

1. Brian Barry, *The Liberal Theory of Justice* (London: Oxford University Press, 1973), p. 50.

2. C. B. Macpherson, "Rawls' Models of Man and Society," *Philosophy of the Social Sciences* 3 (December 1973), pp. 341-347.

3. Kai Nielsen, "Class and Justice," in John Arthur and William Shaw, eds., *Justice and Economic Distribution* (Englewood Cliffs, NJ: Prentice-Hall, 1978), pp. 225-245.

4. C. B. Macpherson, "Revisionist Liberalism," in C. B. Macpherson *Democratic Theory: Essays in Retrieval* (London: Oxford University Press, 1973), pp. 77-94.

5. Barry, *Liberal Theory of Justice*, ch. 16.

6. Macpherson, "Rawls' Models of Man and Society," p. 341. Macpherson cites John Rawls, *A Theory of Justice* (Cambridge, MA: Harvard University Press, 1971), p. 78.

7. C. B. Macpherson, *The Life and Times of Liberal Democracy* (London: Oxford University Press, 1977), p. 11.

8. Macpherson, "Rawls' Models of Man and Society," p. 342.

9. Nielsen, "Class and Justice," p. 238.

10. Raymond Aron, "Two Definitions of Class," in Andre Beteille, ed., *Social Inequality* (Baltimore: Penguin, 1969), p. 75.

11. Ibid.

12. Rawls, *Theory of Justice*, p. 91.

13. Ibid., p. 92.

14. See Barry, *Liberal Theory of Justice*, pp. 45-46.

15. Rawls, *Theory of Justice*, p. 97. In separating these systems, pluralists can argue that a democratic politics is consistent with considerable economic inequality. Rawls's combination of these systems has an egalitarian implication. The combination, plus the first (and prior) principle's designation of the "fair value of liberty," makes it hard to see how a democratic polity can coexist alongside acute inequality in economic distribution.

16. Ibid., p. 98.

17. Macpherson, *Life and Times of Liberal Democracy,* p. 12. I find the notion of a "one-class society" conceptually odd. Doesn't the existence of one class entail the existence of another? There can no more exist one class in society than there can exist but one hand in a round of applause. Yet I see Macpherson's point. He wants to emphasize how a society of independent producers differs from other social formations.

18. Rawls, *Theory of Justice,* p. 274.

19. Ibid., p. 280.

20. Nielsen, "Class and Justice," p. 228. To say that Macpherson's "one-class society" resembles Rawls's "property-owning democracy" is not to say that the two phrases express the same concept. Macpherson has in mind the Jeffersonian-Rousseauist concept of individual households owning privately the land, tools, and means of production on which they work; Rawls's concept entails individuals owning privately shares of stock in various large-scale enterprises in an advanced industrial economy. Both systems are similar, however, in the important respect that they involve widespread private ownership of the means of production.

21. James E. Meade, *Efficiency, Equality, and the Ownership of Property* (Cambridge, MA: Harvard University Press, 1965), ch. 4, 5.

22. In addition to the left critics considered in this article, see also R. P. Wolff, *Understanding Rawls* (Princeton, NJ: Princeton University Press, 1977), pp. 128, 195; Barry Clark and Herbert Gintis, "Rawlsian Justice and Economic Systems," *Philosophy and Public Affairs* 7, 4 (1978); Benjamin Barber, "Justifying Justice," *American Political Science Review* 69 (June 1975), p. 672; David Schweickart, "Should Rawls Be a Socialist?" *Social Theory and Practice* 5 (Fall 1978); Robert Amdur, "Rawls and His Radical Critics," *Dissent* (Summer 1980).

23. Rawls, *Theory of Justice,* p. 112.

24. R. H. Tawney, *The Acquisitive Society* (New York: Harcourt Brace Jovanovich, 1920), p. 20.

25. Joan Robinson, *An Essay on Marxian Economics* (London: Macmillan, 1966).

26. Milton Friedman, *Capitalism and Freedom* (Chicago: University of Chicago Press, 1962), pp. 165-166; also see H. B. Acton, *The Morals of Markets: An Ethical Exploration* (London: Longman, 1971), pp. 62-64; and Frank Knight's seminal essay, "The Ethics of Competition," in Frank Knight, *The Ethics of Competition and Other Essays* (London: George Allen & Unwin, 1935).

29. Friedrich Hayek, *The Mirage of Social Justice* (London: Routledge & Kegan Paul, 1976), p. 74.

28. Ibid., p. 94; also see Robert Nozick, *Anarchy, State, and Utopia* (New York: Basic Books, 1974), pp. 187-188.

29. Rawls, *Theory of Justice,* p. 75.

30. Ibid., pp. 102, 101.

31. Ibid., p. 72.

32. As previously noted, in a property-owning democracy citizens do receive some income from property ownership. The point is that this income results in negligible differentials. Even in socialism, where productive property is owned by the state, citizens receive income, in the form of the social dividend or societywide profit sharing, from property.

33. Macpherson, "Rawls' Models of Man and Society," p. 341. Macpherson says: "The central concern of *A Theory of Justice* remains the justification of unequal life

prospects for members of different social classes." Rawls writes: "What, then, can possibly justify this kind of *initial* inequality in life prospects?" (emphasis added), p. 78.

34. Rawls, *Theory of Justice*, p. 73.

35. Ibid.

36. Barry, *Liberal Theory of Justice*, p. 51.

37. Rawls, *Theory of Justice*, p. 107. For a nice treatment of the causal relation between self-respect and unequal distribution under the difference principle, see Amy Gutmann, *Liberal Equality* (London: Cambridge University Press, 1980), pp. 135-138.

38. Rawls, *Theory of Justice*, p. 84.

39. "Each can be offered a variety of tasks so that the different elements of his nature find a suitable expression"; Rawls, *Theory of Justice*, p. 529.

40. Norman Daniels, "Meritocracy," in Arthur and Shaw, eds., *Justice and Economic Distribution*, p. 174.

41. "The concept of justice as a *fundamental* ethical concept is really quite foreign to utilitarianism. A utilitarian would compromise his utilitarianism if he allowed principles of justice which might conflict with the maximization of happiness. . . . He is concerned with the maximization of happiness and not with the distribution of it"; J.J.C. Smart, "Distributive Justice and Utilitarianism," in Arthur and Shaw, eds., *Justice and Economic Distribution*, p. 104.

42. Rawls, *Theory of Justice*, p. 26.

43. Nielsen, "Class and Justice," p. 235.

44. Nielsen, "On the Very Possibility of a Classless Society: Rawls, Macpherson, and Revisionist Liberalism," *Political Theory* 6 (May 1978), p. 198.

45. Rawls, *Theory of Justice*, p. 15.

46. Ibid., pp. 101-102.

47. Ibid., p. 315.

48. Ibid., p. 307.

49. Ibid., p. 306.

50. The assumption is that there would be an adequate supply of labor for enjoyable jobs even though these jobs paid less income. "Thus the Aristotelian Principle characterizes human beings as importantly moved not only by the pressure of bodily needs, but also by the desire to do things enjoyed simply for their own sakes, at least when the urgent and pressing wants are satisfied. The marks of such enjoyed activities are many, varying from the manner and the way in which they are done to the persistence with which they are returned to at a later time. Indeed, we do them without the incentive of evident reward, and allowing us to engage in them can itself act often as a reward for doing other things"; Rawls, *Theory of Justice*, pp. 431-432.

51. Nozick, *Anarchy, State and Utopia*, pp. 155-160.

52. Rawls, *Theory of Justice*, p. 74; see also pp. 277, 300, 511.

53. Nielsen, "On the Very Possibility," p. 201.

54. Macpherson, "Rawls' Models of Man and Society," p. 342.

55. Rawls, *Theory of Justice*, pp. 243-250, 213-216, 547-548.

56. Ibid., p. 248.

57. Ibid,. p. 246.

58. Ibid., p. 548.

59. Ibid., p. 547.

60. Ibid.; see note 55.

61. In one of his Marxist moments, R. P. Wolff asserts that it is utopian "in the sense that the theories of the early French socialists were utopian"; Wolff, *Understanding Rawls*, p. 204.

62. Schweickart, "Should Rawls Be a Socialist?" p. 23.

63. If the Marxist account of the history of capitalist development is true, it would be the case that capitalism *was* less unjust than alternatives. There *were* no viable alternatives. In our epoch, however, a socialist prospect exists, and if socialists have a generally correct account of capitalism and socialism, (1) the latter leaves the worst-off class better off than does capitalism, and (2) even if both systems leave the worst-off class in the same condition absolutely, socialism would be preferred because of lesser relative inequality among classes and because of capitalism's moral arbitrariness in distributing on the basis of luck. It is an additional empirical question whether socialism can outperform a propety-owning democracy in these respects.

64. In other words, what provides "incentives" for productive contribution in a well-ordered society are the principles of justice that govern distribution. These just incentives are not capitalist market incentives and so Macpherson is wrong in asserting, over and over again, that Rawls "makes the application of his difference principle hinge on capitalist market incentives"; C. B. Macpherson, "Class, Classlessness, and the Critique of Rawls: A Reply to Nielsen," *Political Theory* 6 (May 1978), p. 210.

65. Rawls, *Theory of Justice*, p. 274; emphasis added.

66. Ibid., p. 270.

67. Ibid., p. 273.

68. Ibid., p. 277.

69. Ibid., p. 283.

70. Barry, *Liberal Theory of Justice*, ch. 16; and especially Brian Barry, *Political Argument* (London: Routledge & Kegan Paul, 1965), chs. 7, 13.

71. See Ernest Mandel, *Marxist Economic Theory*, Vol. 2 (New York: Monthly Review Press, 1968), pp. 654ff.

72. August Heckscher, "Public Works and Public Happiness," *Saturday Review* 4 (August 1962); cited in Barry, *Political Argument*, p. 233.

73. See Richard Titmuss, *The Gift Relationship* (London: Allen & Unwin, 1970).

74. Rawls, "Fairness to Goodness," *Philosophical Review* 84 (October 1975), p. 551.

75. Richard Flathman, *The Practice of Rights* (London: Cambridge University Press, 1976), p. 184.

76. Ibid., p. 187.

77. Rawls, *Theory of Justice*, p. 264.

78. Besides Barry, *Liberal Theory of Justice*, see Milton Fisk, "History and Reason in Rawls' Moral Theory," in Norman Daniels, ed., *Reading Rawls: Critical Theories of A Theory of Justice* (New York: Basic Books, 1976), pp. 53-80. Consider one of Barry's examples: Suppose I value the ideal of racial integration. "By integration I refer to the belief that it is a desirable state of affairs for people who differ in certain respects to mix socially and to share the same clubs, churches, political parties, housing areas, shops, schools, theatres, swimming pools, etc." "Integration" is different from the value of "non-discrimination," which "refers to the belief that there is something degrading in treating differently people who differ in certain ways (e.g., the color of their skin.)" It is possible for the requirements of one value to conflict with those of the other. "For example, the only way of achieving racial integration in an area [where there are, e.g., already in existence

truly 'separate but equal' facilities] may be to have a quota system. Without such a guarantee 'tipping' is almost certain to take place. But a quota system involves treating people differently according to their race"; *Political Argument,* pp. 122-123. I take the upshot of Barry's distinction to be that justice, among other values, may conflict with integration, a value in its own right. Barry's point prompts one to wonder whether appeals to justice, when justifying preferential discrimination policies of the sort being, or supposed to be, implemented in the United States, can possibly work. Such policies may be basically unjust for reasons brought out, for example, by Alan Goldman, *Justice and Reverse Discrimination* (Princeton, NJ: Princeton University Press, 1979); the policies may be nonetheless justified morally by an appeal to the ideal of integration. It is doubtful, though, that in a society permeated with liberal values such an appeal would carry much persuasive force.

79. Karl Marx, *Critique of the Gotha Programme,* in Karl Marx and Friedrich Engels, *Selected Works,* 2 Vols. (Moscow: Foreign Languages Publishing House, 1955), Vol. 2, pp. 21-25.

80. See previous discussion in this article.

81. I have discussed at greater length some of the logical problems in Marx's attempt to explain the move from justice to communism, in "Alienation and Justice in the Market," *American Political Science Review* 72, 3 (September 1978), pp. 871-887; reprinted in John Burke et al., eds., *Marxism and the Good Society* (London: Cambridge University Press, 1981).

Arthur DiQuattro teaches politics at Reed College. He has published on topics in political philosophy, political economics, and philosophy of social science in journals such as American Political Science Review, Political Theory, Review of Radical Political Economics, Sociology and Social Research, *and* Social Theory and Practice *(forthcoming).*

Reason and Feeling in Thinking about Justice*

Susan Moller Okin

Recent feminist scholarship has challenged the corpus of Western political thought in two new ways. Some works focus first on either the absence or the assumed subordination of women in a political theory, and then go on to ask how the theory would have to change in order to include women on an equal basis with men. Some focus more immediately on how the gendered structure of the societies in which theorists have lived has shaped their central ideas and arguments and consider how these ideas and arguments are affected by the adoption of a feminist perspective.[1] In this paper, I hope to contribute something to the second project. I raise, though do not by any means fully answer, some questions about the effects that assumptions about the gendered structure of society have had on thinking about social justice. In so doing, I suggest that some recent distinctions that have been made between an ethic of justice and an ethic of care may be at least overdrawn, if not false. They may obfuscate rather than aid our attempts to achieve a moral and political theory that we can find acceptable in a world in which gender is becoming an increasingly indefensible mode of social organization.[2]

* This paper has benefited from the comments and criticisms of Sissela Bok, Joshua Cohen, George Pearson Cross, Amy Gutmann, Robert O. Keohane, Will Kymlicka, Robert L. Okin, John Rawls, Nancy Rosenblum, Cass R. Sunstein, Joan Tronto, and Iris Young. Nevertheless, I regret that I have not been able to respond adequately to all of their objections and suggestions.

1. Works falling primarily within the first category include Lorenne Clark and Lynda Lange, *The Sexism of Social and Political Thought* (Toronto: University of Toronto Press, 1979); Jean Bethke Elshtain, *Public Man, Private Woman: Women in Social and Political Thought* (Princeton, N.J.: Princeton University Press, 1981); and Susan Moller Okin, *Women in Western Political Thought* (Princeton, N.J.: Princeton University Press, 1979). Works within the second include Mary O'Brien, *The Politics of Reproduction* (London: Routledge & Kegan Paul, 1981); and Judith H. Stiehm, ed., *Women's Views of the Political World of Men* (Dobbs Ferry, N.Y.: Transnational Publishers, 1984). The essays in Carole Pateman and Elizabeth Gross, eds., *Feminist Challenges: Social and Political Theory* (Boston: Northeastern University Press, 1987) span both categories.

2. For example, see Carol Gilligan, *In a Different Voice* (Cambridge, Mass.: Harvard University Press, 1982); and Nel Noddings, *Caring: A Feminine Approach to Ethics and Moral Education* (Berkeley and Los Angeles: University of California Press, 1984). See Owen Flanagan and Kathryn Jackson, "Justice, Care and Gender: The Kohlberg-Gilligan Debate

Ethics 99 (January 1989): 229–249

I shall focus on two major philosophers—primarily Rawls, and Kant as a major influence on him—and consider how their assumptions about the division of labor between the sexes, with women taking care of the realm of human nurturance, have a fundamental effect upon their accounts of moral subjects and the development of moral thinking. This is exemplified in their tendencies to separate reason from feelings and to require that moral subjects be abstracted, in their deliberations, from the contextuality and contingencies of actual human life.

John Rawls's *A Theory of Justice* has been the inspiration, in one way or another, for much of contemporary moral and political theory.[3] I am not going to focus primarily here on what it says—or, as it happens, mostly does not say—about women and gender. I am going to focus on the effects of assumptions about gender on central aspects of the theory. I shall first outline Kant's and Rawls's contrasting accounts of how one learns to be a moral person. I shall then argue that, despite this important area of contrast, the strong influence of Kant leads to Rawls's expressing his major ideas primarily in the language of rational choice. This leaves them unnecessarily open to two criticisms: that they involve unacceptably egoistic assumptions about human nature and that they are of little relevance to actual people thinking about justice.[4] Whereas Rawls's theory is sometimes viewed as excessively rationalistic, individualistic, and abstracted from real human beings, I will argue that, at its center (though frequently obscured by Rawls himself) is a voice of responsibility, care, and concern for others. This paper is, in part, an attempt to develop a feminist approach to social justice, which centers on a reinterpretation of Rawls's central concept, the original position.

In another sense, however, the paper is a feminist *critique* of Rawls. For he, unlike Kant but in line with a long tradition of political and moral philosophers including Rousseau, Hegel, and Tocqueville, regards the

---

Revisited," *Ethics* 97 (1987): 622–37, for a valuable alternative approach to this issue, which focuses on recent moral development theory, especially the Kohlberg-Gilligan debate, and provides an excellent selective list of references to what has rapidly become a vast literature. See also Gertrud Nunner-Winkler, "Two Moralities? A Critical Discussion of an Ethic of Care and Responsibility versus an Ethic of Rights and Justice," in *Morality, Moral Behavior, and Moral Development*, ed. W. Kurtines and J. Gewirtz (New York: Wiley, 1984), pp. 348–61; Joan Tronto, " 'Women's Morality': Beyond Gender Difference to a Theory of Care," *Signs: Journal of Women in Culture and Society* 12 (1987): 644–63; and Lawrence Blum, "Gilligan and Kohlberg: Implications for Moral Theory," *Ethics* 98 (1988): 472–91.

3. John Rawls, *A Theory of Justice* (Cambridge, Mass.: Harvard University Press, 1971). Subsequent references to this book (*TOJ*) will be given parenthetically in the text.

4. Thomas Nagel, "Rawls on Justice," in *Reading Rawls*, ed. Norman Daniels (New York: Basic, 1974), pp. 1–16 (reprinted from *Philosophical Review*, vol. 72 [1973]), makes the former argument; Michael J. Sandel, *Liberalism and the Limits of Justice* (Cambridge: Cambridge University Press, 1982) makes both arguments; the latter argument is made by both Alasdair MacIntyre, *After Virtue* (Notre Dame, Ind.: Notre Dame University Press, 1981); and Michael Walzer, *Spheres of Justice* (New York: Basic, 1983), and *Interpretation and Social Criticism* (Cambridge, Mass.: Harvard University Press, 1987).

family as a school of morality, a primary socializer of just citizens. At the same time, along with others in the tradition, he neglects the issue of the justice or injustice of the gendered family itself. The result is a central tension within the theory, which can be resolved only by opening up the question of justice within the family.

THE KANTIAN HERITAGE

Why did Rawls cast his theory, or much of it, in the language of rational choice? Why did he present it this way rather than as a theory that requires empathy even on the part of those artificial moral agents who inhabit the original position, and that requires not only empathy but far-reaching benevolence on the part of ordinary human beings who are prepared to abide by the principles of justice? Only the Kantian heritage can explain these things. The way Rawls presents his theory of justice reflects both Kant's stress on autonomy and rationality as the defining characteristics of moral subjects and his rigid separation of reason from feeling and refusal to allow feeling any place in the formulation of moral principles. Rawls says of Kant, "He begins with the idea that moral principles are the object of rational choice. . . . Moral philosophy becomes the study of the conception and outcome of a suitably defined rational decision" (*TOJ*, p. 251).[5] He frequently and explicitly acknowledges the connections between his theory and Kant's. The concept of the veil of ignorance, he says, is implicit in Kant's works, and the concept of the original position is an attempt to interpret Kant's conception of moral principles as formulated under "conditions that characterize men as free and equal rational beings" (*TOJ*, p. 252).

The Kantian connection, I suggest, made it extremely difficult for Rawls to acknowledge any role for empathy or benevolence in the formulation of his principles of justice and, instead, impelled him in the direction of rational choice. Kant is abundantly clear that feelings are to have no place in the foundations of morality. "No moral principle is based," he says, "as people sometimes suppose, on any *feeling* whatsoever. . . . For feeling, no matter by what it is aroused, always belongs to the order of *nature*."[6] He does not say so here, but he clearly means "nature, as contrasted with freedom." Kant so rejects the idea that feelings have anything to do with moral motivation that he considers that an act that is in accordance with duty, but is performed out of love or sympathetic inclination, has "no genuinely moral worth." It is only when such actions are performed from duty—because the moral law requires them—that they have moral content.[7]

5. See also John Rawls, "Kantian Constructivism in Moral Theory," *Journal of Philosophy* 77 (1980): 515–72.

6. Immanuel Kant, *The Doctrine of Virtue, pt. 2: Metaphysic of Morals*, trans. Mary J. Gregor (New York: Harper & Row, 1964), p. 33.

7. Immanuel Kant, *Groundwork of the Metaphysic of Morals*, trans. H. Paton (1948; reprint, New York: Harper & Row, 1964), pp. 66–67.

Kant is able to conclude that feeling and love have no part in the foundations of morality only because he neglects a very important type of human love. In *The Doctrine of Virtue*, he classifies love into two types. One he calls "practical love" or benevolence; this, he says, sometimes *results* from the performance of the duty to help others. Kant discusses the saying "you *ought* to *love* your neighbour as yourself." He says it "does not mean: you should immediately (first) love him and (afterwards) through the medium of this love do good to him. It means, rather: *do good* to your fellow-man, and this will give rise to love of man in you."[8] Such moral feelings, far from leading to principles of morality, can only follow from principles established independently of them. Kant does not, however, regard them as morally insignificant, since the moral feeling that follows from the thought of the law can be a significant factor in making us conscious of our obligations.[9] The other type of feeling Kant recognizes is called "pathological feeling" or attraction. "Pathological," as used here, does not mean that there is anything *wrong* with it, as it would signify in modern usage, but simply that it is "affective." As contrasted with moral feeling, which "can only follow from the thought of the law," pathological feeling "precedes the thought of the law." Being contingent and subject to change, belonging to the order of nature rather than to the order of autonomy or reason, however, this type of feeling can play no part in the formulation of the moral law.

Kant's brief account of moral education, as presented near the end of *The Doctrine of Virtue*, reflects this account of the relation (or, rather, comparative lack of it) between feelings and moral thinking. The moral catechism Kant presents in the form of a dialogue between teacher and pupil is, as he says, "developed from ordinary human reason." The teacher questions the pupil, and then "the answer which he methodically draws from the pupil's reason must be written down and preserved in precise terms which cannot easily be altered, and so be committed to the pupil's *memory*." These memorized pieces of reasoning are then supplemented by "*good example*" on the teacher's part, as well as his pointing out the "*cautionary* example" of others.[10] Subsequent to formulating principles on the basis of reason, the pupil becomes conditioned, by imitation, into virtuous inclination and action.

This arid presentation of moral education is closely related to Kant's incomplete account of the varieties of human love, which in turn is made possible by the fact that women play only a peripheral role in his philosophy. His reduction of love to two types, the moral feeling of benevolence that follows from the recognition of duty, and the affective love that he calls "mere inclination," leaves out at least one very important kind of love. This is the love that is typified by parent/child relations, under favorable

8. Kant, *The Doctrine of Virtue*, pp. 62–63.
9. Ibid., p. 59.
10. Ibid., pp. 151–52; emphasis in the original.

circumstances at any rate. It is usually made up of elements of affective love and of benevolence, but it also involves far more. The benevolence in it does not spring from the recognition of duty, and the affection in it is usually far from being "mere inclination," with the fickleness suggested by those terms. It is a kind of love that develops over time and that has its origins in attachment so close that, for the young infant, it constitutes complete psychological identification. It is fed by attachment, continued intimacy, and interdependence. On the other hand, it is a kind of love that has disastrous consequences if there is no willingness on the part of the parent to recognize and to appreciate differences between the child and her- or himself. This kind of love is fundamental to human life and relationship since it is the first kind of love we experience (if our circumstances are fortunate) regardless of our sex, and it has, of course, constituted throughout history a much larger part of women's than of men's experience.

Kant seems to have been unable to perceive either the moral relevance or the moral potential of this kind of love. This is probably due to the fact that, accepting without question the gendered division of labor that prevailed around him, he defined a moral world that excluded women. That may seem too extreme a statement. Let me point out, however, that while in most of his central works of moral philosophy Kant defines the moral subjects of whom he speaks as not only human beings but also "all rational beings as such," in less noticed works from the earliest to the last, he makes it clear that women are not sufficiently rational and autonomous to be moral subjects. In an early essay, entitled *Observations on the Feeling of the Beautiful and Sublime,* he says of women that their "philosophy is not to reason, but to sense."[11] Their virtue, unlike men's, is to be inspired by the desire to please; for them, he asserts, there is to be "nothing of duty, nothing of compulsion, nothing of obligation!"[12] In one of his very last works, the *Anthropology from a Pragmatic Point of View,* although, most uncharacteristically, he says that male and female are both rational beings, he takes back any thought of moral autonomy in the case of a married woman, by pointing out that she is necessarily subject to her husband and a legal minor. "To make oneself behave like a minor," he says, "degrading as it may be, is, nevertheless, very comfortable."[13] It is not difficult to tell, from such remarks, where women stand (perhaps it is more appropriate to say "where women *sit*") on Kant's moral scale.

11. Immanuel Kant, *Observations on the Feeling of the Beautiful and Sublime,* trans. John T. Goldthwait (Berkeley: University of California Press, 1960), p. 79. Kant's word is *empfinden.* It is sometimes, with equal appropriateness, translated as "to feel." I am grateful to Suzanne Altenberger for advice on this matter.

12. Ibid., sec. 3, p. 81.

13. Immanuel Kant, *Anthropology from a Pragmatic Point of View,* trans. Victor Lyle Dowdell (Carbondale: Southern Illinois University Press, 1978), pp. 216, 105.

Thus the moral division of labor between the sexes is very clear in Kant's writings. The virtues he assigns to women, as appropriate for their role in the gendered social structure, and particularly within the family, are virtues ranked far lower than the virtues assigned to men. As Lawrence Blum says about the moral rationalist, in a discussion of Kant and Hegel: "It is the male qualities whose highest expression he naturally takes as his model. In the same way it is natural for him to ignore or underplay the female qualities as they are found in his society—sympathy, compassion, emotional responsiveness. He fails to give these qualities adequate expression within his moral philosophy. The moral rationalist philosopher thus both reflects the sexual value hierarchy of his society and indirectly gives it a philosophic grounding and legitimation."[14]

Thus, Kant neglected the moral significance of an extremely important kind of human love, and of the moral qualities that can arise from it, because of his devaluing of women and exclusion of them from the realm of moral subjects. While endorsing what Blum says above, Jean Grimshaw has recently argued, in her excellent book *Philosophy and Feminist Thinking*, that, although Kant implicitly excludes women from his philosophical ideals, he "could, without inconsistency, have retained his view about 'moral worth', but changed his view of women."[15] I do not think he could, for though women are so peripheral as to be virtually absent from his moral world, the role they are assumed to play behind the scenes would appear to be necessary for its continuance. Women as Kant perceived them, inspired by feeling and by the desire to please, provide both the essential nurturance required for human development, and a realm of existence without which the moral order he prescribes for the world outside the family seems intolerable in its demands.[16] Kant's exclusion of women is of significance not only for women; it has a distorting effect on his moral philosophy as a whole.

To the extent that it derives from Kant in some of its basic assumptions about what it means to be a moral subject, Rawls's theory of justice suffers to some extent from this same distortion. As I will argue, Rawls is unwilling to call explicitly on the human qualities of empathy and benevolence in the working out of his principles of justice and in his lengthy description of the process of deliberation that leads to them. However, his original

---

14. Lawrence Blum, "Kant's and Hegel's Moral Rationalism: A Feminist Perspective," *Canadian Journal of Philosophy* 12 (1982): 296–97.

15. Jean Grimshaw, *Philosophy and Feminist Thinking* (Minneapolis: University of Minnesota Press, 1986), p. 49.

16. A possible response to this might be to suggest that a twentieth-century Kantian, not regarding the remaining social subordination of women as natural, would view both men and women as equally moral subjects with the same moral worth. But unless the conceptions of a moral subject and moral worth were to be relevantly adapted, this would result in family life's being governed by principles as strictly rationalist as the moral world outside rather than as providing a haven from this world, as Kant seems to have envisaged.

position consists of a combination of assumptions—mutual disinterest and the veil of ignorance—that, as he says, "achieves the same purpose as benevolence" (*TOJ*, p. 148). Before going on to discuss this, however, let us look at Rawls's account of how people develop a sense of justice. For despite his Kantian assumptions about rationality and autonomy, and the related rational choice language of much of his theory, Rawls's account of moral development is very different from Kant's and indicates clearly that rationality is not a sufficient basis on which to found or sustain his theory of justice.

RAWLS AND THE SENSE OF JUSTICE: THE SIGNIFICANCE OF GENDER

There is little indication, throughout most of *A Theory of Justice*, that the modern liberal society to which the principles of justice are to be applied is deeply and pervasively gender structured. As I shall argue, this neglect of gender has major implications for the practical feasibility of Rawls's principles of justice. In particular, there is very little mention of the family, the linchpin of the gender structure. Although Rawls, for good reason, mentions the "monogamous family" in his initial list of major institutions that constitute the "basic structure" to which the principles of justice are to apply, he never applies the two principles of justice to it. In fact, his assumption that those in the original position are "heads of families" prevents him from doing this (*TOJ*, p. 128). A central tenet of the theory, after all, is that justice characterizes institutions whose members could hypothetically have agreed to their structure and rules from a position in which they did not know which place in the structure they were to occupy. But since those in the original position are all heads of families, they are not in a position to settle questions of justice *within* families. In fact, if we discard the "heads of families" assumption, take seriously the notion that those in the original position are ignorant of their sex as well as their other individual characteristics, and apply the principles of justice to the gender structure and the family arrangements of our society, considerable changes are clearly called for.[17]

Instead, apart from being briefly mentioned as the link between generations necessary for Rawls's "savings principle," and as an obstacle to fair equality of opportunity, the family appears in Rawls's theory in only one context (albeit one of considerable importance): as the earliest school of moral development. Rawls argues, in a much neglected section of part 3 of *A Theory of Justice*, that a just, well-ordered society will be stable only if its members continue to develop a sense of justice—"a strong and normally effective desire to act as the principles of justice require" (*TOJ*, p. 454). He specifically turns his attention to the question

17. Susan Moller Okin, "Justice and Gender," *Philosophy and Public Affairs* 16 (1987): 42–72.

of childhood moral development, aiming to indicate the major steps by which a sense of justice is acquired.

In this context, Rawls *assumes* that families are just, though he has provided no reasons for us to accept this assumption (*TOJ*, p. 490). Moreover, these supposedly just families play a fundamental role in moral development. The love of parents for their children, coming to be reciprocated in turn by the child, is important in his account of the development of a sense of self-worth. By loving the child and being "worthy objects of his admiration, . . . they arouse in him a sense of his own value and the desire to become the sort of person that they are" (*TOJ*, p. 465). Healthy moral development in early life, Rawls argues, depends upon love, trust, affection, example, and guidance (*TOJ*, p. 466).

Later in moral development, at the stage he calls "the morality of association," Rawls perceives the family, which he describes in gendered terms, as a "small association, normally characterized by a definite hierarchy, in which each member has certain rights and duties" (*TOJ*, p. 467). It is the first of many associations in which, by moving through a sequence of roles and positions, our moral understanding increases. The crucial aspect of the sense of fairness that is learned during this stage is the capacity to take up the different points of view of others and to see things from their perspectives. We learn to perceive, from what they say and do, what other people's ends, plans, and motives are. Without this experience, Rawls says, "we cannot put ourselves into another's place and find out what we would do in his position," which we need to be able to do in order "to regulate our own conduct in the appropriate way by reference to it" (*TOJ*, p. 469). Participation in different roles in the various associations of society leads to the development of a person's "capacity for fellow feeling" and to "ties of friendship and mutual trust" (*TOJ*, p. 470). Rawls says that, just as in the first stage certain natural attitudes develop toward the parents, "so here ties of friendship and confidence grow up among associates. In each case certain natural attitudes underlie the corresponding moral feelings: a lack of these feelings would manifest the absence of these attitudes" (*TOJ*, p. 471).

This whole account of moral development is strikingly unlike that of Kant, for whom any feelings that did not follow from independently established moral principles were morally suspect. Unlike Kant, with his arid, intellectualized account of moral learning, Rawls clearly acknowledges the importance of feelings in the development of the capacity for moral thinking. In accounting for his third and final stage of moral development, where persons are supposed to become attached to the principles of justice themselves, Rawls says that "the sense of justice is continuous with the love of mankind" (*TOJ*, p. 476). At the same time, he allows for the fact that we have particularly strong feelings about those to whom we are closely attached and says that this is rightly reflected in our moral judgments: even though "our moral sentiments display an independence from the accidental circumstances of our world, . . . our natural attachments to particular persons and groups still have an appropriate place" (*TOJ*, p. 475). His differences from Kant's views are clear from his indications that empathy, or imagining oneself into the place of others, plays a major role in moral development. It is not surprising that he turns away from Kant, to moral philosophers such as Adam Smith, Elizabeth Anscombe, Philippa Foot, and Bernard Williams, in developing his ideas about the moral emotions or sentiments (*TOJ*, pp. 479 ff.).

In Rawls's summary of his three psychological laws of moral development (*TOJ*, pp. 490–91), the fundamental importance of loving parenting for the development of a sense of justice is manifest. The three laws, Rawls says, are "not merely principles of association or of reinforcement . . . [but] assert that the active sentiments of love and friendship, and even the sense of justice, arise from the manifest intention of other persons to act for our good. Because we recognize that they wish us well, we care for their well-being in return" (*TOJ*, p. 494). Each of the laws of moral development, as set out by Rawls, depends upon the one before it, and the first assumption of the first law is: "given that family institutions are just. . . ." Unlike Kant, with his nameless, but no doubt male, tutor, Rawls frankly admits that the whole of moral development rests upon the loving ministrations of those who raise small children from the earliest stages, and on the moral character of the environment in which this takes place. At the foundation of the development of the sense of justice, then, are an activity and a sphere of life that—though by no means necessarily so—have throughout history been predominantly the activity and the sphere of women.

Rawls does not explain the basis of his assumption that family institutions are just. If gendered family institutions are *not* just but are, rather, a relic of caste or feudal societies in which roles, responsibilities, and resources are distributed, not in accordance with the two principles of justice but in accordance with innate differences that are imbued with enormous social significance, then Rawls's whole structure of moral development seems to be built on uncertain ground. Unless the households in which children are first nurtured, and see their first examples of human interaction, are based on equality and reciprocity rather than on dependence and domination, as is too often in fact the case, how can whatever love they receive from their parents make up for the injustice they see before their eyes in the relationship between these same parents? Unless they are parented equally by adults of both sexes, how will children of both sexes come to develop a sufficiently similar and well-rounded moral psychology as to enable them to engage in the kind of deliberation about justice that is exemplified in the original position? And finally, unless the household is connected by a continuum of associations to the larger communities within which people are supposed to develop fellow feelings for each other, how will they grow up with the capacity for enlarged sympathies such as are clearly required for the practice of justice?

On the one hand, Rawls's neglect of justice within the family is clearly in tension with his own theory of moral development, which *requires* that families be just. On the other hand, his conviction that the development of a sense of justice depends on attachments to and feelings for other persons, originating in the family, is in tension with the "rational choice" language that he frequently employs in laying out his theory of justice. I shall now look at this prevailing mode of interpreting Rawls and then go on to suggest an alternative account of the original position, which is both consistent with much that he says about it and much more compatible with his own account of moral development. It is this alternative account of what goes on in the original position that leads me to suggest that one is not forced to choose between an ethic of justice and an ethic of sympathy or care, nor between an ethic that emphasizes universality and one that takes account of differences.

THE ORIGINAL POSITION

The original position is at the heart of Rawls's theory of justice. It is both his most important contribution to moral and political theory and the focus of most of the controversy and disputes that the theory still attracts more than fifteen years after its publication. How the original position is understood and interpreted is extremely important for both the internal coherence and the persuasiveness of the theory. First I shall lay out briefly the set of conditions that Rawls calls the original position. Then I shall look at the way that Rawls presents it, at least some of the time, a presentation that I think has led to some of the criticisms that have been made of it. Then I will explain my alternative reading, which I think is faithful to Rawls's essential meaning. This alternative reading suggests that Rawls is far from being a moral rationalist and that feelings such as empathy and benevolence are at the very foundation of his principles of justice. The alternative reading, I suggest, leaves the original position, and indeed the whole theory, less susceptible to criticism.

In sum, Rawls's specifications for the original position are as follows: the parties are rational and mutually disinterested, and while no limits are placed on the *general* information available to them, they deliberate behind a "veil of ignorance" that conceals from them all knowledge of their individual characteristics: "No one knows his place in society, his class position or social status, nor does anyone know his fortune in the distribution of natural assets and abilities, his intelligence, strength, and the like. [Nor do the parties know] their conceptions of the good or their special psychological propensities" (*TOJ*, p. 12). The critical force of the original position can be appreciated from the fact that some interesting critiques of Rawls's theory have resulted from others' interpreting the original position more radically or broadly than its creator did. Beitz has argued, for example, that there is no justification for not extending its application to the population of the entire planet, which would lead to challenging virtually everything that is currently assumed in the dominant "statist" conception of international relations.[18] Some of us, feminist critics, have suggested that if we do away with the "heads of families" assumption, and take seriously the fact that those behind the veil of ignorance cannot know their *sex,* we must engage in a radical questioning of the gender structure, which Rawls himself leaves virtually unmentioned.[19]

In *A Theory of Justice* itself, Rawls foresees that problems will arise if readers focus separately on each of the assumptions made about parties in the original position, rather than taking the device as a whole. He warns that the theory may be interpreted as based on egoism if the mutual disinterest assumption is taken in isolation from the other specifications: "the feeling that this conception of justice is egoistic is an illusion fostered by looking at but one of the elements of the original position" (*TOJ,* p. 148).[20] He also addresses in advance those who are likely to ask, having taken note of what would be decided in the original position, what relevance it may have for actual human beings who know who they are and what their social position is. He responds like this:

> The conditions embodied in the description of this situation are ones that we do in fact accept. Or if we do not, then we can be persuaded to do so by philosophical considerations of the sort occasionally introduced. Each aspect of the original position can be given a supporting explanation. Thus what we are doing is to combine into one conception the totality of conditions that we are ready upon due reflection to recognize as reasonable in our conduct with respect to one another. Once we grasp this conception, we can at any time look at the social world from the required point of view. [*TOJ,* p. 587][21]

On the other hand, in a recent response to critics, Rawls says something that does not seem easy to reconcile with this conception of the original position as an explicitly moral point of view that we can adopt in real life by thinking in the appropriate way. He first reiterates the ideas expressed in the passage I just quoted, by saying that we can enter the original position at any time, simply by reasoning for principles of justice as we would if constrained by its restrictions (on our knowledge, motivations, and so on). But then he adds to this the following: "When, in this way, we simulate being in this position, our reasoning no more commits us to a metaphysical doctrine about the nature of the self than our playing a game like Monopoly commits us to thinking that we are landlords

---

18. Charles Beitz, *Political Theory and International Relations* (Princeton, N.J.: Princeton University Press, 1979).

19. See Jane English, "Justice between Generations," *Philosophical Studies* 31 (1977): 91–104; Deborah Kearns, "A Theory of Justice—and Love: Rawls on the Family," *Politics* 18 (1983): 36–42; and Okin, "Justice and Gender."

20. See also Rawls, "Kantian Constructivism," p. 527.

21. See also ibid., p. 518.

engaged in a desperate rivalry, winner take all."[22] This juxtaposition of the original position as a moral point of view, a way of reasoning about principles of justice, with the original position as analogous to a game, without moral significance, identifies a tension in the way the original position is presented throughout Rawls's works. In order to see what leads to such criticisms as I have mentioned above, and to consider how they can be fully answered, it is important to look at each side of this tension, in turn.

First, I shall look at how central aspects of the Kantian heritage—especially the presentation of moral subjects as, above all, rational, autonomous, and freed from contingency—influence Rawls in the direction of perceiving what he is doing as a branch of rational choice theory. Given this interpretation, the Monopoly analogy is perfectly appropriate. Then I shall sketch out an alternative reading of the theory, and of the original position in particular, which explains better what it is that makes it into an appropriate "moral point of view" that we can be persuaded to accept. I shall pay particular attention to the question, What do we have to be like, in order to be prepared to take up this point of view and to formulate our principles of justice in accordance with its demands? This is the crucial issue on which I think some parts of Rawls's theory are misleading, due to his identification with Kantian ways of thinking about the foundations of principles of justice and right.

THE "RATIONAL CHOICE" INTERPRETATION AND ITS IMPLICATIONS

Rawls states early on and repeats a number of times throughout his construction of the theory of justice that it is "a part, perhaps the most important part, of the theory of rational choice" (*TOJ*, p. 16). Recently, he has said that this was a "very misleading" error and that "there is no thought of trying to derive the content of justice within a framework that uses an idea of the rational as the sole normative idea."[23] Once we look at the implications of the rational choice reading of the theory, I

22. John Rawls, "Justice as Fairness: Political, not Metaphysical," *Philosophy and Public Affairs* 14 (1985): 239.

23. Rawls, "Justice as Fairness," p. 237, n. 20. Rawls's movement in this direction is already clearly apparent in the first of the Dewey lectures (Rawls, "Kantian Constructivism"), where he pays much attention to the distinction between the rational and the reasonable. Here, the rational still denotes the advantage of the individual, as in rational choice theory, but the reasonable is defined by moral conceptions such as reciprocity and mutuality. Principles are reasonable only if they are publicly acceptable by moral persons as fair terms of cooperation among them. Rawls seems to draw a clear distinction between thinking about justice and thinking about rational choice when he says: "Familiar principles of justice are examples of reasonable principles, and familiar principles of rational choice are examples of rational principles. The way the Reasonable is presented in the original position leads to the two principles of justice" (p. 530). He also states clearly that, in his theory, "the Reasonable presupposes and subordinates the Rational" (p. 530). See especially pp. 517–22 and pp. 528–30.

suggest that we will be able to see why Rawls has reconsidered it. Purging the theory of the rational choice connection and its implications strengthens it and renders it far less vulnerable to some of its critics.[24]

Let us first look at how Rawls conceives of his theory as a branch of rational choice theory. First, he associates the rationality and mutual disinterest of the parties with rational choice theory (*TOJ*, pp. 13–14). The actors in such a theory are assumed to be egoists, and while Rawls specifies that his parties are not to be understood as egoists in the colloquial sense of being interested only in such things as wealth, prestige, and domination, they *are* to be conceived of as "not taking an interest in one another's interests" (*TOJ*, p. 13). The rationality of the parties is also specified as that standard in economic or other rational choice theory— as instrumental rationality, or "taking the most effective means to given ends" (*TOJ*, p. 14). Rawls explains a number of times that these assumptions are made about the parties in the original position in order that the theory not depend on strong assumptions. He says, for example, that "the original position is meant to incorporate widely shared and yet weak conditions. A conception of justice should not presuppose . . . extensive ties of natural sentiment. At the basis of the theory, one tries to assume as little as possible" (*TOJ*, p. 129; see also pp. 18 and 583). At this point, however, one needs to take heed of Rawls's own warning not to focus on the individual assumptions made about the parties in the original position but to look at the concept as a whole. Rawls claims that each of the assumptions "should by itself be natural and plausible; some of them may seem innocuous or even trivial" (*TOJ*, p. 18). The question is, however, how weak do the assumptions look when considered *together*? And is it possible, considering them together, still to conceive of the theory as an example of rational choice theory?

In rational choice theory, choice under certainty requires the individual to have both vast quantities of relevant knowledge about the environment and a well-organized and stable system of preferences.[25] It is on the basis of these, but especially the knowledge of his or her "independent utility

24. See n. 4 above. In addition, a number of rational choice theorists have criticized Rawls's conclusions as much too egalitarian to have emerged from a situation of rational choice (see, e.g., David Gauthier, *Morals by Agreement* [Oxford: Clarendon Press, 1986], pp. 245–67).

25. Conventional rational choice theory distinguishes three modes of deliberation and choice, correlated with three different sets of assumptions about what is known by the actors. Choice under certainty depends on the actors knowing with certainty the outcome of each choice and the utility of that outcome. Choice under risk occurs when all the possible outcomes and their utility are known, as well as the probabilities of their occurrence. Choice under uncertainty occurs when knowledge of the probabilities is absent or incomplete. These nomenclatures are not always strictly adhered to. Rather confusingly, the actor's preparedness to take risks is a more important factor in the case of the third set of assumptions (see John C. Harsanyi, *Rational Behavior and Bargaining Equilibrium in Games and Social Situations* [Cambridge: Cambridge University Press, 1977], chap. 3). I am grateful to Richard Arneson for helping me to correct some confusions in this part of the paper.

function" that individuals are presumed able to choose, from the alternatives open, the option that will permit each to reach the highest attainable point on his or her preference scale. In conditions where this knowledge about individual preferences is presumed not available, reasoning in accordance with abstract probabilities comes into play. We must compare the specifications of Rawls's original position with these assumptions.

In Rawls's account of the original position, mutual disinterest and instrumental rationality feature only in conjunction with the veil of ignorance. On the one hand, the parties try to maximize what rational choice theory calls their "utility functions." They realize that, as individuals *having* distinct ends and interests (even though these are not revealed to them) they all have an equal stake in promoting and protecting what Rawls calls the "primary goods"—those basic liberties and goods that are prerequisite for the pursuit of distinct ends and interests. In this respect, then, as Rawls acknowledges, there might as well be just one person behind the veil of ignorance since the deliberations of all are identical. On the other hand, the parties do not have any knowledge of their separate, distinct, individual interests. Rawls says of them that "in choosing between principles each tries as best he can to advance *his interests*," and that he will rank the options "according to how well they further *his purposes*," and so on (*TOJ*, pp. 142, 143; emphasis added). But what sense does it make to talk of mutually disinterested individuals pursuing their interests when, to the extent that their interests are distinct and differentiated, they have no knowledge of them? Clearly, choice under certainty, which requires both the knowledge of outcomes and of the utility of these outcomes, is ruled out. The branches of rational choice theory that remain potentially applicable are choice under risk and choice under uncertainty.

Choice under risk, however, involves taking into account the probability of the occurrence of different outcomes. Rawls does not allow this to happen, by specifying that the veil of ignorance "excludes all but the vaguest knowledge of likelihoods. The parties have no basis for determining the probable nature of their society, or their place in it" (*TOJ*, p. 155). As he points out, this stipulation means that the parties "have strong reasons for being wary of probability calculations if any other course is open to them" (*TOJ*, p. 155). Thus choice under risk is ruled out. Rawls says, indeed, that "the veil of ignorance leads directly to the problem of choice under uncertainty" (*TOJ*, p. 172). There is, however, no generally accepted theory of rational choice under uncertainty, and we must still ask: How *do* the parties deliberate, in coming to their conclusions?

Rawls further reduces the applicability of rational choice theory by specifying that the parties are to have no knowledge of their aversion from or propensity for taking risks. By prohibiting the parties from having any knowledge of *either* the probabilities themselves *or* their own attitudes toward taking chances, Rawls decisively rules out the modes of deliberation that rational choice theory typically turns to under such conditions as otherwise defined. When he specifies the situation as one of choice under uncertainty, he suggests another possible mode of reasoning: "Of course, it is possible to regard the parties as perfect altruists and to assume that they reason as if they are certain to be in the position of each person. This interpretation of the initial situation removes the element of risk and uncertainty" (*TOJ*, p. 172). Rawls does not consider himself to be taking this route, believing as he does that it leads to classic utilitarianism rather than to the two principles of justice.[26] But, as I shall argue, because he reduces the knowledge of those in the original position to the point where they cannot employ probabilistic reasoning and cannot be assumed to take risks, Rawls *does* have to rely on empathy, benevolence, and equal concern for others as for the self, in order to have the parties come up with the principles they choose, especially the difference principle. This takes him far from anything in rational choice theory.

Rawls compares the assumptions he makes about those in the original position with other assumptions that include benevolence. He considers whether his own theory requires that the parties be moved by benevolence or by an interest in one another's interests. And he states clearly that "the combination of mutual disinterest and the veil of ignorance *achieves the same purpose as benevolence. For this combination of conditions forces each person in the original position to take the good of others into account*" (*TOJ*, p. 148; emphasis added). It is important to pause and think about this statement. For what it means is that it is only because those in the original

26. In sec. 30 of *A Theory of Justice* Rawls discusses the ethical position that would be adopted by a perfect altruist (a person "whose desires conform to the approvals of . . . a rational and impartial sympathetic spectator"). Imagining himself in the place of each person in turn, the perfect altruist is supposed to arrive at classical utilitarian conclusions since "sympathetically imagined pains cancel out sympathetically imagined pleasures, and the final intensity of approval corresponds to the net sum of positive feeling" (p. 187). It is not clear to me why the imagining of the altruist should involve the conflation of all persons into one that results in adoption of the classical principle of utility. I agree with Nagel (Thomas Nagel, *The Possibility of Altruism* [Princeton, N.J.: Princeton University Press, 1978], p. 138), who concludes that "this situation is unimaginable, and in so far as it is not, it completely distorts the nature of the competing claims." Rawls then imagines the benevolent person in another way—as one who "is to imagine that he is to divide into a plurality of persons whose life and experience will be distinct in the usual way . . . [with] no conflation of desires and memories into those of one person." Under *these* conditions, Rawls thinks that "the two principles of justice . . . seem a relatively more plausible choice than the classical principle of utility" (p. 191). It seems completely reasonable that a benevolent spectator who imagined experiencing the distinct lives of all those concerned separately (the only way that makes any sense to me) would be more likely to adopt the two principles than the classical principle of utility. It is implausible to expect that the pains experienced in one life would be balanced off by the pleasures experienced in another—even if lived by the same person (see Nagel, *The Possibility of Altruism*, pp. 140–42). Rawls argues that a party in the original position, who knows that he will live *one* of the lives, but does not know *which* one, will be even less likely to favor aggregative solutions, or to trade off the pains of some against the pleasures of others. But he resists the idea that such a party needs benevolence since he considers that the veil of ignorance and mutual disinterestedness serve as its functional equivalents.

position are assumed to be behind the veil of ignorance that they can be presented as the "rational, mutually disinterested" agents characteristic of rational choice theory. They can be perceived as thinking only for themselves, *only* because they do not know *which self* they will turn out to be and, therefore, must consider the interests of all possible selves equally.

Having stated that his assumptions achieve the same purpose as that of benevolence, Rawls goes on to argue that his assumption of mutual disinterest and the veil of ignorance has enormous advantages over the assumption of benevolence plus knowledge since the "latter is so complex that no definite theory at all can be worked out." Too much information is required, and unanswered questions remain about the "relative strength of benevolent desires." His assumptions, by contrast, he says, have the "merits of simplicity and clarity," as well as the advantage of being "weak stipulations" (*TOJ*, pp. 148–49). The illusion that the stipulations are weak is not hard to dispel; it is only if they are considered in isolation from each other (just what Rawls warns us against) that they can be seen as weak. In fact, the veil of ignorance is *such* a demanding stipulation that it converts what would, without it, be self-interest into benevolence or the equal concern for others. As for the advantage of simplicity and clarity, when we look at the original position in the only way in which it is intelligible (which is far distant from any rational choice theory), we find that it cannot escape most of the complexities of benevolence plus knowledge. To be sure, the issue of "the relative strength of benevolent desires" is not a problem for those behind the veil of ignorance: since one does not know which person one will turn out to be, one's rational self-interest presumably directs one to being equally concerned for each. But in order to think reasonably in the original position, one must presumably have knowledge of the essential aspects of the lives of persons of all different imaginable types and in all different imaginable social positions. In the absence of knowledge about their own particular characteristics, those in the original position cannot think from the position of *nobody* (as Rawls's desire for simplicity might suggest); they must think from the position of *everybody*, in the sense of *each in turn*. This is far from a simple demand.[27]

In fact, when we consider the reasoning engaged in by the parties in the original position, we can see that this *is* what they do. For example,

27. In a later discussion, Rawls again suggests significant differences between the reasoning of the parties and the self-interest characteristic of conventional rational choice theory. He says: "In the original position we may describe the parties either as the representatives (or trustees) of persons with certain interests or as themselves moved by these interests. It makes no difference either way, although the latter is simpler and I shall usually speak in this vein" (Rawls, "Kantian Constructivism," pp. 524–25). As I have suggested, the latter description is not simpler. For in a situation in which the identity and particular characteristics of the self are unknown there is no difference between self-interest and the representation of the interests of others. Whichever description Rawls chooses, the complexities are the same, and neither can be equated with the situation in rational choice theory.

in formulating the principle that protects equal liberty of conscience, Rawls makes it clear that the parties, who of course do not know what their moral or religious convictions are, "must choose principles that secure the integrity of their religious and moral freedom" (*TOJ*, p. 206). But in the absence of knowledge about the self, including the absence of probabilities, the only way to do this is to imagine oneself in the position of those whose religious practices and beliefs or lack thereof will require most tolerance on the part of others—the religiously "least advantaged," one might call them. It is not easy for an essentially nonreligious person, trying to imagine her- or himself into the original position, to adopt the standpoint of a fundamentalist believer; nor is it easy for a devoutly religious person to imagine the situation of a nonbeliever in a highly religious society. To do either requires, at the very least, both strong empathy and a preparedness to listen carefully to the very different points of view of others.

This method of thinking in the original position is most obviously required in the formulation of the difference principle. There, the maximin rule "directs our attention to the worst that can happen under any proposed course of action, and to decide in the light of that" (*TOJ*, p. 154). In considering permissible inequalities, "one looks at the system from the standpoint of the least advantaged representative man" (*TOJ*, p. 151). And, of course, once we challenge Rawls's traditional belief that questions about justice can be resolved by "heads of families," the "least advantaged representative woman," who is likely to be considerably *worse* off, has to be considered equally. Especially for those accustomed by class position, race, and sex to privilege, wealth, and power, a real appreciation of the point of view of the worst-off is likely to require considerable empathy and capacity to listen to others.[28]

On this interpretation, the original position is *not* an abstraction from all contingencies of human life, as some of Rawls's critics, and even Rawls himself at his most Kantian, present it. It is, rather, as Rawls's own theory of moral development strongly indicates, much closer to an appreciation and concern for social and other human *differences*. Neither does it seem that the theory requires us to regard ourselves as "independent in the sense that our identity is never tied to our aims and attachments," as Sandel says that it does.[29] For there is nothing implausible or inconsistent about requiring us to distance ourselves from our particular aims and

28. For a very interesting discussion of the problems of considering "the other" in moral and social theory, see Joan Tronto, "Rationalizing Racism, Sexism, and Other Forms of Prejudice: Otherness in Moral and Feminist Theory" (Hunter College of the City University of New York, Department of Political Science, New York, 1987, typescript). Compare Kenneth Arrow, *Collected Papers: Social Choice and Justice* (Cambridge, Mass.: Harvard University Press, Belknap Press, 1983), pp. 98, 113–14, for doubts about whether different people with different life experiences can ever have the same information, and can therefore achieve the criterion of universalizability that is required by a theory of justice.

29. Sandel, p. 179.

attachments for the purpose of arriving at principles of justice, while acknowledging that we may to some extent identify with them as we go about living our lives. The original position requires that, as moral subjects, we consider the identities, aims, and attachments of every other person, however different they may be from ourselves, as of equal concern with our own. If we, who *do* know who we are, are to think *as if* we were in the original position, we must develop considerable capacities for empathy and powers of communicating with others about what different human lives are like. But these alone are not enough to maintain in us a sense of justice. Since we know who we are, and what are our particular interests and conceptions of the good, we need as well a great commitment to benevolence; to *caring* about each and every other as much as about ourselves.

Rawls states clearly in several passages that abiding by the principles of justice that would be chosen in the original position requires motivations on the part of real human beings—especially the powerful and privileged—that are far from being self-interested: "To be sure, any principle chosen in the original position may require a large sacrifice for some. The beneficiaries of clearly unjust institutions (those founded on principles that have no claim to acceptance) may find it hard to reconcile themselves to the changes that will have to be made" (*TOJ*, p. 176). But he also speaks of a sense in which abiding by the principles of justice is in the self-interest of all—in the sense of *moral* self-interest. In the well-ordered, just society, "everyone's acting to uphold just institutions is for the good of each. . . . When all strive to comply with these principles and each succeeds, then individually and collectively their nature as moral persons is most fully realized, and with it their individual and collective good" (*TOJ*, p. 528).

All this takes us very far from the language of rational choice, which may explain Rawls's subsequent rejection of his own initial characterization of his theory. In such language, there is no room for a distinction between self-interest and moral self-interest. As I have suggested, Rawls's theory is much better interpreted as a theory founded upon the notion of equal concern for others than as a theory in which "mutual disinterest" has any significance, except as but *one* of several assumptions in a construction that serves not simply as a "device of representation" (as he has called the original position) but also as a device of empathy and benevolence. Indeed, such an interpretation is supported by much of Rawls's own text, and especially by his theory of moral development. On the other hand, it requires that the theory be purged of all suggestions that it is a part of rational choice theory.

It will perhaps be useful to place my reinterpretation of Rawls in the context of the contrasting arguments of several other feminist theorists. For it challenges the views of some who have found such theories of justice to be either incomplete or unacceptable from a feminist point of view. Gilligan, for example, in her critique of the moral development theory of the Kohlberg school (which owes much to Rawls's work on justice), contrasts the morality of care, contextuality, and concern for others with the morality of justice, rights, and rules. She associates the former voice primarily with women and the latter with men.[30] As I have argued elsewhere, many of the respondents whom Gilligan identifies as speaking in the "different voice" use it to express as fully universalizable a morality of social concern as respondents who express themselves in the language of justice and rights.[31] Thus the implication frequently drawn from her work, that women's morality tends to be more particularistic and contextual, appears to be unfounded. Here, by arguing that Rawls's theory of justice is itself centrally dependent upon the capacity of moral persons to be concerned about and to demonstrate care for others, especially others who are most different from themselves, I have presented another piece of argument that questions the wisdom of distinguishing between an ethic of care and an ethic of justice.

In Noddings's view, justice has been much overrated as the fundamental virtue, and principles have been overvalued as a tool for thinking about ethical problems.[32] These mistaken emphases are attributed to an overly individualistic and abstract male bias in moral philosophy. Justice itself, according to this view, should be at least supplemented, if not supplanted, by an ethic of caring, in which one's responsibility to care for those close to one takes priority over or entirely replaces what have generally been regarded as obligations to a broader range of people, or even humanity at large. While the feminist interpretation of Rawls that I have presented above argues that feelings such as caring and concern for others are essential to the formulation of principles of justice, it does not suggest that such principles can be replaced by contextual caring thinking. The problem, I suggest, is not principles or rules per se but the ways in which they have often been arrived at. If the principles of justice are founded, as I have suggested that Rawls's are, not on mutual disinterest and detachment from others but on empathy and concern for others—including concern for the ways in which others are different from ourselves—they will not be likely to lead to destructive rules that have tragic consequences when applied to those we love.[33]

The argument presented above also contrasts with recent work on theories of justice by Young and Benhabib. Young argues that the ideal of impartiality and universality in moral reasoning is misguided and works in opposition to feminist and other emancipatory politics because it attempts to eliminate otherness and difference and creates a false dichotomy between reason and feeling.[34] She thus finds Rawls's theory

30. Gilligan.

31. Susan Moller Okin, "Thinking Like a Woman," in *Theoretical Perspectives on Sexual Difference*, ed. Deborah Rhode (New Haven, Conn.: Yale University Press, in press).

32. Noddings.

33. Compare ibid., p. 44.

34. Iris Marion Young, "Toward a Critical Theory of Justice," *Social Theory and Practice* 7 (1981): 279–301, and "Impartiality and the Civic Public," in *Feminism as Critique*, ed. Seyla Benhabib and Drucilla Cornell (Minneapolis: University of Minnesota Press, 1987).

to be as rationalist, monological, and abstracted from particularity as Kant's. Benhabib makes the closely related claim that, in universalistic moral theories, such as Kohlberg's and Rawls's, "ignoring the standpoint of the concrete other leads to epistemic incoherence." In Rawls's original position, she claims, "The *other as different from the self*, disappears. . . . Differences are not denied; they become irrelevant." With only a "generalized other," Benhabib remarks, "what we are left with is an empty mask that is everyone and no one."[35]

I have attempted here to respond to such feminist critiques of Rawlsian thinking about justice by disputing the dichotomies they draw between justice and care, in the works of Gilligan and Noddings, and, in the works of Benhabib and Young, between impartiality and universalizability on the one hand, and the recognition of otherness and difference on the other. I have argued that Rawls's theory of justice is most coherently interpreted as a moral structure founded on the equal concern of persons for each other as for themselves, a theory in which empathy with and care for others, as well as awareness of their differences, are crucial components. It is, certainly, the case that Rawls's construction of the original position is designed so as to eliminate from the formulation of the principles of justice biases that might result from particular attachments to others, as well as from particular facts about the self. Surely impartiality in this sense is a reasonable requirement to make of a theory of justice.[36] But nevertheless, as I have argued here, the only coherent way in which a party in the original position can think about justice is through empathy with persons of all kinds in all the different positions in society, but especially with the least well-off in various respects. To think as a person in the original position is not to be a disembodied nobody. This, as critics have rightly pointed out, would be impossible. Rather, it is to think from the point of view of everybody, of every "concrete other" whom one might turn out to be.

For real people, who of course *know* who they are, to think *as if* in the original position requires that they have well-developed capacities for empathy, care, and concern for others—certainly not self-interest and instrumental rationality. In order to develop the sense of justice that is required of people if a well-ordered society is to have any hope of

---

35. Seyla Benhabib, "The Generalized and the Concrete Other," in Benhabib and Cornell, eds., p. 89 and passim.

36. The pitfalls of rejecting the goals of impartiality and/or universalizability, and of associating women or feminist theory with such a position, seem to me to be underestimated in the arguments made by Benhabib, Noddings, and Young, as well as in the implications drawn by Gilligan from her data. As I have argued elsewhere, to the extent that findings about women's moral development are interpreted to mean that women are more attached than men to particular others and less able to be impartial or to universalize in their moral thinking, they seem not only to misread the data but to reinforce the negative stereotyping of women that has been employed to exclude them from political rights and positions of public authority (Susan Moller Okin, "Thinking Like a Woman").

being achieved or, once achieved, preserved, human beings must be nurtured and socialized in an environment that best develops these capacities in them. By acknowledging the importance of such feelings for the development of a sense of justice, Rawls breaks away from the rationalist Kantian mode of thinking that casts a strong influence over much of his theory. To the extent that these aspects of the theory are emphasized, and it is thereby freed from some of its most Kantian language and assumptions, it is less open to some of the criticisms that have been made of it—and especially of its central concept, the original position. But such an emphasis at the same time draws attention to the fact that the theory as it stands contains an internal paradox. Because of Rawls's assumptions about the gendered family, he has not applied the principles of justice to the realm of human nurturance, which is so crucial for the achievement and the maintenance of justice.

Toward a New Feminist Liberalism: Okin, Rawls, and Habermas

AMY R. BAEHR

While Okin's feminist appropriation of Rawls's theory of justice requires that principles of justice be applied directly to the family, Rawls seems to require only that the family be minimally just. Rawls's recent proposal dulls the critical edge of liberalism by capitulating too much to those holding sexist doctrines. Okin's proposal, however, is insufficiently flexible. An alternative account of the relation of the political and the nonpolitical is offered by Jürgen Habermas.

Susan Moller Okin, John Rawls's foremost feminist critic and advocate, defends his idea of the original position as a tool for criticizing social structures that, she argues, unjustly disadvantage women (Okin 1989, 1994; Rawls 1971, 1993). If Okin is right, this would establish a strong link between a liberalism grounded in justice as fairness and the central goals of the women's movement. As the possibility of a coherent liberal feminism rides on some such link, Okin's work is of central importance. I began this study perplexed by the fact that Okin is quite confident that justice as fairness requires that the family be structured according to principles of justice whereas Rawls, despite his silence on this issue, would seem to have to reject this claim. In large part what I do here is explain their disagreement and try to make it fruitful to constructive feminist thinking about liberalism.

In this essay I argue that Okin raises a question central to liberal feminism: How liberal must the "background culture" of a society be to support a liberal "political culture"? Feminists will recognize this as one version of the question concerning the relation between the private and the public realms. After showing how this question is developed in Okin's work, I argue that both Rawls and Okin fail to offer acceptable ways to conceive of this relation. In conclusion I offer an alternative approach to the question, culled from Jürgen

Hypatia vol. 11, no. 1 (Winter 1996) © by Amy R. Baehr

Habermas's recent work in political theory, that I argue is more appropriate and more fruitful to feminist ends (Habermas 1992).[1]

In particular, in the first part of this essay I focus on Okin's response to Rawls's A *Theory of Justice* (Okin 1989; Rawls 1971). I show how Okin argues that the difference principle should be applied directly to the family and explain why Rawls would not have us do so. I then show how Okin's claims amount to a critique of the institution of the gendered family. In this section I also take the opportunity to make some clarificatory remarks about gender and liberal feminism. In the second part I turn to Okin's response to Rawls's *Political Liberalism* (Okin 1994; Rawls 1993). I concur with Okin's claim that her critique of the gendered family comes into even greater conflict with Rawls's recent emphasis on the stabilizing role justice as fairness is to play in a pluralistic society than it did with Rawls's original formulation in *Theory of Justice*. From Okin's perspective, Rawls's turn to what he calls political liberalism represents a turn toward toleration of sexism. Through a discussion of Rawls's notion of a reasonable comprehensive doctrine, I show that Rawls and Okin differ on what doctrines may be called reasonable. I argue that Rawls illicitly builds into his notion of reasonableness a distinction between political and nonpolitical spheres. I argue as well, however, that Okin's argument for seeing the family as political relies too heavily on the model of the original position, a tool unsuited to this task. I argue finally for a more fruitful way of thinking of the relation between the political and the nonpolitical.

OKIN'S *JUSTICE, GENDER, AND THE FAMILY*

Okin's Use of the Original Position

I have reconstructed Okin's use of Rawls's original position in *Justice, Gender and the Family* (Okin 1989) in three steps. First, Okin stresses that as sex is a morally arbitrary characteristic, it would be veiled in the original position (1989, 101). Rawls himself makes this claim (1975, 37). Choice behind a veil of ignorance is motivated by no differentiating characteristics of persons (such as sex) but rather by the desire, common to all parties, to secure the largest possible share of a set of primary goods. This gives us good reason to believe that parties behind the veil of ignorance would reject principles that distribute goods according to sex group-membership, or according to membership in any group whose common feature is morally arbitrary, for that matter. This prohibition can be used as a tool for feminist critique. It is a weak tool, however, because a liberal society may officially reject sex-specific distributive principles—outlawing official discrimination, for example—but still be characterized by large-scale sex-linked disadvantage produced and reproduced in the private sphere. If the original position's critical potential reached only to this prohibition on sex-specific distributive principles, persistent patterns of inequality established in the private realm but with influence on the political could be thought benign, as the result of the exercise of citizens' personal autonomy.[2]

Okin's second step addresses this weakness. Making (limited) use of Michael Walzer's notion of complex equality, Okin points out that inequalities in the family seep into and affect the distribution of goods in spheres clearly subject to principles of justice on an egalitarian liberal view (Okin 1989, 174, 182; Walzer 1983).[3] Even if we assume that the family is not the subject of political justice, we can express concern for relations in the family by pointing to this seepage. For this seepage works to maintain a distribution of benefits and burdens in society according to sex.[4] Egalitarian liberals must be concerned with such seepage as they tend to tie the legitimacy of social arrangements to (among other things) a certain measure of manifest (and not simply formal) equality among citizens. This measure of manifest equality is to obtain between citizens in their relations generally in the "background culture" (or private realm) of a society.[5] Thus to point to this seepage of inequality from the family into the economy and politics is to establish a strong ground for addressing inequalities in families as the cause of inequalities clearly seen as political. This focuses our attention on the relation between the realization of the political values of justice and patterns in a society's "background culture," the egalitarian intuition being that certain background conditions securing manifest equality must obtain in order to support the realization of the political values in the foreground.[6]

And finally, with Rawls, Okin claims that despite the ostensibly private nature of the family, it is part of the "basic structure" of society to which, according to Rawls, principles of justice are to be applied (Rawls 1971, 7; 1993, 259; Okin 1989, 94). According to Rawls, the basic structure is "the way the major social institutions fit together into one system"; it includes "the political constitution, the legally recognized forms of property, the organization of the economy, and the nature of the family" (Rawls 1993, 258). Beyond this initial agreement, Okin's treatment of the fact that the family is part of the basic structure is importantly different from Rawls's. Okin argues that parties to the original position—thought of as individuals and not as heads of households—deliberating about principles of justice for the basic structure of society would have the family be directly subject to the two principles of justice. I call this the position that the family must be *maximally* just.[7] In contrast, Rawls's position is that the principles of justice are not to be applied directly to any one institution but to the basic structure as a whole. Rawls does not give us a rule for determining how particular institutions must "adjust to the requirements that this structure imposes in order to establish background justice" (Rawls 1993, 261). He tells us that "an institutional division of labor must be established between the basic structure and the rules applying directly to particular transactions" (284), suggesting that some institutions may proceed according to principles inherent to them but that the role of justice is to continually adjust the results. Rawls also points out that the system taken as a whole may be just even where some single institution is unjust (Rawls 1971, 57). This may be the case when relations in one institution make up for injustice in another. The claim of justice as fairness is that the system of institutions as a whole must be just. Thus *Theory of Justice* does not rule out state intervention in the family to satisfy the difference principle, but it says little about what sorts of adjustments may be required of the family to make it a part of a basic structure that is, overall, just. What is clear is that, for Rawls, justice does not necessarily require that the difference principle in particular be applied directly to the family. I take Rawls to mean that the precise way in which a system of institutions is to satisfy the difference principle in particular is a question for a constitutional convention or a parliament and not for parties to the original position.[8]

Of these three steps, the first, concerning sex-blind principles, is uncontroversial for all liberals. The second, concerning the relation of the background culture to political culture, is an issue that has occupied traditional liberals from John Stuart Mill to John Rawls. I devote considerable attention to the issue in what follows. I argue that Okin points to the right question: How liberal must a background culture be to support a liberal political culture? But I argue that her solution—step three, to apply the principles of justice directly to the family—is problematic.

Maximal Versus Minimal Justice in the Family

To see how Okin's proposal for justice in the family differs from the common egalitarian liberal view, consider this distinction between two senses in which we can think of the family as subject to the values of justice. J. Donald Moon writes: "Many activities and concerns that fall within the household—for example, the treatment of various family members . . .—are, in the liberal conception, properly part of the public sphere, while various activities that were once public—notably, religious worship and festivals—are, in the liberal conception, private. The liberal distinction between public and private does not depend on whether an activity is conducted in the presence of unrelated 'others,' but on whether it is the *kind of activity* that the civil authority may regulate" (Moon 1994, 152).

Moon goes on to specify what "kind of activity" he has in mind. "Inasmuch as human rights can be violated in the personal sphere, the liberal agrees that the personal is the political. Liberalism requires that the civil authority step in to prevent domestic violence, marital rape, and child abuse: privacy does not protect activities that violate the rights of others, no matter where they are conducted" (Moon 1994, 152). Moon's view is that families ought to be just in what I call a *minimal* sense. For Moon, the application of some version of Rawls's first principle, protecting the "liberty and integrity of the person" (Rawls 1993, 291), is the appropriate response to violations of human rights in the family. In addition, for egalitarian liberals like Moon, something like the difference principle is applied to society as a whole, that is, to the system of institutions that make up the basic structure of society, to ensure that inequalities in society in wealth and other basic goods are regulated to the benefit of the least well off (Rawls 1971, 57). And how specific institutions should be arranged in order to fulfill this overall condition is a question for a constitutional convention or a parliament.

In contrast, speaking of "the internal justice of the family," Okin claims that the difference principle ought to be applied *to the family itself* (Okin 1989, 94). I call this making the family *maximally* just. Application of the first principle to the family, as we saw in the Moon quote, is relatively straightforward, for it applies to relations between any individuals, regardless of social roles. Application of the difference principle, however, requires a delineated sphere within which a distributive scheme is to be instituted. And it makes a difference if we take that sphere to be the system of institutions that make up the basic structure or if we take it to be the particular institution of the family. The most important difference is that inequalities permitted under the first application may be impermissible under the second. Indeed, this is Okin's intention: to make more rigorous the requirements that the two principles can place on the family. An example of this strengthening of the requirements of justice in the family is Okin's proposed intrafamilial redistribution enforceable with state power.[9]

Okin effectively changes how relations in the family may be thought to be unjust. Moon's approach claims that family relations ought not violate the first principle, but that they are not the kind of relations that come into direct conflict with the second. Only relations among citizens generally may be thought to violate the second. In contrast Okin writes, "The family [should] be constructed in accordance with the two principles of justice" (1989, 97).

The Critique of the Gendered Family

It is important to note that Okin is not simply advocating a redistribution of wealth in the family, giving women and girls "their fair share." To do so would be to treat the symptoms and not the cause of sex inequality. Rather, Okin sees her argument as a critique of the system coupling the status of the least well off (in the family) with a specific sex, a system enshrined in the gendered family. To be a traditional wife or daughter is to be less well off than one's husband or father or brother in terms of wealth and social power. On Okin's view, the state must move as far as possible to eradicate the system that ensures and reproduces this coupling, again both because the gendered form of inequality in the family as such is unjust and because inequality in the family undermines fair equality of opportunity and establishes sexed patterns of inequality elsewhere.

The system coupling the status of the least well off (in the family) with a specific sex is the system of sex roles. Of these roles Okin writes, "If any roles or positions analogous to our current sex roles—including husband and wife, mother and father—were to survive the demands of the first requirement [the equal opportunity requirement], the second requirement [the difference principle] would prohibit any linkage between these roles and sex" (Okin 1989, 103). Foremost on the list of those factors enforcing the linkage is, of course, the wide array of practices that make up traditional gendering, where gender identity is taken to be the psychological link between biological sex and social role. Okin writes, "Gender, with its ascriptive designation of positions and expectations of behavior in accordance with the inborn characteristic of sex, could no longer form a legitimate part of the social structure, whether inside or outside the family" (1989, 103). Thus gender, as Okin understands it, is incompatible with the—suitably altered—liberalism of justice as fairness. This claim about gender requires clarification. To this end I make a short excursus.

Excursus on Gender

Okin takes "gender" to mean "the deeply entrenched institutionalization of sexual difference" (Okin 1989, 6). By "institutionalization" I take Okin to mean that, under a gender regime, sexual difference determines in large part the distribution of benefits and burdens. As we have seen, on Okin's view, justice as fairness—suitably altered—opposes such institutionalization, and thus opposes gender. It opposes gender because parties to the original position would reject sex-specific distributive principles, because gendered inequality in the family seeps into and affects sexed patterns of inequality elsewhere, and because parties to the original position would see gender's breeding ground—the family—as violating the principles of justice.

But this way of talking—saying that justice as fairness opposes gender—may lead to the conclusion that it opposes all psychosexual distinctions among persons and requires androgyny. Indeed, Okin herself has seemed to suggest this conclusion: "If principles of justice are to be adopted unanimously by representative human beings ignorant of their particular characteristics and positions in society, they must be persons whose psychological and moral development is *in all essentials identical*" (Okin 1989, 107).

This is not a new concern, for liberal feminisms have often been accused of requiring androgyny (Jaggar 1988, 38). In the case of Okin, however, I think that this worry is unfounded because it rests on an equivocation on the word "gender." Consider the distinction between two uses of the word "gender." Gender-1 is what Okin calls the institutionalization of sexual difference such that benefits and burdens are distributed according to sex. If we take gender-2 to mean simply the psychosexual component of identity, then we may claim that justice in the family requires opposing some destructive versions of gender-2, but certainly not that it opposes gender-2 as such. In other words, being nondestructively butch or femme—to name two well-known genders-2—is not in itself in conflict with liberalism. Thus we can oppose gender-1 while affirming gender-2 as compatible with an Okinist liberalism. Indeed, if liberalism did require the abolition of differences in gender-2, it would lose a great deal of its appeal. For, as far as we know, genders-2 will continue to differ.[10] And it makes as little sense to want to eradicate them as it does to want to eradicate differences in persons' reasonable comprehensive doctrines.

We are also, then, in a good position to interpret the following claim of Okin's that is initially troubling: "If principles of justice are to be adopted unanimously by representative human beings ignorant of their particular characteristics and positions in society, they must be persons whose psychological and moral development is *in all essentials identical.* This means that the social factors influencing the differences presently found between the sexes—from female parenting to all the manifestations of female subordination and dependence—would have to be replaced by *genderless* institutions and customs" (Okin 1989, 107). I understand Okin to be claiming, not that gender-2—the psychosexual component of identity—is in principle incompatible with the unanimous acceptance of principles of justice, but rather that persons must share certain basic capacities to a requisite degree. Okin takes those capacities for autonomy to be infringed upon by "all the manifestations of female subordination and dependence." It would be a misunderstanding, I believe, to claim that these capacities are incompatible with some gender-2. We need not identify subordination and dependence with feminine, or any other, genders-2.[11]

The main point of this section is that Okin takes justice as fairness—suitably altered—to be critical of the traditional family with its gendering that includes the ascription of roles according to sex. This proposition is shored up by the claim that the capacities for political and personal autonomy are damaged by the forms of female subordination and dependence characteristic of the traditional family. Thus for Okin, justice as fairness includes ideals of *maximal justice* for the family that must be institutionalized along with the other conditions necessary for background justice.

OKIN AND RAWLS ON POLITICAL LIBERALISM

In this second part I explain how Okin's use of the original position comes into conflict with Rawls's new emphasis on the stabilizing role justice as fairness is to play in a pluralistic society. According to Rawls, political liberalism owes its attractiveness, in part, to its being the subject of an overlapping consensus of diverse but reasonable doctrines. This attractiveness is bought, however, at the price of depoliticizing ideals of the family as too contentious to win such diverse support. To illustrate this, I show how Rawls's view is tolerant of sexist doctrines where Okin's is not. I argue that such tolerance on Rawls's part is, however, the result of his building into the concept of a reasonable doctrine a line between a political and a nonpolitical sphere. I then propose a better way of thinking about the relation between the nonpolitical and the political culled from Jürgen Habermas's recent work in political theory.

The Liberal Feminist Critique of the Gendered Family
and an Overlapping Consensus of Reasonable Comprehensive Doctrines

In a recent essay Okin argues that her original claim—that justice as fairness, suitably altered, opposes the traditional family—is in tension with Rawls's new emphasis on the stabilizing role that justice as fairness is to play in a pluralistic society (Okin 1994; Rawls 1993). This new emphasis is the result of Rawls's reception of some criticisms of his earlier work. One line of criticism urged that Rawls withdraw the universal claim of justice as fairness. Some argued that the original position does not represent an Archimedean point from which questions of justice may be settled with the kind of universal validity claimed by Kant's categorical imperative. It represents rather a clarification of modern Western values. Rawls has accepted this reading and has argued that justice as fairness draws on certain ideals latent in the political culture of the Western democracies and thus that its validity is limited to cultures sharing those ideals (Rawls 1980).[12] In addition, some questioned even the validity of the moral claims of justice as fairness within our own culture, arguing that they are incompatible with the sort of moral pluralism that characterizes liberal cultures like our own.

In *Political Liberalism* (1993), Rawls continues a line of argument from an earlier article (1985), that justice as fairness is indeed a moral theory but not a "comprehensive" one, not one claiming validity for all (or many) spheres of life—as Mill's or Kant's liberalisms did (Rawls 1993, 89-129). Justice as fairness is not such a comprehensive conception but rather a political conception, a moral theory designed only for the basic structure of society and not for other spheres. The diverse doctrines that citizens in a pluralistic society hold apply to these other nonpolitical spheres. Giving an example of what makes a doctrine comprehensive, Rawls writes: "A moral conception . . . is comprehensive when it includes conceptions of what is of value in human life, and ideals of personal character, as well as *ideals* of friendship and *of familial* and associational *relationships*" (1993, 13; my emphasis). Thus if *Theory of Justice* leads us to believe that the family may be subject in some way to principles of justice—insofar as it is part of the system of institutions that makes up the basic

302

structure of society—*Political Liberalism* reminds us that adjusting the family to the requirements of justice may not meet with the kind of overlapping consensus that we may expect to find in a pluralistic society concerning other measures.[13] Indeed, Rawlsian political liberalism seems to permit state power to support only minimal justice in the family. This includes, as I have shown, protection against domestic violence, marital rape, and incest. *Theory of Justice*, in contrast, seems to permit the submission of the family to some requirement set by the application of the difference principle to society as a whole, perhaps even Okin's proposal to redistribute wealth within the family. Thus political liberalism represents a weakening in liberal commitment to family justice.

Rawls holds that limiting the claim of justice as fairness to the political makes it a more viable conception. This is because, according to Rawls, citizens may affirm justice as fairness as a doctrine for this structure while still affirming their own comprehensive doctrines. Justice as fairness can be affirmed as a "module" by citizens holding diverse but reasonable doctrines with reasons stemming from within those doctrines (Rawls 1993, 145). Indeed, according to Rawls, reasonable doctrines are those that can provide reasons for affirming justice as fairness—or some similar political doctrine. Thus justice as fairness need not replace doctrines that citizens hold. Rawls believes that, all things being equal, this would make a society governed by justice as fairness more stable than a society that required its citizens to give up their comprehensive doctrines in order to affirm its political doctrine.[14]

One way of showing the contrast between political liberalism and Okin's feminist uses of justice as fairness is to show how within political liberalism doctrines may be called reasonable—and thus not contrary to liberalism's basic political values—even if they include sexist "modules."[15] Let us look at two examples.

Consider comprehensive doctrines that advocate the use of state power to enforce the masculine monopolization of economic power and political authority. Such doctrines count as unreasonable on both Okin's and Rawls's views for clearly Rawlsian reasons. Although I discuss in more detail below what constitutes the "reasonableness" of doctrines, let it suffice to say here that such doctrines are unreasonable because they deny basic values of justice as fairness, such as equal opportunity in a clearly public realm (Okin 1989, 174). They advocate the distribution of wealth and political influence according to sex. And they advocate the use of state power to enforce their view.

Where Okin and Rawls part company, I believe, concerns those doctrines that can be party to an overlapping consensus about justice as fairness as a political doctrine, and yet advocate that women exclusively take on "private" duties in the family such as child care, care for the elderly, cooking, and cleaning. Such doctrines count as unreasonable on Okin's view, but, I believe, not on Rawls's. Okin's view is supported by the following claims. Such a doctrine effectively denies women fair equality of opportunity because, as we saw, inequality in the family seeps into and causes inequality elsewhere. And it denies women the maximal justice in the family that Okin argued parties to the original position would require.

I believe that a Rawlsian, however, would hold that the doctrines in question could be based on perfectly reasonable (and personal) convictions about women's natural abilities, about the benefits of female parenting, about female fulfillment, or about a divinely ordained social order. Central to the reasonableness of such doctrines is that they do not advocate using state power to enforce a public caste system. Such views and views with vestiges of these ideas are part of many doctrines commonly held today that—for a Rawlsian, I believe—must be thought capable of being party to an overlapping consensus of reasonable doctrines.[16] To understand these differences between Okin and Rawls's approaches, consider the notions of "reasonableness" and "the political" (and "the nonpolitical") that are central to political liberalism.

Reasonableness

Rawls offers two criteria for being a reasonable person. First, reasonable persons desire to engage in fair cooperation on terms others might reasonably be expected to endorse, and they are willing to abide by such terms provided others do (Rawls 1993, 49). Second, reasonable persons accept the "burdens of reason." That is, they recognize that persons may, through the normal use of their faculties, come to very divergent views, and they "recognize that [their] own doctrine has, and can have, for people generally, no special claims on them beyond their own view of its merits" (Rawls 1993, 60). Now what makes a *doctrine* reasonable? "A reasonable doctrine is one that can be affirmed in a reasonable way" (Rawls 1993, 60 n. 14). Rawls also holds that reasonable doctrines can come to consensus on his conception of justice. He writes, "I . . . assume . . . that the case for the stability of justice as fairness, or some similar conception, goes through" (Rawls 1993, 66). Because the model of the original position is central to justice as fairness, this amounts to the claim that reasonable citizens "cannot require anything [of one another] contrary to what the parties as their representatives in the original position could grant" (Rawls 1993, 62).

Okin's work invites us to notice the following about this notion of reasonableness. If reasonable citizens "cannot require anything [of one another] contrary to what the parties as their representative in the original position could grant," but Rawls stipulates that the principles they must arrive at may not have implications for the internal structure of the family—because it is private—*Rawls has written into the idea of reasonableness a distinction between the political and the private.* The feminist intuition is that it is unreasonable to expect parties to the original position (who may turn out to be women), or members of a constitutional convention or a parliament, for that matter, some of whom presumably are women, to accept this distinction between the political and the nonpolitical. Indeed, Okin's claim is that parties to the original position would reject it. Let us look more closely at the distinction between the political and the nonpolitical.

The Political (and the Nonpolitical)

One way that traditional liberals have distinguished between political and nonpolitical institutions is by reference to the involuntariness of political association and the voluntariness of private associations. Rawls makes claims that seem to support this. He argues, for example, that a conception of justice is political if it applies only to the basic structure of society; this structure is special, according to Rawls, because citizens are involuntarily subject to it. Rawls writes, "Membership in our society is given . . . [W]e cannot know what we would have been like had we not belonged to it (perhaps the thought itself lacks sense)" (Rawls 1993, 276). With respect to nonpolitical associations Rawls writes, "We may assume that each party . . . has various alternatives open to them, that they can compare the likely advantages and disadvantages of these alternatives, and act accordingly" (1993, 275). On this view, justice as fairness secures citizens a sphere for personal autonomy by carving out a private sphere. It secures them political autonomy despite the involuntary character of political association insofar as they are subject to only those arrangements that they could reasonably be expected to accept.

In sharp contrast, feminists see the background culture, the sphere of supposedly voluntary associations, as a sphere within which a remarkable consensus among comprehensive doctrines (namely sexist ideology) helps maintain distinct patterns of distribution that clearly reproduce themselves "behind the backs" of persons party to them. Indeed, much feminist work has focused on showing the involuntariness of social relations traditionally thought nonpolitical. On this basis feminists have, as has Okin, sought to recast what counts as political: hence the slogan "The personal is political."[17] To claim that women or girls *choose* disadvantage in the family and its attendant economic and political disadvantage is simply counter-intuitive. Where Rawls sees free and equal citizens benignly affirming diverse comprehensive doctrines, Okin sees enough consensus in comprehensive doctrines in (at least our) background culture that gendered distributive patterns espoused in that consensus are maintained. The idea is that sexism is the subject of an unspoken overlapping consensus, something like what Carole Pateman has called the "sexual contract" (Pateman 1989). Principles rejected by parties to the original position as candidates for political principles are the de facto distributive principles operating in the background culture. The liberal feminist claim is that a political theory that does not challenge these principles tacitly approves of them.

Continuing the logic of this view, to point out the nonvoluntary aspects of the family is to give reason for seeing the family as subject to the two principles of justice—either in the indeterminate sense suggested by Rawls's A *Theory of Justice* or in the maximal sense suggested by Okin's *Justice, Gender, and the Family*. But this way of making the distinction between the political and the nonpolitical is not very fruitful. For once we recognize that little of human social life is radically chosen, as it is assumed on this view, the very distinction between political and nonpolitical loses its sense.

Although Rawls and Okin make claims that support this view, they also both offer a better way of understanding the distinction.[18] They begin with the normative conception of the person that lies at the foundation of Rawls's theory of justice. According to this conception, citizens have two moral powers: the power to conceive and revise a conception of the good life and the power to propose and abide by fair principles of cooperation. These are the powers of personal and political autonomy respectively. Rawls writes, "Since citizens are regarded as having the two moral powers, we ascribe to [the parties to the original position] two corresponding higher-order interests in developing and exercising these powers" (1993, 74). The line dividing the political from the nonpolitical here can be thought of as *an enabling condition* for the exercise of both powers. Thus drawing the line improperly can jeopardize the exercise of these powers. From this perspective, Okin's concern seems to be that drawing the line in such a way that leaves the political too narrow (and the nonpolitical too broad) jeopardizes citizens' political autonomy—that is, jeopardizes their "right" to live under basic conditions that they can reasonably be expected to accept. Rawls's concern seems to be that drawing the line such that the political is too broad (and the nonpolitical too narrow) jeopardizes citizens' personal autonomy—that is, jeopardizes their "right" to conceive and pursue a life of their own choosing (of course, within the constraints of political justice). Clearly, the goal is to get the line just right. How do Okin and Rawls propose to do this?

Okin's approach begins with the idea that because the line dividing the political from the nonpolitical is an enabling condition for the exercise of the two moral powers, for which parties to the original position have a higher-order interest, it should be of interest to them. And Okin thinks we get the line just right if we draw it where parties to the original position would draw it. There are some problems with this strategy, however. Consider first that Okin herself proposes a flat principle of equality between adult members of a domestic partnership. This flat principle—demanding, for example, the equal division of a paycheck—is quite different from the difference principle.[19] The difference principle would suggest that inequalities among adult members of a domestic partnership are permissible if they raise the level of well-being of the least well off. But this could potentially justify traditional sexist inequalities. The flat principle of equality reflects the idea that work outside and work inside the home are of equal value to the household and should be equally remunerated. This principle is a better one, for it represents the equal standing of adults in a partnership and models such equality to children.

This leads me to believe that even Okin does not entirely endorse the application of both of Rawls's principles directly to the family. Clearly we need ways to protect women from vulnerability in domestic partnerships, and ways to ensure that girls are raised to have opportunities and self-respect equal to those of boys. But to do this we need not apply Rawls's two principles of justice directly to the family. We may retain the Rawlsian stipulation that parties to the original position deliberate about principles of justice to govern the system of institutions that makes up the basic structure of society, and not about principles for particular institutions. Drawing out the implications of these principles for particular institutions is, on this Rawlsian view, a task for a constitutional convention and for a parliament. And if we continue to hold, as Okin encourages us to, that the family is part of this basic structure, then we may foresee many ways in which the family may be regulated so as to achieve a basic structure that is just. And we can combine these with those that compensate for injustice in the family through indirect means. Which of these methods will be most effective and most in harmony with other social goals we embrace is a question that will meet with differing answers in different contexts. This way we leave the line between the political and the nonpolitical flexible in a way that Okin's proposal does not.

Of course Rawls does insist that parties to the original position deliberate about principles for the basic structure of society. And on his view, precisely how particular institutions are to be adjusted to satisfy the requirements of the two principles is an issue for a constitutional convention or a parliament and not a question for parties to the original position. This would leave the line between the political and the nonpolitical flexible, except for the fact that, as we saw, Rawls's current view appears to fix that line with the family on the nonpolitical side. This is done to make justice as fairness a more palatable conception for a pluralistic society that includes sexist doctrines. But, as I have shown, this attempt to fix the line between the political and the nonpolitical is unreasonable; it holds the normative insights of the original position hostage to a patriarchal status quo.

The Habermasian Alternative

The Habermasian alternative that I sketch here is controversial.[20] My intention is merely to present this alternative (without considering criticisms of it) and to indicate how I think it avoids the pitfalls of Okin's and Rawls's views. Okin proposes that we draw the line between the political and the nonpolitical from the perspective of parties to the original position. This proposal lacks flexibility and leads to conclusions we may not want to accept. Rawls's position seems to be that we draw the line ultimately from the perspective of the comprehensive doctrines that characterize the background culture. But this proposal is flexible in the wrong way and lacks a critical edge.

On the Habermasian view, we begin with the same normative conception of the person Rawls and Okin begin with. Habermas takes as basic "the idea of autonomy, according to which persons act as free subjects to the extent that they follow those laws which they have given themselves, in accordance with intersubjectively ascertained insights" (Habermas 1992, 537).[21] This basic notion of autonomy takes the form of both personal and political autonomy— they are, in Habermas's terminology, co-original (gleichursprünglich) (1992, 138). This means that the rights delineating a sphere of private autonomy and those delineating a sphere of political autonomy may not be normatively ordered. Neither set of rights is normatively prior or more basic, and thus neither set may be instrumentalized to, or derived from, the other. However, although personal autonomy is not to be instrumentalized to political autonomy, we can say nothing about what the content of a private sphere should be unless citizens exercise their political autonomy to give it this content. And clearly, if citizens are to be able to exercise their political autonomy equally, certain enabling conditions must obtain in the background culture of society. On my reading of Habermas, these conditions determine how much and what kind of manifest equality must characterize the background culture of society.

In an interesting discussion of feminist concerns with the paternalism of the social welfare state, Habermas takes up the following question: How can we determine when state intervention undermines the private autonomy of citizens? (Habermas 1992, 503). Habermas answers: Citizens must decide politically where to draw the line between the political and the nonpolitical guided by the concern that the line must enable citizens to realize their role as participants in the political process. And for Habermas, realizing this role implies much more than voting in general elections (1989). It includes participation in public discourse in the public realm, in the "open and inclusive network of overlapping publics" which serves to frame issues as political in the first place (1992, 373). He writes: "The unequal distribution of basic goods diminishes the . . . rationality of collective decisions. Thus a policy of compensation for the unequal distribution of available social goods can be justified as measures enabling citizenship [Staatsbürgerqualifikationspolitik]" (504).

To insist that the line between the political and the nonpolitical be drawn guided by the concern for enabling political participation permits us to focus attention on the basic structure of society (as Rawls does), but does not make any institutions off limits for adjusting. This is more flexible than Okin's approach, and has greater egalitarian implications than Rawls's. For a principle requiring that level of manifest equality necessary (in Rawls's terminology) to secure the fair value of the political liberties is more demanding than the difference principle (Cohen 1989, 18; Baynes 1992b, 159-60). And its egalitarian implications insist on more than simply an equitable distribution of wealth but focus our attention on all those conditions (including those particular to women's situation) that disable citizens from exercising their political liberties (Baynes 1992b, 161). This level and kind of equality will surely come into conflict with some of the doctrines citizens hold—especially those doctrines that insist on maintaining women's disadvantage. But feminists should take such a conflict as a sign that we are getting our political theory right and not letting its normative content be held hostage by a patriarchal status quo.

NOTES

I thank Andrew Altman, Kenneth Baynes, Ellen Feder, Eva Kittay, Kevin Melchionne, and an anonymous *Hypatia* reviewer for their comments on this paper.

1. For feminist work on Habermas, see Meehan (1995).

2. Many feminists have contributed to our knowledge concerning just how patterns of inequality in the private realm influence public inequality. Besides Okin, see for example Kittay (1995) and Held (1987).

3. Okin takes from Walzer the idea that seepage from one sphere to another is a sign of injustice. Okin clearly does not agree that spheres should have differing regulative principles, for she takes the principles of justice to be regulative in many spheres (Okin 1989, 174, 182; Walzer 1983).

4. The gendered family undermines equality of opportunity of wives primarily through the double burden of work outside the home and traditional women's work in the home. The daughter's equality of opportunity is jeopardized both by her taking on of a disproportionate amount of work in the home and by the traditional gendering to which she is subjected, gendering that predisposes her to enter a disadvantageous marriage.

5. For example, Rawls writes, "Certain background conditions are necessary if transactions between individuals are to be fair: these conditions characterize the objective situation of individuals vis-à-vis one another" (1993, 269).

6. We can imagine two types of policies based on this normative concern for seepage. One type attempts to cause a "reverse seepage." An example of this would be encouraging girls' sports in public schools. The idea here would be that the forms of self-confidence fostered in girl's sports may seep back into the family. The other type would attempt to treat the inequality in the family itself. Examples of this are socially supported pay for housework or Okin's example of an intrafamilial redistribution of wealth, discussed in note 10.

7. In her book *Justice, Gender, and the Family*, Okin convincingly argues that Rawls's initial insistence that parties to the original position be heads of households

amounted to a tacit gendering of those parties as male. Any agreement struck by one gender is, of course, a violation of the deeper contractualist claim that the acceptability of social arrangements is their acceptability to each, regardless of particularizing characteristics (Okin 1989).

8. For example, Rawls writes, "Which [economic] system . . . most fully answers to the requirements of justice cannot, I think, be determined in advance . . . It depends in large part upon the traditions, institutions, and social forces of each country, and its particular historical circumstances" (Rawls 1971, 274).

9. Okin suggests that "employers make out wage checks equally divided between the earner and the partner who provides all or most of his or her unpaid domestic services" (1989, 181). It is important to note that the paycheck proposal is meant to satisfy the requirements of maximal justice in the family. Other more common feminist proposals Okin makes—quality subsidized child care, parent-friendly working conditions, equity in schooling, enforced child support and alimony—aspire to sex equality by tinkering with the system of basic institutions that makes up the basic structure while avoiding direct political intervention in the family.

10. And there will continue to be variation within genders.

11. This is a very important issue, for genders can take on destructive forms—for example, selfless femininity and abusive machismo. Carol Gilligan's description of conventional level care reasoning, requiring the submerging of self into other, would be an example of destructive feminine gender (Gilligan 1982). There is much more to be said on this issue than I can say here. I wish simply to claim that a liberal feminist need not hold that having a gender-2 (masculine, feminine, or some other gender) by itself rules out also having certain autonomy capacities.

12. For an overview of debate on this point see Baynes (1992a).

13. In other words, for Rawls, we cannot expect to find ideals for the family among those ideals that later find a place in a constitution. Nor, I should add, should we expect to find much consensus at the legislative stage. This suggests not only that Okin's policy suggestions redistributing wealth within the family may not meet with agreement at either stage, but that many comprehensive liberal proposals such as parental licensing may not expect to meet with agreement. On this topic see Kymlicka (1991). On the four-stage sequence to which I refer here, see Rawls (1971, 195). Bruce Ackerman even suggests that the difference principle itself does not survive Rawls's turn to political liberalism. See Ackerman (1994).

14. Clear examples of such regimes would be the illiberal regimes of state socialism and theocracy, but, so the reasoning goes, comprehensive liberalisms would also be unstable.

15. Rawls uses the term "module" to refer to the way in which a political conception of justice can be embedded in a person's comprehensive doctrine. See Rawls (1993, 145).

16. Examples of such doctrines may be found in traditional religious groups. As Okin writes, "Rawls's inclination is to find religions reasonable" (Okin 1994, 31).

17. Some writers on feminism have wrongly cited the slogan as "The personal is the political." This way of putting it equates the two where, I believe, feminism wants to realign their relation.

18. Without providing the arguments here, I (as do Rawls and Habermas) reject the natural rights approach. See Martin (1985, 31). See also Habermas (1992, 117).

19. I thank Andrew Altman for this point.

20. See the recent exchange between Rawls and Habermas (Rawls 1995; Habermas 1995).

21. All references are to the German edition. All translations are mine.

REFERENCES

Ackerman, Bruce. 1994. Political liberalisms. *Journal of Philosophy* 91(7): 364-86.
Baynes, Kenneth. 1992a. Constructivism and practical reason in Rawls. *Analyse & Kritik* 14: 18-32.
———. 1992b. *The normative grounds of social criticism: Kant, Rawls, and Habermas.* Albany: SUNY Press.
———. 1995. Democracy and the Rechtsstaat: Habermas's *Faktizität und Geltung.* In *The Cambridge companion to Habermas.* See White 1995.
Cohen, Joshua. 1989. Deliberation and democratic legitimacy. In *The good polity: Normative analysis of the state.* See Hamlin and Pettit 1989.
Gilligan, Carol. 1982. *In a different voice: Psychological theory and women's development.* Cambridge: Harvard University Press.
Habermas, Jürgen. 1989. *Structural transformation of the public sphere: An inquiry into a category of bourgeois society.* Cambridge: MIT Press.
———. 1992. *Faktizität und Geltung: Beiträge zur Diskurstheorie des Rechts und des demokratischen Rechtsstaats.* Frankfurt: Suhrkamp.
———. 1995. Reconciliation through the public use of reason: Remarks on John Rawls's *Political liberalism. Journal of Philosophy* 92(3): 109-31.
Hamlin, A., and P. Pettit, eds. 1989. *The good polity: Normative analysis of the state.* New York: Blackwell.
Hanen, Marsha, and Kai Nielsen. 1987. *Science, morality, and feminist theory.* Calgary: University of Calgary Press.
Held, Virginia. 1987. Non-contractual society: A feminist view. In *Science, morality, and feminist theory.* See Hanen and Nielsen 1987.
Jaggar, Alison. 1983. *Feminist politics and human nature.* Totowa, NJ: Rowman and Littlefield.
Kittay, Eva. 1995. Taking dependency seriously: The family and medical leave act considered in light of the social organization of dependency work and gender equality. *Hypatia* 10(1): 8-29.
Kymlicka, Will. 1991. Rethinking the family. *Philosophy and Public Affairs* 20(1): 77-97.
Martin, Rex. 1985. *Rawls and rights.* Lawrence: University Press of Kansas.
Meehan, Johanna. 1995. *Feminists read Habermas: Gendering the subject of discourse.* New York: Routledge.
Moon, J. Donald. 1994. *Constructing community: Moral pluralism and tragic conflicts.* Princeton: Princeton University Press.
Okin, Susan Moller. 1989. *Justice, gender, and the family.* New York: Basic Books.
———. 1994. *Political liberalism,* justice, and gender. *Ethics* 105(1): 23-43.
Pateman, Carole. 1989. *The sexual contract.* Stanford: Stanford University Press.
Rawls, John. 1971. *A theory of justice.* Cambridge: Harvard University Press.
———. 1975. Fairness to goodness. *Philosophical Review* 84(4): 536-54.
———. 1980. Kantian constructivism in moral theory. *Journal of Philosophy* 77(9): 515-72.

———. 1985. Justice as fairness: Political not metaphysical. *Philosophy and Public Affairs* 14(3): 223-51.

———. 1993. *Political liberalism*. New York: Columbia University Press.

———. 1995. Reply to Habermas. *Journal of Philosophy* 92(3): 132-80.

Sunstein, Cass. 1993. *The partial constitution*. Cambridge: Harvard University Press.

Walzer, Michael. 1983. *Spheres of justice: A defense of pluralism and equality*. New York: Basic Books.

White, Stephen K. 1995. *The Cambridge companion to Habermas*. New York: Cambridge University Press.

Acknowledgments

Lyons, David. "Rawls Versus Utilitarianism," *Journal of Philosophy* 69 (1972): 535–45. Reprinted with the permission of the Journal of Philosophy, Inc., Columbia University, and the author.

Kavka, Gregory S. "Rawls on Average and Total Utility," *Philosophical Studies* 27 (1975): 237–53. Reprinted with the permission of Kluwer Academic Publishers. Copyright 1975 D. Reidel Publishing Company.

Barry, Brian. "Rawls on Average and Total Utility: A Comment," *Philosophical Studies* 31 (1977): 317–25. Reprinted with the permission of Kluwer Academic Publishers. Copyright 1977 D. Reidel Publishing Company.

Nielsen, Kai. "The Choice between Perfectionism and Rawlsian Contractarianism," *Interpretation* 6 (1977): 132–39. Reprinted with the permission of *Interpretation*.

Buchanan, Allen. "Distributive Justice and Legitimate Expectations," *Philosophical Studies* 28 (1975): 419–25. Reprinted with the permission of Kluwer Academic Publishers. Copyright 1975 D. Reidel Publishing Company.

Sher, George. "Effort, Ability, and Personal Desert," *Philosophy and Public Affairs* 8 (1979): 361–76. Copyright 1979 by Princeton University Press. Reprinted by permission of Princeton University Press.

Ball, Stephen W. "Maximin Justice, Sacrifice, and the Reciprocity Argument: A Pragmatic Reassessment of the Rawls/Nozick Debate," *Utilitas* 5 (1993): 157–84. Reprinted with the permission of Edinburgh University Press.

Hill, Thomas E., Jr. "Kantian Constructivism in Ethics," *Ethics* 99 (1989): 752–70. Reprinted with the permission of the University of Chicago Press.

Beitz, Charles R. "Justice and International Relations," *Philosophy and Public Affairs* 4 (1975): 360–89. Copyright 1975 by Princeton University Press. Reprinted by permission of Princeton University Press.

Pogge, Thomas W. "An Egalitarian Law of Peoples," *Philosophy and Public Affairs* 23 (1994): 195–224. Copyright 1994 by Princeton University Press. Reprinted by permission of Princeton University Press.

Feinberg, Joel. "Duty and Obligation in the Non-Ideal World," *Journal of Philosophy* 70 (1973): 263–75. Reprinted with the permission of the Journal of Philosophy, Inc., Columbia University, and the author.

Pritchard, Michael S., and Wade L. Robison. "Justice and the Treatment of Animals: A Critique of Rawls," *Environmental Ethics* 3 (1981): 55–61. Reprinted with the permission of Environmental Philosophy, Inc.

Singer, Brent A. "An Extension of Rawl's *Theory of Justice* to Environmental Ethics." *Environmental Ethics* 10 (1988): 217–31. Reprinted with the permission of Environmental Philosophy, Inc.

Nisbet, Robert. "The Pursuit of Equality," *Public Interest* 35 (1974): 103–20. Reprinted with the permission of *The Public Interest.* Copyright 1974 by National Affairs, Inc.

Macpherson, C.B. "Rawls's Models of Man and Society," *Philosophy of the Social Sciences* 3 (1973): 341–47. Reprinted with the permission of Sage Publications, Inc.

DiQuattro, Arthur. "Rawls and Left Criticism," *Political Theory* 11 (1983): 53–78. Reprinted with the permission of Sage Publications, Inc.

Okin, Susan Moller. "Reason and Feeling in Thinking about Justice," *Ethics* 99 (1989): 229–49. Reprinted with the permission of the University of Chicago Press.

Baehr, Amy R. "Toward a New Feminist Liberalism: Okin, Rawls, and Habermas," *Hypatia: A Journal of Feminist Philosophy* 11 (1996): 49–66. Reprinted with the permission of Indiana University Press.